INSIGHT GUIDES

Created and Directed by Hans Höfer

SOUTH AMERICA

Edited and Produced by Tony Perrottet
Principal Photography by Eduardo Gil

Editorial Director: Brian Bell

APA PUBLICATIONS

This book provides an overview of a continent whose rich culture has so far survived the impact of tourism better than most places in the world. As a result, it is a rewarding place to visit, and *Insight Guide: South America* vividly portrays its attractions. In addition, the 190-title Insight Guides series includes another 13 books devoted to individual South American countries or cities.

For these reasons, it lends itself especially well to the unique approach developed since 1970 by Insight Guides. Each book in the series encourages readers to celebrate the essence of a place rather than try to reshape it to their own expectations and is edited in the belief that, without insight into a people's character and culture, travel can narrow the mind rather than broaden it.

Perrottet

Insight Guide: South America is carefully structured. Each of the 10 countries explored starts with an introductory essay on its history and culture. This is followed by a comprehensive run-down on the main cities and regions worth visiting. Finally, a listings section provides all the necessary addresses and telephone numbers. Complementing the text, remarkable photography sets out to communicate as directly as possible life as it is lived by the local people.

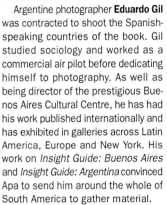

The book was masterminded by **Tony Perrottet,** an Australian journalist based in New York and editor of several other Insight Guides. He first visited South America as a foreign correspondent in the 1980s and vividly remembered tales of relatives who once worked on Chile's Patagonian sheep farms. Having worked on both *Insight Guide: Buenos Aires* and *Insight Guide: Argentina*, Perrottet was a natural choice to look after *Insight Guide: South America*. Apart from editing the book, he wrote the chapters on Argentina, Colombia and Bolivia and the sections on the remote Paine in southern Chile and riverboat journeys in the Brazilian Amazon.

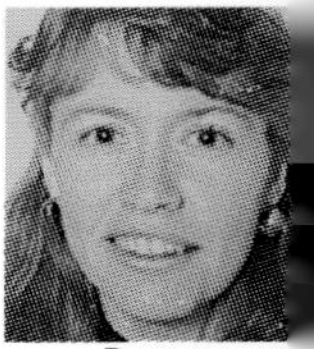

Dempsey

Argentine photographer **Eduardo Gil** was contracted to shoot the Spanish-speaking countries of the book. Gil studied sociology and worked as a commercial air pilot before dedicating himself to photography. As well as being director of the prestigious Buenos Aires Cultural Centre, he has had his work published internationally and has exhibited in galleries across Latin America, Europe and New York. His work on *Insight Guide: Buenos Aires* and *Insight Guide: Argentina* convinced Apa to send him around the whole of South America to gather material.

Journalist **Mary Dempsey** was responsible for writing the Peru chapter of the book. Born in Toronto and raised in America's Midwest, Dempsey developed "an incurable case of wanderlust" while studying journalism and political science – which finally led her to working on newspapers in Caracas, Venezuela. Perrottet caught up with her in Peru where she was writing for US publications and was working as South American correspondent for *TravelAge* magazine.

Doyle

Carson

The special section on trekking in the Andes was put together by the head of the South American Explorer's Club in Lima, **Betsy Wagenhauser**. At first intending to be in Peru for only a few months, she stayed on to become an organizer of this crucial information

Wheaton

Welna

M. Smith

Gil

center for travelers and she brings her years of experience of life and conditions in the Andes to the section.

Sean Doyle came to Latin America as part of his many peregrinations around the world, exploring everything from the plains of India to the streets of New York. After a childhood in the tropical north of Australia and an English Literature degree from Sydney University, Doyle turned to travel – finally spending many months in Ecuador and the Galápagos Islands which he thoroughly researched for this book.

Elizabeth Kline, one of the most experienced writers on Venezuela, covered the country for this edition. Her books include *Kline's Guide to Camps, Posadas and Cabins* and *A Travellers's Guide to Venezuela.*

Returning to Apa for this volume was **Kathleen Wheaton**, project editor for the acclaimed *Insight Guide: Spain* and *Insight Guide: Buenos Aires*. A native Californian with a passion for Hispanic culture, Wheaton studied Spanish at Stanton University and fiction writing at Boston. She lived in Spain for two years before developing an interest in Latin America – giving her a particular perspective and approach for the Uruguay and Paraguay chapters.

Also a veteran of Apa's *Insight Guide: Buenos Aires*, National Public Radio correspondent **David Welna** used his intimate knowledge of Latin America to write the Brazil chapter. Born in Minnesota, USA, Welna took his degree in Latin American studies before moving to Argentina prior to the Malvinas/Falklands War in 1982. He later moved to Rio de Janeiro in Brazil to report for NPR, the Canadian Broadcast Corporation and Monitor Radio.

Michael Smith spent four years studying Latin American affairs in the United States before heading for Santiago, Chile, to work as a foreign correspondent. He put together the chapter on Chile with his Chilean-born wife, **Cecilia Valdes-Smith**, with whom he now lives in New York. Both work on North American newspapers, but dream of the Andes and South Pacific.

The photographs of Brazil were mostly taken by **H. John Maier Jr**. The American-born Maier produced shots for the entire *Insight Guide*: *Rio de Janeiro* and carried on the good work here, traveling around South America's largest country in search of materials. He later moved to Rio de Janeiro to work for the Time-Life News Service and contribute to world magazines.

Special thanks must go to **José Araujo** of Aerolineas Argentinas in Washington, who helped organize transport, as well as to **Rick Alvares**, manager of AeroPeru in Miami. Around South America, the Apa team was particularly helped by **Roberto Begg** and **Diana Wilson** of City Service travel agency in Buenos Aires, **Teresa Anchorena** of Argentina's Directora Nacional de Artes Visuales, as well as **Darius Morgan** of Crillon Tours in La Paz.

Thanks must also go to Lima Tours and Explorama in Peru, El Dorado tours in Colombia, Candes Turismo in Venezuela and Sports Tour in Chile – all of whom gave assistance vital to completing this project.

The expanded Travel Tips section for this updated edition was researched and written by Insight Guides' South America correspondents.

CONTENTS

The Southern Cone

Maps

TRAVEL TIPS

BODYBOARD
KI TANGA

XYZ
XYZ

CUBA
HAITI
PUERTO RICO
JAMAICA
DOMINICAN REPUBLIC
LESSER ANTILLES
Caribbean Sea
NICARAGUA
Barranquilla
Cartagena
Maracaibo
Caracas
TRINIDAD/ TOBAGO
Atlantic Ocean
COSTA RICA
PANAMA
Cuidad Bolivar
Georgetown
Paramaribo
Medellín
VENEZUELA
Buenaventura
Bogotá
Cerro Marahuaca
2579
SURI NAME
FRENCH GUYANA
GUYANA
Cali
COLOMBIA
Quito
Mitú
Rio Negro
Barcelos
Amazonas
ECUADOR
Guayaquil
Chimborazo
6310
Manaus
Altamira
Belém
São Luis
Fortaleza
Iquitos
Benjamin Constant
PERU
Marabá
Teresina
Natal
Cruzeiro do Sul
Prainha
Trujillo
Pôrto Velho
Recife
São Francisco
Maceió
BRAZIL
CORDILLERA
Lima
Cuzco
Salvador
Ica
Lago Titicaca
BOLIVIA
PLANALTO DE MATO GROSSO
Brasília
Vitória da Conquista
6425
Nevado Coropuna
La Paz
Santa Cruz
Pico da Bandeira
Arica
Lago Poopó
Belo Horizonte
2890
Pacific Ocean
Paraguay
Iquique
DE LOS
São José do Rio Prêto
Victória
Volcán Llullaillaco
6739
GRANCHACO
PARAGUAY
Antofagasta
Salta
Rio de Janeiro
Asunción
Paraná
Foz do Iguaçu
Sao Paulo
Curitiba
Resistencia
Laguna Mar Chiquita
Cerro Aconcagua
6959
Pôrto Alegre
CHILE
Santa Fe
Córdoba
Rio Grande
Volcán Maipo
5323
URUGUAY
Santiago
Buenos Aires
Montevideo
ANDES
ARGENTINA
RIO DE LA PLATA
Concepción
Mar del Plata
Bahia Blanca
Colorado
BAHIA BLANCA
Negro
Valdavia
Atlantic Ocean
Osorno
3554
Monte Tronador
PATAGONIA
Comodoro Rivadavia
ARCH. DE LOS CHONOS
GOLFO SAN JORGE
Desado
Monte Fizroy
3375
FALKLAND ISLANDS /
ISLAS MALVINAS
Santa Cruz
BAHIA GRANDE
ARCH. REINA ADELEIDA
Punta Arenas
Rio Grande
I. GRANDE DE TIERRA DEL FUEGO
I. DE LOS ESTADOS
South America
1000 km

THE UNDISCOVERED CONTINENT

"South America is a man with a moustache, a guitar and a revolver." That is how foreigners see the continent, according to the Colombian novelist Gabriel García Márquez. More than any other continent, South America has been the victim of stereotypes and misconceptions. Most people see it as one huge and mysterious jungle, a mountainous wasteland or a backward rural world languidly lost in an eternal *siesta*.

But from the moment you step out of an aircraft anywhere in South America, it's obvious that the images fail to capture even a fraction of the reality. There are mighty rivers, wilderness and final frontiers here, but also ancient civilizations and dazzling new cultures. Along with the Amazon basin and its "Wild West" outposts, South America offers the Parisian salons of Buenos Aires and stylish resorts along the Caribbean. While the Andes might be littered with Indian villages that have hardly changed for centuries, visit the glittering cities of Brazil and you will find a lifestyle so modern and energetic it will leave you breathless.

The countries in South America share a common history – thousands of years of Indian cultures broken by European intrusion 500 years ago; colonial rule followed by bitter wars of independence; then an unsteady progress at the fringe of world events. Despite these shared experiences, each country retains its own character, dictated as much by accidents of fate as by South America's wild geography.

Four distinct groups of countries emerge: first, to the north (*page 31*), are Colombia and Venezuela, with mixed populations divided between rugged mountains and the languid Caribbean coast.

Second comes the Andean heartland of South America (*page 73*): Peru, Ecuador and Bolivia are the most Indian countries on the continent, clustered around the barren highlands where the Inca Empire once ruled and now the least developed parts of the continent.

To the east (*page 173*), the giant Brazil is in a world of its own, separated from the Spanish-speaking neighbors by a Portuguese heritage. Everything from the language and architecture to the sheer pace of life is unique in this whirlwind country that never seems to sleep. On its borders is Paraguay, at the heart of the continent, "an island surrounded by land".

Finally, in the south (*page 237*) are Chile, Uruguay and Argentina. The most European and prosperous of South American republics, they have the wide empty spaces that stretch along the spine of the Andes to the last stop before Antarctica: Tierra del Fuego.

Preceding pages: a typical Peruvian rug; dancing in a Rio carnival procession (Brazil); Machu Picchu, the "Lost City" of the Incas (Peru); a reed boat in Lake Titicaca (Bolivia); colonial city of Potosí (Bolivia); a lazy day at the beach in Rio; and singing in a bar in San Agustín (Colombia).

THE CARIBBEAN NORTH

Both Colombia and Venezuela are countries divided: although stretching along the blue Caribbean coast, their backbones are rugged mountain ranges. The sagging palms and golden sands of the tropical coast are so remote from the cool and misty highlands that you could be excused for thinking you were in a separate world altogether. This dual landscape is reflected in the people. The highlanders are mostly *mestizos*: mixed European and Indians (so misnamed ever since Christopher Columbus thought he had reached the Indian subcontinent in 1492). But on the coast there is a strong black and *mulatto* element, the descendants of slaves brought across the Atlantic from Africa.

The coastal cities have a relaxed languor that suits the tropical heat, while life in the mountain cities is more serious and hectic. Highlanders see the coastal folk as lazy, rum-soaked and given to sexual excesses; while mountain people are regarded on the coast as a taciturn and stuck-up bunch, unable to enjoy the pleasures of life.

One of the wildest of South America republics, Colombia has a past of gold-seeking and violence that fits its passionate population. The landscape is no less dramatic: high in mist-laden mountains are the capital Bogotá (*page 41*) and the famous ruins of San Agustín (*page 47*), while down on the coast (*page 50*) is the Spanish fortress city of Cartagena (*page 53*), once guarding bullion against the English sea-dogs of old. The treasures were worth fighting for: country has the finest gold museum on the continent (*page 44*).

Extending alongside is Venezuela (*page 59*), the birthplace of South America's favorite hero, Simon Bolívar. The pace and modern glitter of the capital Caracas (*page 64*) only makes Venezuela's countryside seem all the more quiet and remote, ranging from the colonial charms of Mérida (*page 66*) to the bizarre land formations of the Guayana Highlands (*page 67*).

Preceding pages: young boy in a restaurant (Caribbean coast); and an Amazon riverboat. Left, a perfect morning on the Caribbean coast of Venezuela.

COLOMBIA: THE LAND OF "EL DORADO"

The colonization of Colombia was shaped by a recurring Spanish dream: the legend of "El Dorado", an empire of gold and emeralds that would yield untold wealth to its discoverer. Hundreds of conquistadors, searching vainly for the promised land, perished in the steaming jungles and icy mountains of this wild country. Over the years, Colombia did yield riches, but never in the quantities that the Spaniards dreamed of. From that wild, frustrated and often violent start, the nation has taken an equally unruly course – until the present day, where in political life it can be difficult to distinguish just where reality ends and dream begins.

Courtesy of New York Public Library

The gold-dazed Europeans: Although the country bears his name, the explorer Christopher Columbus never set eyes on Colombia. It was his companion, Alonso de Ojeda, who first landed on the Caribbean coast in 1499, and was astonished by the wealth of the local Tairona Indians.

Colombia boasted no highly-developed civilizations to compare with those of the Incas or Aztecs, covering vast areas with grand capitals and great armies. Instead, it developed with about a dozen smaller cultures scattered around the country. Long before the Spaniards arrived, San Agustín and Tierra-dentro in the central highlands were flourishing centers of Indian tribes who have left behind mysterious monoliths and tombs. Still powerful in the 16th century were the Muisca, Tairona, Sinu and Quimbaya cultures.They shared a common expertise with gold unparalleled in South America. Seeing the Indians wearing items of the precious metal for religious and decorative purposes, the first explorers expected to find massive reserves.

The famous myth of "El Dorado" was born with rumors of the Muisca culture near present-day Bogotá. During religious rituals, these Indians did, in fact, throw gold offerings into the sacred waters of the Laguna de Guatavita, while the chief, covered in gold dust, bathed by its shores – hence "El Dorado", or "The Gilded One". But the Spaniards' feverish imaginations expanded on reality, and within several years of Colombia's discovery, teams were searching for everything from solid gold mountains in the Sierra Nevada de Santa Marta to vast cities of emeralds in the Amazon jungle.

With so many gold-crazed conquistadors

roaming through the country, permanent colonial settlements soon sprang up. Santa Fe de Bogotá, for example, was founded when three separate expeditions arrived at the heart of Muisca territory from Quito, Venezuela and the Colombian coast, all lured by tales of precious metal. Others disappeared into the countryside, as Indians realized there was no quicker way to be rid of the invaders than to tell them a land of gold was "somewhere near, just over the horizon".

The various Indian civilizations were brutally wiped out in the process, with the inhabitants brought into slavery alongside the black prisoners shipped over from Africa. Those who trusted the Spaniards were soon betrayed; any opposition was crushed with the help of the newly arrived armored horses, striking fear into the hearts of native warriors. By the end of the 16th century most of Colombia's present-day cities had been founded, and the country had been put under the colonial rule of the Viceroy of Peru.

The Spanish yoke: Colonial rule in Colombia was no less brutal than in the rest of Latin America. Along with slavery and hunger, the Spaniards imposed harsh taxes, *encomiendas* and the Inquisition. Attempted rebellions during the 18th century by Indians and *mestizos* – those of native American and Spanish blood – were crushed with studied cruelty, ensuring that nothing would interfere with the draining of the continent to finance Spain's endless wars in Europe.

But at the same time, a new national consciousness was arising amongst the *criollos*: those who were white, but Colombian-born. In the wake of the French and North American revolutions, followed by the occupation of Spain by Napoleon, several Colombian towns began to declare their independence. The first to do so were Cartegena and Mompos, and a new central state body was set up in Bogotá.

Simon Bolívar, *El Libertador,* the man who would become the hero of South America's independence struggle, came to prominence in neighboring Venezuela. He fought a brilliant campaign in 1813, winning six battles in quick succession against the royalist forces. But the tide turned with the defeat of Napoleon in Europe, and the Spanish crown began the reconquest of its rebellious colonies. Within a couple of years, Bolívar was forced to retreat to Jamaica.

Then, in 1818, Bolívar landed again on the Venezuelan coast. This time, with an army of

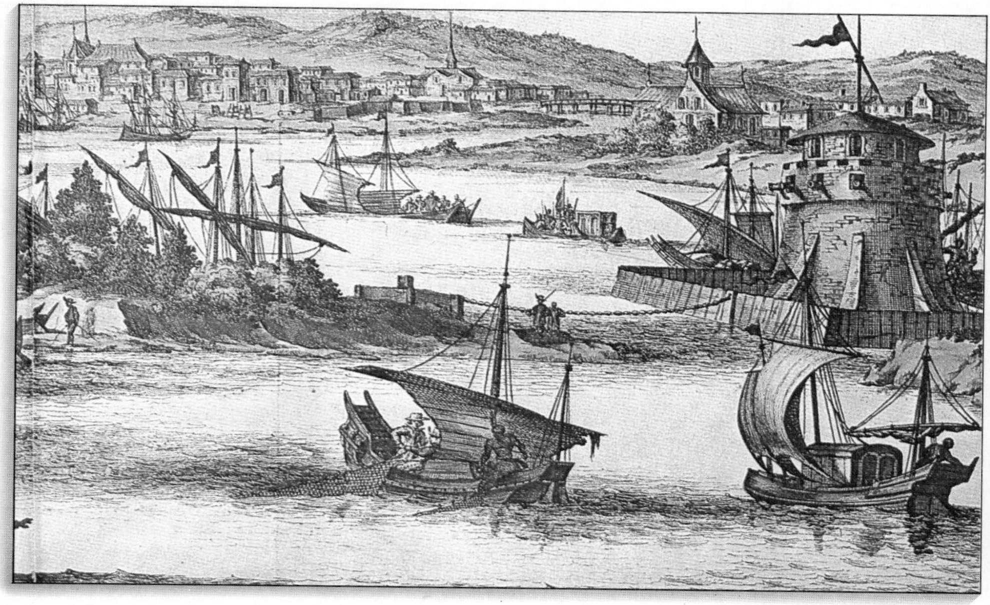

Preceding pages: mask from the Gold Museum. Left, Muisca Indians turn their king into "El Dorado", the Gilded One. Above, 18th-century etching of the fortified colonial port, Cartagena.

horsemen and a contingent of British veterans from the Napoleonic wars, he began the struggle once again from the beginning. Victory followed victory until the battle of Boyacá on August 17, 1819, after which Bolívar could march in triumph through the gates of Bogotá.

The fragments of a dream: Drunk on victory, the revolutionary congress in Venezuela promptly declared *la Gran Colombia*: a new state that would unite Venezuela, Colombia and Ecuador. It was Bolívar's plan for a unified, centralized state, and the hero was elected president. But opposition to many of his ideas was already powerful and the congress chose Fransisco de Paula Santander, who favored a loose federation of states, as vice-president.

While Bolívar was away liberating the Andean regions, *la Gran Colombia* fell apart. Within a decade, Venezuela and Ecuador had seceded. Bitterly disillusioned and wracked by illness, Bolívar retired to die alone in Santa Marta in 1830. His final judgement on his countrymen was that "America is ungovernable. He who serves a revolution plows the sea."

Less than two decades after Bolívar's lonely death, Colombia was on the verge of civil war. The two political currents, centralist and federalist, that had been born in the independence struggle, were formalized into parties: the Conservatives wanted a country run from the capital in Bogotá, while the Liberals wanted a federal system, giving the provinces more self-control. The division erupted soon after, and the rest of the 19th century was marked by 50 insurrections, eight civil wars and several constitutions.

The most violent of the civil wars, the War of the Thousand Days, began in 1899 and was won by the Conservatives at the cost of 130,000 lives. After all the bloodshed, little had changed for most Colombians: the government was still in the hands of the *criollo* minority who paid scant attention to the *mestizos*, *mulattos*, blacks and Indians who made up the bulk of the population. Meanwhile, the US took advantage of Colombia's chaos to foment a secessionist movement in Panama, then a Colombian state. Soon afterwards, work began on the Panama canal. The US President Theodore Roosevelt, before being given the Nobel Peace Prize, boasted "I took the Canal Zone and let Congress debate." The Colombian government begrudgingly accepted the loss in 1921.

The period of relative peace in the first decades of this century unfortunately proved only to be the calm before the storm. It was

Above, crowds in the streets of Bogotá, 1948.

a time when the United Fruit Company of the United States created huge banana plantations along the coast, paying workers starvation wages and, in 1928, ending a long-running strike by using the Colombian Army to machine-gun unionists in front of the railway station in San Juan de la Cienega.

As the banana boom died, coffee became the new hope for the Colombian economy. Many hoped that the crop would create a new class of small landowners who would consolidate democracy, but the pattern of large plantations repeated itself. Small fluctuations in the world price would devastate whole areas of the countryside.

Unprecedented brutality: But the scene was being set for the most spectacular bloodbath in Colombian history, known simply as *La Violencia*, "the violence". A popular Liberal politician by the name of Jorge Eliecer Gaitan was pushing for real political change. When he was gunned down in the streets of Bogotá in 1948, a spontaneous explosion of frustrations brought crowds to the streets of the capital, smashing windows, burning houses and shops. This so-called *Bogotazo* was followed by civil war in the countryside, with fighting between peasants, police and soldiers reaching unprecedented brutality.

At least 300,000 people lost their lives in the conflict, and whole villages were massacred by opposing groups who had no real idea of how their ideologies differed. But by 1953, many of the armed peasant groups in the countryside were beginning to develop a clearer revolutionary philosophy. The Liberal leaders in the cities, who had maintained a gentlemanly tone in their manifestos throughout the bloodshed, suddenly realized that they had unleashed forces which might lead to more profound changes in society. They quickly patched up their differences with the Conservatives, and united in the fear of a communist advance.

Both sides supported a military coup and the repression of guerrilla s. In 1957, Liberals and Conservatives signed an agreement known as the National Front, in which they agreed to share power for the next 16 years. Once again, after all the carnage, the same politicians were back in power, ensuring that nothing would really change. Meanwhile, the various peasant armies in the countryside dragged on their battle with the Armed Forces, a fight that continues to this day, giving Colombia the dubious honor of having the oldest guerrilla forces in the continent.

Experiments with peace: The National Front formally came to an end in 1974, but continued in modified form for another 12 years. In 1982, President Belisario Betancur attempted a creative way to end the guerrilla conflict and offered amnesty to anyone laying down their arms. One guerrilla group, the FARC (Fuerzas Armadas Revolutionarias de Colombia) even created its own political party, the Unión Patriótica. This brave "democratic opening" of Colombia's political institutions finally failed when the M-19 guerrilla group took over the Palace of Justice in Central Bogotá. In the ensuing battle, more than 100 were killed, including 11 judges of the Supreme Court.

Drugs economy: Since then, the signs for Colombian politics have been contradictory. The presidency of Virgilio Barco opened the way for full competition in democratic elections but the government had a battle against a new force – the Medellín drug cartel that controlled 80 percent of the world traffic in cocaine. Boss of this cartel based around the mountain town of Medellín, was Pablo Escobar, who by the end of the 1980s had an estimated wealth of $3 billion, making him the 14th richest man in the world, according to *Forbes* magazine. The evil trade undoubtedly helped the economy and largely protected Colombia from the ravages of the 1980s recession.

Escobar died in a hail of bullets in 1993, and the biggest drugs' cartel subsequently fell to the barons in the neighbouring town of Cali. Over the next two years the authorities had a number of successes, not least when the treasurer of the Cali cartel fled the country and gave himself up to the US Drug Enforcement Adminstration. Among the damaging claims he made was that president Samper had used $6 million of drugs money to fund his 1994 election campaign.

Despite this image of chaos – and the occasional sign that goes up on highways telling people not dump corpses – visitors are unaffected by the violence, which occurs in remote jungle and mountain areas. The country remains one of the friendliest and most fascinating on the continent, as thousands of tourists discover every year. Nobody who visits Colombia fails to be impressed by its creative energy and quixotic beauty.

DAVIVIENDA
COLMENA

BANCO CA

BOGOTÁ: INTELLECTUAL HUB

Shrouded by clouds in the midst of the northern Andes, the city of **Bogotá** is where Colombia's contradictions collide. It has grown 20-fold in the second half of the 20th century, and the layers of history peel away like the rings of an onion: outlying slums give way to towering skyscrapers of polished steel and glass; grand government palaces are followed by quaint English mansions; and its centre is colonial Spanish with flower-covered courtyards and viceroyal monuments of stone and weathered brass.

This city of the highlands, 8,670ft (2,642 meters) up, has been looked upon with incomprehension by people of the Colombian coast, who see its inhabitants as closed, cold and aloof. Reflecting a popular view, writer Gabriel García Márquez once described Bogotá as "a gloomy city where on ghostly nights the coaches of the viceroys still rattled through the cobbled streets" and "32 belfries tolled a dirge at six in the afternoon". But the image has never worried *Bogoteños*, who see themselves as intellectual and cultured, in a city which easily outstrips in cosmopolitan pace whatever else Colombia can offer.

Anything and everything can be found in Bogotá's chaotic avenues. It is a city of opulent restaurants, teams of homeless kids, vendors selling emeralds, peasants in ponchos, endless traffic jams and walls covered with graffiti. But above all, it is the intellectual hub of Colombia, a place where – despite a complete lack of government aid to the arts – you can find dozens of theaters, vibrant university life, classic museums, streets full of bookshops and avant-garde art galleries, all in a creative tumult that has had Bogotá dubbed "the Athens of South America".

Orientation: For most people, the first glimpse of Colombia is Bogotá's **El Dorado airport**, impressively efficienct and possessing the world's second-largest landing field. Surrounding the airport are miles of glasshouses, growing the flowers that are one of Colombia's lesser-known exports.

The best view of the city is from the top of the **Cerro de Montserrate**, which can be reached by a funicular railway and cable car. Every Sunday, traffic is blocked and *Bogoteños* stroll to the summit, where an amusement park is set up alongside a statue of *El Señor Caido* (the fallen Christ). Down below, the city is arranged in a warped grid, with numbered *calles* running east-west and *carreras* running north-south.

On the way down, at the foot of Montserrate, call in at the **Quinta de Bolívar**, a magnificent colonial mansion with expansive lawns and gardens that was once the home of Simon Bolívar (1783–1830). It is now a museum, full of paintings depicting *El Libertador*, his mistress and his battles as well as many of his personal effects. Wreathed with roses are cannons from the general's greatest victory, the Battle of Boyacá.

The city center: A good place to start exploring Bogotá is in the heart of the old city, the **Plaza de Bolívar** – with a

Preceding pages: Central Bogotá by night. Left, Bogotá Cathedral, Plaza Bolar. Right, letting loose at a Bogotá nightclub.

statue of the Liberator at its center, naturally. Three Spanish conquistadors coming from different directions met here in 1538 to found a town in the fertile lands of the Muisca Indians, near the local capital of Bacata. Despite killing the Indians and later one another with surprising rapidity, the outpost grew into a city which, by the time of independence, would be declared the capital of Gran Colombia.

Today the plaza is not surrounded by colonial buildings but by more recent architecture. To the south stands the **Capitolio Nacional**, looking like a classic Greek temple, where the Colombian Congress sits. Beyond that is the **Palacio Presidencial**, which was sacked in 1948 during the uprising known as *El Bogotazo* and not restored until 1979. Every day at 5pm there is a changing of the guards, whose uniforms were modeled on pre-World War I Prussian outfits, complete with shiny silver spikes on their helmets.

On the western side of the plaza is the **Cathedral**, which was begun in 1565, knocked down by an earthquake two centuries later and only completed after Colombia's independence. Alongside are the **Capillo del Sagrario**, and the sumptuous **Teatro Colón**, the city's principal theatre, which can only be visited during performances.

To the north of the square is where the **Palacio de Justicia** once was. Taken by guerrilla s in 1985, it was left with a gaping hole in its side from the ensuing fire fight with the Army. It remained unoccupied for several years afterwards until the decision was finally made to level it.

The colonial quarter: A short stroll from the plaza takes you into Bogotá's colonial quarter, **La Candelaria**. The single-story whitewashed buildings creep up a hillside, their red tile roofs and decaying cupolas stretching out to the city center. One of the finest buildings of the area has been turned into a hotel and restaurant, La Hostería de la Candelaria, on Calle 9 No 3–11, where the rooms are all tastefully decorated with antiques and set around a sleepy

Hotel interior Villa de Avila near Bogotá.

courtyard bathed in the light of another epoch.

Like all of South America's colonial cities, Bogotá is a feast for those passionate about religious art. The **Iglesia de Santa Clara** (Calle 9, Carrera 8), built during the 17th century, has a sumptuous interior with works by the most famous of Bogotá's painters at the time, Gregorio Vasquez de Arce y Ceballos. On a less sublime note, history records that the church became notorious for the kidnapping of several novices – on one occasion, the artist Vasquez himself being implicated and spending a spell in prison.

Heading back into the modern city, it is worth wandering along Avenida 19, to see the amazing range of books on display. Colombia is South America's largest exporter of the printed word. Nearby, on Calle 18A/Carrera 1 is the **University of the Andes**, which is one of the continent's most respected centers of learning set around a relaxing and conducive campus.

To get a taste of the flourishing emerald business, head for the corner of Avenida Jimenez and Carrera 7. Colombia controls 60 percent of the world's production of these precious green gems, and many fortified shops sell them to travelers who have a few thousand dollars to spare. Emeralds are graded by their brilliance, color and purity, and every shop has special lights and filters to detect fakes.

The most famous museum in Bogotá is the **Museo del Oro** (*see page 44*). But also worth visiting is the **Museo Nacional**, set in a building known as the Panopticon. Designed as a prison by an Englishman, Thomas Reed, early last century, it was the latest in European architectural ideas, built so that each of the 200 cells could be observed from a single vantage point. It was used as a prison until 1946 and it has now been lovingly restored so that each of the corridors houses a different episode from Colombian history – from pre-Columbian through to the present, with the lower level devoted to art.

A cathedral of salt: Traveling along a highway two hours north of Bogotá, through the lush countryside once ruled by the Muisca, a morning excursion can be made to the famous **Cathedral of Zipaquira**, carved out of solid salt. The salt mines had been worked for centuries by the local Indians when the Spanish came and took them over. By the 1920s, such a large cavern had been dug that the Banco de la República decided to build a cathedral inside.

Carefully cut from a mountainside above the small town of Zipaquira, a tunnel leads into the darkness with the thick aroma of sulfur heavy in the air. Finally an altar appears silhouetted in the distance: the cathedral itself is 75 ft (23 meters) high and has held more than 10,000 people at one time, but the walls are black, giving the unsettling sensation of walking through space. Despite the lack of color, they are 75 percent pure salt – as can be affirmed by a quick taste – and mining is still going on elsewhere in the mountain. Colombians will proudly tell you that the mountain could keep the world supplied with salt for more than 100 years.

ltar of e Salt athedral, paquira.

The Lure of Colombian Gold

Protected like Fort Knox, the Museo del Oro (Gold Museum) in the heart of Bogotá is unsurpassed. Its breathtaking collection of bracelets, earrings, masks, statues and rings runs to more than 29,000 pieces from a dozen pre-Columbian cultures, all revealing a mastery of technique that leaves modern jewelers astounded. Just to spend an afternoon in the museum makes a visit to Colombia worthwhile.

The range of gold items surviving from the cultures in Colombia is far more impressive than those that remain from the grander South American civilizations of Peru – the Gold Museum in Lima is a pale collection of tinsel in comparison to its counterpart in Bogotá.

This is largely because of the impatience of the gold-crazed Spanish conquistadors. Arriving from the Caribbean coast, they sacked and looted their way through every Indian tomb they could find, stripping local nobles of the metal they wore for religious or decorative purposes. But the Spaniards had neither the time nor the energy to search deep below the surface of the earth for the occasional piece of jewelry from long-forgotten cultures. Much more profitable was the pillage of the Inca empire to the south, already centralized and organized to facilitate shipments of cargoes back to Europe, while new mines in the Andes were yielding wealth that made the few trinkets of the Colombian natives seem like drops of water in the ocean.

Thus the great art of the Incas and other Peruvian cultures, easily robbed by the Spaniards, was melted down into gold bars to be shipped back to the royal coffers, while the jewelry of the Colombian cultures was not discovered until the more selective hunters and treasure seekers of later years; not just by archaeologists but by the ever-present and adventurous *guaqueros* or grave robbers who have scoured the countryside for generations.

The metal-working tradition of the Americas developed over some 30 centuries from the middle of the second millennium BC up to the arrival of the Europeans in the 16th century. The work done in Colombia is considered remarkable. Its technology embraced all the known gold working techniques then available in the New World and its diversity is extraordinary: each of the cultures, isolated by the country's wild and inhospitable geography, developed its own peculiar style.

Hammering was without doubt the most primitive technique for making gold objects, although great skill is required to manage the metal. Some cultures in Colombia developed smelting, using combinations of alloys to strengthen the gold. Joining techniques were perfected to connect sheets of gold into more complex figures, and it is probable that the technique of lost-wax casting – using molds of wax models which dissolve on contact with the alloy – was first developed in Colombia.

Pre-Columbian Indians used gold for decoration and religious rights, such as burial, recognizing the value of a metal which did not tarnish and could be easily sculpted: the jewelry made from gold was reserved for the highest figures in tribal society. Clear guidelines were laid down as to who could and could not wear the metal, while in some areas it was also used as an item for trading.

Run by the government-owned Banco de la República, the Museo del Oro is in the center of the capital at the Parque de Santander (closed Mondays). The grand building is like a fortress. Armed guards, vaults and video surveillance are only part of the measures taken to protect the priceless collection.

The museum, which is closed on Mondays, has video shows several times a day in English, and a free tour can be booked in advance at the office on the second floor.

The first level of the museum outlines the various styles of the pre-Columbian cultures: it shows the hammered breastplates of the Calima region near the Pacific, the delicate necklaces of the Muiscas around modern-day Bogotá, the figurines of the Narinos, pendants of the Quimbayas and polished eagle statuettes of the Taironas. There are countless nose-rings, masks and scepters, as well as tiny model birds which, when placed in wind tunnels, have proved to be aerodynamically highly advanced – a fact that inspired the writer Erik von Daniken to claim that they were designed by aliens.

Also on this level is an excellent model of La Ciudad Perdida, the Lost City of the Taironas that was found near Santa Marta in 1975. Several times larger than Machu Picchu in Peru, the discovery is considered to be one of this century's most important find in South America, though continuing finds, such as the recently excavated Sican site in Peru, show there may still be many treasure waiting to be found.

One of the museum's prize possessions is a tiny boat created by the Muisca people, showing the ritual of throwing gold into Lake Guatavita as an offering to the gods, while the chief gilded himself with gold, giving rise to the first myth of "El Dorado". The piece was found during one of the many dredging and diving projects around the lake.

Other priceless items include two crosses from the Spanish colonial period, studded with emeralds, diamond and images of angels. They both belonged to impoverished orders of nuns, who only recently agreed to sell them to pay off debts.

But the climax of any visit to the museum is the huge strong-room on the top floor. Only 20 people at a time are allowed to enter the room which is in complete darkness – until the lights are dramatically turned up to reveal more than 12,000 pieces hanging around the room, almost blinding in their brilliance. Piped Indian music transports visitors to the mysterious golden world whose reality can only now be guessed at.

Left and right, crafted Indian treasures in the Gold Museum, Bogotá.

San Agustín: Heart of the Countryside

One of Colombia's most surprising destinations is the small village of **San Agustín** in the mountains near the Ecuadorian border. It is famous for its ancient stone statues, mysterious remnants of a lost culture from one of the most important archaeological sites in South America. But visitors also stay for the wild scenery of the surrounding Magdalena Valley and for the atmosphere of the village itself, where slow rural rhythms, hardly affected by the outside world, take you into the heart of the Colombian countryside

Running through San Agustín are mostly dirt roads, lined by low Spanish houses. Layers of red-tiled roofs lead past a white church tower to the surrounding hills, covered by banana trees. The mountains beyond are a rich green because it rains every day for nine months of the year in a light, erratic drizzle; but even if the rain stops, the humidity can be stifling and the white streets blinding.

There are not many cars in the village, and those that function are old and clapped-out. Transport is mostly by horse: on every corner are cowboys in ponchos, wide-brimmed hats and leather boots, standing by their trusty steeds. Although a handful have sold out to motorbikes, the conversion has not affected their swaggering.

The village's isolation has limited its compromises to tourism. A "new road" has to be cut through the mountains to the nearest town **Popoyán**, a colonial gem that was nearly levelled by an earthquake in the early 1970s. Even Land-Rovers find it rough going over rocks and mud, plowing over a mountain pass to get there.

The most obvious outside influence is San Agustín's few new restaurants and artisan shops. But enough travelers make the journey to ensure that a classic tout is waiting for any jeep, usually a teenager with slicked black Elvis Presley hair, jeans and an "I Love New York" T-shirt. Within seconds he can arrange cheap hotels, cheap food, cheap horses or a ready supply of Colombia's more notorious commodities.

Baffling figures: In a continent full of strange remnants of ancient cultures, the statues of San Agustín have continued to baffle archaeologists. Around 500 figures have been found in the surrounding Magdalena Valley: some resemble masked monsters, others clearly eagles, jaguars or frogs.

Nobody knows who carved the statues or for what reason. Even today, investigators can only date the civilization from between the 6th and 12th centuries AD. Some experts argue that it was earlier, others that it grew later and was suppressed by the Incas, since this was the northernmost point of their empire.

Some of the statues are arranged neatly in archaeological parks near the village, with little umbrellas over them to keep off the rain. Within walking distance are the **Bosque de los Estatuas**, with more than 35 figures, and the **Alto de los Idolos**, where the largest statue is 23ft (7 meters) high. Four Mesitas, labelled

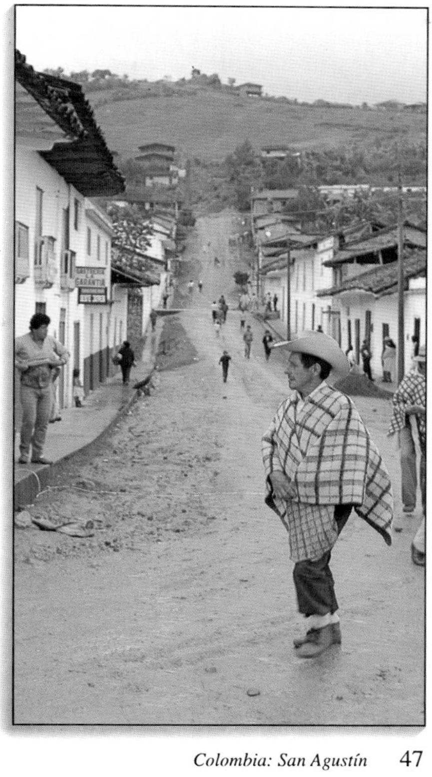

eft, ysterious atue of the agdalena alley. Right, e muddy reets of San justín.

from A to D, are also nearby: these are ancient burial sites with mounds, statues and funeral temples.

Most exciting to visit are the statues further in the countryside. Many can be reached only on horseback as the paths are difficult and often knee-deep in mud. The landscape is spectacular, with dramatic canyons and gorges over-looking rivers and crashing waterfalls. It can be a somewhat perplexing experience to force through thick undergrowth and confront a stone image poking its tongue out down the valley to ward off an unknown threat.

Rhythms of the countryside: Once the stone statues have been visited, San Agustín can become a difficult place to leave. This is not just because rains sometime cut off the roads: some travelers stay for weeks, forgetting their timetables and relaxing into the slow pace of the village.

Every hour of the day provides a different view of Colombia from the cliché to the totally unexpected. Mornings begin in the coffee shops around the village, where old men get out their playing cards, some young men start on a beer, and the women listen to a radio which is never properly tuned.

Although the surrounding countryside grows some of the world's finest coffee beans, the cafes serve only instant. The alternative is a tea bag, while the adventurous can go for a *te doble*, or "double tea", which turns out to be two tea bags in one cup.

Meanwhile the shopkeepers stand in their doorways to catch the morning sun and nod hello to passers-by. A few Indians carry chipped wood into town for sale. Hammering starts up in the leather shops which make saddles and boots, while cowboys gather on their corners to watch the women walk by.

The village market gets under way. Goat cheese *empanadas* are fried up, banana soup brewed and lumps of meat boiled. Juice shops lay out their papayas, pineapples and mangoes, as well as novelties peculiar to Colombia.

Right, coach and horses: coming home from the market, San Agustín.

Caribbean Coast

Arriving from the highland capital of Bogotá in Colombia's Caribbean coast, gently washed by the waveless sea beneath crystal clear skies, is like stepping into a completely different world. It is as if there were two separate countries: one cool and remote, the other tropical and sensual.

Rum and sun: A gateway to the coast and to many attractions of the north is **Santa Marta**, the capital of Magdalena province. One of the most pleasant cities in Colombia, it was founded by the Spaniards in 1525, but there are few remaining colonial charms in the popular modern resort town in recent years. Instead, visitors come here for more simple pleasures: to loll in the sun along **El Rodadero beach**, considered the best in Colombia; to stroll up and down the tourist promenade while being bombarded by *salsa;* or simply to take a seat in one of the many outdoor bars, sip on a rum cocktail and enjoy the view across the bay to the rocky island of **El Morro**.

Santa Marta is also a convenient jumping-off point to the **Tairona National Park**. This stretch of untouched jungle is at the foot of the **Sierra Nevada de Santa Marta**, a pyramid-shaped mountain that drops sheer into the Caribbean. Once the territory of the Tairona Indians, the park attracts day visitors and overnight campers, who walk through its many paths to find a remote tropical hideaway for complete isolation.

The nearby **Santuario de Flora y Fauna Los Flamencos** is a new nature reserve which, as the name suggests, is full of pink flamingoes. Living in large colonies, they seem to wallow in shallow water near coastal lagoons and can be seen from well-marked paths.

Lost City: Santa Marta is also the place to reach **La Ciudad Perdida**, the Lost City of the Taironas that was only found in 1975. Larger than Machu Picchu in Peru, the discovery is considered the most important in South America this century, confirming that the Taironas

The sun goes down over the Caribbean.

were not just major craftsmen but had built one of the largest cities on the continent, with wide boulevards and roads connecting it to the outside world.

The city was found by *guaqueros* or grave robbers in the tropical jungle of the Sierra Nevada. Calling it *El Infierno Verde* (the green hell), they fought over the finds and tombs until the government stepped in, placing an army post at the site. Today it can be reached in 20 minutes by helicopter or in three days on foot. Archaeologists are still working to find more of the golden jewelry for which Colombia is famous.

The site is impressive, with many paths and buildings cut from the ever-encroaching jungle. But despite the work done so far, in the absence of any written records on the site, archaeologists can only guess when it was built – probably in the 13th century – and what disaster or war led the inhabitants to disappear without a trace.

ɬany on the ɔast are escended om African aves.

García Márquez country: Although not aware of it, the first image many foreigners have of South America comes from the Caribbean coast of Colombia, thanks to the works of national author and Nobel prize winner Gabriel García Márquez. His writings have preserved the life and history of the region, and today the small town of **Aracataca** where he was born and raised – and which he fictionalized as the town Macondo in his 1967 novel of magic realism, *One Hundred Years of Solitude* – can be easily visited to get a glimpse of coastal life.

Buses leave several times an hour from the Santa Marta terminal, winding past the nearby swamps before heading inland to Aracataca. Nothing distinguishes the town from the thousand others like it in Colombia: its streets are wide and empty; the houses have rusting tin roofs and walls peeling from age. There is a plaza with a statue of Bolívar, an old church tower, several shabby billiard halls and a couple of empty restaurants. The air tastes of sugar in the morning and of dust in the afternoon, while the tropical heat builds steadily during the day until it becomes almost unbearable.

But tucked away in a back street is a modest building with the sign: GGM MUSEUM. In a garden full of chickens is the house where García Márquez was born in 1928 – wooden, whitewashed and without a stick of furniture inside. Today a "cultural center", it usually has a number of young boys on its porch learning somewhat painfully how to play the saxophone.

After visiting this shrine to the author, the real attraction of Aracataca is the fact that it is a typical coastal town with the peculiar atmosphere of the Caribbean. Old ladies wander past with colored rollers in their hair, using battered parasols to keep out the sun; unemployed men in singlets sit in the shade, looking melancholically at the sky; little girls in freshly pressed white frills climb up and down the broken seats in the plaza; someone might be polishing up a 1950 vintage Chevrolet, one of the few cars in the town; and yellow butterflies drift oblivious to the distant afternoon storm clouds that roll over the surrounding hills.

CARTAGENA: ROMANTIC CITY

Of the many colonial jewels in South America, **Cartagena de Indias** is perhaps both the most romantic and least known. Placed on the tropical Caribbean coast, saturated by heat, music and feverish dreams, this fortress city of the Spaniards is a living museum. Just walking its streets recalls the days of bloodthirsty pirates, galleons full of bullion, and swordfights beneath the palm trees.

But Cartagena is also a growing city, with beaches, nightclubs, bars and restaurants. It offers the easy-going, languid attitude of Colombia's coastal people, as well as their love for rum, dancing and basking in the sun.

Spain's New World fortress: The history of Cartagena reads like an adventure comic. Founded in 1533 by the first of Spain's scurvy-ridden conquistadors, the town quickly blossomed to be the main colonial port on the Caribbean and the gateway to the whole South American empire. But as the wealth plundered from Indians piled up in galleons to be taken to Cadiz, the city became a target of every pirate and desperado cruising the Caribbean seas.

During the 16th century, Cartagena was besieged no less than five times by buccaneers and cutthroats. The most dramatic was by the English sea-dog Sir Francis Drake, who sacked the port in 1586 and extorted a 10 million peso ransom from the inhabitants. This was shipped back to England for Queen Elizabeth, along with the bodies of several crocodiles, blasted from the nearby swamps with cannons and stuffed with straw.

Soon afterwards, the Spanish crown decided to create fortifications so powerful that the port would be impregnable. Stone ramparts and battlements were constructed over many decades, the like of which the Americas had never seen. The pirate attacks continued, but never with the same success: Cartagena was even able to survive several sieges by the English and the French.

Left, horse and buggy at La Puerto del Reloj. Below, the docks at Cartagena.

Exploring the old city: Arriving in Cartagena from the airport, a highway passes along Marbella beach towards **Las Murallas**, the stone ramparts that still surround the old city. Many small forts, where cannons and other defensive weapons were placed to ward off sea attacks, remain intact.

The colonial section of Cartagena is only a small part of the metropolis, which has a booming port and a petrochemical industry, but it contains enough relics to warrant several days' exploration. Centuries ago the city was divided by a channel that separated the more affluent areas of **El Centro** and **San Diego** from the poorer **Getsemaní**. Today the waterway has been filled in and is the more modern area called **La Matuna**.

A good place to start is the **Plaza de Bolívar**, where people still come to lounge in the shade of sagging trees during *siesta* time. Facing the plaza is the **Palacio de la Inquisicion**, one of Cartagena's finest buildings. Its baroque stone entrance is topped by the Spanish coat of arms and along its walls are elegant wooden balconies. Serving a more gruesome purpose was the small window at the side of the entrance, where the faithful could come to denounce their brethren for heresy, blasphemy or witchcraft.

The palace has now been turned into a museum, recalling the fearful proceedings of the Holy Inquisition. It contains examples of torture instruments and a model of Cartagena in 1800, along with fine original maps. Now decorated with contemporary etchings of witches and sorcerers, the room upstairs was where inquisitors sat at their desks to interrogate victims. Despite the terrible reputation of the Inquisition, only 12 people were actually put to a public *auto-da-fé*, burning alive in the plaza for their sins. When Cartagena declared its independence, this palace was one of the first places that the angry crowd came to sack.

Adjoining the Plaza Bolívar is the town **cathedral**, which looks more like a fort than a place of worship. Three

ortress at an ernando.

blocks to the south is the **Plaza de la Aduana**, once used as a parade ground for troops, and now based around a statue of Christopher Columbus. Call in at the **Museo de Arte Moderno** in the former Royal Customs House, then take a stroll under the **Puerto del Reloj**, which once linked the inner walled town to Getsemaní by a drawbridge over a moat.

Following closely the city wall around to the south, you will run into the **Iglesia y Convento de San Pedro Claver**, named after a Spanish monk who spent his whole life looking after the black slaves brought over from Africa. Nicknamed the "Slave of the Slaves", St Peter Claver (1580–1654) was the first person to be canonized in the New World.

Today the three-story monastery is a haven of solitude and peace, with arched stone patios built around a garden of flowers and foundations. Pairs of colored macaws scrabble along tree branches and a wire cage contains a pair of toucans. The remains of St Peter himself are kept on display in the church next door; although he may only be a skeleton, the religious robes are kept starched and clean.

There are dozens of other colonial houses, churches and monuments worth visiting in Cartagena, and the best way to find them is by accident, by simply walking around, glancing in through doorways to shady courtyards and watching the daily life in the city. Drop in at the colonial **Casa de la Candelaria** – once a noble's mansion, now a restaurant – then stroll around the city walls in the afternoon sun to **Las Bovedas**. These were built two centuries ago as dungeons, with walls 50ft (15 meters) thick. Today the buildings are used for tourist shops, a coral museum and bar.

Barriers of stone: The whole of the old city was turned into a fortress, but the Spanish decided that this was not enough to keep their gold secure and even more extraordinary fortifications were built in key points.

Looming over the city from the San Lorenzo hill is the impregnable **Castillo**

Dancing the cumbia.

de San Felipe de Barajas. A complicated system of batteries, tunnels and hiding places was engineered from massive chunks of stone to ensure that no enemy could survive an assault. The tunnels, which can be visited, were constructed so that any sound would echo and warn guards of approaching soldiers. Meanwhile, the view over the old city from the castle is one of the best in Cartagena.

Located at the entrance to Cartagena Bay is the **Fuerte de San Fernando**. A huge chain was hung between it and another outpost at the opposite side of the bay to prevent surprise attacks. Many films on the colonial period have been shot in its well-preserved interior. The fort can only be reached by water and a colony of cheap restaurants and souvenir shops has cropped up nearby, somewhat detracting from the period effect. But once inside, local guides will take visitors to the darkest corners of the fort, built to contain sufficient troops and supplies to survive any siege in which they would be cut off from the rest of the city.

For an energetic walk to round off visits to the historical sites, climb the large hill behind the city to the **Convento de la Popa**. The Augustinians built a wooden chapel at the summit in 1607, soon replaced by a monastery with an image of the patroness of Cartagena, La Virgen de la Candelaria.

Facing the sea and a river: Just near the Puerto del Reloj is the city's dock area, **La Muelle de los Pegasos**. It is usually full of fishing and cargo boats, as well as the wooden riverboats that come by canal from the Magdalena river. All along this area are small juice stalls offering concoctions from more than a dozen fruit varieties, and where you can take a seat and watch the port life go by. On the other side of the port is a box-like **Convention Center**, once supposed to be one of the most modern in South America but looking decidedly out of place with its ugly, angular design.

Also departing from La Muelle are the many tourist boats offering services to the **Islas del Rosario**. Only a couple of hours away by high-speed motor, these tiny islands have the turquoise waters and golden sands that tourist brochures of other places offer, but never seem to deliver. Although part of a national park, many houses have been built on the islands – even though some are barely big enough to balance a basic structure.

For a taste of the local seafood, there is no more pleasant way to spend an evening than to stroll up **Avenida Venezuela** and call in at the *ostrerias*, small booths selling delicious shrimp and oyster cocktails. Take a seat, buy one of the city's excellent local beers, listen to the inevitably blaring *salsa* music and enjoy a sea breeze and the atmosphere of the Caribbean.

For more sophisticated fare and nightlife, the best place to head for is **Bocagrande**, several minutes out of town by taxi. Its long beach has attracted hotels and restaurants, turning it into a Colombian resort. Although the beach is not as spectacular as many would have you believe, the food and dancing is the best Cartagena can offer.

panish unnel inside he fortress t San ernando.

todas
ertas
CHEQUE MERCANTIL
ABRA 24

VENEZUELA: BIRTHPLACE OF "THE LIBERATOR"

Venezuela – literally, "Little Venice" – was first seen by Europeans on 1 August 1498, when Christopher Columbus sighted the Orinoco River on his third voyage to the New World. The country's imaginative name was conferred soon afterwards by the Italian explorer Amerigo Vespucci (1451–1512), who compared Indian lake dwellings to the houses and canals of his native Venice.

Although one of the first parts of Latin America to be settled, Venezuela remained a sleepy and malaria-ridden backwater of the Spanish Empire for three centuries. Conquistadors in search of gold and pearls quickly followed the first explorers. The native Carib and Arawak Indians could raise no effective resistance and the invaders established their first permanent settlement at Cumana in 1520.

As in Colombia, expeditions went into the wilderness in search of "El Dorado", often never to return. The conquistadors reasoned that gold was to be found in the most tropical regions, and so plunged deeper into the Amazon in search of further Aztec or Inca empires.

Eventually, the Spaniards gave up the hunt for instant wealth and turned to agriculture. To help them, settlers rounded up Indian slaves to found and build Barqisimeto, Valencia and Caracas, and it was not until a century and a half later that they began to spread out and settle the vast *llanos* or grasslands in the country's south. Even today these regions are only sparsely inhabited.

The March of "the Liberator": The soporific calm of colonial Venezuela, punctuated by three brief rebellions against Spain, was broken at the beginning of the 19th century with the rise of General Simon Bolívar, *El Libertador,* who was born in Caracas in 1783 and whose memory is worshipped in every part of South America. Short in stature, thin and wiry, a fine horsemen and swimmer, Bolívar displayed superhuman energy. He inspired the passionate devotion of his soldiers and the praises of everyone from South American patriots to foreign romantics such as the English poet Lord Byron, who named a boat *Bolívar* and planned to sail it to Venezuela.

Together with his trusty lieutenant Antonio José de Sucre (1795–1830), Bolívar took the fight against Spain as far south as the frontier of Argentina. He picked up the revolutionary banner from Fransisco Miranda, a leader betrayed by his companions to the royalists, and in 1806 set up a provisional government in the town of Angostura, now called Ciudad Bolívar.

Bolívar rounded up a motley army of horsemen from the *llanos* and some 5,000 British veterans fresh from the Napoleonic wars in Europe. After initial victories, he faced a reinforced royalist army from Spain and was forced to retreat to the island of Jamaica. On his return to the continent, he won a string of brilliant victories against the Spaniards, culminating in the battles of Varas and Boyacá in Colombia. From there he headed into Ecuador and Peru, meeting the Argentine general San Martín on the way. In all these conflicts, Venezuelan troops made up a large part of Bolívar's armies. Up to a quarter of the country's population may have perished in the struggle for independence. But the Libera-

Preceding pages: river scene at La Llovizna near Puerto Ordaz, Venezuela. Left, one of the many new skyscrapers in Caracas, capital of Venezuela. Right, Simon Bolívar, who broke Spanish rule in much of South America.

tor's great dream of a unified republic called Gran Colombia fell apart even as he watched. Venezuela, like the rest of South America, drifted into civil war and anarchy. Bolívar died in 1830 a crushed man, alone and bitter in a country retreat, cursing the continent to which he had devoted his life.

The land of oil: Venezuela entered the 20th century deep in debt, its ports blockaded by the fleets of creditor nations. Then, in 1917, oil was found, transforming it from a vagabond nation into Latin America's richest.

The derivatives of "black gold" were needed to work the factories and automobiles in Europe and the United States, and within years Venezuela had not only paid off its debt, but was rolling in new wealth. Its dictator, Juan Vicente Gomez, an uneducated *mestizo* who had worked on cattle ranches, made sure that Venezuela would be attractive to foreign investors, turning Caracas into a consumer capital and covering Lake Maracaibo with spider-like rigs and throbbing oil pumps.

Oil towns sprung up overnight, with bars, gambling dens and brothels, where prostitutes were known by such names as "The Derrick" and "The Hoist". Native communities were robbed of their lands to set up oil fields, all fenced in and with their own police.

The President's family and friends flaunted their wealth around the world, joining Texas oil barons in their search for new forms of ostentation. Gomez rewarded cronies with petroleum shares and gifts, including one to the archbishop who gave the President special dispensation to eat meat on Good Friday.

The massive profits rarely reached the bulk of the Venezuelans, who moved in increasing numbers from the countryside to the crowded capital. The country had some of the world's biggest superhighways, but health and education standards had changed little. Gomez's death in 1935 led to riots and strikes, until a clique of military officers and landowners took power. Coup followed coup before Colonel Perez Jimenez came to the helm, crushing all opposition, but also putting some oil money into public works and into accommodation for laborers. Finally, in 1958, amid riots which killed 600 people in the capital, Jimenez was overthrown by younger military officers. Democratic elections were held and for 30 years Venezuela enjoyed the continent's most stable rule, with successive governments passing on power in a peaceful and orderly way.

The decline of "black gold": In 1980, Venezuela's petroleum sales were bringing in US$18 billion, about 95 percent of its export revenue. However, with the worldwide crash in oil prices the days of easy money ended. The first dramatic effect was felt with "Black Friday", February 18, 1983, and the beginning of a series of rapid-fire measures, including exchange controls and immediate devaluation of the national currency, the bolívar. The real crisis was not felt until Carlos Andrés Pérez returned for a second presidential term in 1989, riding on the popularity from his first time in office in 1974–79. His tough economic measures led to two bloody military coup attempts that year, with government forces turning back disorganized rebels.

Pérez survived the coups, but on May 20, 1993, he was indicted by the Supreme Court on charges of corruption for alleged misuse of secret funds. The Senate voted to remove him from office and he was convicted in 1996, but with credit for several months in jail, and because of his age (over 70), he completed his brief sentence at home.

Rafael Caldera, who had been president 1969–74, was re-elected in 1994, based on his reputation for honesty and promises not to devalue the bolívar or impose exchange controls. His honesty may hold true, but his promises did not. Faced with mounting foreign debt, the failure of 17 financial institutions representing nearly half the total of the nation's deposits, massive capital flight, and the public's lack of confidence, the value of the bolívar was slashed and exchange controls simultaneously imposed from June 1994 to April 1996. A system of "bands" was imposed to "prevent shocks", but the bolívar was heavily devalued, hitting Venezuelans hard, and making it a bargain destination for tourists.

Characterized by a lack of any coherent plan, the Caldera administration played up the IMF's announcement that the government's "Venezuela Agenda" was on the right track. But talk rather than action followed promised cuts in government spending to attack the fundamental problem: huge public debt which continued to mount.

Crime has risen with the economic woes. Robberies directed against the "haves" has turned them into prisoners of their privilege, living behind high walls and guarded doors. Meanwhile violence among the poor in the Caracas *barrios* is increasing.

But Venezuela has tremendous potential for economic growth. It has a proven desire for a democratic system. The first direct elections for state governors and municipal officers were held in 1989, and recent years have seen the rise of active neighbourhood associations in the cities. They are tackling local social and economic problems which mainstream politics, through corruption and patronage, still fails properly to address.

Left, steamers on the Orinoco at the turn of the century. Above, young bohemians gather at the Caracas bookstore in the 1920s.

Caracas: Capital of Contrasts

Venezuela's capital is a city of dramatic contrasts. The first view is a shock for most foreign visitors. Hillsides surrounding the resort-lined access road from the airport and on slopes ringing the center of the metropolis are blanketed with thousands of haphazardly constructed *ranchos* – shacks largely inhabited by illegal aliens and poor people from the interior of the country. The central valley and upscale residential areas of the east and south show a quite different side: modern, attractive, affluent.

Centro is the traditional heart of the city and **Plaza Bolívar** is the core of its historic zone, with treasures including the 19th-century **Capitolio** (the nation's capitol); 17th-century **cathedral**; **Casa Natal**, birthplace of the liberator of South America, Simón Bolívar and the next-door **Museo Bolivariano**, with mostly military-related memorabilia associated with him; **Concejo Municipal**, birthplace of Venezuela's call for independence (visit the unpublicized but fascinating **Museo Criollo** inside, which has a display of miniatures created by Raúl Santana depicting every aspect of *criolla* life at the turn of the century, along with paintings by the impressionist Emilio Boggio); **Casa Amarilla**, a former jail and a presidential residence, and now offices of the Foreign Ministry) and **Gobernación** (seat of government of the Distrito Federal, with art gallery on the ground floor) facing the northwest corner of the plaza; and the **Iglesia de San Francisco**, begun in 1575, with gorgeous gilded altars lining its walls, and connected **Palacio de las Letras**, the academies of history, language, and science. All these are within a block or two of the plaza. The striking twin-tower pink and gray **Panteón Nacional**, resting place for more than 130 of the nation's greatest heroes, is several blocks north of the cathedral.

Though it will require a taxi ride if you are on foot, well worth the effort is a visit to the excellent colonial art mu-

Preceding pages: crossing Venezuela's great river, the Orinoco River. **Below** view of Caracas, one of South America's busiest cities.

seum, **Quinta de Anauco,** in San Bernardino. Surrounded by gardens cultivated with plants of the period, this elegant colonial home, built in 1797, has been restored and filled with outstanding colonial art and furnishings.

Financial hub: Interspersed with colonial gems in Centro are sleek glass-faced skyscrapers, harboring the nation's financial, business, and political movers and shakers. Shoppers here can delight in the nine-story gold center, **La Francia,** facing the Plaza Bolívar, or small shops with shoes, clothing and jewelry stretching east from the plaza to the **La Hoyada** Metro station.

Chuao has the city's largest shopping center, soon to be superseded by others under construction. It has most attractive mall, **Centro Ciudad Comercial Tamanaco (CCCT)**, filled with top-of-the-line shops, restaurants, night clubs, travel agencies, Viasa's office with advanced luggage check-in service, a supermarket, and the four-star all-suites Hotel C.C.T. Facing it is the distinctive **Cubo Negro** (black cube) office building, one of the many examples of attention-grabbing contemporary architecture in the city), with a dramatic hanging kinetic sculpture by Venezuelan artist Jesús Soto,

Traffic and parking are perennial headaches in Caracas but the fast, clean, economical subway system, the Metro de Caracas, takes you across the city in minutes. Though a slower option, there is also a non-stop flow of dirt-cheap buses that go everywhere. Taxis are numerous and inexpensive, but few drivers speak English, so have addresses written in Spanish if you can.

A few minutes east from *Centro* (the northeast exit from the **Capitolio** Metro station is closest to the plaza, diagonal from the capitol), you can get off at the **Bellas Artes** stop where one block to the south is **Parque Central**. This massive urban renewal project has 56-story twin towers, seven 44-story apartment and commercial units and with the outstanding **Museo de Arte Contem-poráneo de Caracas Sofía Imber**, with sculpture garden and restaurant. There is also a fabulous hands-on children's museum, **Museo de los Niños**, and the **Museo Teclado**, a keyboard museum with weekly concerts. Nearby is the spectacular **Teatro Teresa Carreño** complex and the **Teatro Rajatabla**, home of a popular alternative theater group.

Other attractions here are the **Museo de Ciencias Naturales** and **Museo de Bellas Artes**, with international contemporary art, and **Galería de Arte Nacional** showing Venezuelan artists, approached on weekends through lines of local artisans' stands. Behind them is the sprawling **Los Caobos Park** and in the background the **Ibrahim bin Abdulazis al Ibrahim Mosque**, the largest in South America.

Continue on the Metro to **Plaza Venezuela,** then walk eastward to **Chacaíto** along the kilometer-plus "gran avenida" of **Sabana Grande.** This wide pedestrian boulevard is lined with shops, sidewalk cafés, and chess tables, where office workers often spend their lunch hour. It is delightful by day, best avoided by night when hookers and transvestites take over and the adjacent hotels are primarily rented by-the-hour.

A little further east, exit the Metro at **Parque del Este** to explore the 81-hectare (200-acre) park by Brazilian landscape architect Roberto Burle Marx, with planetarium, mini-zoo and artificial lake. The **Museo de Transporte** facing its east side is connected by walkway over the busy freeway.

Among the city's other parks, two blocks south of **Plaza Venezuela**, with a giant central fountain, is the **Jardín Botánico** which has extensive gardens, an arboretum of some 100,000 trees and sculptures by national artists. Or take the No. 2 spur of the Metro from the Capitolio station to the **Zoológico** stop to visit the 486-hectare (1,200-acre) "no cages" **Caricuao Zoo**.

The greatest concentrations of upscale restaurants are found in the commercial zone of **Las Mercedes** in the shopping center of the same name. **La Candelaria**, just east of Centro, is an eminently Spanish sector famous for its dozens of traditional restaurants and tascas, bars which feature many hearty appetizers known as *tapas*.

MÉRIDA, THE ROOF OF VENEZUELA

The Andean states of **Trujillo** and **Mérida** are perhaps the most picturesque regions of Venezuela. There are regular flights, but this area should be visited by car to take in the breathtaking landscapes, explore the quaint villages, stop at wayside restaurants to savor trout or smoked cheese on a wheat flour *arepa* washed down with warm spiked anise-flavored *calentado* or creamy eggnog-like *ponche andino*, and admire colorful flowers bordering glacier-fed lakes.

The most scenic route calls for joining the **Transandean Highway** via **Guanare**, heart of the central farmlands, where a side trip a few kilometers to the south possible to the impressive **Templo Votivo Nacional de la Virgin de Coromoto**, inaugurated in 1996 by the Pope and dedicated to Venezuela's patron saint. Or you can go via **Boconó**, with a beautiful drive through coffee-growing areas to this "garden city of the Andes" and side trips to **Tostos** and picturesque **Niquitao** to the south.

Regardless of entry point, just south of Valera, one passes through **La Puerta**, "the doorway to the Andes", the beginning of a journey through soaring, velvety green mountains, some cut with terraces, some simply cultivated on seemingly impossibly steep slopes where oxen plow.

The first paved road arrived here in the 1950s and things haven't changed much since then. Houses have walls of pounded earth or stacked stone, central courtyards and tile roofs. Hardy residents, draped with ponchos against the morning chill, sell produce and crafts along the way. Visitors are likely to encounter some sort of religious or folkloric celebration on any visit, announced with the shooting off of rockets and processions.

The *páramo*: The area around **Paso Pico El Aguila**, Venezuela's highest paved road, traverses the treeless, enchanting high moors known as the *páramo*, where the *frailejón*, with fuzzy silver-green leaves and bright, tall-stem yellow flowers, dominates the landscape. In nearby **Apartaderos** is the **Observatorio Astronómico Nacional del Llano del Hato**, with four giant telescopes and visiting hours for celestial observation, plus a museum.

Sierra Nevada National Park borders the east side of the highway from **Santo Domingo** and has many hiking trails for which the Inparques office in Mérida sells a detailed map. The principal entrances are by the park guard station of **Laguna Mucubají**, the largest of Mérida's 200 trout-filled glacial lakes, called *lagunas*, on the Santo Domingo route, and via the park's administrative center at **Mucuy**.

A touristy, but nonetheless interesting stop not far north of the city of Mérida is **Los Aleros**, the reproduction of an entire Andean village as it typically would have looked before the highway came through.

Natural high skyline: Forming the impressive backdrop for the city of **Mérida**, the state capital, are the country's highest peaks: **Bolívar**, **Humboldt**, **La Concha** and **Bonpland**, all over 16,000 ft (4,900 meters). Unless one is bent on scaling these chilly crests, or going by mule to visit one of the quaint villages in remote high valleys such as **Los Nevados**, simply viewing them in the background can be enjoyed in the year-around spring-like weather of Mérida. For the adventurous, all the paraphernalia of mountain sports and activities is available in the city.

Known as "the city of gentlemen", Mérida (founded in 1558) has the highest and longest **cable car** in the world, recently restored and climbing to 15,486 ft (4,720 meters). during its run of 7½ miles (12km). The city has a massive, eclectic **cathedral** with pelican-shaped rain spouts, and the **Universidad de Los Andes**. On Av. 2 at Calle 29 is **Heladería Coromoto**, in the *Guinness Book of Records* for having more flavors of ice cream than anyone else in the world – more than 540 at the last count.

Continuing south from Mérida, down through **San Cristóbal**, the capital of Táchira state is an enjoyable and beautiful drive where you can see the more tropical side of the Andes.

GUAYANA HIGHLANDS: THE LAST FRONTIER

The vast southern sector of Venezuela, encompassing Delta Amacuro, Bolívar, and Amazonas states, is referred to as the **Guayana Region**, named after its base, the **Guayana Shield** formed out of pre-Cambrian rock up to 2.5 billion years old and among the most ancient on the continent.

A particular feature of the region are *tepuys*, plateaux of stone soaring majestically above the floor of the savannah or jungle. The most famous of these are **Roraima**, subject of Sir Arthur Conan Doyle's *Lost World*, and **Auyantepui**, from which **Angel Falls** drops. Because of the isolation and great temperature changes, from freezing nights to tropical days, many plant and animals species have evolved there which are found nowhere else in the world.

Great Savannah: The paved road, completed in 1991, linking Ciudad Guayana with **Santa Elena de Uairén**, at the frontier with Brazil, has contributed to opening up the southern part of the state to tourism, permitting even city cars to traverse the length of Canaima National Park and its famous **Gran Sabana** a great savannah, dotted with moriche palms and settlements of Pemón Indians. Like exclamation points are the stately *tepuys* in distance, including the famed **Roraima,** the highest of all the *tepuys* of the Guayana Shield. There are numerous impressive falls along highway, such as **Kama-merú** and **Quebrada de Jaspe**, with the bed of the river and stair-step falls glittering with semi-precious reddish-orange jasper. There are many places for basic lodging.

One of the country's principal tourist destinations is the area around the community and lagoon of **Canaima** in the northwest corner of the 12,600 sq. mile (30,000 sq. km) **Canaima National Park**. Access is only by air and visitors can opt for day tours from Caracas (Maiquetía), Porlamar and Puerto Ordaz, or stay over at one of the many cabins or rustic shared rooms in hammocks.

The principal draw here is the proximity to **Angel Falls** (named for an American bush pilot, Jimmy Angel, who is credited for "discovering" it in 1935 (though not only Indians, but other adventurers recorded its presence before that), the longest free drop (2,648 feet) of water in the world, and the full length of the falls plummeting 3,212 feet (likewise a world record) from the edge of **Auyantepui,** also known as "Devil's Mountain", the park's largest *tepuy*, covering 700 square kilometers.

Weather permitting, visitors get a look at the falls from the air, both as they arrive and leave. Though Auyantepui and its famous falls is not visible from the camps at Canaima, excursions of several days duration by dugout canoe and on foot are offered, but *only* in the rainy season from May to November.

The main camp area is in a beautiful setting in front of the lagoon, with low, wide **Hacha Falls** at the far side and *tepuys* in the background. More recently, another popular destination, **Kavac**, has been developed at **Kamarata,** also with access to the falls only by plane.

mong the aterfalls in e tropical ainforests of e Guyana ighlands

THE ANDEAN HIGHLANDS

Clustered around some of the most inhospitable territory in South America are the countries of the Andean highlands: Peru, Ecuador and Bolivia. The area was home to extraordinary civilizations for thousands of years before being finally united by the Inca empire in the 14th century. Although the the Incas were the most famous rulers of South America, they lasted for only a brief moment of glory before the Spanish conquistadors crushed them into submission. The colonists subsequently kept themselves distant from their subjects and to this day the old Inca lands are dual societies: one Indian, impoverished and traditional; the other *mestizo* or white, looking to Europe or the United States for cultural inspiration.

Nowhere is this more so than in the Inca heartland of Peru. The capital, Lima (*page 85*), lies on the barren coast facing the sea, while the ancient capital of Cuzco (*page 93*), regarded by the Incas as the navel of the world, remains in the mountains, nursing its shattered past. From these two cultural poles Peru's many wonders can be reached : to the south, the baffling Nazca lines (*page 88*) and in the north the ancient adobe city of Chan Chan (*page 112*). The world's highest railway runs east of Lima to Huancayo, connecting with the colonial city of Arequipa (*page 100*) and onwards to the shores of Lake Titicaca (*page 118*). Thousands flock here every year to trek in the Andes (*page 102*) or delve into the Peruvian Amazon (*page 108*), now being opened up to settlement at breakneck speed.

To the north of Peru is the Republic of Ecuador. Rarely making a mark in regional history, this compact country can be explored in short jumps from the mountain capital Quito (*page 128*), a colonial gem now placed on the World Heritage list. Nearby are the unique Otavalo Indians (*page 130*), using their weaving to attract new wealth, while a short jump east lands you in the steamy Oriente jungle (*page 132*). A train ride through the "Avenue of the Volcanoes" (*page 134*) ends on the Pacific beaches of Ecuador's coast (*page 136*) – several hundred miles beyond which are the country's pride and joy, a biologist's dream untouched by interfering humans: the unique Galápagos Islands (*page 139*).

Across from Lake Titicaca is the land-locked mountain country of Bolivia. The most Indian and poorest of South America's republics, Bolivia is a mash of ancient traditions and colonial relics. Carved from the bleak *altiplano* or "high plane", La Paz is the highest capital city in the world (*page 153*). Still in the shadow of spectacular peaks is the nearby Yungas region (*page 160*), a sub-tropical refuge of banana, coffee and coca leaf. Back again in the windswept heights is the town of Potosí (*page 164*), once the Spanish empire's main source of silver and still a mining town.

Preceding pages: the Bolivian Andes; and Quechua Indians at a wedding near Cuzco, Peru. Left, Quechua woman with llama near Cuzco (Qosqo).

PERU: CRADLE OF THE INCA EMPIRE

Peru was the center of the Inca Empire that once stretched the length of South America, and vestiges of this amazing civilization still awe visitors. But long before the Inca Empire flourished, Peru was home to dozens of equally intriguing cultures, whose remains lie scattered around the country.

As early as 100 BC the Chavin Indians were producing sophisticated drawings and pottery in a civilization stretching along Peru's barren coastline. At around the same time, the Paracas Indians wove fanciful fabrics using techniques that cannot be reproduced even to this day. They practiced trepanation, a primitive form of brain surgery, as well the intentional deformation of babies' skulls for the sake of fashion.

The Moches, meanwhile, showed a singular touch for realism, as they recorded in painful detail their daily life on pots and vessels, showing the illnesses they suffered, the instruments they played, the way they delivered children, their sexual practices, the fruits they ate and the animals they raised. Scientists say they may have been the region's best metallurgists, electroplating gold centuries before the Europeans.

Just before the rise of the Incas, the most expansive Indian culture was that of the Chimus, who controlled most of the northern Pacific coast and successfully irrigated the desert. The most important remainder of the Chimu civilization is the adobe city of Chan Chan outside Trujillo. Covering 8 sq. miles (20 sq. km), it was Peru's largest prehispanic city and housed a civilization that fished, produced crafts and attained superb goldworking skills. Tied to the sea and its rhythms, the Chimus worshipped the moon. They were conquered by the Incas in 1450.

The Children of the Sun: Tradition has it that the Incas began when brother and sister Manco Capac and Mama Ocllo were sent by the sun god Inti to civilize mankind. The couple emerged from the waters of Lake Titicaca and, gold staff in hand, began their divine task of finding a spot where the staff would sink easily into the ground. That place was Cuzco and there Manco Capac taught the men to farm and Mama Ocllo taught the women to weave. The Inca dynasty started regionally and the empire did not come into being until the reign of Inca Pachacutec, who began a great expansion, conquering other Indian nations, creating a state religion and turning Cuzco into a glittering capital as large as any city in Europe.

Perhaps one reason the Incas – literally, Children of the Sun – developed their civilization so rapidly is that they did not destroy the Indian cultures they vanquished. Instead, they left the conquered nations to live as they always had, except that they were required to worship the sun as their supreme god. The Incas sent teachers and craftsmen to the conquered nations to study them and adopt their medical advances, weaving and pottery techniques and irrigation skills. The Inca dynasty lasted only just more than a century (from AD 1400 to 1532) but it is considered one of the most advanced of all times.

The Incas called their empire Tawantinsuyo – the four quarters – and with Cuzco (now known by the older spelling of Qosqo) as its center, it consisted of Chinchaysuyo in the north, Contisuyo in the south, Collasuyo in the high plateau near Lake Titicaca and Antisuyo to the east. The Incas built a highway network from southern Colombia to south of what is now Santiago, Chile, with side roads leading into Argentina. The Peruvian desert, one of the world's driest, was irrigated and crops were stored in silos to avert hunger in the kingdom. The Spanish later borrowed Incan metallurgy skills in mining the gold, silver and copper so abundant in Tawantinsuyo. And Incan architecture was so fine that cities such as Machu Picchu still stand and a razor blade cannot be inserted in the mortarless joints of its stone buildings. Yet all this was achieved without any knowledge of the wheel or the written word.

The Conquest: How did a handful of raggedy Spanish soldiers manage to conquer the most powerful dynasty in South America? They were, simply, in the right place at the right time.

When Francisco Pizarro landed in Peru in

Preceding pages: Plaza de Armas, Cuzco. Left, Spanish conquistadors forcing Indians to carry their baggage on expeditions.

1532, he found a country recovering from the ravages of a civil war. For 40 years beforehand, Inca Huayna Capac had reigned from Cuzco, the capital of the Empire, and Quito, the northern capital. In both cities, he had a son – one legitimate, the other illegitimate. When Huayna Capac died, both claimed to be heirs to the throne, and the Inca Empire suffered its first internal war. At about the time the illegitimate son Atahualpa had defeated his brother and was tying the severed head of the enemy army's general to his belt, Pizarro and his conquistadors were arriving in his empire.

The Spanish quickly took advantage of the confusion from the five-year civil war, as well as Indian legends that predicted the arrival of tall white gods sent by the sun. The Spaniards' weapons, sailing ships and horses – never seen before by the Indians – gave credence to their divinity. When Pizarro invited the Inca Atahualpa to meet them in the northern town of Cajamarca, he unsuspectingly agreed.

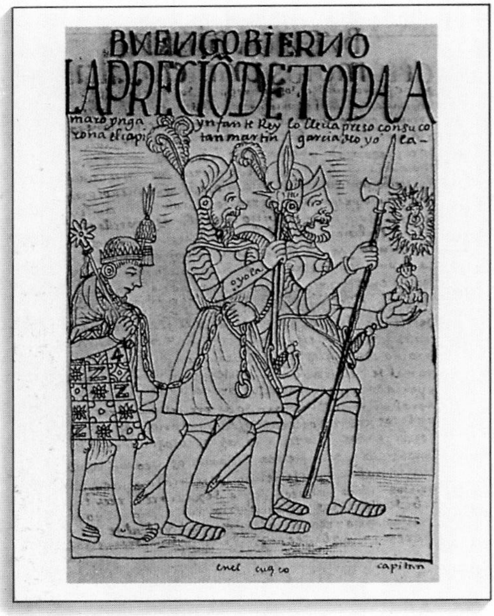

The meeting was a trap. Pizarro and his men, hidden in ambush when the emperor arrived with his entourage, greeted them with cannon blasts and a cavalry charge. Thrown into disarray, thousands of the Inca guards were slaughtered mercilessly and Atahualpa himself captured.

The conquistadors proceeded to demand a massive ransom for the emperor's life: Pizarro ordered a large room in an Inca palace filled once with gold and twice with silver. The Incas searched the empire to supply the metals, which had only ceremonial value for them. But as soon as the demand was fulfilled, Pizarro had Atahualpa strangled.

Some say that the Spanish killed the Inca to punish him for the death of his brother Huascar during the civil war. Others say it was for blasphemy because Atahualpa rejected a proferred Bible – having little use for it, never having seen a book. Either way, it may have been a chess game that tipped the scale. During his nine-month imprisonment, while Indians were sending gold and silver-laden llamas to Cajamarca with his ransom, Atahualpa passed his days watching his guards play chess. He eventually learned the game and, in a key match between two soldiers, indicated to one how to win the game. When those same soldiers voted whether the Inca's life should be spared, he was condemned to death on the margin of one vote – that of the Spaniard who lost the chess match.

With Atahualpa dead, the Inca Empire fell apart. The Spaniards marched on Cuzco and began wholesale pillaging of every scrap of precious metal they could find, destroying temples and magnificent works of art in the process. Indians were enslaved and forced to work in mines. The collective farming system at the base of the Inca society was devastated, as were the aqueducts used to provide irrigation. Catholicism was imposed and colonial administrators installed to rule Peru with an iron fist, sapping the country's resources for use in Europe.

Despite all this, the Indian culture could not be crushed. Often accepting superficial changes, its traditions have survived. A remarkably large percentage of the Indians in remote villages still speak only the Quechua and Aymará tongues. Much of their dress has changed since Inca times, but the rituals and fiestas have persisted – only changing the names to fit in with Christian lore. And the haunting Andean music still survives, using the same instruments and tunes that were played long before the Spaniards came to plunder the Inca lands.

Colonial rule: With the Indians vanquished, Pizarro founded Lima in the valley running along the Rimac River. Initially the buildings in the new city were rustic one-story wood and mud structures, with the exception of the impressive cathedral.

Under the Spanish, Lima grew and prospered. As it expanded, so did its religious zeal, prompting some to dub it the "Rome of South America". Churches and monasteries sprang up, each more ostentatious than the next. By 1606, there were at least 15 temples and convents apart from the cathedral. Eight years later, Lima's population had swelled to 26,500; of the total, 10 percent were nuns, bishops, priests or monks. With them, eventually, came the terror of the Holy Inquisition, which meted out its frightful tortures in Peru from 1570 to 1761.

During this growth period, little outside the capital was developed and Peru's fast-paced commerce was centered on the mining of precious metals. The wealth that soon came to the country was reflected in the continual construction and the increasing use of finer building materials, including woods from Panama, marble from Italy and Spanish tiles. The 1687 earthquake that destroyed most of Lima only served to give its inhabitants a chance to rebuild – on an even more grandiose scale.

Interiors of homes were decorated with cloths from Venice, Holland, and Brussels and, by 1629, there were at least 200 fine carriages roaming Lima's streets. Even the lower class citizens had jewels. In keeping with the religious fervor of the century, the faithful attempted to outdo one another with offerings of gold and silver, the construction of altars of fine stone and donations of silks brought from Europe and now guarded in religious art museums across Peru.

If the 17th century was Lima's religious period, then the 18th century was its romantic era when poetry, promenading and pomp were the mainstay. It was during this time that the *tapadas* appeared, the shockingly sensual upper class *mestizo* women. It wasn't long before a rivalry arose between these flirtatious *tapadas* and the more reserved Europeans. While the Spanish females cinched their skirts to show their tiny waistlines and fluttered fans before the eyes of admirers, the *mestizos* narrowed their skirts to emphasize their ample hips and bared their arms. But they always kept their faces veiled – with the exception of one eye. French feminist Flora Tristan, visiting her father's homeland, described the *tapada's* Moorish costume as a "skirt... so tight that it allows

Left, Indian artist Felipe Huamán Poma de Ayala shows the Spaniards leading the last Inca to execution. Above, Hatunrumiyoc, the famous Twelve Angled Stone in Cuzco (Qosqo).

just enough room to put one foot in front of the other and to take very little steps. This costume so alters a woman – even her voice since her mouth is covered – that unless she is very tall or very short, lame, hunchbacked or otherwise conspicuous, she is impossible to recognize. I am sure it needs little imagination to appreciate the consequences of this time-honored practice which is sanctioned or at least tolerated by law." Those "consequences" ranged from men unknowingly flirting with their own wives on the street to infidelity on the part of the *tapadas*.

It was during the days of the *tapadas* that Peru's most famous romance was born – the affair between the young, vivacious Perricholi and the aging Viceroy Manuel Amat y Juniet. Tongues wagged viciously when Amat lost his head for the Perricholi, whose real name was Micaela Villegas, after seeing her sing and act onstage in Lima. He built her a mansion, gave her a gilt carriage and fathered her child before he was ordered back to Spain. Their love story inspired Verdi's opera *La Perrichole*; the title uses the nickname that stuck to Micaela when Amat furiously called her a half-breed bitch on a Lima street one night. The Spanish translation, *perra chola*, was mispronounced by the toothless Amat, who had a strong Catalan accent.

While the upper class Peruvians lived well, served by black and Indian slaves, they could not ignore the cries for independence coming from Argentine General José de San Martín in the south and from Venezuelan Simon Bolívar in the north. The 1800s brought revolution to Peru.

There were heated political discussions in the cafes and streets as well as talk of conspiracies and secret agents sent by San Martín to sow discontent against the government. When the liberation armies finally arrived in Peru, the upper class *mestizos* took up the cry for independence, angered by the inferior status they held compared to Spanish-born residents, as well as the high taxes and trade restrictions imposed by Spain. San Martín proclaimed Peru's independence in Lima on July 28, 1821, although most of the country was still held by the Spanish crown. Under an agreement reached between San Martín and Bolívar – after they argued over whose troops would liberate Peru – the Venezuelan finished the job of freeing the country and, in 1826, the last Spanish troops surrendered.

The first years of independence saw few real changes in the way Peruvians lived. But midway through the century, military man Mariscal Ramón Castilla took over the presi-

Above, a military outpost overlooking Lima at the end of the 19th century.

dency, and under his rule modernization shook the country. Basic services such as water and street lights were installed in Lima and a rail line – the first on the continent – linked the capital with the nearby port of Callao. Castilla abolished slavery and directed approval of the 1860 national constitution. However, the growth of the country in those decades was set back by the losses and destruction incurred during the bloody War of the Pacific, which lasted from 1879 to 1883 and in which Chile took over a section of the mineral-rich desert in southern Peru. (Bolivia lost its only port to Chile in the same war, ending up a landlocked nation.) Chilean soldiers sacked public treasures and artwork in Lima, burned the library and easily defeated armed men and children before heading even farther north. Many of the monuments in city plazas across Peru pay homage to those who died in that war.

Despite these tumultuous changes in the 19th century, life continued much as in the 17th for the bulk of the population: the Indians living in the highlands. The two worlds of Peru, the Indian and the "European", were drifting even further apart.

A divided nation: Of all of South America, Peru saw the most important clash between the native and European cultures – a clash that continued to modern times, proving fertile ground for terrorism in the highlands, an energetic chaos in Lima and an amazing creativity. Like most Latin American capitals, the past two decades have seen massive migration from the interior of the country. *Campesinos* sold their last cow or llama, packed up their bundles and took the first bus – or in many cases, the first passing truck – to Lima in search of a better life. They left a beautiful countryside void of schools, hospitals, electricity or running water. And they flocked to a city that does not have the housing, buses or schools to handle a burgeoning population of 6½ million.

Ever since colonial days, Peruvian Indians have shown an amazing aptitude for survival. In recent years that resourcefulness has ranged from earning a living selling loose cigarettes and lottery tickets in downtown Lima to the emergence of *ambulantes* – vendors selling from temporary kiosks set up wherever the fancy strikes.

Unlike Chile, where dictators were unheard of until General Augusto Pinochet took over in a 1973 coup, Peru has been run by a number of military strongmen. Most intriguing among them was the left-wing military dictator General Juan Velazco Alvarado, who undertook a flawed agrarian reform program, temporarily turned over the biggest newspaper – *El Comercio* – to a peasant group and renamed all of Lima's streets after national heroes. An example is Avenida Woodrow Wilson, which the dictator relabeled Garcilaso de la Vega after the *mestizo* who chronicled the Spanish conquest of Peru.

Sprinkled among these dictators have been 30 elected presidents, all of them conservatives until the 1985 election of Alan García Pérez of the left-of-center party APRA. The charismatic García drew popular support from the poor and non-urban dwellers who cheered his decision not to pay the foreign debt incurred by past governments.

But the US cutoff in development aid, the unwillingness of businesses to invest in the country and political maneuvering by the far left and far right – both hoping a García failure would open the way for them to take control in the next election – sent the nation of nearly 20 million into an economic crisis in late 1988 after two years of growth. Prices of food and gasoline doubled overnight on more than one occasion, the currency devalued rapidly, and people spent days in passport lines before heading to Venezuela or the United States in search of jobs.

The political division and social upheaval accompanying García's presidency opened the way for an independent candidate, Alberto Fujimori, to take over as president. Having attracted controversy for temporarily dissolving Congress after he took power, Fujimori got the economy sufficiently under control to win a second term in 1995.

He also succeeded in weakening the guerrilla group Sendero Luminoso (Shining Path) whose activities in the mountains had severely affected tourism in the 1980s. After waging a savage campaign against the guerrillas, government forces captured their leader, Abimael Guzman, in 1992. Since then many other leaders have defected, making Peru's hinterland once again safe for trekkers.

Peru remains a divided nation. With most of the country living in bitter poverty, the challenge is still to break out of its colonial past, resolve its internal conflicts and end the cycle of economic dependency.

LIMA: CAPITAL OF THE NEW WORLD

Spanish conquistador Francisco Pizarro considered the site where he founded Lima on January 18, 1535, inhospitable: rain seldom fell, earthquakes were common and winter was a time of gray skies and dreary wet fog. But his soldiers saw it as the best place for a quick sea escape in the event of an Indian uprising. Little did they suspect this open plain would become the political and military capital of the New World, seeing the reigns of 40 viceroys before the "City of Kings" was declared capital of an independent Peru in 1821.

The city center: The **Plaza de Armas** is where for centuries the power of the new colony was concentrated and it remains one of the city's most active and attractive squares. At its center are rose gardens, a stone fountain and park benches that draw young couples looking for a place to chat, countless shoeshine boys and families in their Sunday best posing for photos. A favorite photo is one with the **Palacio Presidencial** in the background. The foundation of this building is the same that Pizarro built, but its facade was changed in the early 1900s during the dictatorship of Augusto Leguia.

When President Alan García took power in 1985, he eliminated the Prussian-style helmets and elaborate uniforms the president's military guard had worn for years, calling them too showy. You can see their more modern garb every day at 1pm during the ceremonial changing of the guards, who are still fond of the goosestep.

The best spot for viewing the ceremony is the wide front balcony of the **Palacio Municipal**. The original structure used as city hall burned down in 1923 but its neoclassical replacement is impressive, with marble stairways, gilt mirrors and crystal chandeliers. Don't leave without seeing the library. This small room with massive leather chairs, huge wooden tables and a smell of old books offers a calming respite from the traffic outside. Its circular stairway was hand-carved from a single piece of Nicaraguan cedar.

Across the square, the **Archbishop's Palace** has one of the most beautiful wooden balconies in the city. Take a peek in the archbishop's patio before heading next door to the **Cathedral**, which contains Pizarro's remains.

A few blocks away is the jewel of Lima's old churches, the **San Francisco Monastery**. Lovingly repaired after every earthquake that damaged it for the past four centuries, this cloister features fine mosaic tiles from Seville, frescoes discovered – to the delight of art historians – when an earthquake demolished portions of an outer wall, and an impressive collection of religious art. But most fascinating are its catacombs – underground tunnels and burial pits that served as Lima's cemetery through the colonial period.

Behind the Palacio Presidencial is the **Desamparados Train Station**, the city's first iron building. Brought in pieces by boat from England and rebuilt here in 1908, it is the depot for all trains

Preceding pages: dusk at the Plaza San Martín, Lima. Left, girls wait at the doorway of the Lima Cathedral. Right, colonial wooden balconies grace Lima's buildings.

out of the capital. Also behind the president's office is the bridge that leads to **Rimac**, one of Lima's oldest neighborhoods, named after the river that flows along its edge. A working-class *barrio*, where women in doorways chat with their neighbors while children play rough games of soccer in the streets, it once was the city's top spot for promenading. Then, the stars were the *tapadas* – seductive women whose skirts shamelessly showed their tiny feet, whose necklines were scandalously low and whose heads and shoulders were covered by a veil that bared only one eye. In the afternoons, they were most likely to be found on the **Alameda of the Descalzos**, courting and flirting but never lifting their Moorish-style veils to reveal their identities.

This promenade, built in 1611, is lined with Italian marble statues representing the months of the year and bordered by lawns and flowers. It leads to the **Convento de los Descalzos**, or Monastery of the Shoeless, whose friars wore only sandals on their feet.

As religious as it was opulent, Lima was home to two of South America's most famous saints: Rose of Lima and Martín de Porres. Rose, who died of tuberculosis at age 31, had a fervent following during her short lifetime and she was credited with curing thousands, performing innumerable miracles and even saving the city from pirate attacks which, along with fires and earthquakes, were the scourge of Lima. For Martín de Porres, fame came after his death. While alive, he lived with the monks in the **Santo Domingo Monastery** in Jirón Camaná but was barred from becoming a priest because he was black. His duties in the monastery included working as the janitor, and statues and paintings of the saint usually show him with a broom in hand. Both saints are buried in Santo Domingo, which is open to visitors.

Lima's religious devotion may have been proportional to the terror inflicted by the Holy Inquisition. Chills will run up your spine when you descend into the depths of the **Inquisition Museum** in Plaza Bolívar. Gruesome tortures were

The changing of the guard in the Plaza de Armas.

inflicted to obtain "confessions" of heresy, Judaism and witchcraft. The guilty had their property confiscated by the church and were promptly marched off to the Plaza de Armas to await their fate, which ranged from public flogging to burning at the stake.

Lima's most active square is **Plaza San Martín**, linked to the Plaza de Armas by the pedestrian walkway **Jirón de la Unión**, once the most fashionable shopping district in the Peruvian capital and still a lively place where you can buy silver items, browse in bookstores and chuckle over the endless variety of goods sold by street vendors who block the walkway until passing policemen shoo them off. Plaza San Martín is where most of the money changing houses are located (alongside the Gran Bolívar Hotel) and it is usually jammed with people lounging on the grass, eating their lunches or watching the caricaturists, charlatans and gypsies who frequent the plaza. Its recent salmon-colored paint job caused a stir; Limeños claimed it was fine during their sunny summer but too dreary when the winter fog (*garua*) arrives.

From downtown, it's a quick cab ride to the suburb of **Miraflores**, the stomping ground of the children of Peru's wealthy families. Here you can people-watch at outdoor cafes, shop or enjoy good meals and music. The pretensions of the Miraflores youths – the *Mirafloriños* – are described with precision in the novels of Mario Vargas Llosa. Miraflores is the best place for theaters, trendy boutiques and nightclubs.

Nearby is **Barranco**, the romantic bohemian neighborhood made immortal in Peruvian waltz and still home to the city's best artists, poets and jazz bars. Here you'll find the lover's lane, **Puente de los Suspiros**, or Bridge of the Sighs, lined by fragrant jasmine trees and hyacinth bushes. It heads down to a lookout point over the Pacific Ocean, and to a stairway to the beach for those in good shape. Strolling here at sunset you may hear Peruvian flute music or Argentine tangos wafting from windows as you pass.

oney hangers ear the laza San artín.

THE NAZCA LINES

"The lines are like precious parchment, very fragile, that needs to be guarded jealously." —Maria Reiche

Until the 1930s **Nazca** was like any other small Peruvian town with no claim to fame, except that you had to cross one of the world's driest deserts to reach it from Lima. But it is that desert – a sketching pad for ancient Indians – that has since drawn thousands to this sun-bleached colonial town of 25,000 and made the pampa, or plain, north of the city one of the greatest scientific mysteries in the New World.

The Nazca lines are a series of drawings of animals, geometric figures and birds ranging up to 1,000 ft (300 meters) in size, scratched on to the arid crust of the desert and preserved for about 2,000 years owing to a complete lack of rain and special winds that clean – but have not erased – the pampa.

It wasn't until 1939 that Paul Kosok, a North American scientist flying over the dry coast in a small plane, noticed the lines that previously were believed to be part of a pre-Inca irrigation system. A specialist in irrigation, he quickly concluded this had nothing to do with water systems. By chance, the day of the flight coincided with the summer solstice and, making a second pass over the area, Kosok discovered that the line of the sunset ran tandem to the direction of one of the bird drawings. He immediately dubbed the Nazca pampa "the biggest astronomy book in the world".

But it was a young German mathematician who became the expert on the lines and put the backwater on the map. Maria Reiche was 35 when she met Kosok and served as his translator at a seminar on the lines. She had arrived in Peru eight years earlier to teach the German consul's children in Cuzco (Qosqo). After Kosok's speech, she spoke with the scientist and he encouraged her to study the pampa. She dedicated the next half century to the task.

Aerial view of the mysterious lines in the desert.

Unraveling the mysteries: An 86-year-old woman in 1990, blinded by glaucoma and her movements restricted by Parkinson's disease, Reiche could no longer see the lines that she studied, measured, cleaned and charted daily from both the air and a 50-ft (15-meter) high metal platform she built. But she had developed the most widely accepted theories on the hundreds of delicate drawings that cover a 31-mile (50-km) belt between Nazca and Palpa.

"This work was done so that the gods could see it and, from above, help the ancient Peruvians with their farming, fishing and all their other activities," said Reiche, who called the pampa an "astronomical calendar". For example, she speculated that the drawing of the monkey – her favorite representation– is the Indian symbol for the Big Dipper, their constellation representing rain. When rain was overdue – a common occurrence in this plain where it only rains the equivalent of about half an hour every two years – the Indians sketched the monkey so the gods, looking down, would be reminded that the earth was parched.

Reiche also broke the key to the puzzle on how the Indians could have made the huge sketches with such symmetry. She determined that they used a basic unit of measurement, probably the distance from their elbows to their forefingers, and based all calculations upon this. As for symmetry, Reiche believes they used ropes tied to stakes to form circles and arcs that they cut with straight lines.

There are, of course, those who do not accept Reiche's theories, denying that the ancient Indian culture would have drawn something they themselves could not see. Because the drawings can only be seen from the air, the International Explorers Club set out in 1975 to prove a theory that the Nazca Indians had aircraft. The Explorers Club made a hot air balloon, the Condor I, out of cloth and reed and flew it for 60 seconds, reaching an altitude of 300 ft (100 meters). But the flight proved little.

Writings from the planets? The most damaging theory about the Nazca lines came seven years earlier when Erik Von Daniken published *Chariots of the Gods*, in which he put forward the argument that the pampa was part of an extra-terrestrial landing strip – an idea that Reiche discarded impatiently.

Von Daniken's book drew thousands of visitors to the lines, but newcomers in search of the drawings set out across the pampa on motorcycles, four-wheel-drive vehicles and even horses, leaving the unerasable marks of their visits. Now it is illegal to drive or even walk on the pampa: Reiche used the profits from sales of her book, *Mystery on the Desert*, to pay four guards to keep a constant watch on the plain.

Reiche's last trip to the pampa was in 1987 with Phyllis Pitluga, the US astronomer Reiche chose as her successor. Although she does not live in Peru year round and still retains a post at the Max Adler Planetarium in Chicago, when in Nazca Pitluga gives a daily lecture about the pampa.

There is a metal ladder at the side of the Pan American highway if you want to view the pampa from ground level, although there is not much to see from so low. The best way to capture the impact of the lines is to fly over them. AeroCondor offers flights from Lima, Ica and the small airport in Nazca, and flights can be booked at the Alegria, Montecarlo, Nazca and Turistas hotels. Flights last up to 45 minutes and can be bumpy. A lunch and a stop in the **archaeological museum** in downtown Nazca is included in the day-long Lima package. Aeroica in Nazca also has 45-minute flights over the lines. If you want to make the flight more economical, it is possible to wander over to the Nazca airstrip and wait around for pilots who are willing to bargain on the price for carrying tourists over the lines.

From the ground, the Nazca pampa is hot, dry and dusty, but from the air it is an amazing puzzle that will thrill you as you try to decipher the lines and figures they represent. Unfortunately, unless you take the AeroCondor flight from Lima, the only way to reach Nazca is by bus – a trip that can take up to eight hours from the Peruvian capital.

THE GREAT TRAIN RIDE TO HUANCAYO

The trip to **Huancayo**, Peru's most popular Sunday fair, takes your breath away – literally – because to reach this town you must take a trip on the world's highest single-gauge rail line.

Leaving Lima's Desamparados depot, this engineering marvel built by eccentric North American Henry Meiggs is more than 600 miles (1,000 km) of zigzags, tunnels and trestles. Those who survive the curves must still conquer the altitude – and the task is formidable. Crossing the hauntingly beautiful Andes, which have lured poets and hindered economic development, the train reaches altitudes so extreme that conductors run up and down the aisles administering oxygen to any passengers who fall victim to the flu-like symptoms of *soroche*, or altitude sickness. Indians claim the headache and breathlessness of *soroche* can be relieved by drinking *mate de coca*, a tea brewed from coca leaves. *Soroche* usually peaks just as the train does at Ticlio, a spot 15,800 ft (4,800 meters) above sea level and marked only by a Peruvian flag atop a mountain. At this altitude there are no trees or vegetation and passengers speak in whispers. Only the clicking of cameras and the sound of the struggling train engine break the silence.

Vendors sell to tourists on the train to Huancayo.

Moonlike landscape: The rugged landscape begins to soften and llamas reappear on the hillsides as the train begins its descent past the mining town of La Oroya and the raging Mantaro – the River of Destiny. It was on its banks that the Huancas Indians stood up to the conquering Incans and, later, where the Spanish wrestled control from the Incan nation. Bloody battles were fought beside the Mantaro during the Peruvian struggle for independence and when Chilean soldiers invaded the region during the Pacific War a century ago.

The highland's violent past contrasts with the tranquility at one of the more unusual stops en route to Huancayo. That is **Ocopa**, little more than a monastery tucked away in a eucalyptus grove and home to one of the continent's finest libraries. To go there, you must leave the train at Jauja and take a bus or cab to the **Santa Rosa de Ocopa Monastery**, opened by Franciscan monks in 1725 as the jumping-off point for missionaries planning to convert the Amazon Indians to Catholicism. The missions met with some resistance, as evidenced by the monastery wall bearing the portraits of 54 priests who died at the hands of the indigenous people. Those who escaped the rainforest kept journals that were key in mapping paths through the Amazon in later years.

The overpowering scent of eucalyptus and a calming silence greet you on the walk up the long driveway to the well-kept monastery. At its doorway Indian women, their children at their heels, sell local sweets.

The monastery's tiled corridors and flowering patios lead to its prize: its library with volumes dating back to 1490. Many arrived in the saddlebags of European priests who crossed the Andes on mules. In the years since, the cool dry mountain air has acted as a natural preservative for the library's 25,000 volumes. The oldest and most valuable are centuries-old biology, astronomy and theology books from Europe and some of the first diaries describing the Spanish conquest of the New World. The monastery has recently been opened to overnight guests.

Health cures in the Andes: Returning to **Jauja**, where you left the train, you will find no decent overnight accommodations but it is a delightful place to pass a few hours. It was the first capital of Peru, but Francisco Pizarro had to transfer the title to Lima when his soldiers protested they were too far from a sea escape route. Jauja's cathedral with 14 side altars, the Chapel of Carmen with silver altar columns and a handful of colonial buildings are evidence of the Spanish presence.

Jauja was once home to Peru's tuberculosis sanatorium, now a general hospital, and the Indian women wandering the main plaza selling fresh bread claim that the village never has a day without sunshine.The town's sun and the dry mountain air once lured tuberculosis sufferers from all parts of Peru.

Huancayo, at the end of the rail line, has lost its Andean charm as it has grown but its Sunday market is still one of the best in Peru. The market is increasingly overrun with modern goods, ranging from pots and pans and sewing machines to tennis shoes and spare tires. But mixed among the merchandise is a quality selection of woven belts and tapestries. If you look closely, you may even be able to find some with train engine designs in tribute to the metal monster that linked this town with the rest of the country. Embroidered skirts and shawls, delicately carved gourds, leather goods, alpaca blankets and handknit items are spread out on Huancavelica Street every Sunday.

In Huancayo, you will also have the best selection of regional food, including trout and *Papa a la Huancaina* – boiled potatoes covered in a spicy cheese sauce. For the brave, guinea pig is available fried or stewed.

ypical
ndean
arket.

CUZCO, CAPITAL OF THE INCA EMPIRE

The Indians selling goods in Cuzco's market speak Spanish with tourists and Quechua with one another. The buildings behind them are colonial style, built on Incan foundations. The elaborately carved facades on the city's many churches have detailed scenes of angels, saints and biblical characters – but their facial features are Indian. Cuzco today stands as a living testimony to the fact that the Incan civilization – one of the world's most sophisticated – could not be erased.

Of course, the Cuzco of today is dramatically different from the awesome city that Francisco Pizarro and his conquistadors found when they reached the capital of the Inca Empire, home to that kingdom's nobelmen, priests and their servants. Five hundred years ago, an estimated 15,000 people lived in the city, which was connected to the rest of the empire thanks to the *chasquis* – the long-distance runners who carried news and messages from the four corners of Tawantinsuyo to its capital. It is now a fairly modern Andean community with a population of about 140,000 and daily rail, plane and bus service to Lima.

Cradle of an empire: The name Qosqo means "bellybutton" or "navel" in Quechua because the Indians considered the navel the center or source. When the Spanish headed here after executing the last Inca, Atahualpa, in Cajamarca, they entered the fertile valley where Cuzco is located to find a lush green countryside filled with fields of corn and golden and purple patches where kiwicha and quinua, varieties of amaranth, were planted.

Corn was perhaps the most valuable crop in the kingdom. It was used for bartering and as a food staple that appeared in everything from main dishes to the alcoholic *chicha*, prepared by young women who chewed the corn, then spit it into jars where it fermented with their saliva. The amaranth, a grain high in protein that grows well despite extremes in temperature and moisture, nearly fell victim to the Spaniards' attempts to "civilize" the Indians. The conquistadors called it the "subversive grain" because it made the Indians healthy and, thus, harder to enslave. Pressured by the Spanish, the Vatican eventually outlawed its cultivation and consumption. But now, four centuries later, kiwicha and quinua once again flourish in the Sacred Valley of the Incas and Peruvians use the grains in everything from soup to cookies.

During the Indian reign, anyone entering Cuzco was greeted by the phrase, "*Ama Sua, Ama Quella, Ama Lulla*" – "Don't lie, don't steal, don't be lazy," summing up what was important in this cooperative society. Laziness, in fact, was a capital offense punishable by death. Although royalty and priests were exempt, everyone else in an Incan community was required to work on projects such as roads, irrigation ditches and aqueducts owing to an Indian philosophy that if all participated, all would take care of the finished product. When the Spanish took control of this country

eft, aditional eaving ethods near uzco. Right, elling local elicacies in e Plaza de rmas.

those cooperative projects – known as *mingas* – were replaced by forced labor. But like many other things imposed by the Spanish, they were not completely replaced; today there are still *mingas* in the Peruvian highlands. Women begin preparing a community meal on *minga* day while the townspeople, regardless of age, set to work.

At its peak, Cuzco was a city with sophisticated water systems, paved streets and no poverty. But that does not mean it was always a city of wise and competent leaders. One Inca chief, Urco, was behind such atrocities that his name was erased from Incan history and his mention forbidden. Another hung his enemies along the roadsides in the empire's cities – a gruesome message for the disloyal. Yet another had the entire population of a nearby city executed for the rape of a virgin selected to dedicate her life to the sun cult. But these excesses fail to overshadow the magnificence of a civilization whose architecture could not be destroyed and whose feats could not be matched.

The most startling and curious characteristic of Cuzco at first glance is its architecture. Huge walls of intricately fit stone pay testimony to the civilization that 500 years ago controlled much of the South American continent. The Spaniard's attempts to destroy every trace of the "pagan" Incan civilization proved too ambitious a task and the Europeans ended up putting their own buildings on the indestructible Incan foundations, often using the same huge rocks that had been cut by the Indians. The cathedral in Cuzco is made in part from stones hauled from Sacsayhuamán, the Incan fortress outside the city.

Walking into the past: To explore this intriguing city, the **Cathedral** is a perfect place to start. It is located on the **Plaza de Armas** which, in Incan times, was known as Huancaypata and in addition to being the exact center of the empire was the spot where the most important religious and military ceremonies were held. Although the most spectacular view of the Cathedral comes after dark when its dramatic lights turn

View of Cuzco from Sacsayhuamán.

the plaza into a breathtaking sight, its interior can only be seen during the day – and you won't want to miss it.

Built on what once was the palace of Inca Viracocha, the Cathedral mixes Spanish Renaissance architecture with the stone-working skills of the Indians and took a century to build. Its Maria Angola bell in the north tower can be heard up to 25 miles (40 km) away. Made of a ton of gold, silver and bronze, the more than 300-year-old bell is reportedly the largest on the continent.

El Triunfo church, to the right of the Cathedral, was built in honor of a Spanish victory over the Indians, who unsuccessfully tried to burn the thatched roof chapel that originally stood on the site. On the other side of the Cathedral is the **Church of the Holy Family**. At only 250 years old, it is one of Cuzco's "newer" structures.

In a city with so many churches, it is an honor to be dubbed the "most beautiful" and that is exactly the title that belongs to **La Compañía**, sitting on what once was the palace of Inca Huayna Capac on the main plaza. Construction of the church, with its intricate interior, finely carved balconies and altars covered in gold leaf, took nearly 100 years to complete.

The street to the side of this baroque church leads to what was the most important place of worship in the Inca Empire. Now the **Santo Domingo Church**, this was once known as Koricancha – Temple of the Sun – and was the most magnificent complex in Cuzco. Walls there were covered in gold, and windows were constructed so the sun would enter and cast a near blinding reflection of golden light off the precious metals inside.

Spanish chronicles tell of how the Europeans were stunned when they saw Koricancha's patio filled with life-sized gold and silver statues of llamas, trees, fruits, flowers and even delicately handicrafted butterflies.

Virgins of the sun: In modern Cuzco, yet another Christian enclave was formerly used as an Incan holy place. This is the **Santa Catalina Convent** that

elow, Indian 'oman sells er weavings. **ight**, the olonial treets of uzco.

centuries ago housed a different group of cloistered women – the Chosen Women, or virgins who dedicated their lives to the sun god. Now a colonial-style building occupied by Roman Catholic nuns, this was home to 3,000 women who were trained to serve their heavenly husband, the sun, or attend to the pleasure of his earthly son, the Inca.

An important contribution to the art world stems from the mixing of the Indian and Spanish cultures and the latter's failure to obliterate everything that was Incan. This dark religious painting style – touched with brushings of gold – is known as the School of Cuzco. In these paintings you will see archangels dressed as Spaniards and carrying European guns, but surrounded by cherubs with Indian facial features. School of Cuzco paintings of the Last Supper show Christ and his Indian-looking apostles dining on guinea pigs or Peruvian cheese. Scenes of the crucifixion depict a Christ hung on a cross decorated with Indian symbols.

A fine collection of this art, which flourished from the 16th through 18th centuries, is found at the **Museum of Religious Art** on Calle Palacio heading downhill from the Plaza de Armas. This building, where once stood the palace of Inca Roca, has Moorish features and complicated carvings on its doors and balconies. And just outside this building is the **Twelve Angled Stone**, a masonry masterpiece left by Incan architects who proved no stone was too irregular to be fitted without mortar.

The easiest way to see Cuzco's landmarks is to buy a $10 ticket that allows you to visit the **Regional History Museum**, Santa Catalina, Koricancha, the Cathedral and the **San Blas Church** – with its elaborate solid wood pulpit carved by an Indian craftsman – as well as half a dozen Incan ruins in the Sacred Valley outside of Cuzco.

The valley of ruins: The best known of these ruins is the overwhelming fortress of **Sacsayhuamán**, a bold example of the Incan architectural skills. Made of massive stones – including one weighing 125 tons (117,000 kg) – this military

Below, crowd watches Festival of the Sun ritual at Cuzco. Right, the Inca's throne, Machu Picchu.

MACHU PICCHU

The mystery of Machu Picchu did not start in 1911 when Hiram Bingham stumbled on the snake-infested mountaintop citadel hidden by a vast tangle of vines and trees. This site on the steep summit overlooking the raging Urubamba River was always a mystery – because only a chosen few in the Inca Empire were allowed to glimpse it. To call it a "lost city" is misleading; it was more like a sanctuary.

Machu Picchu means "Old Peak", and the higher Huayna Picchu (Young Peak), stands vigil over it. The only ways to reach the site today are along the Inca Trail or on the four-hour bus and train service from Cuzco. At 3,000 ft (900 meters) lower than Cuzco, this area is semi-tropical and a lush green covers the terraced gardens. Much like Pachacamac and other less important temples in the Inca Empire, Machu Picchu was home to priests, high functionaries, craftsmen and servants and, most importantly, the *mamacunas*, or virgins chosen to dedicate their lives to the sun god.

Machu Picchu was a city without poor, a city of streets, aqueducts where crystal clear waters still run, of liturgical fountains and walkways. Despite Bingham's discovery, the city remained inaccessible until the 1940s when an archaeological expedition working at the site discovered the Inca Trail cutting through the Valley of the Incas to the citadel.

The fate of this city's inhabitants remains unknown. Spanish chronicles of the Cuzco area make no mention of the city. Theories of its demise range from speculation that its occupants fell victim to epidemics to suggestions they were ostracized – and forgotten – in the bloody political disunity sweeping the empire before its fall. The Incas left no written record.

Excavations at the site have only added to the mystery. In all, the skeletons of 173 people were found; 150 were women. No gold objects were discovered. At the tomb of the high priestess, as Bingham called it, the remains of a woman and a small dog were found along with some ceramic objects, two broaches and woolen clothing. The woman had suffered from syphilis.

Although you'll enter the ruins at the Hotel Turistas, the only entrance to the city in ancient times was the narrow doorway at the southwest section of the citadel. The city's 12 acres (5 hectares) of cultivated land were farmed on narrow terraces on the steep slopes of the mountaintop and the thousands of steps connecting them have survived for centuries. It is believed that crops were harvested two to three times a year under the sunny blue skies of this city, although some terraces were reserved solely for the growing of brilliantly colored flowers.

The city is divided into sections: the cemetery, the jails, the small dwellings and the temples. The Temple of the Three Windows allows sun to pass through its windows to the Sacred Plaza and probably played an important role in sun rituals. Climbing higher is the astronomical observatory and Intiwatana, the curious-shaped stone block believed to have been a solar clock or, as some claim, "the hitching post to the sun", where the sun's rays cast shadows used in planning seasonal activities and religious ceremonies.

Also notable is the Torrejon, or huge round tower on the summit.

Some of the buildings in Machu Picchu were two stories high, originally topped with sharply-peaked straw roofs. What especially amazes architects today is the precision with which the stones for the buildings were cut and assembled.

On the slope in front of the city is the Condor Stone, a flat altar in the image of a condor's head and body. A hole at the front of the head leads below to a small cave; it is believed that sacrifices took place on the altar and the blood from those ceremonies collected in the cavern below.

A steep path rises from the site to the top of Huayna Picchu. At a distance, the exuberant vegetation of this neighboring mountain peak covers its stairways and terraces but the trail is an easy one. At the skirt of Huayna Picchu is the construction known as the Palace of the Moon, and from the summit there is an extraordinary view of the ruins and the Urubamba valley. ■

complex overlooking the city of Cuzco has a double wall in zigzag shape. It also marks the birthplace of the river that runs under Cuzco, channeled through stone conduits honed by the ancient Indians, invisibly supplying the city with water. Archaeologists estimate that tens of thousands of workers labored on this massive structure for more than seven decades, hauling the immense stone blocks that make up its double outside walls and erecting the near indestructible buildings that made the complex one of the most wondrous in all the empire. You can take the short hike to the fort – keep in mind, however, that it is uphill from the city. Or hire a cab to take you up and wait for you. This is one of the area's most spectacular spots to take photos at dawn.

If you're looking for a quiet place for a picnic lunch or for reading, Sacsayhuamán is the spot. Perched on a stone, you will have an amazing view of the red tile roofs of Cuzco and the lush fields of the surrounding valley. Pay no attention to the llamas wandering among the ruins; they won't bother you if you don't bother them.

Annually thousands of tourists and Cuzco residents step back centuries into time to celebrate Inti Raymi, the Incan feast of the winter solstice on June 24 at Sacsayhuamán. There is a procession, ceremony and symbolic sacrificial offering by costumed Indians and much merrymaking at the event.

Less than 4½ miles from Sacsayhuamán is **Qenqo**, an Incan shrine whose architectural features include an 18-ft (5-meter) high stone block that *Cuzqueños c*laim looks like a puma. Its name means labyrinth and this ceremonial center – dedicated to the worship of the mother earth – includes water canals cut into solid rock and a subterranean room.

Farther along the road to Pisac is a smaller fortress, **Puka Pukara**, believed to have guarded the road and the Sacred Valley of the Incas. Like Machu Picchu it has hillside terraces, stairways, tunnels and towers. To the north is **Tambomachay**, the sacred bathing place for

Inca ruins at Pisac.

the Incan rulers and their royal women. A hydraulic engineering marvel, its aqueduct system still feeds crystalline water to a series of showers.

From there you head down some 1,500 ft (400 meters) into the valley on the curvy road leading to **Pisac**, a friendly village known for its good fishing, Sunday market and the ruins above the town. To reach the ruins, climb past the mountainside terraces (Indian children will serve as guides for a small fee). This high-altitude hike may leave you winded and your heart pounding, increasing the likelihood you will be grateful when you turn a bend in what appears to be an isolated trail only to find yourself face to face with an Inca Kola vendor.

The stones making up Pisac's buildings are smaller than those at Sacsayhuamán but the precision with which they are cut and fit will still amaze you, as will the lovely view here.

If you plan to do a full circuit of the valley, then continue onto the great fortress of **Ollantaytambo**, 45 miles (72 km) from Cuzco. This elegant and intricate complex is made of rose-colored granite and has temples, baths and impressive military installations.

Back in Cuzco, stroll around and look at the artisan work for sale. The best quality goods are found in the stores, including those around the Plaza de Armas, although some bargains can be obtained from the Indian women selling items on blankets under the archways along the square. Cuzco is dependent on tourism and some visitors feel literally assaulted by the women, men and children who pester them to buy goods.

In the evenings, highland music can be heard wafting out of restaurants all over the city and one of the finest floor shows is at **El Truco**, where the pisco sours pack a wallop and the musicians and dancers are first rate. Eating a plate of *anticuchos* – a shish kebab of beef heart – and watching the performers in their traditional clothing, singing in Quechua and playing reed flutes makes you forget temporarily that the Incas lost their showdown with the Spanish.

:low, the rtress of ıcsayhuamán, nere the eatest battle :tween the ıanish and cas was ught. Right, young ıechua girl.

AREQUIPA: SECOND CITY OF PERU

Although **Arequipa** was far from Lima and isolated between desert and mountains when the country was young, it was on the route linking the silver mines of Bolivia to the coast. For that reason, it grew to be the Peruvian town with the largest Spanish population and the strongest European traditions. Today, with distinctive buildings of white volcanic stone, it remains Peru's second most important city.

In 1541 the King of Spain granted this oasis at the foot of the Misti volcano the title "Most Noble, Most Loyal and Faithful City of the Ascension of Our Lady of the Beautiful Valley of Arequipa." The Aymará Indians, who lived in this valley beside the Chili River, called it Ariquepa (*sic*) or "The place behind the pointed mountain."

Arequipa's **Plaza de Armas** is one of Peru's most beautiful. One full side is occupied by the massive **cathedral**, rebuilt twice in the early 19th century after it was destroyed by fire and earthquake. Its clock is the city's unofficial timepiece and the place where any disputes over punctuality are settled. Make sure you see the cathedral's organ from Belgium and its elaborately carved wooden pulpit, the work of French artist Rigot in 1879.

Two-story arcades grace the other three sides of the plaza, where palm trees, old gas lamps and a fountain amidst an English garden attract strollers and those looking for a park bench.

Centuries of earthquakes: The city is full of dignified patricians' homes built in the 18th century and which have, for the most part, withstood the tremors that regularly shake this city. The one-story colonial structures are replete with massive carved wooden doors, grilled French windows and high-ceilinged rooms clustered around spacious central patios. The best for visiting are **Casa Ricketts**, built as a seminary in 1738 and now used as a bank, the 200-year-old **Casa de la Moneda** or former mint and the

The spaciou[s] central Plaza of Arequipa.

Casa Moral, named after the venerable mulberry tree on its patio.

No visit would be complete without a stop at **La Compañía** church. The sacristy's ceiling is covered with miniature paintings and carvings of crimson and gold. The view from La Compañía's steeple is fabulous, especially at sunset when the late afternoon light casts a pink, then mauve, glow to the city's white sillar rock buildings.

The most astonishing stop in Arequipa is the **Santa Catalina Convent**, opened in 1970 after 400 years as a cloister for nuns. Despite the fact that its doors were closed all that time, there was little heed paid to the nuns' vows of poverty and silence. During its heyday, this convent's sleeping cells were more akin to the chambers in European palaces than austere retreats, with English carpets, silk curtains, cambric and lace sheets and tapestry-covered stools. As for silence, French feminist Flora Tristan, visiting the convent in 1832, said the nuns – daughters of aristocrats – were nearly as good at talking as they were at spending huge sums of money. Each had her own servant and dined with porcelain plates, damask tableclothes and silver cutlery.

When the convent opened its doors two decades ago, its anecdotes and scandals were resurrected. But don't believe it when they tell you the story of Sister Dominga, the 16-year-old who entered the convent when her betrothed left her for a rich widow, then staged her own death to escape. This beautiful young woman really did place the body of a deceased Indian woman in her convent bed one night then set the room on fire, but the whole thing occurred at another cloister in Arequipa – **Santa Rosa**. The Mother Superior refused to believe rumors that the young nun was really alive and living outside the cloister until Dominga sent her a message demanding return of the dowry she had paid to enter the convent.

Independent spirits: Arequipeñas are a proud lot and a century ago they started a movement to secede and form an independent country. Even today Lima residents heading to the "City of White" jokingly ask one another if they've remembered to bring along passports.

Outside of Arequipa, set in a beautiful countryside, is **Sabandia** and a flour mill that was restored, stone by stone, in 1973. Two hours away and drawing nearly as much tourist attention as the city itself is the **Colca Canyon**, which Peruvians claim is the world's deepest at more than 3,000 ft (900 meters), deeper than the Grand Canyon. From the Colca River at its base to the mountains above, the chasm reaches depths of 11,000 ft (3,400 meters). A series of canyon trips, usually starting with a bus ride from Arequipa then a switch to *burros* (donkeys) or trekking, allows you to explore this rift full of small towns seldom visited by outsiders. Look up and you will see condors.

To unwind in Arequipa in the evening, do what the locals do and head to a *picantería* for a cold Arequipeña beer and some spicy stuffed peppers, rabbit or marinated pork. Your beer will be accompanied by a dish of *cancha* – salty fried corn for munching.

ıside the anta atalina onvent, for enturies losed to the utside orld.

TREKKING THE ANDES

The great Andes, at 4,500 miles (7,200km) the longest mountain chain in the world, forms the backbone of western South America. It stretches from Colombia down to southern Chile and Argentina, and is made up of dozens of parallel mountain ranges known as *cordilleras*. In Peru, these cluster together providing trekkers with easy access to some of the highest peaks outside of the Himalayas.

Except for the most rugged and remote areas, the Peruvian Andes are not altogether untouched wilderness. Every piece of arable land is farmed in a variety of geometric shapes, ranging in colors from deep green to warm gold. It is into these areas that trekkers wander along well-used paths, sometimes pausing to allow a herd of llamas, or goats or sheep to scramble by, crossing high passes at altitudes above 13,000 ft (4,000 meters), and marveling at how a remote area on a distant continent can be so spectacular.

It is the presence of a living culture that makes trekking in Peru a unique experience. There is always the opportunity to stop and have

a conversation, or a word, or few simple hand signals with local inhabitants. Many of the older *campesinos*, especially the women, speak little Spanish and Quechua, the language of the Incas, is most often heard. The people are reticent with strangers but there is usually someone who will initiate a conversation by asking the passing *gringo* or foreigner, the time of the day – even though the *campesinos* can accurately tell the time without the benefit of any timepiece. The question is merely a device for conversation.

Passing these remote, populated areas is like stepping back into the past. One or two-room huts constructed of crude mud bricks and topped

by local Indians. Most people who go trekking in Peru want to get far away from the 20th century and become acquainted with the timeless indigenous lifestyle.

The formidable Peruvian *sierra*, or mountainous region, was conquered by the Incas, whose terraced system of agriculture enabled large areas of steep yet fertile land to be cultivated. This system is still employed in some areas, and countless remains of ancient terracing give an insight into the productivity achieved by this civilization.

The mountain Indians, or *campesinos*, cultivate numerous small plots of ancestral land. During growing season the hillsides are plowed

with *ichu* grass have changed little in design since Incan times. There is no electricity, and fresh running water is drawn from a nearby stream. Small courtyards house chickens and *cuy*, or guinea pig which are considered a delicacy in the *sierra*; corn and other grains can often be seen drying in the midday sun. Though the scene provides an interesting glimpse of an ancient lifestyle, it can make the trekker seem out of time and place.

Trekking is not the same as mountain-climbing. Most treks are simply extended walks along steep paths that can be attempted by any reasonably fit and healthy person. When planning a trek, one of the best places to start is the South American Explorer's Club in Lima. Their office at Avenida Portugal 146 keeps an invaluable stock of reports on trails, maps and books and the knowldegeable staff are more than willing to give advice to both beginners and experts.

Usually treks begin in the Andean *altiplano* at around 13,100 ft (4,000 meters), then descend to warmer climates – so bring a down jacket or warm clothes for the first few nights. A tent and a good sleeping bag are essential. To be certain of good quality equipment, it is best idea to bring your own but if the idea of lugging a tent and bag around does not appeal, these can be hired for several dollars a day in the major trekking centers high in the Andes: Cuzco in the south, Huaráz in the north, and La Paz just over the border in in Bolivia. Make sure you check the quality of what you hire, since items can often be the worse for wear.

Before setting off, spend a couple of days getting used to the thin high-altitude air around Cuzco and Huaráz, or you will find yourself becoming quickly exhausted. Food for treks can be bought at both of these places but don't expect the convenience dried meals or range of luxuries that can be found in Western stores. Take as much as will be needed for the duration since it is unlikely that anything can be bought on the way other than the occasional piece of bread or fruit in the most popular areas. A gas or kerosene burner for cooking is essential: there is no wood for fires at higher altitudes, and using up the scarce reserves at lower levels only adds to the serious problem of soil erosion that plagues the area. And of course no litter whatso-

Left, snow on the Andes. Above, an Indian woman tends her flock of llamas on an Inca road.

ever should be left behind. Guides are available but not necessary. The *sierra* of Peru offers unlimited trekking possibilities, but a few special places are an inevitable draw.

The Inca Trail: Of all the popular treks in South America, the three-to-five-day hike along the Inca Trail to Machu Picchu is the best known. The adventure from Cuzco begins with a four-hour train ride along the Urubamba River, known by the Incas as the Sacred Valley. Legions of early-rising *campesinos* loading and unloading their marketable goods at every stop crowd together in what begins to look more like a cattle car than a passenger train. At Kilometer 88 the train pauses briefly allowing hikers to disembark. Here at the trail head a footbridge temporarily separates the trekker from a rich history dating back more than 400 years. Trail permits costing around $15, which include entrance to the Machu Pichu site at the journey's end, can be bought here.

The first 7 miles (12 km) meander through easy terrain of dusty scrub rushes, low-lying hills, and a few primitive huts. It is the arrival at the foot of Warmiwañusqa pass that pitifully teases the hiker. Beyond it lies a wealth of Inca ruins, but struggling to the top of this 13,000-ft (4,000-meter) pass is no small challenge. The hiker soon identifies with its name. In English it translates as "Dead Woman's" pass.

From here Inca history begins to unfold. The small guard post of Runkuraqay, overlooking the valley and often shrouded in early-morning mist, is the first reward of the Inca Trail. Like a treasure hunt, the jewels become finer as the hike proceeds. Farther along, the more elaborately-constructed ruins of Sayajmarka ("dominant town") perch on top of a narrow cliff. The fine stonework for which the Incas were famous is apparent. An incredible "paved highway" snakes along the valley below, masterfully constructed by a people the Spaniards did not consider civilized.

Puyapatamarka ("cloud-level town") is fascinating for its circular walls and finely engineered aqueduct system which still provides spring water to the ancient baths. Below another surprise awaits. Along the road to Wiñay Wayna, huge steps like a stone stairway almost half a mile in length, lead down into high jungle. This stretch of the trail was only discovered in 1984. Before then, a modern footpath served to reach the same ruins. Tenaciously clinging to a steep hillside, the last set of ruins is also the most stunning. Wiñay Wayna presents an astonishing picture when first seen from a distance. That something so complex could be constructed in a ravine so vertical is beyond comprehension.

An hour away lies the jewel in the crown – Machu Picchu. The high pass of Intipunku, the Sun Gate, provides the first glimpse of the fabled city. This is the culmination of days of walking; the immersion into an ancient culture complete. Arriving as the Incas did centuries ago, the trekker begins the final descent into Machu Picchu, sharing a path with history.

The Auzangate Loop: The Cuzco area is rich in superb trekking possibilities. Considered by many seasoned hikers to be one of the finest areas is the route around the mountain peak of Nevado Auzangate (20,900 ft/6,400 meters). A truck from Cuzco is the usual transport, and the village of Tinki the destination for the start of this trek. The eight-hour ride is hot and dusty by day, and bitterly cold at night, which gives apt preparation for the day ahead.

The route of this five-day trek leads through one valley after another, each divided by passes nearing altitudes of 16,000 ft (5,000 meters). Inviting hot springs welcome the hiker at the start, and give a warm goodbye at the finish. Huge moraines, rock and silt deposits left behind by the Ice Age, and glacial lakes, each a breathtaking, yet different, shade of blue, provide plenty of visual feasts for the days ahead. The close-up views of Auzangate are spectacular, and frequent. At one point along the trail, the tongue of a glacier extends down within walking distance. A little exploration will reveal a huge ice cave within. It is easy enough to break the few icicles concealing the entrance, and roam through its numerous chambers.

Wild vicuña, a cameloid cousin to the llama, are elusive creatures valued for their fine wool. Herds of these skittish beasts are often seen, but only from a distance. Their domesticated relatives, llamas and alpacas, also graze along the route, usually tended by traditionally dressed *campesino* children.

Camping at night near inhabited areas will often reward the trekker with gifts of warm boiled potatoes brought around by a generous local. Nothing is asked for in exchange, but a sharing of food is the common response, and greatly enhances the evening meal. In spite of the strenuous effort required, the days pass too quickly and in almost no time the final hot spring is reached, and the last of the dust washed away. What remains are sore muscles and, for a longer time, fond memories.

Cordillera Blanca: Eight hours by bus north of Lima is one of the finest trekking areas in all of South America. For its diversity and large number of mountain peaks clustered so conveniently in one central area, the Cordillera Blanca is a trekkers' paradise that you won't want to leave in a hurry.

Left, party of trekkers gathers in a mountain valley. Right, enjoying the freedom of trekking.

The small city of Huaráz, largely rebuilt after a devastating earthquake in 1970, is the hub for all hiking activity, There are regular flights up from Lima which is an eight-hour bus ride away, and frequent local buses transport enthusiasts to a variety of trail heads. Hikes of anything up to ten days are possible, combinations producing even more possibilities if desired. Lack of imagination is the only limiting factor.

The Cordillera Blanca is full of striking views and wonderful adventures. The highest mountain in Peru, Huascaràn (22,200 ft/6,800 meters), and the most beautiful in the world,

Alpamayo (19,500 ft/5,900 meters), are just the toppings on an already rich cake. Glacial lakes dot the landscape, and fresh running streams serve up tasty trout to even the most amateur of fishermen. The days are warm and the air scented with eucalyptus. Snow-covered peaks towering overhead provide a perfect backdrop.

It is no wonder that by the middle of May the area is bustling with *gringos*, and only begins to settle down by the end of October when the rainy season takes hold. It is an area unsurpassed for first-time trekking in Peru, but wonderful experiences here have a disastrous effect on other hiking areas: one just never gets to them. ■

PERUVIAN AMAZON

Three-fifths of Peru is jungle – **the Amazon**. Despite the encroachment of modern man, this is where adventures can still happen and the exotic reigns. Here the "roads" are rivers and the vehicles are colored motorboats and canoes. It is the home of witchdoctors and folk medical experts, who say that its steamy borders might contain anything from new contraceptives to a cure for cancer.

The remotest frontier: The Amazon is the one place the Incas never succeeded in penetrating. When the Spanish conquistadors arrived, they heard wild tales of a golden city hidden in the heart of the jungle. In their search for El Dorado, they found nothing but disease and hostile Indians, although the legend of the golden treasure lives on.

The Spanish explorer Francisco de Orellana is credited with discovering the Amazon River. He named it after the fierce female warriors in Greek legend when he erroneously took the long-haired Yagua Indian men, who confronted him wearing fiber skirts, for women.

A later Spanish expedition was fictionalized in the 1973 Werner Herzog film, *Aguirre, the Wrath of God.* This starred Klaus Kinski as the demonic Aguirre, who killed for pleasure during his 1560 trek through the jungle, along the Amazon River to what is now Venezuela and out to the Atlantic Ocean.

In later years, the search for gold was replaced by missionaries' quest to "convert the savages" by teaching them to take up farming, to adopt a sedentary lifestyle and to send their children to mission schools. The indigenous people did not succumb easily and from the late 1600s to the mid-1700s they managed to keep the jungle free of a European invasion, thanks to an uprising led by Juan Santos, a Jesuit-educated Quechua Indian who united warring tribes to expel the Europeans.

The missionaries eventually returned and, in modern times, the Catholic presence in the rainforest has received strong competition from evangelists, especially those from the United States.

Rubber fortunes: The colonization of the Amazon was consolidated at the end of the 19th century with the rubber boom. The period was one of overnight wealth for US and European rubber barons and overnight enslavement for the Indians in the rainforest.

The best-known of the rubber barons was Carlos Fitzgerald – or Fitzcarraldo, subject of Herzog's 1982 film of the same name– the son of an English immigrant and a Peruvian woman. Accused of spying for Chile during the 1879 war with Peru, Fitzcarraldo fled to the Amazon where he made a great fortune in rubber and became obsessed with a plan to travel from the Ucayali River (which later is the Amazon) through the Madre de Dios River by steamship. Although only an 8-mile (13-km) isthmus separated the two, it was widely believed impossible to cross from one to the other.

Although his quest failed, steamships later made the trip – effectively linking

Preceding pages: Amazon village, Peru. **Left**, Indians practice their blow-dart technique. **Right**, a multi-colored macaw.

the Atlantic and Pacific oceans – when thousands of Indians hauled the ships across the isthmus.

Fitzcarraldo and other rubber barons had no cause to miss Europe; they imported every luxury that struck their fancy. Their women were dressed in the latest Parisian fashions, the men drank imported wines and European theater and opera stars regularly performed in the midst of one of the world's densest jungles. But the opulence ended in 1920 when rubber grown in Asia and Africa began to compete on the world market.

Peru's most important rubber boom city – and the largest city in the Peruvian Amazon – is **Iquitos**. The old days of wealth are still evident in the houses covered with Portuguese tiles and, on the **Plaza de Armas**, in the ramshackle two-story metal house designed by Gustave Eiffel for the Paris Exhibition of 1889 and transported to Iquitos piece by piece by rubber magnate Jules Toth. On the waterfront of Iquitos is the colorful **Belén** port, where all of the houses float on rafts.

From here, irregular riverboat services run to Leticia in Colombia and onwards to Manaus in Brazil, preserving a taste of the days when air travel was unknown and the only way to reach Iquitos was after weeks of journeying.

Exotic wildlife: Although it is a bustling city of 400,000 one only has to go a short distance from Iquitos on the Amazon, Yanamono or Manatí rivers to be in virgin jungle. On the way are the rustic wood and palm houses on stilts inhabited by the *ribereños* or mestizos who live on the river and speak a lilting Spanish reminiscent of Brazilian Portuguese. Exotic birds fly in and out of vine covered trees, attracting bird watchers from around the globe, while brilliantly colored butterflies, tapirs, monkeys, wild pigs and pink river dolphins fascinate newcomers.

Tourists generally stay in lodges in the jungle, the oldest and most recommended being the three **Explorama** complexes, ranging from the ultra modern Explorama Inn with electricity 24 hours a day and private bathrooms in

At the floating markets of Belén, near Iquitos.

every cabin to the primitive Explornapo camp where kerosene lamps, night walks and mosquito netting tents add to the mystique.

The *ribereños* and Indians in this part of the Amazon live isolated lives except when they head off in their dugout canoes or hitch a ride on the "river buses" – boats which cruise up and down the Amazon collecting passengers and their cargoes of bananas, yuca, corn, dried fish and chickens headed for Iquitos. These people live off paiche, dorado and piranha fish.

Another important Amazon city is **Pucallpa**, a frontier lumber town and the last navigable port for ocean-going vessels on the Amazon. It is 6 miles (9 km) from **Lake Yarinacocha**, a 14-mile (22-km) body of water luring tourists fascinated by its spectacular sunrises and sunsets, its fishing and the undisturbed Shipibo Indian villages along its banks. Its forests are full of cedar, pine, mahogany and bamboo and serve as home to nearly a thousand bird species, endless varieties of butterflies and exotic mammals – including sloths. Local boats called *pekepekes* after the chugging sound made by their small motors are available for hire for day trips to some of the isolated villages or to see the Shipibos and buy their hand-painted pottery and textiles.

Farther south is **Puerto Maldonado**, just a few hours by river from one of the world's most important wildlife reserves and capital of the least populated, least developed and least explored province – or department – in Peru. The **Manu National Park**, covering more than 5,000 sq. miles (13,000 sq. km), has everything from ocelots and jaguars to alligators and otters.

More than 500 bird species have been identified by its research station. A trip to Manu usually is accompanied by camping on the banks of the Madre de Dios, or the River of Serpents as the Indians call it. Closer to Puerto Maldonado is the smaller **Tambopata Wildlife Reserve** with bird, dragonfly and butterfly species – including some that only recently have been identified.

undreds of irdwatchers ock to the mazon Basin very year.

Chan Chan and Northern Peru

Trujillo, the "travelers' resting place" along the Spaniards' route between Lima and Quito, is a graceful coastal city. Founded in 1535 and named after Francisco Pizarro's birthplace in Spain, it soon became worthy of the title the "Lordliest City" and even today its well-preserved wooden balconies – designed so upper class women could look out but their jealous husbands' rivals could not look in – and ornate window grills pay testimony to the colonial days.

More recently, the city is famous for being the first in Peru to declare independence from Spain, while in 1932 the Trujillo Massacre began when APRA crowds were turned on by the Army.

The best place to start exploring Trujillo is the **Plaza de Armas**, bounded by city hall, the bishop's palace and the newly-renovated Cathedral with its marble pillars and gilt hand-carved wooden altars. The colonial building next to the Cathedral is the **Hotel Turistas**, one of the finest hotels in the state-run chain.

Girl at a fiesta in Trujillo.

Off the main square, colonial mansions abound. **Casa de la Emancipación** is typical of the houses built in the 16th and 17th centuries and contains much of its original furniture. Although earthquakes and remodeling over the centuries have taken their toll, there are other mansions worth seeing, including **Casa de Mayorazgo**, **Casa Urquiaga** and **Casa Bracamonte**. Or stop by the **Casa Ganoza**, now an art gallery, and the **Palacio Iturregui** which houses the Central Club.

Further vestiges of the days of wealth are found on the sugar *haciendas* outside the city. Land reform in the 1970s turned most into cooperatives but the opulence of the past is still evident. The most impressive are **Casa Grande** and **Hacienda Cartavio**, from where sugar comes for Cartavio Rum.

Meanwhile, Trujillo's prehispanic past is on display at the University of Trujillo **Archaeological Museum**. There is another impressive archaeological collection at the **Cassinelli Museum** in a former service station north of Avenida España, the elliptical street where once stood the wall to protect the city from pirate attacks.

An adobe city: On the fringe of Trujillo are the ruins of **Chan Chan**, possibly the world's largest adobe city at the time it was discovered by the Spanish. Made up of seven citadels spread over 8 sq miles (20 sq km) and enclosed by a massive adobe wall,

Chan Chan was home to the Chimus, who fished and farmed, worshiped the moon and left no written records. Under a hot sun, it is an eery silence that greets you at this ancient city. On its walls are carvings of fish, sea birds, fishnets and moons. The Chimus had such a sophisticated aqueduct and irrigation system that they were able to turn the arid wasteland around them into fertile fields of grains, fruits and vegetables. It wasn't until the Spanish sabotaged those water conduits, forcing the Chimus to leave the protection of the city, that the Europeans were able to conquer the Indians.

Three hours to the north is the tiny town of Lambayeque and the **Brüning Museum**, which has Peru's finest non-private gold collection and the fabulous finds from the **Sipán** archaeological dig (*see "Digging for the Past" on the following page*). Visitors can see the digs and view the tomb of the Lord of Sipán. Nearby is the new excavation at the **Túcume pyramids** – a project originally directed by Norwegian Thor Heyerdahl. A steep stairway at Túcume takes you to a lookout point over the pyramids and a picnic area is located at the entrance of the site.

Where the last Inca met his fate: Historically, the most important northern city is **Cajamarca**. Now a cattle and dairy area where you can find some of Peru's best cheese, this is the city where the Incas and Spaniards had their showdown. According to Spanish chronicles, the Inca Atahualpa was taken prisoner after offending the Europeans by accepting a proferred Bible then, after touching, smelling and listening to it, tossing it to the ground as useless.

In an attempt to rescue him, Indians from all over the empire brought gold and silver, filling the **Rescue Room**, a block from the Plaza de Armas, twice over with silver and once with gold. But the effort was futile and the Spaniards garrotted the last Inca on the main square.

That square, now the Plaza de Armas, is the hub of this slow-paced city of 120,000 and is ringed by colonial buildings and two churches – the Cathedral and lovely San Francisco Church. Opened in 1776, the **Cathedral**'s carved wood altars are covered in gold leaf and its facade is intricately carved volcanic rock. But conspicuously absent are its bell towers, which were left unfinished to protest Spain's tax on churches. **San Francisco**, older and more ornate, has the city's **Religious Art Museum** and eerie catacombs.

Also on the plaza is **Salas Restaurant**, described by one *Cajamarquino* as the "city's nerve center". Not only is it *the* place to catch up on the latest news and gossips, but it has the city's best home cooking.

han Chan, e largest dobe city in e world.

In 1996 the largest tomb excavated in the Americas was unearthed at Sican, northern Peru. It was 50ft (15 meters) deep and contained a high priest or prince, aged 25–30, wearing a spectacular gold mask with emerald eyes. In the tomb with him were many brilliant artifacts including a gold and copper, gold gloves and 80 sq ft (7.5 sq meters) of gilded cotton cloth. There were also the skeletons of 24 women, possibly sacrificed at his death. The whole burial complex is made up of 14 tombs, the second largest of which contained 500kg of

gold, and it forms part of the square mile capital of pre-Inca Peru dating from the 9th–10th centuries. It is just another find in a dazzling history of archaeological discoveries.

Richest find: Only a few years before the Sican discovery archaeologists in northern Peru followed a bloody trail of thievery to the intact tomb of a Moche warrior-lord, the richest documented burial chamber ever uncovered in the Americas, and renewed concern over archaeological excavations and their looting. Not since Harvard's Hiram Bingham stumbled on to Machu Picchu in 1911 and Peruvian Julio C. Tello uncovered the first Paracas funeral bundle on the Pacific coast some 18 years later have scientists been so enthusiastic about obtaining new information on the ancient Indian cultures that were sacked and vanquished by the Spanish conquistadors 500 years ago. The continuing excavation at Sipán (*see Northern Peru on the previous page*) promises to provide crucial new evidence about the life of the Moches, a sophisticated Indian civilization that left no written word but whose ceramics have been used to unravel some of the secrets of their society.

The Moches were fine potters and, for tourists, it is most often their *huacos eroticos* – erotic ceramics – that shock and amuse with their graphic portrayals of sexual acts, birth, death and scenes from everyday life. Medical researchers have used the ceramics to conclude that ancient civilizations suffered from modern-day ills, including venereal disease, blindness and even cancer. Women's role in that culture, based on what is shown in the pottery, was one of submission. And, indeed, the remains of three concubines – their feet cut off possibly to symbolically prevent them from leaving their master's grave – were buried alongside the Moche lord in the Sipán tomb.

Theories about the Moches have received ample broadening from the Sipán excavation but scientists predict the best is yet to come.

"This is a very dynamic project," says Walter Alva, the Peruvian archaeologist in charge of the Sipán dig, financed in part by the National Geographic Society. "We are still digging and it is very probable that we'll find other tombs."

Alva knows there was at least one equally fabulous tomb at the same site, but grave robbers reached it first. Alva was pulled into the project when local police in February of 1987 called him to say they had confiscated some pre-Columbian treasures headed for the black market. As director of the Brüning Museum in Lambayeque, Peru's best non-private gold museum, Alva was accustomed to the constant trafficking of archaeological artifacts. But he had no idea of the immense value of what the police would show him – copper masks, a gold face mask with silver and lapis lazuli eyes, detailed larger-than-lifesize peanuts of solid gold and various ornaments and ceramics.

Facing the grave robbers: Alva and his assistant began holding all-night vigils at the Sipán ruins, discovering to their dismay that the grave robbing continued. Police started surprise raids on the homes of the townspeople suspected of trafficking in the goods. During one raid, the police fatally shot a grave robber, shocking the tiny town of Lambayeque and leaving the archaeologists fearful the dead man's family would seek revenge.

Although funds were eventually obtained to begin the excavation of the site, the Sipán incident called attention to the problem of looting at ancient Indian sites, a custom that first began in Peru in the 1500s when the Spanish soldiers began sacking Incan burial grounds. The determination of the grave robber, or *guaqueros* as they are known in Peru, was so great that at one point in time they diverted the Moche River so they could tunnel under a pyramid. The fact that the Sipán tomb was found intact is what makes its discovery so special.

Until now, scientists have had access to a large number of ceramics, ornaments and even precious artifacts taken from a grave here or an ancient temple there but never have they been able to stumble upon an intact Moche grave. The Moches preceded the Incas by some 1,200 years and irrigated a fertile, but dry, valley with

Left, piece from the recent discovery at Sipán in the Museo Brüning, Chiclayo. Above, "the house of the Grandson" near Huaráz.

such success that they were able to sustain a population estimated at about 50,000. But they never had a system of writing.

"Sipán is going to help us fill a vacuum in the continuum and help us know more about the life, the technology, the social structures and the interactions the Moches had with other Indian groups," Alva says.

At Sipán, archaeologists found feathered headdresses and jewelry of copper, gold, turquoise and silver. The man buried in the grave may have been a warrior priest interred in what his discoverers have dubbed a "cocoon of tribute" with precious metals adorning his body and placed above and below him. Christopher Donner, an archaeologist from the University of California at Los Angeles, speculates from the presence of concubines, guards and even a dog in the grave that the deceased was a warrior priest.

Another unusual aspect of the Sipán dig is that the Moche lord was buried within a wooden coffin – the first time such a burial box has been discovered. Experts at the dig had to use air-squeeze bulbs to gently blow away the dust after they opened the coffin and began painstakingly sifting through layer after layer of clay ceramics and beakers, gold ornaments and other priceless artifacts. Many of the items taken from the dig were sent to Germany for examination, along with the remains of the Sipán lord which will undergo sophisticated forensic tests before returning to be put on display at the Brüning Museum.

Thor Heyerdahl's dig: Peru is a paradise for those interested in ancient Indian cultures. For decades, sporadic excavations have been going on at the massive adobe city of Chan Chan as scientists try to unravel the story of how the Chimu Indians lived. In the highlands near Cajamarca, University of Tokyo archaeologists annually dig at Kuntur Wasi and Huacaloma, covering the sites with dirt when the rainy season begins.

One of the most intriguing projects was set up under the direction of the Norwegian explorer Thor Heyerdahl. His dig at Túcume, not far from Sipán, brings together a team of European and Peruvian archaeologists funded by Heyerdahl's Kontiki Museum. Túcume, a plain of 27 arid hills which actually are pyramids covered by centuries of dust and dirt, is one of the few spots where grave diggers have not entered since the time of the Spanish conquest. That's because the Spanish, wanting no interference from the Indians, began rumors that the devil lived among the pyramids – more than enough to scare off superstitious *guaqueros*.

City sites: Even within Lima there are remains of pre-Incan settlements, largely adobe structures. One is found at the Parque de las Leyendas zoo and playground. In the suburb of San Isidro, brilliant red bougainvillea grow beside the pre-Incan burial site of Huallamarca. It has a small museum with mummies and such artifacts as cloths, baskets and drinking gourds.

The most important archaeological site near Lima is Pachacamac. Many of the pyramids that once made up this site are still covered in sand. Rising to prominence in about AD 700, this pre-Incan shrine was later used as an Incan temple for adoration of the sun god and it is believed that the Inca Huayna Capac once had a residence here. Francisco Pizarro used the buildings for a residence of his own.

Although Peru has strengthened its laws on the sale of archaeological artifacts large quantities of items continue to leave South America clandestinely each year. Just as disturbing for archaeologists is the tendency of squatters to use foundations or materials from ancient ruins to construct their own dwellings. This has occurred at Chan Chan, some adobe ruins in Lima and Sacsayhuaman outside of Cuzco. The Peruvian government admits it does not have the money to protect these historical sites.

In contemporary times, Bingham's discovery of the enigmatic Machu Picchu ruins atop an Andean peak marked one of the most well-known archaeological discoveries in Peru and converted the city – an architectural marvel – into the most visited tourist spot on the continent. Peruvian officials are currently in negotiations with Harvard University in an attempt to recuperate the Machu Picchu ceramics and artifacts taken to the United States by the Bingham expeditions.

After Bingham, Tello's discovery of the Paracas Indian burial grounds exposed the world to the fine fabrics those desert Indians wove and buried with their dead – and which the arid Nazca desert has preserved for centuries. In Paracas, cotton and fiber clothes found at the necropolis show a sophisticated knowledge of animal and vegetable fibers and dyes, plus an expansive repertoire of designs. Weavers today still are unable to imitate the techniques that gave birth to these antique cloths. The finest collection is on display at the Amano Museum in Lima.

Right, rainbow carving at La Huaca.

TITICACA, SACRED INCA LAKE

When Peruvians talk of **Titicaca**, the world's highest navigable lake, they never fail to mention that it has waves. That's their way of emphasizing the size of this bright blue body of water separating Peru and Bolivia. And large it is, covering more than 3,000 sq. miles (8,000 sq. km), with more than 30 islands. But don't let the sunny skies and gentle spread of the land surrounding Titicaca fool anybody into thinking it is hospitable. Not surprisingly its waters are frigid year round, as it lies at 13,000 ft (4,000 meters) above sea level.

According to folklore, it was from Titicaca that one of the most important Indian cultures the world has ever known – the Incas. For them, the lake was sacred and its islands holy. The story goes that when the Spanish reached Cuzco, the Indians took the 2-ton (1,800-kg) gold chain of Inca Huascar from its resting place at Koricancha, the Temple of the Sun, and hurled it into the lake to hide it from the invaders. Some years ago the French oceanographer Jacques Cousteau spent eight weeks with a mini-submarine exploring the lake. He found no gold but he did discover a 20-inch (50-cm) tri-colored frog that apparently never surfaces.

Floating islands of reed: Titicaca's surface is broken by islands, the best known being the floating reed islands of the Uros Indians. According to local superstition, black blood coursed through the Uros's veins, allowing them to survive the freezing nights on the lake. The last full-blooded Uro died in 1959 but the island's current inhabitants, who are a mix of Uro, Aymará and Quechua Indians, follow the Uro ways. They fish, hunt birds and live off the lake plants, including the all-important reeds used to make their homes, build their boats and form the base of their islands.

Nearby is **Taquile**, the island of weavers. The king of Spain awarded it to a man who turned it into a colonial hacienda, then the Republican period saw it

Reed boat near the Uros Islands.

designated as an island prison, but the Taquiles have gradually managed to regain ownership of their ancestral island. Since 1970 they have been running their own tourism operations in a bid to ensure the old ways are not lost with the arrival of visitors.

There are no hotels on Taquile but islanders willingly open their homes to overnight guests, and there are small eating establishments specializing in the local delicacy: lake trout.

Like the Uros, the Taquile Indians are extremely poor. A US anthropologist who has lived on the island says this poverty has bred a cooperative lifestyle and has won the islanders their reputation for hospitality. "No one robs here because one person alone can't survive," she says. "The most important thing on Taquile is respect and personal pride."

While on the island, buy textiles from the weaving cooperatives. Most of the items are knitted from finely spun sheep's wool dyed red and blue, although the colors and weaves depend on the wearer's role in the community. In fact, an outfit can tell a person's age, social position and marital status. Single men, for example, wear knit hats with white tufts on top. Married men's hats have red tufts. Some of the belts are seasonal, with certain colors reserved for special times of the year.

More textiles can be purchased at **Amantaní**, a peaceful island with temples and a throne of carved stone on one shore. A steamship service to the islands offers half-day trips aboard a British vessel that was carried piece by piece on trains to the lake before World War II. The ship, the *Ollanta*, stops at Amantaní, Taquile, **Soto** and **Esteves** islands. The latter, connected to Puno by a causeway, has a luxury hotel run by the government hotel chain.

Back on solid land: On the Peruvian side of Titicaca is **Puno**, founded in 1668 by the Count of Lemos and once was one of the continent's richest cities because of its proximity to the Laykakota silver mines. These days it is an unattractive commercial center, capital of Peru's *altiplano*, the harsh highland region better suited to roaming vicuñas and alpacas than people. But outside Puno you'll find **Sillustani**, with a circular burial tower or *chullpas* overlooking Lake Umayo, and **Chucuito**, a village sitting upon what was once an Incan settlement. Stop by the Santo Domingo Church in this *altiplano* village. **Juli**, formerly the capital of the lake area, has four beautiful churches under reconstruction and is the city where you can catch the hydrofoils to Bolivia.

Puno is the "Folklore Capital" of Peru. It has won that distinction by being home to dozens of energetic dances, including the Devil Dance performed during the feast of the Virgin of Candelaria. Dancers, fiercely competing to outdo one another, dress up in grotesque masks and colorful clothing for a non-stop profusion of street entertainment. And when there is no riotous festival – which isn't often – you can sit back with a fermented corn liquor drink called *chicha* and listen to Puno's beautiful cane flute music.

A llama looks inquisitive.

ECUADOR: ON THE SIDELINES OF HISTORY

When South America's two greatest liberators, Simon Bolívar and José de San Martín, arranged their only meeting – lasting two days in July 1822 and ending in bitter disagreement – it was on Ecuadorian soil. Their main concerns were the formation of Gran Colombia and the liberation of Peru. The land on which they stood was of secondary importance, as it was only part of grander designs: this has often been Ecuador's fate.

Since the arrival of the Incas in the southern highlands in the mid-15th century, the various regional masters have ruled from distant capitals. The attempt to impose order on this small country, divided so distinctly into the coastal, mountain and Oriente regions, has been an ongoing and often futile process whether under the Incas, the Spaniards, or democratic independence.

Knowledge of pre-Inca Ecuador is fragmentary. Stone Age tools discovered near Quito dating from around 9000 BC are the earliest signs of habitation, while archaeologists have found various later cultures – such as that based in Manta – skilled in metallurgy, ceramics and weaving.

During the 10th century, the Caras – the forefathers of the modern *Otavaleños* – ascended the Rio Esmeraldas and settled in the Quito area. They built an observatory to mark the solstices, and identified the equator as "the path of the sun". They were animists who worshiped the sun, and believed the moon was inhabited by humans. They grew corn and wheat and kept sheep, but their economy was based on weaving, and the law required women to spin wool whenever possible – even when walking mountain trails.

Their successors were the Duchicela dynasty which established the Kingdom of Quito, a powerful confederation based on strategic alliances which became the Incas' main regional rival. The Inca invasion of present-day Ecuador was aimed at the conquest of Quito. They first encountered the southern Cañari Indians who fought for several years before being subdued by the Inca Tupac-Yupanqui, who took 15,000 hostages. He constructed a major city called Tomebamba on the site of present-day Cuenca: stonemasons were summoned from Cuzco to build a Temple of the Sun, and palace walls were plated with gold.

The Spanish chronicler Cieza de León

visited the largely ruined city in 1547 and found fully-stocked warehouses, barracks for the imperial troops, and houses formerly occupied by "more than two hundred virgins, who were very beautiful, dedicated to the service of the sun".

Fall of the Incas: Ecuador soon played an important part in the collapse of the Inca Empire. Huayna Capac, the son of Tupac by a Cañari princess, succeeded his father to the throne in 1493. He grew up in Ecuador and married, in turn, a Duchicela princess. Their son, Atahualpa, was bequeathed the throne along with his half-brother Huascar when Huayna Capac died in 1527, thus splitting the empire, for the first time, between Quito and Cuzco. Civil war ensued for the next five years, until Atahualpa defeated and killed his brother after a major battle near Ambato in central Ecuador. In this way, the Inca Empire, after years of refined centralization and uniformity, was severely weakened at precisely the moment in history that Francisco Pizarro began his conquest.

The first Spaniards to set foot on Ecuadorian soil were an exploratory band dispatched by Pizarro from Colombia. They landed near Esmeraldas in September 1526, and found sufficiently favorable conditions to prompt Pizarro himself, with a mere 13 men, to sail south a year later. Visiting an Indian town at Tumbes, he noticed large quantities of gold and silver, and needed no further encouragement. Late in 1530, having traveled to Spain to secure the patronage of Charles V and the title of Governor and Captain-General of Peru, Pizarro returned to Ecuador. This time he came prepared with 180 men and 27 horses, and he marched southwards, reaching Cajamarca in 1533.

While Pizarro captured, ransomed and subsequently executed Atahualpa – having first baptized him – his lieutenant Sebastian de Benalcázar battled his way northwards to Quito. Arriving in late 1534, he found the city in ruins: Rumiñahui, Atahualpa's general, had destroyed and evacuated it rather than lose it intact to the Spaniards. Benalcázar refounded Quito on December 6, 1534, while Rumiñahui was captured, tortured and executed the following month.

Bloodthirsty rulers: Spanish rule was firmly established in Ecuador from this time onwards, but for decades the conquistadors continued to double-cross and murder one another. From the dawn of the colonial era, Ecuadorian politics was frequently a contest

Preceding pages: Indian procession, near Quito. Left, Spanish engraving of the early conquistadors. Above, path through a cacao plantation, c. 1890.

of personalities, of greedy and brutal individuals who refused to compromise. This legacy is evident through the age of the *caudillos* in the 19th century and on to the modern era of the military dictator, from whom Ecuador has suffered its share.

In 1541, Gonzalo Pizarro dispatched his lieutenant Francisco de Orellana to explore the Amazon in search of El Dorado. For 18 months, Orellana and his men drifted down the river; they found no gold, but enacted the first trans-continental crossing, finding themselves on the Atlantic coast of Brazil.

Ecuador was initially administered by the Spanish as a province of the vice-royalty of Peru. The conquerors brought with them horses, cattle and pigs, and Ecuador was the site of the first cultivation of wheat and bananas in South America. They also brought diseases such as cholera and syphilis which decimated the indigenous populations of urban centers but had little impact in the more remote mountain regions.

Spanish settlement was relatively light in comparison with other colonies like Mexico and Argentina, and racial intermixing was limited.

Colonial administration was based on the *encomienda* system, under which land was distributed among the Spaniards. They were responsible for the productivity of their plot and the conversion of the Indians living there. In return for these "services" to the people, the Spaniards assumed the haughty rights of a feudal lord. Taxation in the form of animals and vegetables was exacted, and labor was unrewarded. Should the Indians object to these conditions, the *encomenderos* held power over life and death.

This brutal system was preserved after independence in the form of huge estates or *latifundis* owned by a fraction of Ecuador's wealthiest *criollo* families. Long overdue land reforms were enacted in 1964, which freed the Indians from compulsory agricultural labor. Often, however, it was unproductive land which was redistributed, and many *haciendas* remained intact – governments being reluctant to attack the wealthiest and most powerful class, the landowners.

Rebellions and coups: The injustices of Spanish rule – the exclusion of the ruled from all privileges, the seizure of all arable land and the enslavement of the Indians as peasants – prompted several violent uprisings. The first of these was the Alcabalas Revolution of 1592–93, when the populace, with the active support of the lower clergy, rebelled against increased taxes on food and fabrics. After 10

Above, Ecuadorian militia on parade in a mountain village.

months' agitation, 24 conspirators were executed and their heads publicly displayed in iron cages.

Foremost among these early revolutionaries was a *mestizo* named Eugenio Espejo, who founded a liberal newspaper which satirized the excesses of colonialism. He was imprisoned several times, exiled and finally died in jail in 1795. Today he is remembered with affection, having the National Library and many streets named after him.

Ecuador's first step towards independence was also its first coup – many more would follow. In August 1809, members of the *criollo* oligarchy seized power for 24 days in Quito before being displaced and executed. Years of subsequent agitation culminated in Guayaquil's declaration of independence in October 1821 with the support of Bolívar and San Martín. Following the decisive battle of Pichincha in May 1822, when forces led by General Sucre defeated the royalist army, Quito was liberated. Ecuador became part of the new nation of Gran Colombia and remained so until its dissolution in 1830, when full independence was attained.

The nature of politics since then has been typical of many South American republics. Power has alternated between the Liberals and the Conservatives, with their respective strongholds on the coast and in the mountains, while the Oriente has been completely neglected until the discovery of oil in 1967. The first president, a Venezuelan called Flores, established the tone by arranging with his successor, Rocafuerte, to alternate occupancy of the presidency. He broke this deal, retained control of the army, and bribed Rocafuerte into exile. Finally ousted in 1845, he organized a Spanish invasion of Ecuador which was only averted by Great Britain's intervention. National development since then has been sporadic and almost incidental. Two of the best-remembered presidents, Moreno and Alfaro, were both assassinated by their opponents – one shot, the other slain by an incensed mob.

Stumbling into the 20th century: Against this savage backdrop, the exporting of bananas, coffee, cocoa pods and Panama hats blossomed. The sole beneficiaries, however, were the ruling oligarchy of a few hundred *criollo* families and the foreign companies who controlled the industries. For decades Ecuador has been the world's largest exporter of bananas, but until the 1960s the entire industry was owned, as it was throughout Central America, by the Boston-based United Fruit Company. Until the recent growth of the oil industry, bananas accounted for most of Ecuador's total export earnings – and the fact that all the profits left the country is one reason why Ecuador has remained so poor for so long.

Prosperity has not been helped by Ecuador's neighbors occupying large chunks of its territories in wars. The most dramatic loss came in 1942, when Peru took most of the southern jungle region known as El Oro – an area rich in precious metals and oil, a nd where the country's best coffee was grown. This remains Ecuador's foremost international dispute, occasionally threatening to blow up into another full-scale war. A three-month conflict in 1995 cost both sides hundreds of casualties and had a damaging effect on the Ecuadorian economy.

Twentieth-century Ecuador has experienced mainly military rule, the latest period of which was from 1972 to 1979. In 1978, the army drew up a new constitution under which an election was successfully held the following year. Ecuador became the first Latin American country to return to democracy after the military era which engulfed most of the continent throughout the 1970s, and national politics have been stable since then.

Leon Febres Cordero, a Conservative elected in 1984 was kidnapped by troops loyal to a high-ranking general who was in jail for attempting two coups. Febres secured his release after 11 hours by granting the general an amnesty

Elections in 1988 brought to power President Rodrigo Borja Cevallos, a Social Democrat from Quito. During his presidency inflation fell, the foreign debt was serviced regularly and foreign investors continued to be attracted. These trends continued under his successor, Sixto Duran Ballen, of the Christian Social Party, who introduced an unpopular privatisation program, but many were surprised that Abdala Bucaram, "El Loco" (the Crazy), was elected in 1996: one of his campaign tricks was to take off his belt and threaten to thrash the rich. It will take more than just thrashing the rich to resolve the more deeply rooted problems of regionalism, land reform and widespread socio-economic inequality which remain unchecked.

ORANGINE
REFRESCANTE

INSTANTE
COPIADORA DE LLAVES
DE
TALLER
EL
GANSUA

OLD QUITO: A WALKING TOUR

Old Quito displays Spanish colonial architecture at its finest. Walls of brilliant whitewash, deep blue railings and green tile rooftops dazzle the eye, conjuring a period when the city was a peaceful provincial capital dedicated to the creation of artistic beauty. Earthquakes in 1587, 1768 and 1859 caused severe damage to many churches, which nevertheless number a staggering 87. In 1978, UNESCO declared Old Quito a World Heritage site, acknowledging its historic value and ensuring that modern development will not spoil its unique and harmonious atmosphere.

Cultural potpourri: The Spanish past blends with modern cosmopolitanism as members of Ecuador's many ethnic groups make Quito their home. Life on colorful **Calle Cuenca** contrasts with the city's characteristic affluence. Fleshy black women sell tropical fruits, papayas, passionfruits, pineapples and a dozen varieties of bananas. An Indian newspaperwoman with a baby at her breast pierces the sound of footsteps with a rasping street voice, crying *Comercio, Hoy* in a nasal refrain.

Above it all stands the **Church of San Francisco**, the first major religious construction in the continent and the spiritual heart of the city. Begun a few days after Spanish settlement in 1534, it took – in true Ecuadorian form – 70 years to complete. Ascending the stairs from the plaza is a revealing cultural experience, a progression from music shops playing the latest hits and displaying album covers of scantily-clad women, up past the blind and crippled vendors of candles and incense, and in through the huge doors to the silent, sanctified interior.

The creaking wooden floor contrasts with the spectacular baroque carvings of the main altar and the statue of Our Lady of Quito, a fine example of the "Quito school of art". This style, a blending of Spanish and Moorish techniques with the indigenous imagination, grew out of an institution started by Friar

Preceding pages: on the road to the Statue of the Virgin in Quito. Below, colonial Quito, now on the World Heritage list.

Joedco Ricke, who was also South America's pioneer wheat farmer.

From San Francisco, it is a short walk through the clothes market on Calle Cuenca to **La Merced**, which contains paintings depicting scenes from Quito's past: Sucre riding gloriously into battle, volcanoes erupting, and suspiciously docile Indians being converted.

Two blocks away is the **Plaza de la Independencia**, where the heroes of 1809 are immortalized. Today, *Quiteños* sun themselves, read the morning newspapers, and put the swarming shoeshine boys to work. Here is the **Presidential Palace** with its traditional guards and a mural by Guayasamin depicting Orellana's descent of the Amazon.

The adjacent **Cathedral**, finished in 1706, is where Ecuador's illustrious lie: the tombs of Sucre and Flores are here, and a plaque shows where Moreno died of gunshot wounds in 1875. Among the collection of paintings inside is the *Descent From The Cross* by Caspicara, perhaps colonial Ecuador's best Indian artist. A mere 25 years ago, Ecuador's poverty was such that these showpiece buildings, the symbolic cornerstones of church and state, went without paint. Today, however, they shine.

One block south of the **Church of San Augustín**, where the first declaration of independence was signed, is **Calle Espejo**, the only pedestrian thoroughfare in Old Quito. Nearby is the magnificent **La Compañia**, built by the Jesuits between 1605 and 1768. Containing an estimated seven tons of gold, it is Ecuador's most ornate church. The remains of the *Quiteño* saint Mariana de Jesus lie beneath the solid gold main altar, and there is a bizarre collection of colonial art: one painting graphically depicts the grades of punishment reserved for sinners in Hell, with adulterers and fornicators having the most unpleasant fate.

From 1828 until his death in Colombia two years later, Sucre lived a block from here: his house is now a museum, affording a rare glimpse of period aristocratic home life. It has a plaque which rather ambiguously celebrates the "valor, heroism and virility" of both Spaniards and Ecuadorians at the battle of Pichincha. A statue of Sucre occupies the Plaza of Santo Domingo, opposite the church of the same name, which is best seen at night when its domes are floodlit. Inside is an altar to St Judas, patron saint of "desperate causes", where satisfied worshipers have posted "thank you" notices.

The best-preserved colonial street is **Calle Ronda**, which is entered down a ramp at the motley open-air market on Avenida 24 de Mayo. A quiet, narrow, cobbled lane, it is lined with 16th-century houses with overhanging balconies and heavy grilled doors. This brings you to the **Bridge of the Black Vultures**, where you can climb to the Virgin of Quito at the summit of **El Panecillo**, or "little bread loaf". Unfortunately numerous thieves are at work on the way up. It is therefore most advisable to take a taxi to the summit – and don't go alone. There are sweeping views of the whole valley and, on a clear day, of the snowcapped peaks of **Pichincha**, and **Cayambe** away to the north.

…side the …vish Church … Compañia.

THE OTAVALO INDIANS

The Otavalo Indians are one of America's few indigenous peoples to achieve modern financial security as a direct result of colonial oppression. Forced to become weavers by the Spanish, about half of Ecuador's Otavaleños are today involved in weaving, which has made them the most prosperous Indian group in Ecuador, possibly in all of South America.

The town of Otavalo lies betwen Quito and the Colombian border and there are expatriate commuities in Bogotá and Popayán, Colombia, and scattered throughout Brazil and Spain, they export their finely manufactured textiles to the United States, Canada and Europe, while the bulk of their business remains in South America. Each month a single family may export more than 1,000 embroidered acrylic dresses to Venezuela, or 500 acrylic ponchos to Chile.

The modern Otavaleños are descended from the Cara tribe which expanded from Colombia to the Ecuadorian *sierra* about 1,000 years ago. Settling mainly in the areas of Cayambe, Otavalo and Caranqui, the Caras established trade links with neighboring tribes, particularly in the Oriente. They bartered cotton and blankets, along with dogs and salt, in exchange for *achiote* (a plant from which dyes are extracted), parrots and monkeys. Then, as now, a traveling class of merchants conducted this commerce.

The inherent ingenuity of the Caras – their legacy to the Otavaleños – brought them prosperity until the arrival of the Incas in the late 15th century, which marked the beginning of 500 years of colonization, imposed labor and beliefs. After 17 years of fighting, the Inca Huayna Capac took Caranqui and massacred thousands of Caras as punishment. Large numbers of Caras were transported to Peru while loyal Inca subjects were settled Cara territory and their descendants dress distinctly to this day. The Incas introduced coca and llamas, an excellent source of wool, but they was too shortlived to seriously influence Otavaleño culture.

The longterm influence arrived wiuth the Spanish. Under the new colonizers, coca was banned and llamas were killed for their flesh and hides. The *encomienda* system was established in Otavalo, putting Spanish settlers in control of an area and its indigenous inhabitants. The first weaving *obraje* (workshop) was set up in the 1550s with 500 workers, some as young as nine years old.

In 1581, regional administration passed directly to the Spanish crown. Modern tools were introduced and within 50 years the Otavalo *obraje* was the most productive in Ecuador. Indians labored 14 hours a day manufacturing cotton cloth, woollen blankets and rope for export. It was hard and dispiriting work and in 1648 one *obraje* in Peguche was closed down because the number of suicides among workers had grown to alarming proportions.

Cultural oppression accompanied economic slavery. The Spaniards, like the Incas, sought uniformity among their subjects. The Otavaleños were forced to learn Quechua to facilitate their conversion to Christianity, although the Otavaleños' Catholicism today has a special flavor, incorporating ancestral beliefs about the mountains and evil spirits.

The commercial success of the Otavaleños, combining intense labor and new techniques such as the use of synthetic dyes – which permits the exact repetition of a particular shade – has brought them considerable fame. Friedrich Hassaurek visited the area in 1863 and observed the use of imported silk in *obrajes* in Atuntaqui and Cotocachi, where 6,000 cotton ponchos were manufactured each month. In 1917, a local weaver began copying the then-fashionable Scottish tweed, the success of which led to the international recognition of the abilities of the *Otavaleños*. *National Geographic* did a feature on them in 1929, and 20 years later they were the subject of a detailed anthropological study.

Land reforms enacted in Ecuador in 1964 abolished the *wasipungo* system, based on enforced Indian labor. In its place, each family was assigned a minimum of 12.5 acres (5 hectares) of arable land. These reforms were frequently ignored: as recently as 1978, troops evicted Indians from a *hacienda* they had occupied in La Bolsa. Nevertheless, the *Otavaleños* could now work as they wished.

The first store selling woven products opened in Otavalo in 1966, and within a dozen years there were 75. Weaving has decentralized from the savage *obrajes* and is now a cottage industry. One of the region's most fascinating characteristics is the specialization by different villages in the various crafts.

Every Saturday morning, the usually quiet streets of Otavalo teem with the life of Ecuador's most captivating market. By 9am Market Square, known as Poncho Plaza, is a feast of colors and textures: rolls of cloth, thick blankets, tapestry wall hangings, chunky sweaters, long patterned belts or *fajas* such as the women wind round their waists and *cintas*, tapes they use to bind their long hair. Day-trippers arrive by bus from Quito around 10am.

On the northern edge of town, across the incongruous Pan American Highway, horses, cows, pigs, sheep and goats are sold in hard-fought deals. Most Otavaleño textiles are made of sheep wool, though occasionally vicuña sweaters can be found. Downtown, grilled cow intestines, anaconda skins and fox paw luck charms are available alongside ponchos, shirts, hats, rugs, bags and shoes – or, if you prefer, balls of naturally-dyed wool and cotton.

In traditional fashion, the production of textiles is in most cases still organized around the seasonal demands of agriculture: potatoes, peas and beans are the main crops. The mechanization of the modern textile industry, potentially disastrous for the Otavaleños, has been compensated by tourism and an emphasis on quality goods produced naturally. The lure of tourist dollars has, in the last decade, brought several thousand Indians from their farms to live in Otavalo town.

Clearly though, most Otavaleños prefer village life, and so succeed, as few others do, in bridging the precarious gap between old and new worlds. ■

Left, the Saturday market at Otavalo. Right, *Otavaleña* selling her unique weavings.

THE ORIENTE AND THE AMAZON

Sliding across silver moonlit waters that mirror the silhouetted surrounding trees, the longboat engine fades. The guide has spotted a cayman, the Amazonian alligator; mesmerized, its eyes blaze under the flashlight. It raises its back and tail above the water, threatening the intruders, stares cold defiance, and suddenly vanishes with a lightning thrash.

This is the Ecuadorian **Oriente**, the upper Amazon basin east of the Andes – nowadays known as "the province of the future". It is a place of endless virgin rainforest cut by fast-flowing rivers and inhabited by jaguars, ocelots, anacondas, monkeys, tapirs, fish-eating bats, piranhas and over 450 species of birds. Travel into this primordial region is easier in Ecuador than in neighboring countries as distances here are shorter and transportation quite straightfoward.

Headhunters and Stone Age tribes: The indigenous inhabitants of the Oriente include the Siona, Cofan, Quechua, Quijo and Waorani tribes in the basins of the Napo, Aguarico and Pastazo rivers to the north; and the Shuars, Ashuars and Saraguros in the south. Development has affected the lifestyles of all the tribes, and many traditions have died; such as those of the Shuar, who until early this century would shrink the heads of dead enemies.

Some of the Waoranis, however, retain their Stone Age culture deep in the jungles bordering Peru near the **Rio Napo**. They hunt with spears, blowpipes and poison darts, keep harpie eagles as both pets and watch-dogs, and still make fire by rubbing sticks together. Several missionaries, including, recently, the Bishop of Coca, have actually been killed for attempting to encroach upon their precious culture.

Such disturbances of Indian life date from 1541, when Francisco de Orellana's expedition departed Quito and stumbled upon the headwaters of the Rio Napo. Towns were soon established, as bases for conquest and for conver-

A motorized canoe cuts along the Napo river.

sion. Many were subsequently abandoned due to repeated Indian attack, but the gold prospectors, the Franciscans and the Jesuits, driven by fierce faith in their gods, gradually pushed back the frontiers.

Oil and tourist booms: The loss of most of the Oriente to Peru following the border war in 1941 stirred the government's attention, which was rewarded in 1967 with the discovery of huge oil deposits near **Lago Agrio**. The face of the region has changed drastically since then, with towns constructed overnight to provide services for the booming industry, which quickly became Ecuador's main money-spinner.

This influx of people has sent the wildlife deeper into the forests. **Misahuallí**, the end of the road, is the easiest place to organize tours, though there is little fauna apart from birds and insects in this area.

Six hours down the Rio Napo is **Coca** – a journey past stilt houses with exotic menageries set in rambling banana patches. The farmers load the fruit into their dugout canoes until they barely float, and then paddle precariously off to market.

Feeding the monkeys in a jungle resort.

Settlements beyond Coca are realizations of wild imaginings. Perched above the river is **Primavera**, population 12, with sweeping sunset views. Nearby, the uninhabited **Isla de los Monos** is home to a colony of inquisitive woolly monkeys, one of the largest species in South America which lives among the higher branches of giant fig and breadfruit trees.

Within Ecuador's borders is the greatest variety of jungle vegetation in the continent. This is well represented in the **Taracoa** area, opposite Primavera. The canopy is thickest at a height of approximately 100 ft (30 meters), beneath which grows, in damp dimness, an astonishing assortment of ferns and wild lemon trees with tiny edible ants living inside its stems.

A boardwalk across swamps passes a giant kapok tree, the tallest Amazonian species measuring 200 ft (60 meters) high and 130 ft (40 meters) around the base of the trunk. Indians on the move seek shelter at night in the hollows between its roots. Its branches are cluttered with bromeliads, strangler vines, and the *bella dona*, from which atropine is extracted. The plant's juice has hallucinogenic properties, and is used by Indians in their religious ceremonies. Reeds clogging the banks of the Rio Taracoa teem with tarantulas, and the lake is inhabited by cayman, piranhas and stingrays – a great place for a *daytime* swim.

On **Pompeya Island**, a museum remembers the Quechua practice of placing their dead on uncovered mounds and letting insects devour their flesh. By **Lago Limoncocha** live approximately 300 Quechuas brought here by some 50 American missionary families 25 years ago. The Christian utopia lasted until 1982. Today, the Americans' houses are empty shells undergoing reafforestation. The villagers fish the surrounding waters and ponder the vagaries of destiny. It is a typical Amazonian scenario, quixotic and inscrutable, an instant in the jungle's eternity.

BY TRAIN FROM THE ANDES TO THE COAST

Train travel began in Ecuador in 1910 when the line opened between Quito and the country's largest city, the sea port of Guayaquil, reducing to two days a former nine-day trek along a mule path which was impassable for half the year because of rain. Despite the extraordinary difficulty of the terrain, it is still possible today to travel south along the Andes' Avenue of the Volcanoes from Quito as far as Riobamba, past orchids and palm trees, with tundr vegetation, glaciers and snow visible on the dormant and active volcanoes above. From Riobamba the line descends to Guayaquil, crossing the physical, cultural and cultural barriers between the mountains and the coast.

From Ibarra, in the Andes north of Quito, another spectacular line descends to the sea at San Lorenzo, and is a similarly symbolic link between two contrasting worlds.

Ilbarra is a sleepy provincial capital with approximately 50,000 inhabitants. Horses pull vegetable-laden carts down its cobbled streets; Mt Cayambe, Ecuador's third highest peak at 19,000 ft (5,790 meters) and the only visual link with Quito, shines in frozen splendor. Founded in the early 17th century, Ibarra – along with Otavalo – was completely destroyed by an earthquake in the space of a minute in August 1868. It has been handsomely rebuilt in white.

The journey begins from the antiquated two-platform station at 7am daily and remains a novelty for the locals, as the train is actually a bus on tracks, an *autoferro*. The body of an old Bluebird bus, complete with steering wheel, horn and brakes that feed on sand, has been fitted with a diesel engine and mounted on a railway chassis. The single cabin seats 56 passengers, while another 30 occupy the aisle and the roof. Considering that the train is the only freight and passenger link between the numerous isolated communities along the way, it is invariably crowded.

The descent begins immediately: at an average speed of 15 miles per hour (25 kph), the *autoferro* takes all day to cover the 125 miles (200 km) between Ibarra at 7,250 ft (2,210 meters) elevation and the station in San Lorenzo, a stone's throw from the Pacific. Motion is a matter of brakes being applied to an onward slide, with the land providing momentum. When a little speed is gathered and the carriage starts bouncing precariously, the sensation is like riding a runaway rollercoaster. But it is the characteristic snail's pace that allows an appreciation of the passing landscape, which throughout the morning is quite overwhelming.

Fields of corn and potatoes in the fertile *sierra* give way to rugged dry scrubland at the narrow head of the Rio Mira valley. In a marvelous feat of engineering, the tracks cling to the sheer south side of the valley, crossing spindly bridges over the Mira's tributaries and penetrating 20 tunnels. Surrounding the small town of Salinas, 20 miles (30 km) from Ibarra at 5,300 ft (1,615 meters), are fields of sugar cane and coffee, and rolling grass paddocks where dairy cows graze.

tracks; villagers cultivate corn, papayas and bananas in the dry riverbed as the higher ground is barren and empty.

Shortly after Rio Blanco, 3,000 ft (900 meters) high and 46 miles (75 km) from Ibarra, the line leaves the Rio Mira, which twists northwards over the border into Colombia. Walls of dense tropical vegetation threaten to engulf the tracks as the descent continues through Rocafuerte, the midway junction at Cachaco, and the military checkpoint at Lita, where a religious shrine protects the bridge over a Mira

Here the valley flattens, and the softer subsoils allow the Rio Mira to irrigate the lush hinterland.

At Carchi, a further 12 miles (20 km) and 1,300 ft (400 meters) down, the *autoferro* stops for passengers to eat from trackside stalls. Beyond this point, the population is mainly black, descendants from African slaves transported here by the Spanish in the 17th and 18th centuries to work on the plantations. No more than a score of basic dwellings straddle the

<u>Left</u>, inside the Bluebird, the only way of getting from Ibarra to the remote coastal town of San Lorenzo. <u>Above</u>, the dense tropical vegetation threatens to cover the track.

tributary which is particularly prone to flooding. There are sweeping views of undulating virgin rainforest away to the northern horizon..

Night falls, the air is thick, warm and humid as the train approaches San Lorenzo. It could not contrast more with Ibarra: it is a ramshackle tropical town of about 15,000 with a Caribbean feel, pulsating to the beat of Colombian salsa. There are no road connections with the outside world, only the train and boats that ply the coast to even more isolated towns. Men find work in fishing or repairing the tracks, an ongoing process. Thus the *autoferro* is a livelihood, a link with beyond and, for the visitor, a unique transcultural Ecuadorian experience. ■

COASTAL ECUADOR

Ecuador has always been best known for its mountains. The tropical lowland west of the Andes has – along with its inhabitants, who comprise half the nation – been characterized as savage and uncivilized by the mountain-dwellers, a place to be exploited for its abundance. It is the traditional source of Ecuador's wealth, based on the cash crops of bananas, coffee and cocoa.

Swamps and beaches: Coastal Ecuador begins in the north with **San Lorenzo** and its neighboring villages, collections of wooden stilt houses suspended in steamy, timeless isolation amidst twisting mangrove channels. At La Tola, on the edge of the San Lorenzo Archipelago, the coast road begins, a dusty track through mainly uninhabited swamps bursting with vegetation.

Esmeraldas, strung along the shore of the like-named river, exemplifies urban coastal culture. A city of approximately 100,000, it is loud, vibrant and stay-up-late. Visual images are disparate: among a population chiefly *mestizo* and black, mountain Indians in bowler hats sell fruit from street stalls; Andean panpipe music disturbs Caribbean dance songs and Michael Jackson's rhythms; Chinese restaurants serve sweet-and-sour; and a shopping arcade is christened "Che Guevara".

Southwest of Esmeraldas are some of Ecuador's finest and most peaceful beaches. The road passes through **Atacames**, a small resort town, and on through **Sua**, a beautifully situated, lively fishing village, until finally ending at **Muisne**, with beaches as remote as they are alluring.

The main road south of Esmeraldas follows the languid river through cattle farms and plantations of bananas, palm oil and rubber, rising 1,600 ft (500 meters) to **Santo Domingo de los Colorados**. The name refers to the indigenous inhabitants of the region, the Zatchila or Colorado Indians, whose striking appearance consists of black stripes painted

A vendor prepares refreshing crushed ice a[t] Esmeraldas.

on their faces, and hair dyed red with achiote and cut in a bowl shape. Today they live mainly in areas to the south of town; while retaining their curative knowledge of natural medicine, they dress traditionally only for special occasions.

Perhaps the most scenic of the lowland routes runs from Santo Domingo to **Manta**, the calmest and prettiest coastal city. Lacking the energy of Guayaquil or Esmeraldas, Manta is very much of the sea. On **Tarqui beach**, local fishermen unload their catch of shark, dorado, eel and the odd tortoise, which are cleaned and sold on the sand amidst the aerial frenzy of seagulls and vultures. The **Municipal Museum** houses relics of the ancient Mantans, who enjoyed eating cocoa, worshipping a fertility cult, and tearing the hearts from sacrificial victims of war.

The famous Panama hat: Manta is the gateway to the nearby Panama hat villages. Based in **Montecristi**, this cottage industry has protected the heads of Teddy Roosevelt and King Edward VII, and featured in Renoir's canvasses during its illustrious hundred-year history. Made of reed straw brought on horseback to the homes of aging craftsmen, these hats can take up to three months to weave. They have always been produced in Ecuador exclusively, but were shipped worldwide from Panama, hence the misnomer. Fine wickerwork furniture and sisal hammocks are also manufactured here.

South of the the central coast, all roads lead to **Guayaquil**, Ecuador's largest and liveliest city with approximately 2½ million inhabitants. The Spanish quickly established their regional shipbuilding industry here: enormous 250-ton sailing vessels transported goods from Europe to Lima via Mexico and Panama, and returned laden with gold and silver.

The new, both in technology and in ideas, has always come first to Guayaquil: just as it had public streetcars and gas lighting before Quito, so it was the first city to realize independence in 1821, and has been the bastion of progressive liberal thought in modern Ecuador.

Target for pirates: The city has suffered countless burnings, by pirates on plundering raids during the 17th and 18th centuries; and more recently in 1896 and 1906, when damage was on such a scale that the entire city was rebuilt from scratch. A pleasant walk is along the riverfront **Malecón Simon Bolívar** past **La Rotonda**, commemorating Bolívar's meeting with San Martín; up to **Las Peñas**, the only extant colonial district, and scenic **Cerro El Carmen**.

Shrunken heads from the Oriente, pre-Inca ceramics, colonial religious paintings and a changing modern art exhibition fill the **Municipal Museum**.

Parque del Centenario, where gymnasts and comedians routinely perform, divides Avenida 9 de Octubre, the city's commercial heart. Here, crowds mill outside cinemas featuring blood-and-guts extravaganzas, and every second shopfront is a fast food restaurant. To escape the frenzy, join the locals in a rare moment of tranquility in **Parque Bolívar** – but beware of iguanas lurking in the trees.

anama hats
r sale.

THE GALÁPAGOS ISLANDS

Imagine sailing through fog in an uncharted ocean 600 miles (1,000 km) off the South American mainland, caught in the unknown whirlpools of the shifting Humboldt and El Niño currents. Suddenly, out of the fog, there emerge stark shapes, alien landmasses... This was how the Galápagos Islands were first seen by Europeans. In 1535, the Bishop of Panama was caught in the Doldrums on his way to Peru, drifting without water for three days, before sighting the islands. He and his crew survived on prickly pear juice, and in thanks named the place "The Enchanted Islands."

It is possible that the ancient Mantans, Polynesians and the Incas visited the Galápagos. From their discovery until their incorporation into Ecuador in 1832, the islands served as a refuge for European and American pirates, whalers and sealers. They re-stocked supplies of firewood, water and fresh meat in the form of giant tortoises which – stacked upside down – could remain alive for a year in ships' holds.

Charles Darwin arrives: Just as the islands were undergoing permanent settlement, *The Beagle* dropped anchor in **San Cristóbal Bay** and the 26-year-old naturalist Charles Darwin strode ashore. Previous scientific expeditions had been mounted, including Morrel's in 1825 which witnessed the spectacular eruption of Fernandina's volcano and recorded water temperatures of 150° Fahrenheit (65° Celsius). With Charles Darwin's visit, however, the enormous biological and geological significance of the Galápagos islands was recognized.

Although he stayed for only five weeks in 1835, Darwin made many of the observations upon which he based his theories of evolution and the mutability of species. He noticed 13 types of finch, each with a different beak designed to collect its particular food, ranging from seeds to insects and worms.

The enchantment of the islands suffered dearly over the next century when a penal colony was established on Floreana. Conditions were harsh, administrators gratuitously cruel. The original colonists, some 80 soldiers whose crimes of insurrection had been pardoned, fled the islands' hardships, leaving the prisoners to their fate.

As recently as 1944, a colony was established on Isabela to which increasingly hardened criminals were sent. Escapees were hunted like animals and, when caught, were put to work on the "Wall of Tears", where many were crushed to death by the huge basalt stones they had to carry. The infamy of the place was such that convicts were, upon arrival, reputed to "cry like babies or tremble like terrified women". Following a riot and mass escape in 1958 which terrorized the civilian population, the penal colony was dissolved.

Volcanic birth: This sordid history is strangely suitable to Herman Melville's vision of the islands: "Take five-and-twenty heaps of cinders dumped here and there in an outside city lot; imagine some of them magnified into mountains, and the vacant lot the sea..."

eft, olphins llow a ailing boat the lands. ight, a alápagos rtle.

In fact there are 13 mmajor islands, six small islands and 42 islets spread over 30,000 sq miles (80,000 sq km). The land consists of lava resting on a basalt base, accumulations of volcanic refuse produced by successive underwater eruptions which continue today. The islands have never been connected with the mainland, but emerged from the water individually over a period of a million years. The violence of the goelogical past is most evident on Isabela with its chain of five volcanoes as high as 5,600 ft (1,700 meters). One of them, the **Sierra Negra**, has the second largest crater in the world, measuring 6 miles (10 km) in diameter.

Seeds were transported accidentally by birds and aboard ships. Today the islands support almost 900 plant varieties, the most revered of which is the *palo santo*, found in abundance on **Rábida**. There are six distinct vegetation zones ranging from low level desert to the uppermost *pampa*; a walk up to the old sugar mill on San Cristóbal passes most of them.

On **San Bartolomé**, two sparkling horse-shoe beaches are separated by a narrow strip of semi-tropical forest. From the island's summit, one of the best vantage-points in the archipelago, the rolling lunar wasteland of **Santiago** stretches away to the west – a black mass of swirling lava flows understandably uninhabited. Within this desert, however, is a freshwater spring, which quenched the thirst of many a pirate docked in **Buccaneer Cove**. And doubtless these first visitors watched the flamingoes dance around the nearby lagoon; buried each other up to the neck in the coffee-colored sand of **Espumilla Beach**; and, near **Puerto Egas**, were confounded by the fur seals that swam through an underwater tunnel between the open sea and two small, clear pools.

Beneath the waves: Until they were declared a national park in 1959, the Galápagos supported a singularly bloodthirsty population. What they needed to take the fight out of them was some snorkeling equipment, to enter the wondrous silence of the cool ocean.

Iguana.

Some of the best snorkeling is off far-flung islands like **Española**, which is the only place in the world that the endemic waved albatross breeds. In Gardner Bay, flapping manta rays probably think you are just another sea lion, but the sea lions know better, and an aggressive bull should be given right of way. The females and young are playful; they can recognize the 290 varieties of fish in the water, but a pale figure with a mask and flippers is still a curious sight.

Fernandina holds the largest colony of the world's only marine iguanas. As inquisitive as the two related land species, they are much more dragon-like with their scaly skin – which turns from black to blue and red during mating season – and the row of spines along their back. Being land-dwellers originally, they can submerge for only a few minutes at a time, searching for algae; and upon resurfacing, snort a salty spray into the air. Watching the marine iguana perform these rituals beneath the smoldering **Volcan La Cumbre**, which last erupted in September 1988, is one of the natural world's most primal experiences.

Directly opposite Fernandina is **Urbina Bay**, and one of the few coral reefs in the archipelago. Fish of every color steer clear of the Galápagos penguin, the world's northernmost species whose clowning routines indicate its delight in the equatorial sun. The entrance to nearby **Elizabeth Bay** is protected by a cluster of islands which more penguins share with nesting pelicans which feed on the abundant fish in the cove.

An animal wonderland: Enroute to Floreana, schools of sperm and killer whales cruise the deep waters, and bottle-nosed dolphins surf the bow waves of boats. At **Devil's Crown** – named after the jagged, truncated volcanic cone rising from the ocean – sea lions glide along strong currents, which make for adventurous snorkeling.

The beach on **Point Cormorant**, Floreana's most beautiful location, is dotted with olivine crystals, while the adjacent lagoons teem with flamingoes.

luxury
uiser
sses
tween
ands.

Around the point is the **Bay of Sharks**; its ring of pristine white sand is popular with nesting tortoises. The name refers to the relatively harmless white-tipped shark, which is found mainly here and off San Bartolomé. It is, along with the enormous – up to 50 ft (15 meters) – and equally docile whale shark, the only kind in these waters.

On land, the unchallenged king of the islands is the giant tortoise, the *galápago* itself; the word means English saddle in reference to the shape of the shell. These prehistoric hermits, considered the oldest reptile in existence, can reach 200 years of age and weigh up to 600 lbs (300 kg).

After spending his first night on a beach on San Cristóbal, Darwin took a walk and encountered a "strange Cyclopean scene" – two tortoises enjoying the sun and munching on cactus. One "gave a deep hiss, and drew in its head", the other "slowly stalked away". From such an inauspicious introduction, Darwin became fascinated with the beasts, noticing numerous subspecies with different shaped shells. On rocky, sparsely vegetated islands like Isabela and Española, the tortoises have a longer neck and legs as well as a saddle-shaped carapace, which enable them to reach higher to obtain food. These features are absent from the more cumbersome species inhabiting fertile islands like Santa Cruz.

A delicate ecology: The **Charles Darwin Research Station** was established on Santa Cruz in 1959, upon the centenary of the publication of *The Origin of Species*. One of its most important programs is the controlled hatching of tortoise eggs, a necessary step since the introduction by early settlers of feral dogs, cats, goats, pigs and rats.

Given the chance, these unnatural enemies gulp down baby tortoises. On Pinzón, for example, not one young tortoise has been sighted for nearly 50 years. The feral species likewise destroy much of the vegetation, but have participated in the evolutionary miracle of the Galápagos in at least one respect: the goats on **Santa Fe**, in the absence of

Left, an excursion o[n] a volcanic island. Righ[t,] bright crab.

freshwater, have developed a taste for the sea, and now live on it.

As these pests indicate, man's presence on the islands has until recently been mainly destructive. Scattered among the coves and hills are remnants of commercial ambition and military adventurism, which underline the inhospitable loneliness of these shores. In **Whale Bay** on Santa Cruz, ceramic fragments conjure images of the famous buccaneer Henry Morgan with a blue-footed boobie squawking on his shoulder. Pirates and whalers recorded their passage on the cliff faces of **Tagus Cove** on Isabela: today the graffiti is read mainly by flightless cormorants. A more recent ruin is the incongruous skeleton of an abandoned salt mine dating from the 1960s which sits above Puerto Egas on Santiago.

Drama in the tropics: Floreana has witnessed some mysterious interludes. A Norwegian fishing operation established in the 1920s lasted only eight years: the Ecuadorian government reputedly confiscated their ship, driving the fishermen to alcoholic oblivion. Shortly thereafter, an odd collection of Germans searching for a tropical paradise settled here, among them a baroness and her two lovers, a doctor and his mistress, and another couple.

Melodramas ensued, leading to the death of thirst on Marchena Island of one lover and a Norwegian skipper, abandoned enroute to Santa Cruz. The doctor died inexplicably of convulsions before he could relate the suspicious circumstances. The descendants of the original couple, the Wittmers, still live in **Puerto Velasco Ibarra**. More recently, two other people have disappeared without a trace among the picturesque lava flows.

The Galápagos Islands do not suffer human habitation gladly. They are one of the few places in the world where animals still live undisturbed, and nowhere are the forces of evolution more clearly displayed. To observe these natural processes is to sense a wholly other world, harmonious and beautifully savage. Visitors should leave no scars.

e unique ora of the lands.

AÑO
1997

BOLIVIA: THE TIBET OF SOUTH AMERICA

Just over a century ago, a diplomatic crisis began in La Paz over a single glass of *chicha*. The new British ambassador to Bolivia made the mistake of sneering at this local firewater when served by dictator Mariano Melgarejo. As punishment, he was forced to drink a barrelful of chocolate and was then led through the streets of the capital sitting backwards on a donkey.

When news arrived in London, Queen Victoria was not amused. It is said that she demanded a map of South America, drew a cross through the country and angrily announced: "Bolivia does not exist!"

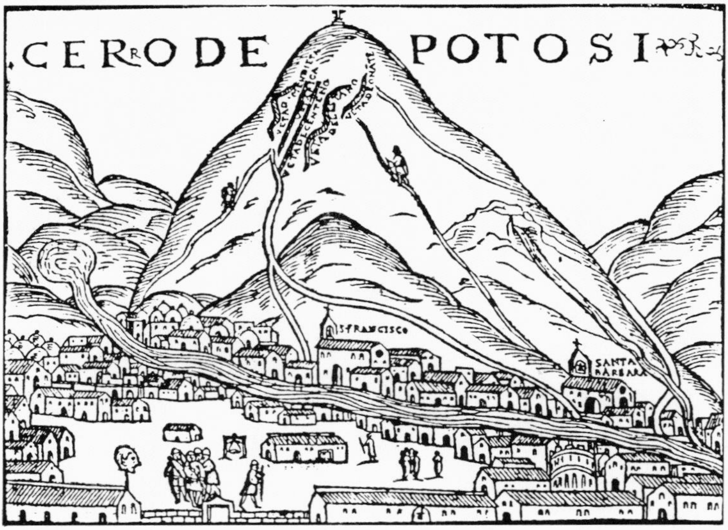

For the rest of the world, Queen Victoria's judgement might as well have been true. Even today, Bolivia remains one of the least-known of South American countries. Exploited and humiliated throughout its modern history, this landlocked mountain nation is the poorest on the continent.

It also has the largest Indian population of any South American republic, with two thirds of the nation full-blooded and many only speaking their native Quechua and Aymará languages. Despite the extraordinary depredations inflicted by the Spanish and the political chaos since independence, their culture has shoiwn surprising resilience.

Fading civilizations: The barren highlands of Bolivia, known as the *altiplano*, were a part of the Inca Empire when the Spaniards arrived in Peru. Before then the *altiplano* had seen a range of ancient civilizations, the most powerful of them centered around the city of Tiahuanaco on Lake Titicaca. Archaeologists are only now beginning to realize the extent of that empire, which probably extended as far north as Ecuador. The Tiahuanaco culture is considered more advanced than the Incan, although many of the stone carvings and hieroglyphics they left behind remain undeciphered. In the absence of written records, what brought about the empire's decline remains a matter for speculation. Certainly, Tiahuanaco was already in decay when the Incas began expanding from Cuzco in the 1400s. It easily became a part of the highly-ordered and efficient Inca realm, and the Aymará Indians became ruled by the Quechua-speaking Children of the Sun.

It wasn't long before the first conquistadors had made their way into what they called "Alto Peru" – modern-day Bolivia – to divide up the spoils. The first was Diego de Almagro, who fell to a Spanish assassin's knife. The city of Chuquisaca (modern Sucre) had already been founded as a base for colonization when in 1544 an Indian named Diego Huallpa discovered silver in the Cerro Rico of Potosí. From that moment, the country's fate was sealed.

The lust for silver: For the next two centuries, everything in Bolivia was geared towards extracting this vein of precious metal, the greatest ever discovered. Conquistadors and missionaries quickly flocked to the Andean city in search of their fortunes. Towns were founded only to supply Potosí with goods traded from other parts of the empire

...ope. Nothing ...he ore and its ...g wilderness, ...ndians. As in ...ems of terrac- ...pair. Christi- ...he conversion ... obvious was ...m of dress for ...sses, odd hats

...in the streets of ...dated 1555, the ...w World mining ..., La Paz, c. 1900.

and plaited hair make up the most famous tourist image of Bolivia today, they were actually first worn by decree of the Spanish king in the 18th century. Even the way women's hair is parted was ordered by the Viceroy of Toledo.

The Indian populations were theoretically free subjects of the Spanish crown, but the protection was a fiction. In reality, they were forced to pay massive tributes, lived at the beck and call of brutal overlords, and were regularly dragged from their agricultural communities to work in the mines of Potosí. Press-ganged into the Cerro Rico, Indians died by the thousands every year in the harsh and brutal conditions. One Dominican monk in 1515 described the Rich Hill as "the mouth of hell", where workers were treated "like stray animals". Meanwhile, colonial Potosí grew to match any city in the Old World.

The amount of silver taken from Potosí is staggering: 16,000 tons (16 million kg) arrived in Seville between 1545 and 1660 – a figure which does not include smuggled metal – an amount three and a half times the entire European reserves of the day. But the wealth did not stay with Spain – it was squandered on its futile religious wars, or wasted by the extravagance of its nobles and clergymen. Almost all of it ended up in the coffers of Flemish, German or English bankers, financing the industrial development of northern Europe while Spain became a backward agricultural nation.

An uncertain independence: Several revolts were led by Bolivian *mestizos* and Indians during the oppressive colonial rule, without managing to shake Spain's iron grip. But as the 18th century ended, independence movements were being kindled around South America. It is little known that the first independence movement in Latin America began, of all places, in Chuquisaca in May 1809, although it was quickly crushed. When General Sucre's victories in Peru put an end to Spanish rule in 1825 , the provinces of "Upper Peru" were declared to be a new republic named in honor of the Liberator, Simon Bolívar: Bolivia.

Although they had nothing in common, these disorganized territories ranging from the Amazon to the icy *sierra* were now forced to make their way as a nation. General Bolívar came to visit the wretched land that would bear his name, passing through the desperately poor countryside to visit La Paz, Potosí and Sucre before dictating an idealistic constitution and returning to Colombia. With the silver of Potosí exhausted and the grasping *criollo* minority now in government, the prospects for the new republic of Bolivia were not promising.

Chaos was not long in coming. An attempt at union with Peru quickly failed, and the young republic launched into an apparently endless series of military governments – averaging around one coup a year since 1825. But despite the apparent chaos at the highest levels of power, little changed for average Bolivians. The coups were mostly bloodless reshufflings in the palaces of La Paz, with wealth and control being kept in the hands of the small number of families descended from the Spaniards who have always run the country.

Meanwhile, Bolivia proceeded to lose large chunks of its territory in one war after another with its neighbors. The most serious loss came after the War of the Pacific (1879–83) when it was deprived of any access to the sea by Chile. Then, in 1903, Brazil annexed a vast stretch of Bolivia's Amazon basin, known to be rich in rubber trees. To round off the losses, Paraguay won much of the southern Chaco from Bolivia in a desperately-fought war in 1932, during which both countries were bled dry.

The only good news seemed to be the discovery of tin by a prospector named Simon Ituri Patino. He found veins in Oruro and

Above, Victor Paz Estensorro is sworn in as President after the 1952 revolution.

Potosí so rich that they could be exported without the need for concentration. The discovery coincided with the developed world's use of the tin can for packaging food.

But the find did Bolivia little good. Patino used the discovery to amass a personal fortune, making himself one of the ten richest people on earth. While Patino lived luxuriously in Europe, he kept miners on starvation wages in conditions hardly better than those imposed by the Spanish in colonial days. Able to command the obedience of presidents and politicians, Patino dealt with industrial disputes by organizing massacres as he vacationed in Switzerland with the crown heads of Europe.

Miners' revolt: The defeat by Paraguay's was the last straw for many Bolivians. A period of intense self-reflection followed the war, creating a growing movement for change. Radicals banded together in the new Movimiento Nacionalista Radical (MNR) behind Victor Paz Estenssoro. Winning the elections of 1951, the party was blocked from office by a military coup and Paz Estenssoro forced into exile in Buenos Aires. But the miners began an armed revolt and after heavy fighting defeated the military. Paz Estenssoro returned to La Paz and the MNR began to put its reforms into action.

In the following years Bolivia saw the nationalization of tin mines, the granting of votes to Indians (previously banned as illiterates) and a wide-ranging land reform. Unfortunately, the mines were still dependent on foreign capital and land given to Indians was in plots too small to be quickly productive. The country's economy began sliding and the MNR finally ousted in another military coup, with the air force taking the precaution of bombing mining camps to break resistance.

Following the coup, dictator followed dictator with monotonous regularity. In 1967, Bolivia gained brief world attention when the hero of the Cuban revolution, Che Guevara, was hunted down and killed in its Amazon jungle, trying to raise the Indians up in revolution. He was unable to provoke support, despite the dismal conditions in which the *campesinos* live.

The 1970s were dominated by General Hugo Banzer Suaréz, who ran Bolivia at the head of a right-wing coalition before finally scheduling elections in 1978. Although he ignored the results when he lost, Banzer finally had to give way to other stronger military leaders. The most infamous of Bolivia's many dictators came to power in 1980 in a coup which cost hundreds of lives: General Luis García Meza sent his tanks into La Paz, rounded up and shot left-wing leaders, and bombed mining camps in Oruro. His period in office is remembered for its extraordinary corruption, with the general inviting men like Klaus Barbie to help organize his security forces and selling off national treasures such as Che Guevara's diary to line his own pockets.

Finally García Meza was driven from power and in 1982 democracy was restored, with the left-wing Dr Hernan Sile Zuazo as President. Unfortunately, the doctor is best remembered for leading Bolivia into one of the world's highest inflation rates, hitting the mind-boggling level of 35,000 percent a year, with the peso at 2 million to the US dollar.

Tin price collapse: In 1985, the presidency was handed over to the octogenarian Paz Estenssoro, who had led the 1952 revolution. The economy was on the verge of collapse, with the major export being the illicit cocaine trade and inflation running at 20,000 percent. Reversing his radical stands of 35 years ago, Paz Estenssoro embraced the conservative policies recommended by the International Monetary Fund and embarked on a dramatic austerity plan. With the collapse of tin prices in 1985 he sacked 20,000 miners from the state-run company COMIBOL, using the military to head off their union protests. Inflation ground to a halt but at the price of massive unemployment.

Bolivia began a facelift to attract foreign investment. and the country began to receive the highest per capita level of foreign aid in South America. Investment was to some extent encouraged to break away from cocaine manufacture. In the early 1990s the US embarked on Operation Support Justice, a highly publicised anti-narcotics programme in Bolivia which included $78 million in aid. But high-profile raids on illegal laboratories led to few arrests and the Americans were shortly asked to leave.

There is still a long way to go before South America's poorest country can begin to solve its income inequalities and to improve the dismal statistics of unemployment and child deaths from malnutrition.

La Paz: The World's Highest Capital

The most dramatic way of arriving in La Paz, the highest capital city in the world, is in the back of a local truck bringing produce from the north. A dirt highway is carved from the side of the Andes, skirting canyons and running along cliffs. In five hours the truck rises more than 9,000 ft (2,700 meters) from dense jungle to the treeless, windswept *altiplano*. The first two hours are the most uncomfortable, thanks to the thick clouds of brown dust billowing from the road. Then the truck passes under a waterfall, soaking everyone to the skin in a freezing downpour. But the most disturbing aspect of the trip, almost spoiling the spectacular views, is the number of wooden crosses placed along the roadside where other trucks have plunged down ravines.

For obvious reasons, many people prefer to fly into La Paz. The views are even more extraordinary as the aeroplane sweeps across Bolivia's highest mountain ranges to dive into the city, which sits in a natural canyon. The one disadvantage is that some travelers arriving in the airport, at an altitude of almost 12,000 ft (3,600 meters), are struck by the vague nausea of *soroche*, or altitude sickness. A day or two of taking it easy is a certain cure.

In such a magnificent setting, La Paz at first seems an ugly blur of orange brick and gray corrugated iron roof. But on much closer inspection, it is one of South America's most unusual and lively cities.

High in the Andes: The streets of La Paz, made of slippery bricks, are steep and tiring in the thin mountain air. They spread out from the **Plaza San Francisco** with its huge stone church containing a statue of Jesus with a blue fluorescent halo. The snowcapped **Mount Illimani**, at more than 19,000 ft (6,000 meters) in height, dominates the skyline from most parts of La Paz.

The city's traditional center is the **Plaza Murillo**, where the Italianate

Preceding pages: view of La Paz. Below, central La Paz at twilight.

Presidential Palace is located – most often referred to as the Palacio Quemado, or Burnt Palace, twice gutted by inflamatory crowds since it was first built in the 1850s . Nearby is the modern **cathedral**. The surrounding streets are the most atmospheric in the city: the **Calle Jaén** is still cobbled and without traffic, lined by preserved colonial buildings. Another atmospheric area is behind the church and monastery of San Francisco near the upper end of the Av Mariscal Santa Cruz. It dates from 1549 and the carvings are rich and ingenious.

The more modern city center has a collection of shabby skyscrapers and streets clogged with traffic.

One of the cultural landmarks of the city center is the cafe of the **Club de La Paz**, on the corners of Avenidas Camacho and Colón. This antique wooden retreat has seen innumerable business and political deals, and was probably where many of Bolivia's coups were hatched. Its conspiratorial atmosphere made it the favorite hangout of Klaus Barbie before he was arrested in the early 1980s and returned to France for trial as a Nazi war criminal.

Witches and markets: But the real attaction of La Paz is the street life. Narrow alleyways stretching all the way up along the hillside behind the Plaza San Francisco are generally packed with Bolivian women in their bright layered dresses and bowler hats, selling blankets, nuts, herbs and – for the *gringos* – woolen jumpers with the image of a llama emblazoned upon them.

Near here is the famous **Mercado de Hechicería**, or Witchcraft Market, where elderly ladies sell magic charms for every possible occasion. You can pick up a small bottle full of colored pieces of wood and oil which, depending on its contents, will give good luck with either love, money or health. A more macabre specialty is dried llama fetuses, traditionally buried in the foundations of any new building to bring good fortune to the occupants.

Also for sale at many markets are plaster figures of an Indian household god Ekeko. This red-nosed grinning

eft, a young cholar eceives his iploma. ight, pretty ndian girl.

character is always loaded down with miniature goods, from sacks of grain to blankets and wads of money. Ekeko is said to bring prosperity and during the Alacitas Fair, at the end of January, you can buy toy houses, sheep or tiny airline tickets for this Bolivian version of Santa Claus – and he will grant you a real one before the year ends.

When visiting these markets, food turns out to be one of La Paz's most unexpected attractions. Vendors sell papaya milkshakes, spiced chicken and rice, fried trout caught in Lake Titicaca or pieces of heart with hot nut sauces skewered on a wire. The markets near Plaza San Francisco have a particularly good range of delicacies, served by ladies grown large on their own cooking. Take a seat at one of the booths for tea and goat cheese in the early afternoon – the perfect vantage point to watch Bolivian life go by. Later in the night, a potent *chicha* might be more appropriate, or the excellent local beer.

An unfortunate past: La Paz also has a number of very odd museums which are forced to commemorate Bolivia's sadly unsuccessful past. The **Museo Murillo** on Calle Jaén is in an old mansion owned by one of the country's greatest heroes: Pedro Domingo Murillo led an unsuccessful revolt against the Spanish in 1909 and was hanged for his efforts. There is a good collection of colonial furniture and a room devoted to medicine and magic.

In the same street, the **Museo de Litoral** has artifacts from the War of the Pacific (1879–83) in which Bolivia was defeated by Chile and lost its only access to the sea. The defiant emblem over the cashier reads: Bolivia Has Not Lost and Will Never Lose Its Right to the Pacific.

Several other museums are worth seeking out. The **Museo Nacional de Arte**, in the 18th-century baroque palace of the Count of Arana, near the cathedral at Calle Socabaya 432, has colonial as well as local paintings. At the **Museo Nacional de Etnografia y Folklore**, in the palace of the Marquis of Villaverde at Calle Ingavi 915 there

A common sight in the Andes: a bus under repairs.

are good cultural exhibits from Ayoreo and Chipaya Indians.

Beyond the city: La Paz is the perfect base for exploring the Bolivian highlands. Day trips can be arranged to some of the most diverse landscapes on earth, from ghostly valleys and ice caves to mysterious ruins and the turquoise waters of Lake Titicaca.

The easiest excursion is to the so-called **Valley of the Moon**. Only 7 miles (11 km) away from downtown La Paz in distance, but light years away in appearance, this is a bizarrely eroded hillside full of pinnacles and miniature canyons. Known technically as "badlands", its desert formations are constantly shifting and can be strolled around for hours, ducking between cacti and around precipices, or simply viewed from a comfortable vantage point.

One and a half hours away from the center of the city by bus is a place for any skiing fanatics: **Chacaltaya**, the world's highest developed ski area. The ski slopes on the side of the mountain runs between 17,000 and 17,700 ft (5,200 and 5,400 meters) and is definitely only for those acclimatized to the altitude. For those less interested in snow sports, the peak still provides some spectacular views of the Andes.

The blue Lake Titicaca: Most visitors to La Paz use the opportunity to visit the Bolivian side of nearby **Lake Titicaca**, the great high-altitude expanse of water shared with Peru. One easy excursion is to the small village of **Copacabana**, famous for its miracle-working Dark Virgin of the Lake, the patron saint of Bolivia. An image of the Virgin was taken to Rio de Janeiro in the 19th century and the village found itself giving its name to a (today more well-known) Brazilian beach.

The Bolivian Copacabana is a quiet and relaxing place, where visitors can stroll along the lakeside or loll in one of the many fish restaurants. But the village comes alive during its regular fiestas, when the Virgin is paraded through the streets, copious amount of alcohol is consumed and any new buses and trucks are solemnly blessed with beer poured

emetery ear La Paz.

over their bonnets. Small rowing boats can be hired to spend a few hours on the water, with the only competition being the occasional fishing vessel or small gunboat from Bolivia's nearly non-existent navy.

For those with a day to spare, row out to the **Island of the Sun**. This lush and idyllic spot contains a sacred rock at its northwestern end, where the Incas believed that their founding parents, Manco Capac and Mama Ocllo, emerged from the waters of Lake Titicaca at the call of the sun god.

For those traveling between Bolivia and Peru, Crillon Tours offers a luxurious hydrofoil service across the lake, visiting both Copacabana and the Island of the Sun en route.

Ancient mystery: Another worthwhile excursion from La Paz is to the splendid ruins of **Tiahuanaco**, on the southern tip of Lake Titicaca. Still being dug by archaeologists, this site is fast becoming one of the most important in South America as evidence emerges about the civilization's extent.

Experts believe that the Tiahuanaco culture, which flowered one thousand years ago, was more advanced than the Incan in art, pottery, astronomy and mathematics. But a mysterious cataclysm hit the majestic city – probably an earthquake – and the civilization fell into decay by the time the Inca armies were marching.

Today, with less than one-sixth of the site excavated, Tiahuanaco is baffling to visit. It boasts a magnificently carved Gate of the Sun, Acapana Pyramid and chambers cut from stone with faces staring from the walls. Many of the images are reminiscent of Mexican and Polynesian art. But archaeologists admit that they are still merely scratching the surface of this remarkable site, guessing at the culture from the few shreds of evidence the past has left behind.

For those whose appetites have been whetted by a visit to the ruins, many of the finds are now housed back in La Paz in the **Museo Nacional de Arqueologia** (on the corner of Frederico Zuazo and Tiwanaku streets).

Left, baptismal goods for sale at Copacabana. Right, musician at a peña in La Paz.

A Night At The Peña

After a long day of wandering the streets of any Andean city – La Paz, Potosí, Cuzco or Quito – the best place to head for is the local *peña*, or folk nightclub. That's where to sit and enjoy the haunting music of the *altiplano* while sipping a cold beer, glass of wine or potent *pisco sour*, made of grape brandy with egg yolk.

Starting off at around 10pm, *peñas* are usually relaxed and informal bars which offer set musical programs. Up to a dozen groups can play on a single night, giving an idea of the range and variety of Andean music; while the rhythms of the *altiplano* are related, every region has its own unique sound. A group from Potosí is quite different to one from the shores of Lake Titicaca, and more different again to musicians from Cuzco in Peru.

In La Paz, the best *peñas* to head for is the Naira at Sagarnaga 161, a dark and intimate hangout with a fine repertory of good musicians. Other well-known *penãs* are in the restaurants Los Excudos on Mariscal Santa Cruz and La Casa del Corregidor.

The basic instruments used are the single-reed flutes (known as *guenas*), deep wooden pipes (*zampoñas*), drums and rattles. The famous *charango* is a miniature guitar made of an armadillo's shell, with 15 strings that the player strums and plucks to create a penetrating, tiny sound. Along with the Andean harp, the *charango* is one of the few examples of local culture mixing successfully with the Spanish. Stringed instruments were one of the few cultural innovations that the Andean Indians were glad to accept from Europe.

The effect of these instruments is mesmerizing. Andean music evokes the loneliness of the bleak and harsh *altiplano*, the almost uncultivatable highlands that Indians refuse to leave, despite the efforts of successive governments to relocate them in the lush Amazon basin.

The music is traditionally played without vocal accompaniment, but in recent decades they have been joined to ballads – called *waynos* – sung in the Quechua or Aymará tongues, or in a mixture of native languages and Spanish. They often deal with the daily lives of *campesinos* in the fields:

Do you want me to tell you
Where I'm from?
I'm from behind that hill,
Amid the carnations,
Among the lilies
My sling is of Castilian fabric,
And my lassoo of merino wool:
Very Long-lasting,
Very strong.

Some of the songs speak of passionate love in the mountains:

Does your heart not pain you?
Do you not weep?
You are my beautiful flower,
My queen,
My lady.

Others are much more progressive:

The priest of Andahuaylas
Keeps telling me to get married.
Maybe he knows, maybe not,
Where I went last night.

As an expression of Indian culture, the music has often had a mixed reception from the country's rulers. On radio, it must compete with the pop from the First World, favored by many of the middle and the upper classes, as well as the salza and samba from other parts of Latin America. At its worst, this cultural cringe was producing Western songs on Andean instruments – like "Rock Around the Clock" on panpipes. But as Indian cultures are increasingly seen as worth preserving, the presence of *altiplano* tunes is definitely growing.

Certainly in the *peñas* they hold full sway. The musicians are often accomplished mimes and the show generally includes a few comics, which manage to be hilarious no matter how little Spanish you know.

Usually the crowd becomes more boisterous as the night goes on, shouting and yelling interjections or whistling to the music. Prodigious amounts of alcohol can be consumed and, if the *peña* is large enough to have a dance floor, the revelries are very likely to continue well into the early hours. ■

Fiesta

Travelers in Bolivia can always tell when a fiesta is on the way. The celebrations begin the night before, when every bar in town fills with drunken revelers. Meanwhile in the streets outside, those sober enough to stand are building wooden platforms from which the next morning's procession can be viewed.

But the preparations have been going on for months. Behind closed doors, hundreds of participants put the last touches to their elaborate costumes, getting ready for their part in the famous *diablada* – the Devil Dance that dates from pre-Inca times, and is central to the fiestas around the country.

This most spectacular cultural expression of Bolivian Indians, is also a central part of the country's biggest celebrations. Carnival in Oruro is the most famous, held for eight days before Ash Wednesday every year. Carnival has also been growing inpopularity in La Paz, where the other major event is the Festival of Jesus held every June.

Eager spectators take their places by dawn, huddling against the cold mountain winds. Soon the street vendors are out in force, most selling cans of beer. Older people turn up their noses at these new-fangled tins, preferring a more potent breakfast of *chicha*, the local maize whiskey. With a few drinks under their belts, by 10am the crowd is ready for the Devil Dance. It follows a ritual pattern that has remained unchanged for centuries. First, the way for the procession is cleared by two figures dressed elaborately as a bear and a condor. Then come the masked dancers, led by Satan and Lucifer, both in scarlet cloaks, with metal serpents twisted around one arm and a trident in the other.

Following these are the hundreds of devils in fantastic outfits, leaping and pirouetting along the steep roads. Their heavy masks are made of plaster, looking more Asian than Latin. They have sprouting horns, bulbous eyes, horsehair wigs and long, glistening fangs. The devils' clothes are also carefully prepared, and these include silk shawls embroidered with dragons, jewelled breastplates and boots sparkling with golden spurs.

Soon the streets are filled with these ferocious-looking figures, interspersed between phalanxes of other dancers dressed as pumas, monkeys or insects. Accompanying them are teams of pipe players or drummers or brass bands playing chaotic tunes.

The lead is soon taken by China Supay, the

Devil's wife, who tries to seduce the Archangel Michael with her wiles. Dancers appear wearing barrel-shaped uniforms with ostrich plumes, bouncing along carrying in their hands such industrial emblems as small wooden sewing machines and trucks in their hands, as each group represents one of the local workers' unions.

Other dancers dress as the Incas, done up in headdresses shaped like the condor, with the sun and the moon embroidered on their chests. Still others appear as the black slaves brought

over by the Spaniards, clanking through the streets in chains. Bolivian girls in pink and black mini-skirts bounce along the steep streets, dancing with men dressed as giant white bears. Teams of pipe players in colored uniforms stumble past, their faces purple from blowing so long and hard in the thin mountain air. Collections of elderly women struggle around the course in bright yellow dresses, followed by their husbands in red, their daughters in green and sons in blue – all dancing to a beat unchanged

Left, preparing for the procession at the Festival of Jesus in La Paz. Above, one of the devils in the *diablada*.

through the ages. The watching crowd, by now yelling and often joining in the dancing, becomes more boisterous as the day progresses and as more alcohol is consumed. Others retire from the fray to pass out in doorways. Most in the procession grab a few cans of beer, which doesn't help their dance steps.

In Oruro, the procession ends up at a football stadium, where dancers perform two masques, like medieval mystery plays. The first is a reenactment of the Conquest by the Spanish, performed, naturally enough, as a tragedy. In the second, the Archangel Michael defeats the forces of evil with his flaming sword, taking on not only the devils but the Seven Deadly Sins as well. The result is announced by the Virgen del Socavon, the patroness of miners, and the dancers enter a chapel to chant a hymn in Quechua.

Despite the Christian gloss over the proceedings, the ritual is a purely pagan ceremony of thanks to Pachamama, the earth mother. It commemorates the struggle between the forces of good and evil on earth. The conquering Spaniards were only able to convert the Indians superficially, changing a few names of deities to fit the formulae of the church – to attempt more would have provoked rebellion. The fiestas acted as a valve for letting off steam.

The *diablada* survived and grew during colonial times as an expression of the Indians' frustration. The Europeans sat on their elegant balconies and looked down on the streets, the subjected peoples were allowed their annual dose of freedom – an act of rebellion that became like a safety valve.

Since independence, the campesinos have felt no more control over their own destinies, still being ruled by the descendants of their former colonial masters who often regard them as little better than animals. The drunken fiestas still give many Bolivian a chance to forget their many problems. For a few days nothing matters, or won't until the hangovers hit. The *diablada* procession breaks up into smaller groups at the end of the day, carousing around bonfires and dancing late into the night.

For several days afterwards revelers can be seen in the streets and dark bars, dressed as demons or mosquitoes, seeking out their Bolivian oblivion. ■

THE YUNGAS: TROPICAL VALLEYS

Sweeping down from the Andean heights near La Paz to Bolivia's steaming Amazon basin is the sub-tropical region known as the **Yungas**. The combination of a warm climate with magnificent mountain views has made the zone a favorite for short visits from the capital and for the growing number of trekkers now flocking to Bolivia.

The Yungas – the name simply means "Valleys" – is in a completely different climatic zone to the Bolivian capital, less than 60 miles (100 km) away on the bleak and barren *altiplano*. The drive to the town is one of the most spectacular in South America, going over a high-altitude mountain pass to dive into fertile valleys with drifting tropical mists, ancient Inca terraces and abundant fruit.

At 5,000 ft (1,500 meters) above sea level, the small town of **Coroico** is the zone's main commercial center. Coroico itself is little more than a tidy main square surrounded by a few cheap restaurants and hotels. But there are plenty of tranquil walks in the dripping green countryside near the town, beyond the plantations growing coffee, coca and bananas. The gentle strolls provide spectacular views of snow-capped mountain ranges on the horizon leading to jungle-covered valleys, as well as to several rivers for swimming.

The best views of the Cordillera Real are from the little church above the town, at the top of Cerro Uchumachi. Also worth calling in on is the **Mothers of Clarissa Convent**, where Bolivian nuns make peanut butter, biscuits and quite drinkable local wine.

The nearby towns of **Sorata** and **Chulumani** are equally relaxing places to visit, both villages with small guest-houses and walks. The roads to both places are magnificent and Sorata in particular is said to have the most beautiful setting in Bolivia. A day hike from Sorata leads to the bat-filled **San Pedro cave**. Less adventurous spirits will be content with strolls through the flower-filled valleys that locals insist was the original sight of the Garden of Eden.

Coroico is enjoying a new popularity as a starting point and a goal for two popular treks, neither of which need any special experience to tackle.

Bolivia's "Inca Trail": The most popular walk begins at **La Cumbre**, the highest point of the road from La Paz to the Yungas. It takes about four days, following an ancient Inca road that is in better repair than the path to Machu Picchu in Peru – although lacking any sites as magnificent as the Inca ruins along the way.

Starting in the freezing and treeless heights, this path quickly descends into the more lush and habitable Yungas. Most walkers advance slowly at first, gasping in the thin mountain air and rhythmically plodding over the chilly pass. At this altitude, there are no signs of human habitation. But further into the valleys, Indian villages begin to appear – often containing many yelping dogs but few people. Along the way are scattered pieces of a large airplane's fuselage, obviously the remnants of a

The view from Coroico

disaster some years ago. Enterprising *campesinos* in one village have used parts of the fuselage to make a bridge over a stream and a set of chicken coops.

More villagers begin walking along the path at lower altitudes, usually Bolivian women weighted down with sacks of potatoes or sticks. Finally the Inca path gives way to dirty Bolivian roads, where passing trucks head to the town of Coroico.

The Gold-Diggers' Trail: Another trek begins where the last left off, in Coroico. Taking a road back into the mountains, the trail runs further down into the **Beni jungle** along the so-called "Gold-Diggers' Trail".

It follows the **Tipuani Valley**, a region first fossicked by the Incas. They exhausted all the surface gold, which was used for ornamental purposes in their temples and art. Today thousands of Bolivians have tossed in their old lives in cities to try their luck in the jungle, now digging tunnels in the hope of instant wealth.

The trail once again follows an ancient Inca road, this time mossy and crumbling, through jungle-clad mountains and dramatic gorges. It passes many small mining communities that can only be reached by foot. A typical outpost is the village of **Fatima**, put together from bamboo and corrugated iron only a few years ago.

But the primitive jungle setting sits incongruously with signs of sudden wealth: makeshift bars have new refrigerators, with crowds of men already drunk on beer at 9am. Residents come panting down the mountainside after trips to the capital carrying portable cassette decks and non-stick frypans.

Other settlements, such as **Llipi**, have up to 600 people living with the overpowering smell of rotting garbage and stale urine. Its main street has 15 bars, six pool halls and three brothels, where miners relax with considerable gusto. The path ends up at the hot and dusty town of **Guanay**, a less than charming Amazon outpost. From there buses can be taken back to Coroico, and further on to the cold heights of La Paz.

oading up r a ride on a uck, the nofficial ıblic ansport of e Andes.

Coca Leaves

O coca leaf, choice coca,
You know my life and destiny;
How I wept in foreign parts,
How I suffered in strange towns.
—Indian song

To the outside world, the small green coca leaf is best known as the raw material for the drug cocaine. But in the Andean highlands of Peru, Bolivia and Ecuador, it has been a part of the traditional Indian culture for over 4,000 years and is still an integral part of daily

life. Coca leaves are for sale in any mountain town market. Ask at a café for *mate de coca*, and you will receive a tea-bag of the leaf for a hot and refreshing drink – normally taken by travelers as the best cure for *soroche* or altitude sickness.

Everyday use: Some 3 million South Americans still chew coca, adding a little bicarbonate of soda to get the saliva going, and keeping a wad of the leaf in their cheeks. It gives energy, and dulls the senses against cold and exhaustion. The biggest consumers have always been miners, who use up to one pound a day.

Coca is also used at every stage of Indians' lives. Before giving birth, a woman chews the leaves to hasten labor and ease the pain. When the child is born, relatives celebrate by chewing the leaf together. When a young man wants to marry a girl, he offers coca to her father. And when somebody dies, *mate de coca* is drunk at the wake and a small pile of leaves is placed in the coffin before burial.

Local soothsayers even use coca to tell the future. Known as *yatiris*, they scatter the leaves over a woolen blanket, recite a prayer in mixed Spanish and Aymará, then read their customers' fortunes.

Ancient tradition: Archaeologists say that coca was first cultivated in the Andes around the year 2,000 BC – or three millennia before the rise of the Inca dynasty. But it was the Incas who turned its production into a monopoly, as one more means of controlling subject populations. Its use was restricted to royalty, priests, doctors and the empire's messenger runners, known to travel up to 150 miles (250 km) a day by chewing the leaves. Trading and bartering with the leaf was common. Some historians say that the Incas even supplied coca to conquered chieftains to ensure their loyalty.

By the arrival of the first European explorers, the Incas had relaxed their monopoly on coca and its use had spread beyond their empire. The Italian explorer-navigator Amerigo Vespucci, arriving in the Caribbean in 1499, noted with distaste that the islanders "each had their cheeks bulging with a certain green herb which they chewed like cattle". The Spanish conquistadors were less fussy: within months of Francisco Pizarro's arrival at the Inca capital of Cuzco in 1533, he found some of his men secretly chewing coca themselves.

The Catholic church first tried to ban chewing of the leaf, denouncing it as "the delusion of the devil". But they quickly changed their tune when it was found that Indians needed it to survive the brutal conditions in the colonial mines and plantations. To keep the captive labor force under control, the church then went into the coca business itself, establishing its own monopoly to keep up the profits.

Back in Europe and the United States, coca was almost unheard of until the mid-1800s, when a chemist in Paris by the name of Angelo Mariani marketed a wine made from the leaf. Immensely popular at all levels of society, this Vin Mariani quickly inspired several American soft drink companies to produce other drinks based on coca, such as Coca-Cola.

At the same time, cocaine was first being developed. The white substance was quickly taken up by such modern luminaries as Sigmund Freud, who called it a "magical substance". Sir Arthur Conan Doyle wrote of his fictional character Sherlock Holmes partaking of cocaine on a regular basis.

A new use: But by the early 1900s, moves were afoot to ban the drug. In the 1970s, cocaine became more popular, especially in the United States. Much of the coca grown in the Andes is now crushed by foot in chemicals, turned into a gummy paste and flown to Colombia. After being refined into powder, the cocaine is then smuggled into North American and European cities.

Scientists who have studied coca agree that there are no dangers at all in chewing the leaf, nor is it addictive in the slightest. But the United States, in trying to solve the domestic social problem caused by cocaine and its derivative "crack" has tried to stop its flow at the source. At various times, it has tried to encourage defoliant or eradication programs.

These have met with little success, and often provoked violent demonstrations by angry *campesinos*. Many Indians defend their traditional right to grow coca. Others, desperately poor, defend the chance to grow a crop which is more durable than rice or potatoes and many times more lucrative when selling it to drug lords.

The coca plant is surprisingly resilient. Growing best in the steep terraces of the subtropical yungas, it can be harvested four times a year and one bush can be productive for several decades. Different types of coca plant are being found adaptable to other climates, allowing production to spread deeper into the Amazon basin.

A new law passed in Bolivia is trying to tackle these problems. It protects the coca-growing region which grow for "traditional" use by *campesinos*. And instead of outright eradication of illegal coca, the government now plans to substitute new crops and indemnify farmers – thus allowing the construction of sorely-needed schools and hospitals in one of the poorest regions of South America. ■

Left and above, gathering the small green coca leaves for sale.

Potosí: Silver City in the Sky

Perched at 13,000 ft (4,000 meters) above sea level in the shadow of a cursed mountain, **Potosí** is the highest city of its size in the world. It was built in this inhospitable location by Spanish conquistadors for just one purpose: silver mining.

Today the Andean city is only a shadow of its former glory, when – during the 1600s – Potosí was as large as London and many times more opulent. But anyone visiting Bolivia should make the journey to Potosí. Not only is it one of the least-touched colonial cities on the continent, Potosí has become, for many, a symbol of Latin America's fate. It proves a rule of thumb: the richest regions in colonial times are the poorest today.

"As rich as a Potosí": Appropriately, **El Cerro Rico**, the Rich Hill, is always visible from the city's streets. The Incas had known that there was silver in the bare red mountain but did nothing to exploit it. The Spaniards, however, with their usually voraciousness, were quick to begin mining, soon discovering that it held the largest silver deposit that the world had ever seen.

A frontier city was quickly created on the bleak mountainside, with conquistadors and missionaries flocking from Spain to win a slice of the fantastic wealth. Local Indians were press-ganged to work in the mines, dying by the thousands in horrific conditions.

Even today, Spaniards use the phrase "as rich as a Potosí" when they try to describe an unimaginable fortune. The city's churches were built with silver altars and the lavish feasts of Spanish nobles glittered with the precious metal. Even the horses were said to be shod with silver in Potosí.

When the silver gave out and the Spaniards left, the city survived on the mining of tin which the colonizers had discarded as garbage. But now tin is almost worthless, and Potosí has become a fascinating relic.

Testimony to the former riches are the scattered crumbling villas, stone carved doorways and forgotten abbeys of the city. Ancient houses teeter from both sides to nearly meet in the middle of narrow, winding streets. Potosí is still crowded with masterpieces of colonial architecture and artworks blending the styles of medieval Europe and pre-Conquest Indian.

The most impressive building in Potosí, and considered one of the finest examples of Spanish civil construction in Latin America, is the **Casa Real de Moneda**. First built in 1542 and reconstructed in 1759, it was used as a mint by the colonizers. Now a museum, it has rooms full of religious art, collections of colonial coins and the original wooden minting machines once worked by negro slaves. Guided tours take up to three hours to work through the many exhibits, which contain anything from altars removed from collapsed churches to relics of Bolivia's many unsuccessful foreign wars. One of the prize displays is a pair of iron strong boxes used to transport silver from the New World to

Entrance to the Casa de Moneda, Spain's mint in the New World.

Spain, using no less than 15 locks to secure them, while a huge gallery makes a valiant but still incomplete attempt to provide portraits of the country's many presidents. (Remember to wear plenty of warm clothes, since the museum is like a refrigerator inside).

Many of the churches are crumbling in disrepair, some so close to collapsing that they are dangerous to enter. A stroll through the city will take you past **San Francisco**, **La Compañia** and **San Lorenzo**, as well as the **cathedral** and **Cabildo** in the main plaza. Wandering through the town you might run into famous old mansions such as the **Casa de las Tres Portadas** on Calle Bolivar 19–21 and the **Crystal Palace** at Calle Sucre 148–156.

Indian cultures: But Potosí is much more than a collection of ruined colonial buildings. Many of the Andean Indians living there and in the surrounding countryside have not changed their lifestyles for centuries. The **town market** is still a fascinating place to explore, full of round women selling produce and butchers carrying whole animal carcasses over their shoulders – usually covered in flies and with the beast's hairy tail still dangling from the meat.

The poorest parts of the city are closer to the Rich Hill, traditionally occupied by miners and their families. A monument to the Bolivian miner has been set up in one of the squares, showing a figure in a metal hat brandishing a rifle. The mining unions of Potosí and Oruro were once the most powerful force in Bolivian politics, but have been all but decimated in the collapse of tin prices.

Few mines still operate. Unemployed men sit glumly in wooden bars where nobody can afford the price of a drink, while churches open their doors to worshipers unable to buy a candle.

The wealth of Potosí proved a curse that is still with the Indians today. The Spanish took their silver by cross and sword, then left with the spoils. Potosí gained nothing by the deal, and the city which helped finance the economic development of Europe has slid deeper into Third World oblivion.

El Cerro Rico, the "Rich Hill" of Potosí.

THE SILVER MINES

Deep in the heart of Potosí's "Rich Hill", dust-covered miners were laughing with the Devil. Chewing coca leaves in a candlelit recess full of putrid air, they paid their respects to a small horned statue, the owner of the silver beneath the ground. The miners visit *El Tío* – "the Old Fellow" – every day to leave a drink or burn a cigarette for luck.

"*El Tío* has always liked tobacco," joked one of the miners, "but these days he only accepts filter tips."

The image of the Devil in the Incarnación mine was made 3,000 years ago by Indian slaves. They were press-ganged by the Spanish to dig silver in Potosí, the largest of South America's colonial mines.

Today, *El Tío* is being visited again. With the collapse of the tin market in 1985, the state mines of Cerro Rico were closed, but since then Bolivian miners have been re-opening old shafts to find the silver that the conquistadors left behind.

But if the Indian miners' superstitions appear to have changed little since colonial days, neither have working conditions. The digging is being carried out in such a primitive and dangerous fashion that many miners accept their work as a kind of death sentence.

Every morning at dawn, the miners gather outside the Incarnación mine on El Cerro Rico. The mountain that once held the world's greatest silver deposit is now a giant slag heap, an unnaturally symmetrical peak riddled with over 5,000 shafts.

Incarnación is only one of the several private mines still operating, to which guides from the city will bring visitors for a small fee. Most people bring a few packets of cigarettes to share with the miners as they spend the first hour of their day sitting in the cold sun, chatting and chewing coca leaves, which in these harsh lands have been in use long before the Incas to ward off hunger and fatigue.

Visiting a mine is not for sufferers of claustrophobia. You need to crouch to just enter the mouth of the diggings, while the miners' antique carbide lamps barely dent the darkness. To round off the nerve-wracking effect, the ancient wooden shaft supports often sag in the middle. Stalactites hang from the rough walls of the tunnel near its mouth, but as the mine descends into the mountain, polar cold shifts to subtropical heat. Many of the shafts can only be passed on hands and knees. The air becomes thick and stale. Workers from the last shift become visible down cracks, stripped to the waist and hacking away with picks.

There are no power tools and no engineers in mines such as Incarnación. Blasting is done with dynamite bought in the supply store in Potosí, and the miners simply withdraw around a corner as the charge goes off. Each worker keeps the ore he finds himself. Miners on the lowest levels must climb long ladders to the surface with sacks of rocks on their backs.

Left and right, miners work inside the "Rich Hill" of Potosí in 18th-century conditions.

The real enemy hereis silicosis, caused by fine dust gathering in the miners' lungs. Within a few years of entering the pit, many feel a heavy weight on their chests. A few years later, they die coughing blood.

Little wonder that Indian tradition holds the metals of Potosí to be the property of the Devil, or that the miners give *El Tío* his daily cigarette for luck.

Group tours lasting four to five hours are organized by recognized guides. Put on your old clothes and take a handkerchief to keep out the dust. A helmet and lamp will be provided. The tour costs around $5 and a donation to the miners' cooperative is appreciated.

THE TROPICAL EAST

Nearly half the South America continent can be described in one tantalizing word: Brazil. Almost as big as the United States and home to 145 million people, Brazil is a world in itself – a sensuous giant that invariably becomes a part of everyone who experiences its pleasures. Brazil the geographic colossus is also a state of mind, one that loosens up even the most cautious of spirits who venture there. That's the power of the Brazilian *jeito*, or way. Relax, hang loose, improvise, and *nao esquente a cabeca*: don't get hot-headed, come what may.

There is a vibrancy to Brazil unparalleled elsewhere in Latin America; the country's cutting-edge innovations and penchant for fads have led many to call it "the California of South America". But for all its laid-back ethos, Brazil is also a dynamo of economic activity. The world's eighth largest population produces the planet's eighth largest economy. Virtually everything one buys in Brazil is made in Brazil. Cars crafted in São Paulo run on fuel grown in fields of sugarcane, as their compact disc players made in the Amazon port of Manaus play tunes from the recording studios of Rio de Janeiro.

As the major port of entry, Rio is where most visitors get their first dazzling impressions of Brazil (*page 185*). But like the iceberg below its tip, there's much more to Brazil than Rio. Nearby is South America's largest metropolis, São Paulo, with 13 million people under its towering skyline (*page 192*). To the northwest lies Brasilia, the pristine architectural wonder that sprang up from the wilderness to become the national capital (*page 194*). Beyond the triangle of political and economic power formed by these three cities are other wonders: the stately colonial cities of Minas Gerais (*page 196*), living monuments of the gold and diamond booms; the inviting beaches and rich Afro-Brazilian culture of the Northeast (*page 199*); the immense rainforests of the Amazon jungle that still cover more than half the country (*from page 206*); the vast marshlands of the Pantanal, a birdwatcher's paradise (*page 214*); and the breathtaking waterfalls of Iguassú (*page 218*).

Completely different but even more isolated from its neighbors is backward, dreamy Paraguay (*page 223*). The capital, Asunción, is probably the slowest of South America's cities, where horse-drawn carts still clatter through the streets beneath statues of forgotten generals – but even that seems hectic when compared to the provincial torpor of the countryside and wastes of the vast and empty Chaco (*page 227*).

Preceding pages: a young Carajás Indian of the Amazon; and statue of former president Kubitschek and the Justice Palace (Brazil). Left, Christ the Redeemer statue (Brazil).

BRAZIL: A WORLD APART

One historical fact has given Brazil a character and culture that set it apart from the rest of Latin America; the first European to set foot there was not Spanish, but Portuguese. Pedro Alves Cabral ran into Brazil quite by accident in 1500 on his way to India. The Portuguese language that Cabral spoke as he planted his nation's flag on the sands of Porto Seguro is still spoken today in Brazil. More significantly, the Portuguese who later settled in Brazil brought with them a seafaring culture more attuned to trading and exploring than to sacking and conquering.

Settlement, sugarcane and slavery: Settlement in Brazil got off to a slow start. While the Spanish conquistadors regarded the New World as a treasure to be plundered, the Portuguese were initially too busy trading with the East (they were the first Europeans to trade with China) to bother much with Cabral's discovery. Indeed, the new territory's only attraction was *pau brasil*, a tree whose wood produced a deep-red dye. It gave its name to the country.

The Portuguese who slowly emigrated to Brazil in the 16th century were mostly ne'er-do-well men in search of a new life. Their attempts to enslave Brazil's indigenous peoples largely failed. Most of the nomadic natives either died of disease or fled inland. Some of the women, however, were taken as concubines, and their children raised as legitimate heirs to their Portuguese fathers.

What historians later termed "the Lusitanian libido on the loose" contrasted starkly with the ideal of racial purity espoused by Spanish settlers in the New World. The racial mixture that was born of necessity in Brazil quickly became a lasting cultural fixture. Adding to Brazil's racial blending was an influx of Africans captured in the Portuguese colony of Angola.

As Europe's taste for sugar grew in the 17th century, so did the demand for slave labor to work Brazil's plantations. Sugarcane imported from the Portuguese Atlantic island of Madeira grew splendidly along Brazil's humid coast, and the economic bonanza that came with it was an inducement to ignore the inhumanity of slavery.

The wealth generated by sugar prompted Portugal to keep a tighter grip on the products of its budding colony. All industry except sugar refining was forbidden, in order to assure Portuguese traders a protected new market. These restrictions were accepted in Brazil at an official level, but they were in fact easily circumvented by smugglers. Such

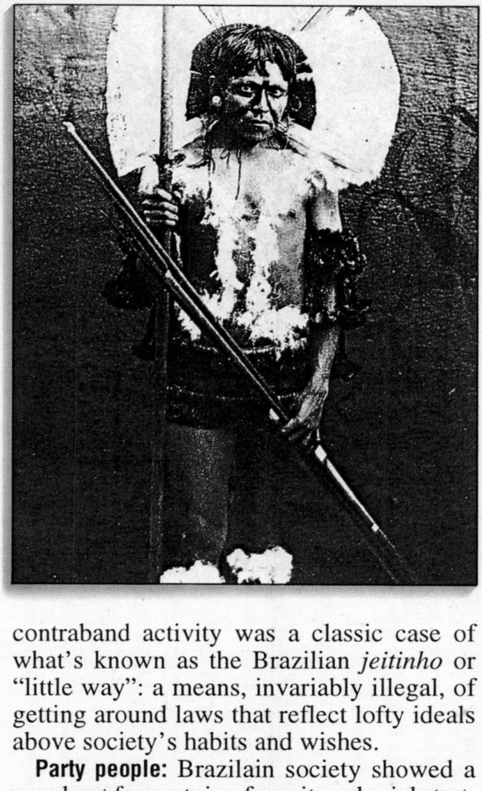

contraband activity was a classic case of what's known as the Brazilian *jeitinho* or "little way": a means, invariably illegal, of getting around laws that reflect lofty ideals above society's habits and wishes.

Party people: Brazilain society showed a penchant for partying from its colonial start. An exasperated Jesuit instructor, José de Anchieta, wrote in the 17th century that his task was complicated "by the nature of the country itself, for it is relaxing, slothful and melancholic, so that all the time is spent in parties, in singing, and in making merry." Beach culture was of course a long way off, but the sugar planters were loath to stray far

Preceding pages: Sugarloaf mountain guards the entrance to Rio's Guanabara Bay. Left, the Rio Carnival. Right, Capoyó Indian dressed in chieftain's costume, from around 1870.

from the Atlantic's pounding surf and settlement was limited to the coastal regions.

Brazil's interior was finally penetrated in the late 1600s. The first pioneers were Jesuits proselytizing Guaraní Indians near what is now Brazil's border with Paraguay. Hard on their heels were Portuguese immigrants too poor to acquire land in the sugarcane-dominated coastal regions. These settlers pushed into what is now the state of São Paulo to raise cattle and plant subsistence crops of corn and rice. Like the wealthy sugar planters whose labor force was mostly black slaves, these farmers also sought bonded workers for themselves. So they organized expeditions to abduct Guaraní Indians who inhabited the region. Known as *bandeirantes* becausde of the banners they marched under, these Indian were attracted to the Jesuit missions where Guaraní people lived in educated, highly productive communities. Despite their barbaric raids, the *bandeirantes* have gone down in Brazilian folklore as brave pioneers who opened up what has become the country's most productive economic region.

Gold and diamond booms: Just when the world market for Brazilian sugar started to go soft around 1700, a new boom shook the country. This time it was gold and diamonds, discovered by the *bandeirantes* in the rugged hill country of Minas Gerais. Most of the gold was sent to the Portuguese crown. But enough remained to build the baroque cities of Ouro Preto, São João del Rei and Sabará. The treasures of Minas Gerais gold were shipped out through Rio de Janeiro, putting the backwater port on the map, and by 1763 Rio had become so important that the Portuguese crown moved the capital there from the sugarcane and slave entrepôt of Salvador in the northeastern state of Bahia.

Other booms followed. Cotton crops replaced sugarcane in many areas as demand for the fiber grew quickly in Europe's newly industrialized textile centers. But the biggest and most lasting boom – coffee – started in the late 18th century and has persisted up to the present. The state of São Paulo was covered with coffee plantations as the craze for drinking coffee spread around the world in the 19th century.

As the Brazilian economy grew, it overshadowed the Portuguese fatherland. This fate was sealed in 1808 when the Portuguese emperor, Dom João, fled Napoleon's army and took his entire court to Brazil. Dom João gave Brazil equal status with Portugal, converting the colony into an empire in its own right. The monarch returned to Portugal in 1821 and left his son, Dom Pedro I, in charge. But when Dom João ordered his son back to

Portugal the following year, Dom Pedro rebelled, shouting "I'm staying!" That, in effect was Brazil's declaration of independence, celebrated every year on September 7.

Emancipation: What ensued were 67 years of stable, independent monarchy. But the practise of slavery was a growing political problem. On his flight to Brazil Dom Pedro had been escorted by British warships, and he now came under increasing pressure from the British to stop the importation of captive Africans for enslavement on plantations. There were then nearly 2 million black slaves in Brazil, twice the number of those Brazilians with purely European ancestry. The British pressure arose in part from a growing public outcry in England against slavery on moral grounds. But the British also considered slave labor unfair competition for their own plantations in the West Indies. When Brazil persisted in the slave trade, British warships attacked and scuttled slave ships headed for Brazilian ports.

Brazil finally outlawed the importation of slaves in 1850, three years after Dom Pedro's son, Pedro II, occupied the throne. The ban is credited to the liberal persuasions of Pedro II, who preferred to promote free immigration from Europe. As the slave trade died, millions of Europeans did flock to Brazil, attracted by cheap farmland in the south. About a third of the newcomers were Italians, a third Portuguese, a sixth Spaniards, while one out of 25 were Germans. Their ability to farm successfully without slave labor contrasted with the owners of sugar and cotton plantations, or *fazendas*, in the north who continued to force slaves to perform their manual labor. As in the United States, the movement for abolition gained momentum in urban centers far removed from the plantations. Parliament finally abolished slavery in 1888, making Brazil the last country to do so in the New World. Abolition proved the death-knell of the empire. Plantation owners, who received no compensation for the slaves they were forced to emancipate, sought to depose Pedro II and turned to the military for support. Military officers were themselves disgruntled, feeling neglected by the emperor since their savage triumph in a war waged against Paraguay 18 years earlier. So in 1889, the army deposed Pedro II, beginning a long tradition of intervention in the country's domestic politics.

Left, slaves selling fruit and vegetables in Rio, c. 1880. Above, many blacks freed from slavery found themselves press-ganged into the army.

A constitutional, republican form of government replaced the monarchy. But relatively few participated in the new political system: only adult males who could read were allowed to vote. The presidency alternated between aristocrats from Minas Gerais and São Paulo, and the military kept an ever watchful eye over the elitist democracy. Meanwhile, another boom hit the economy: this time, it was rubber. The growing demand for tires created a fabulous market for latex tapped from millions of rubber trees growing wildly in the Amazon jungle. But Brazil's rubber monopoly broke after 1912, when plantations in Malaysia started producing much cheaper latex.

An awful lot of coffee: Coffee remained the country's biggest export, and its cultivation spread despite warnings of a glut developing on the world market. Coffee prices collapsed in 1930, and the government toppled with them. It fell to a military putsch engineered by Getulio Vargas, who was governor of Rio Grande do Sul, Brazil's southernmost state. Vargas seized the presidency and won Brazilians' hearts with his populist rhetoric and legislation that blessed organized labor. The so-called "Father of the People" went on to declare himself dictator and establish a corporate state that bore a strong resemblance to Mussolini's Fascism. Bowing to intense pressure from the United States, Brazil fought along with the Allies during World War II. The fall of Hitler and Mussolini prompted Brazilians to reconsider their support for Vargas, and he resigned in November 1945.

Eighteen years of constitutional rule followed, a period of steady economic growth highlighted by the construction of Brasilia as the new capital in the late 1950s, more than 600 miles (1,000km) distant from the former capital of Rio de Janeiro. In the early 1960s, the government faltered as demands grew for more rapid social change. With landless peasants increasing dramatically, land reform became an explosive political issue and the military responded to the growing unrest by seizing power in April 1964.

Miraculous boom: This was the start of the era known as "the Brazilian Miracle". The military's crackdown on leftists (many of whom were tortured and killed) and generous fiscal incentives combined to attract a flood of foreign investment. The Brazilian economy boomed, enriching mostly those who were already wealthy. Disenchantment with military rule grew as the economy took a nosedive in 1980, crippled by enormous bills for imported oil and public works projects, such as a rarely used highway across the Amazon jungle. The military set up a timetable for a gradual retreat from power, and the last of a series of military dictator presidents stepped down in March 1985.

Tancredo Neves, the man chosen by an

electoral college to head the new civilian government, was a longtime opponent of the military. But Neves fell deathly ill on the eve of his inauguration, and his vice-president, José Sarney, was instead sworn in as president. The Sarney government inherited a foreign debt of more than 100 billion dollars, the largest in the Third World. Much of it came from oil imports. Exports of agricultural products and manufactured goods had soared, but the earnings had been absorbed in interest payments on the foreign debt. Sarney, closely allied with the military, quickly lost political support as inflation, which reached 1,000 percent in 1988, continued to ravage the economy.

Economic woes were accompanied by growing street crime. Such anti-social behaviour is relatively recent in Brazil, and is widely considered a product of the tremendous influx of rural Brazilians into large cities since the 1960s. Some were attracted by jobs, but many arrived as refugees from severe droughts in the Northeast. The jobs these people find in the cities rarely pay enough for bare subsistence.

Progress for the poor is also limited by racial discrimination. Although Brazil has been called a racial paradise because of the high number of inter-racial marriages and an absence of open racial conflict, to be black in Brazil almost always means to be poor, and 40 percent of the population is black. But whatever his or her color, there is little chance of a poor Brazilian becoming a rich one.

High performer: The 1990s have seen a great surge forward economically, with successive governments driving through privatization programmes and attracting foreign investment to make Brazil's economy the 10th largest in the Western world with nearly 70 percent of its exports in industrial goods. Huge natural resources, on a par with South

Africa's and Australia's, also ensure that Brazil is a country with a great future. These natural resources also bring responsibilites towards the environment, particularly in the Amazon region, where destruction has been on a massive scale. The Rio Earth Summit in 1992 was a recognition of these responsibilities, but there is a long way to go before real protection is afforded the invaliable Amazonian assets.

Meanwhile natural resources and good housekeeping alone will not solve the intractable problems of income distribution and land tenure which will continue into Brazil's next century.

Left, Rio's Copacabana Palace Hotel, just after completion, c. 1900. Above, view of Botafogo in the early 1900s.

RIO DE JANEIRO, CITY OF FUN

Brazilians call **Rio de Janeiro** *a cidade maravilhosa* – the marvelous city – and they have ample reason to do so. There's the city's stunning setting: flanked to the east by the enormous **Bay of Guanabara** and to the south by the Atlantic Ocean, Rio sprawls around and even up the sides of enormous granite peaks and down to wide sandy beaches. The result of this topsy-turvy topography is a city sculptured around the whims of nature, giving the urban landscape a look that can only be described as sensuous. An Italian statesman gazing over Rio was moved to exclaim, "She's as beautiful as a woman."

And then there are the 10 million people who live in and around Rio. They're known as *cariocas*, and they epitomize the casual, good-natured disposition associated with all Brazilians. Part of the *carioca's* sunny outlook may derive from the smug satisfaction of living in a place most people only dream of, where it's possible to join the fun on the beaches for the price of a local bus fare. Another reason for the *carioca's* friendliness could be the open social scene of Rio. Unlike other big cities, where exclusivity heightens the appeal of social gatherings, in Rio people of all classes throng to public places for fun. The beaches are the biggest attraction, followed by soccer stadiums and carnival street parties. Bars are not dark, enclosed watering holes – in Rio, it's sociable to down a *chopp* out on the sidewalk and perhaps even bang out a samba tune with friends on nearby parked cars.

Uninhibited lifestyle: When it comes to sex, *cariocas* have a reputation for few inhibitions and tremendous appetites. That image developed in part from the bacchanal bashes of the carnival season, in part from the tantalizingly tiny beach attire favored by both genders.

But sex is most frequently a spectator sport. "Tall and tan and lovely... and when she passes each one she passes goes ahh!" moan the mouthwatering lyrics of Antônio Carlos Jobim's *bossa nova* classic, *The Girl from Ipanema. Cariocas* like Jobim find it natural and even wholesome to live in a state of lust that's usually consummated only in their vivid imaginations.

In Rio, you don't have to be gorgeous to be on display – just uninhibited. *Cariocas* are extremely tolerant people (gay men seeking open minds flock to Rio de Janeiro from the rest of Brazil) and everyone can indulge in a little – or a lot of – exhibitionism.

Pleasure became Rio's main moneymaker after 1960, when the seat of government was moved from the seaside capital to landlocked Brasilia. Rio went from being the center of the Brazilian universe to a mere tourist attraction, and it took a long time for the city to come to terms with its new identity. For many years officials were content to let Rio's wonders alone attract visitors, but more recently they have added *jardineiras* that ply the beaches and floodflights at oceanside. For *cariocas,* tourist service is a long way from the past glories of

'receding ages: the prawling *avela* of ochina, the argest in Rio nd a city ithin a city. **eft**, crowds ock to opacabana each on a unny day. **ight**, *arioca* omen are enowned for ieir tiny ikinis.

inhabiting Brazil's capital, but they take comfort knowing that the politicians who moved to Brasilia left their hearts in Rio.

The city center: Most visitor's first encounter with Rio is at **Galeão International Airport**, a sleek modern complex famous for the purring sex kitten voices that announce arrivals and departures. Galeão is built on a man-made island north of Rio, and to the west is a massive swampy area known as the Baixada Fluminense, or Fluvial Lowlands, where two-thirds of the city's inhabitants live. Poor and without attractions, this area is home for most of the city's bus drivers, maids, construction workers and salespeople.

The drive into the city from Galeão passes Rio's port and soon after takes you into the heart of the downtown area. The main thoroughfare, **Avenida Rio Branco**, is lined by skyscraping banks, tourist agencies, and finally the ornate 19th-century buildings of the **Teatro Municipal** (with a splendid ground floor café replete with mosaic tiles), the **Municipality** (whose steps often serve as bleachers for evening concerts), and across the street, the **Biblioteca Nacional** (with neo-classic and art nouveau paintings displayed) and the **Museu Nacional de Belas Artes**, the country's foremost repository of classic Brazilian artwork, with regular exhibitions of contemporary art. Modern art is permanently on display in the exciting **Museu de Arte Moderna** in Avenida Infante D Henrique.

The **Museu Nacional** in the Quinta da Boa Vista was the palace of the emperors of Brazil, and their throne room and reception rooms remain among an eclectic ethnographic and natural history collection.

The place to watch downtown action is the open plaza in front of the **Teatro Nacional**, an area known as **Cinelândia**. Come nightfall it's a kind of Hyde Park – political campaigners, *capoeira* performers, guerrilla theater, and many transvestites. This is also the downtown's only movie theater district. Leading away from Cinelândia on the other

The view from the sand, Copacabana.

side of the Teatro Nacional is a wide pedestrian mall, the **Largo da Carioca**, a favorite redoubt of snake-oil vendors and leather artisans.

For a flavor of what downtown Rio was like before skyscrapers crowded its skyline, wander down sidestreets off Largo da Carioca. Don't miss the stately **Confeiteria Colombo** At Rua Gonçalves Dias 32, with a mirror-lined tea room downstairs and elegant dining room upstairs. Rio's intelligentsia used to gather there before the turn of the century, and the Belle Epoque furnishings evoke those days. Or stroll **Rua da Carioca** for hearty German food and *chopp* at the lively **Bar Luiz**, a downtown fixture for more than a century.

Rising high above Largo da Carioca to the west is the **Santo Antônio Convent**, a complex of religious buildings built between 1608 and 1780. Beside the baroque main church is the lovely **São Francisco da Penitencia Chapel**. To the north stands Rio's cone-shaped **New Cathedral** on Avenida Republica do Chile, finished in 1976. Nearby the cathedral are the **Arcos da Lapa**, a towering 18th-century aqueduct that now serves as a bridge for streetcars, or *bondes* (pronounced "bon-jees"), that shuttle between a station next to the cathedral and the steep streets of **Santa Teresa**.

Artists' quarter: Known for its precipitous topography and grand views, Santa Teresa is for many the most charming of Rio's neighborhoods. Its residents are a mixture of artists and musicians, who've arrived there fairly recently, and wage earners who came before others discovered the charms of living there.

The best way to see the picturesque 19th-century homes that line many of Santa Teresa's streets is to take the yellow streetcars that leave from the cathedral. Leave valuables behind, since the open-sided cars are vulnerable to pickpockets. Be sure to see the **Chácara do Ceu museum** on Rua Martinho Nobre. Its splendid views are matched by its lovely collection of Brazilian and European paintings.

Much of the shoreline between down-

Garlic for sale in a Rio market.

town Rio and the Bay of Botafogo including the **Santos Dumont airport** (where Lockheed Electra turboprops shuttle to São Paulo) is the result of landfill, or *aterro* at the edge of downtown. South along the *aterro* from the business district is a tall stone monument built in honor of Brazilians who died in World War II . To the other side of the road, up on a cliff, is the **Church of Gloria**.

Then comes **Flamengo Beach**, which has a large park between the beach and the road for picnics and soccer matches. Although people do swim at this beach, the polluted state of the Guanabara Bay makes the water less than inviting. The next bay going south is **Botafogo**, a lovely expanse with a marina and several movie theaters near the beach.

Rising like a gigantic granite knee 1,300 ft (400 meters) from the waters of the entrance to Guanabara Bay is **Sugarloaf Mountain**. Cable cars leaving Praia Vermelha beach on the half hour from 8am to 10pm sweep visitors up first to the lower Morro da Urca, with a restaurant and amphitheater, and then on to Sugarloaf. The most interesting time to visit is towards the end of the afternoon, affording views in daylight, dusk and sparkling darkness.

Suburbs on the sand: To the west of Sugarloaf begin Rio's legendary beaches. The first wide arc spans the neighborhoods of Leme to the east and Copacabana to the west, with a naval station at the western point. **Leme** is mostly residential and quiet. Rua Princesa Isabel, which divides Leme from Copacabana, is a favorite with prostitutes, and nightlife in the area tends towards the seedy side.

Copacabana, with 300,000 residents, is Rio's most densely populated highrise neighborhood, and can be quite hectic away from the beach. But it is also a lively place to enjoy street celebrations during carnival and New Year's eve. The magnificent beach itself stretches out almost a block to the water. It's lit by floodlights at night, but stay close to the crowds on the sidewalk to avoid getting mugged. Tourists wandering by the

Left, the affluent sail from Rio to nearby Buzios. Right, snorkeling is one of Rio's many outdoor sports.

water are considered "papaya with sugar" by petty thieves.

After Copacabana comes **Ipanema Beach**, which connects at its western end with another beach called **Leblon**. Both Ipanema and Leblon are largely residential, with fewer hotels than Copacabana. The beaches of these more exclusive neighborhoods are more in vogue with the *carioca* fast-set than traditional Copacabana. Behind them to the north is the freshwater **Lagoa Rodrigo de Freitas**, a large natural lagoon surrounded by highrises and restaurants.

To the north of the lagoon are the **Jockey Club** race track and the **Botanical Garden** on Rua Jardim Botanico. Some 5,000 species of Brazilian plants cover the garden's 250 acres (100 hectares), and though some of the grounds have gone to seed, a visit there is still a pleasure.

Another nature adventure is the ride up the side of **Corcovado (Hunchback) Mountain** in the train leaving from Cosme Velho. At the top, 2,340 ft (700 meters) above the ocean, towers the trademark of Rio, the statue of **Christ the Redeemer**. The road coming down from the statue wends through the tropical lushness of Tijuca National Forest, with several breathtaking lookout points.

South of the sands of Leblon, sprawling up the sides of granite slopes, are two of Rio's biggest *favelas* or hillside shantytowns – **Vidigal** and **Rocinha**. Their residents, who number in the hundreds of thousands, often endure such precarious circumstances in order to live close to their jobs on the south side of the city.

Further to the south is **São Conrado Beach**, a fast-growing suburb still free of the congestion that's endemic to the rest of Rio. Hang-gliders swoop down from the slopes above to wide sand expanses below.

The cleanest beaches lie even further south beyond the primordial plains of **Barra de Guaratiba.** These are the areas not yet fully conquered by "the marvelous city". To see them is to understand the kind of awesome beauty that provided Rio its enduring magic.

mass erobics lass at the raia Do eme.

Where else does an entire country shut down every year for four days and nights of splendid pageantry and joyful debauchery? "Carnaval," says Dinah, a buxom showgirl from the Beija Flor samba school, "is the only thing this country takes seriously."

She may be right. Nothing else merits more months of preparation, more prolonged and devout attention, and a more lavish outpouring of private resources than this annual convulsion that has come to symbolize Brazil, for better or for worse. Extravagance, self-indulgence, exhibitionism, and a kind of gleeful innocence are the basic elements of Carnaval – qualities that color life in Brazil, albeit less intensely, the rest of the year. Carnaval strips away the remaining inhibitions, and revelry reigns. Social scientists often label Carnaval "the great social escape valve" for the cathartic nature of these pent-up urges finding their release during the annual bacchanal – a nation plays out its private fantasies publicly.

The world travel upside-down: Being in Brazil during Carnaval is like living a waking dream, especially for those familiar with the country's erstwhile status quo. Streets normally clogged with fast-moving steel on wheels are reclaimed by revelers on foot; macho men lasciviously parade about in drag; laborers masquerade as 18th-century royalty; mothers dress up like babies; the wealthy watch while the poor perform; people stay up all night and sleep all day.

Carnaval arrived with the Portuguese and was a re-invention of the pagan and later Christian late winter celebrations of Europe. The celebrations are ostensibly the last shot at merry-making before the 40 days of fasting that precede Easter (the world carnival itself is believed to be a derivation of the Italian *carne vale*, or farewell to meat). In Brazilian Carnaval began as the pre-Lenten *entrudo* from Portugal – an aggressive spree of throwing water, mud and flour at unsuspecting passers-by. This unpleasantness, which still characterizes Carnaval in neighboring Bolivia and Argentina, was banned in Brazil in the mid-19th century.

But the Carnaval that Brazil is renowned for – the opulent street parades of Rio de Janeiro – did not become a tradition until the 1930s. That's when neighborhoods started adding choreography, elaborate costumes, and theme songs to their street forays. By 1932 the neighborhood groups had begun to compete and became known as *escolas de samba*, or samba schools. Samba is a derivation of West African rhythms best recognized by the thump-thump undercurrent of the bass drum and in the south of Brazil it has become the signature music of Carnaval.

Today the competition between samba schools is akin to the rivalry between top sports teams. Almost all the major schools are from around Rio, and Carnaval there is charged with suspense over which school will be champion. Months of preparation preceed the brief moments of glory before thousands of live spectators and millions of television viewers. Some of the funding comes from ticket sales and television rights, and much comes from the minimum wage. Most members of the samba schools come from the humblest of Rio's neighborhoods, including the hovels known as *favelas* clinging to steep hillsides. Many of the schools are also underwritten by the kingpins of the local numbers game, who acquire royalty status among the poor for this philanthropy.

Samba schools hold practice sessions for months before Carnaval, to which the public is often invited for a small admission. A theme is chosen for each year's Carnaval, and sambas are composed and costumes designed reflecting that motif. The moment of glory comes at the gates of Rio's one-of-a-kind samba stadium, the Sambadrome, which was designed by the leading architect of Brasilia, Oscar Niemeyer, and erected in 1984. Eighty-five thousand spectators can be seated along this kilometer-long parade strip to watch the samba schools go dancing by.

The "moving opera": To the untrained eye, the samba schools may first appear to be no more than frenetic waves of skin and glitter. But each one has a different story to tell, and the distinct groups, or wings (*asas*), that dance within each school are all chapters of these epics. "The samba school must be seen as a moving opera," says Brazilian anthro-pologist Maria Julia Goldwasser. Unlike opera, the spectators are expected to join in the singing, led by the *puxador* who belts out his samba through a sound system to the chorussed response of the school and crowd.

A night at the Sambódromo can begin at eight and end well after sunrise. For some, it becomes an endurance test to sit (or dance) through it all; many others feel as if they've died and gone to samba heaven. If you can't get a ticket, you can see the schools line up outside in Av Presidente Vargas.

Throughout Brazil, Carnaval is an affair of both streets and clubs. The best street dancing is in Salvador, where musicians called *trio eletricos* play atop deafening soundtracks as the hordes leap around behind them through the city. As in the case everywhere during Carnaval, it's best to dress minimally (shorts or bathing suits) to blend into the crowds and not attract thieves. Many experienced travelers prefer Carnaval in the Northeast. In Recife the preeminent Carnaval music is *frevo*, which ignites passions, while Bahian Carnaval features *afoxé*, monotonous music often sung in African languages by subdued participants in flowing satin robes.

A less frenetic street Carnaval can be found in the two historic cities of Olinda and Ouro Preto, as well as in the outlying suburbs of Rio. In Rio itself, there's dancing both in Copacabana and Ipanema led by traditional neighborhood *blocos*. Class lines seem to dissolve as elated revelers hop together down the streets in camaraderie fueled by generous amounts of beer and *cachaca*, the sugarcane brandy that's ubiquitous during Carnaval.

Carnaval is when the energy of Brazil explodes.

But Carnaval has increasingly moved off the streets and into the clubs in recent years. People go to the clubs both to see and to show themselves. Clubs are where Carnaval's most intense debauchery and exhibitionism goes on. Club Monte Libano's "Night in Baghdad" on Tuesday, the last soirée of Carnaval, undoubtedly has the hottest reputation. The Red and Black Ball and the Gay Ball at the Scala are also big affairs. The most unusual balls are those held in Rio by the city's large transvestite community. These are a showcase for the amazingly deceptive transformations, and the Marilyn Monroe look-alike contest at Sugarloaf Mountain is a must.

Not everyone in Brazil is wild about Carnaval. Many intellectuals sneer at the kitsh, wanton drinking and lewdness that attract so many others to this yearly spasm. But for outsiders, there is probably no better time than Carnaval to see the Brazil of everyone's fantasies. ■

SÃO PAULO: THE BIG METROPOLIS

The first thing that strikes most visitors to the city of **São Paulo** is its sheer enormity. "I had no idea you had things like this down here," exclaimed then-US President Ronald Reagan as he flew over São Paulo by helicopter back in 1982. Home to 13 million *paulistanos*, as the city's natives call themselves, São Paulo is one of the world's largest metropolises and its phenomenal growth shows no signs of abating. Already the city covers nearly a thousand square miles (2,600 sq. km), and it is ringed by suburbs that continue to mushroom.

São Paulo is a center of trade and industry, the workhorse of the Brazilian economy. "São Paulo works so that the rest of Brazil can play," *paulistanos* will tell you. Indeed, two-thirds of the country's industrial goods are produced in São Paulo, including nine out of ten automobiles. *Paulistanos* rightly deserve their reputation as hard workers, and life in their busy city moves at a frenetic pace.

City of individualists: Why *paulistanos* keep their noses so close to the grindstone is a matter of some debate – *cariocas* would say they simply don't know any better. Since its foundation in 1554, São Paulo has always attracted self-reliant individualists – it was Brazil's equivalent to the Old West, and São Paulo today still proudly honors its old trailblazers, the *bandeirantes*. Those who followed the *bandeirantes* came from all over the world, especially in the last century, bringing with them work habits that contributed to the city's industrious ethos. More recent immigrants are from the drought-stricken states of Northeastern Brazil. Poorly educated and without job skills, they end up in the festering slums ringing the city that hold half its population.

São Paulo is not a place to spend one's whole vacation, but it is well worth a visit. Unlike Rio, it is a city whose pleasures are entirely man-made. Typically, the most popular diversion is one

Taking the afternoon su[n] in São Paulo.

that also satisfies biological necessity: eating. São Paulo's enormous array of restaurants are as diverse as they are numerous – a reflection of the city's varied and ethnic makeup. The predominant cuisine is Italian, but there are also many options for Japanese, German, Lebanese and French cooking.

Paulistanos have cosmopolitan tastes, and they consider themselves trailblazers not only in industry but also in the arts. The pride and joy of the city is the MASP, or the **São Paulo Museum of Art**, with a representational collection of more than a thousand exhibits. And every odd-numbered year, São Paulo hosts one of the world's largest periodic art show, the Bienal, a two month-long happening of modern artworks from around the world. The pavilion where the Bienal is held is connected to a permanent collection of modern Brazilian art, housed in the sleek **Museum of Modern Art**.

Beneath the chaos: Perhaps the best way to explore São Paulo is by its clean, fast subway system. Going underground helps cut the effects of the sometimes stinging air population, and it circumvents the maze of usually crowded roadways above. Stop off at **Liberdade**, where Japanese immigrants and their descendants have established the largest ethnic-Japanese colony outside Japan. (Some 600,000 Japanese-Brazilians live in São Paulo). There are many traditional restaurants in the neighborhood, as well as sushi bars, and on Sundays there's a food and crafts fair at **Praça Liberdade**.

ıe concrete ngle ɔwntown.

São Paulo is not all towering monoliths. Neighborhoods such as **Jardim Paulista** or **Jardim America** have streets lined with trees and mansions that are a respite from the rush of downtown. Another favorite oasis is the lovely **Parque Ibirapuera**, São Paulo's Central Park completed designed by Oscar Niemeyer to celebrate the city's 400th anniversary in 1954. It has art museums, the striking **Legislative Assembly**, a **planetarium**, cycle and motorbike circuits and at its entrance, an impressive monument to the Bandeirantes.

Downtown, the place to stroll is around the leafy **Praça da República**. Nearby Avenida São Luiz, Rua Augusta and Rua Barão de Itapetininga are all interesting for shopping. Watch for pickpockets.

Whether you like snakes or not, the **Butantã Snake Farm** should not be missed. Some 80,000 snakes there are milked for venom daily, and serum is prepared for distribution throughout Brazil. There is a museum as well, located at Avenida Dr. Vital Brasil 1500 in the Pinheiros neighborhood.

Nightlife: At night, São Paulo has a wide variety of clubs and cafés to while away the hours. Live music is even more plentiful than in Rio. There's also a counter-culture quarter, the **Bixiga**, centered on Rua 13 de Maio. There are few old buildings left in the city, but the **Teatro Nacional**, which has resident opera and dance companies, evokes the elegant days of 19th-century coffee barons. The city frequently hosts world-class performers – *paulistanos* may be workaholics, but they demand the best when they knock off for some play.

BRASILIA: FUTURISTIC CAPITAL

Rising out of the great scrubby expanses of Brazil's central *cerrado*, **Brasilia** looks more like a gleaming extra-terrestrial settlement than Brazil's national capital. Absent are the familiar red-tile roofs, intimate passageways, and panache of pastel hues found in every other Brazilian city. Brasilia is cool, regimented and an architectural wonder – "a city of the future" that Brazilians are still trying to reconcile with the present. A popular joke has it that there are three great things about Brasilia: its cool air, its enormous sky, and its air shuttle to Rio.

Brasilia, 2,800 ft (1150 ft) up and more than 500 miles from the coast, was built precisely because of its isolation from the great coastal cities. When Juscelino Kubitschek was elected President in 1955, he vowed that before he left office Brazil would have a new capital in its unpopulated interior, and he firmly believed that that capital would be a magnet to pull Brazilians away from their beloved coastline.

By 1956, work had already begun on Brasilia. The city plan, drawn up by urban designer Lucio Costa, consisted of a central line of government buildings crossed by a curved arc of residential buildings – a layout that resembled the shape of an airliner. The architect chosen to design the structures was the Brazilian Oscar Niemeyer, a onetime student of the great modern Swiss architect, Le Corbusier. Work proceeded at a furious pace, and by its inauguration in April 1960, Brasilia already had 100 inhabitants: Kubitschek left office that year seeing his dream come true.

A guess at the future: The new capital spread grandly across the *planalto,* the high plain on which it is built. At the time, Brazil's automobile industry was quickly expanding, so Brasilia was designed with the certainty that everybody would get around in cars in the future. Wide thoroughfares sweep through the city, oblivious to the needs of people on foot. With no sidewalks and few crosswalks, Brasilia has the country's highest pedestrian mortality rate. Its grassy knolls are crisscrossed by red earth paths created by Brazilians who still depend on their feet to get around the capital.

What makes Brasilia such a modern wonder is the graceful, pristine architecture of many public buildings. Almost all of those worth seeing were designed by Niemeyer. They are around the **Praça dos Tres Poderes** – the cockpit in the airplane layout – headquarters of the government's executive, legislative and judicial arms.

Most prominent is the **National Congress**, a low white building with two towers rising from the middle, one occupied by the Senate, the other by the House of Deputies. A huge inverted dish crowns the lower building on the Senate side, symbolizing the senators' lower susceptibility to voters' pressure due to longer terms in office. The Deputies' side is crowned by an open dish, representing the receptivity of congressman who face voters more frequently.

The presidential offices are in the

Palacio do Planalto, which may be visited in office attire. The **Supreme Court**, with columns bathed by artificial waterfalls and a blindfolded sculpture of Lady Justice, is also open for visitors.

Nearby is Brasilia's most celebrated building, the **Foreign Ministry**, or Itamaraty. The building appears to float in the pool of water surrounding it, which is highlighted by a sculpture known as "the meteor".

The roads leading to the "cockpit" are flanked by tall, identical office blocks housing the ministeries. The commercial district lies where the two south and north residential wings intersect with the civic and commercial axis. All this can be seen from the observation platforms of the television tower located near the intersection of the axes.

Dehumanizing logic: The other way to see Brasilia is touring by bus or taxi – this is not a city to stroll about. Everything is laid out in the city according to a master plan, and addresses have a logic unparalleled in the rest of Brazil. Still, Brasilia has the feeling of an enormous housing project built with little concern for its occupants. Residents are segregated according to their income levels, making Brasilia more rigidly class-structured than any other Brazilian city.

Those who built Brasilia – poor migrants from the coastal states – now live on its peripheries in enormous shantytowns. Many work in the city itself as servants, taxi drivers and restaurant workers. Brasilia's 400,000 residents are now only one-fifth of the population in the larger metropolitan area.

A generation of Brazilians has grown up in Brasilia, and many of them are content to stay. Cultural life has broadened in recent years, easing the longings for the music and the good times of Rio. Family ties are no longer exclusively with cities far from the capital. For all its technocratic veneer, Brasilia has established an organic place in the society, remaining a symbol of audacity and still the unfulfilled dream of populating the hinterlands.

eft and elow, the chitectural periments Brazil's tificial city.

Minas Gerais: Old Colonial Style

Nestled in the steep hills north of Rio de Janeiro are some of Brazil's most lovely colonial-era cities, all of them in the large state of **Minas Gerais**. As its name suggests, Minas Gerais is a mining region. In the 18th century it was the world's principal source of gold and today more than half the country's minerals and nearly all its iron ore come from here.

Belo Horizonte, today's capital city of Minas Gerais, is neatly planned and a good base from which to explore the region. Sixty miles (100 km) to the south lies the most prized creation of Brazil's Golden Age, the beautifully preserved city of **Ouro Preto**. Its name comes from the gold encrusted with black iron oxide that was discovered nearby early in the 18th century.

City of gold: The find set off a gold rush, and Ouro Preto soon became the colonial capital of Minas Gerais. The gold lasted more than a century, during which time Ouro Preto and several nearby cities acquired sumptuous baroque churches and mansions, the only lasting heritage of 1,200 tons of gold extracted during that era.

Thanks to the Brazilian government's decision to declare the entire city of Ouro Preto a national monument in 1933, much of its colonial treasures are intact, along with a charming atmosphere of the city's heyday. Cobblestoned streets wend through hilly quarters lined by well-kept colonial homes. Thirteen churches punctuate the city of 24,000 with baroque splendor.

Many of the churches display the genius of the sculptor and architect Antônio Francisco Lisboa, better known by his nickname, *Aleijadinho*, or Little Cripple. Hobbled as an adult by a crippling disease, Aleijadinho nonetheless sculpted some of Brazil's most beautiful and expressive statuary – with his hammer and chisel strapped to his wrists.

Just as Oscar Niemeyer much later imposed his artistic vision on Brasilia, Aleijadinho left his graceful mark not only on Ouro Preto but on many other cities of Minas Gerais. The self-taught artist almost single-handedly shifted the aesthetics of the Golden Age from the box-ish forms of mannerism to the sensuous curves of baroque architecture and decor.

The most striking example of the curvaceous baroque lines of architecture is the exterior of the church of **Nossa Senhora do Rosario dos Pretos**, built by black slaves who ran out of funds for the church's interior. Nearby is the plain-looking church of **Nossa Senhora do Pilar**, whose interior is an orgy of baroque carved angels and gilded walls.

Off the main square, which is named after the 18th-century revolutionary, Tiradentes, is an exquisite example of Aleijadinho's artistry. It's the Church of **São Francisco de Assis**, designed by Aleijadinho and a repository of some of his most moving wood and soapstone figures. The church's interior is painted by the high baroque master Manuel da Costa Athayde.

Ouro Preto has an important mining

school on Praça Tiradentes, and there is a gem museum well worth seeing in the imposing **Governor's Palace** nearby. Information can be found there about the gold and diamond mining that continues in the region.

Treasures of stone: The colonial town of **Mariana**, just to the east of Ouro Preto, is another treasure left by gold barons who expressed gratitude for their good fortune by building extravagant churches. Work by Aleijadinho and Athayde can be found there, as well as a former beating post for slaves marked by a stone monument to Justice.

Twenty miles (30 km) west of Ouro Preto is **Congonhas do Campo**, the site of Aleijadinho's greatest feat: his hauntingly beautiful carvings in soapstone of twelve Old Testament prophets outside the majestic church of Bom Jesus do Matozinho, a shrine for pilgrims. There are also 66 expressive carvings in cedarwood of Christ's Passion by Aleijadinho and his students.

Sixty miles (100 km) to the south is **São João del Rei**, a colonial city of 50,000 with three striking 18th-century churches. There is also beautiful pewterware made at a local factory run by Englishman John Somers. Nearby is the silversmith village of **Tiradentes**, named after the man who agitated for independence from Portugal and ended up being hanged in Ouro Preto.

Two other sites in Minas Gerais deserve attention for their baroque treasures. **Sabará**, 14 miles (22 km) east of Belo Horizonte, has fine examples of Aleijadinho's work in its various churches. Oriental influences, brought by Portuguese Jesuits, are evident in the decor of the city's churches.

The least commercialized of all the colonial towns is **Diamantina**, 80 miles (130 km) north of Belo Horizonte. Once the center of a diamond boom, Diamantina is best known as the birthplace of President Juscelino Kubitschek, founder of Brasilia. There are black statues carved in one of its churches, and instruments of torture are displayed, adding insight into how so many treasures were extracted in Minas Gerais.

Left and below, Ouro Preto is considered Brazil's greatest colonial gem.

SALVADOR AND THE NORTHEAST

The Northeast is quite a different place from the prosperous south. The accent is different, the people more mestizo and less mulatto, the food more fiery and the baren *sertão* is more like an African desert than tropical Brazil.

For the essence of the Brazilian mystique, one must go to where it all began: legendary, lustful **Bahia**, the state where Pedro Alves Cabral established contact between Portuguese and native cultures in 1500. Up the shoreline from that historic encounter is **São Salvador da Bahia de Todos os Santos**, Brazil's first capital and still the richest source of the country's cultural identity. Salvador – also known as Bahia, the name of the surrounding state – is where much of the food, religion, dance and music that characterize Brazil all originated. It was where Catholic Portuguese culture blended with the beliefs and aesthetics of the West African slaves who were brought to work the great sugar plantations of the state of Bahia.

Brazil's party capital: The 1.8 million inhabitants of Salvador, known as *baianos* (pronounced bye-*ah*-nooz), are known throughout Brazil for their laid-back, festive temperament, which has made Salvador a favorite destination for vacationing Brazilians.

The city is convulsed by street celebrations almost every month of the year. Carnival is the biggest – it officially begins a day before carnival in the rest of the country. Unofficially, preparations get going in late November, agitated by commemorations of several religious holidays along the way. Salvador's carnival is entirely participatory – frenzied hordes of minimally clothed dancers revel behind blaring soundtracks carrying live bands known as *trios eletricos*. It is not for the faint-hearted, as the crowds often get unruly and are worked by petty thieves.

The backdrop for all this revelry is a city with a rich heritage from its colo-

Left: fishermen haul in the nets on one of Bahia's many beaches.

nial past and a beautiful natural setting. Salvador is built mostly on a high escarpment overlooking the Bay of All Saints. That upper level of the city is known as **Cidade Alta**, and it is where almost all of the ancient buildings are found. The most charming sector is **Pelourinho**, a borough of pastel-hued 17th- and 18th-century buildings held to be the best representatives of such architecture in the New World.

Here you'll find practitioners of *capoeira*, a kind of foot-fighting martial art originally brought by slaves from Angola, performed to the rhythm of a tambourine and the throbbing sound of a *berimbau*, whose single steel string stretched across a bowed stick resonates in a hollowed gourd attached to the stick. *Capoeiristas* perform on the street for donations, but they also give shows during the evening at a cooking school and restaurant called SENAC along Pelourinho's plaza. It's best to visit Pelourinho in daylight, though, since street crime flourishes after dark.

Pelourinho is also home to a famous black men's fraternal association named Filhos de Gandhi. Thi is a benevolent group connected to the syncretistic Afro-Brazilian religion of *candomble*. They assemble near the plaza for feast days and carnival, dressed in turbans and togas.

Visitors will also notice numerous women street vendors wearing flowing white lace dresses. These are known as Baianas, and they sell spicy and sweet specialties of Bahian cuisine. In general, Bahian cooking is considerably more spicy than elsewhere in Brazil, and generous amounts of coconut oil – *dêndé* – are used. Seafood predominates, and is frequently prepared in stews called *moquecas*.

An elevator not far from Pelourinho connects the Cidade Alta to the lower, more recently constructed **Cidade Baixa**. The main attraction there is the big handicrafts marketplace called the **Mercado Modelo**. The white lace-decorated garments sold there are typically Bahian. For a more authentic market, visit the **Mercado São Joaquim** further

Left, canoes drift along th coast near Recife; belo the Largo do Pelourinho, Salvador.

down the shoreline. It's not the cleanest, but it's a compelling slice of local life.

Pristine beaches: Like Rio, Salvador is a city that lives at its beautiful beaches. The most accessible from downtown is **Barra**, a small but extremely popular stretch. Bars near the beach are often jammed, and the fun continues long after sundown. Barra is at the tip of a long scalloped shoreline of beaches, most of which are shaded by palms and have grassy areas. The best are the farthest out from the city, **Itapoán** and **Piatã**. It's best to hit these beaches on weekends when there are crowds, both for safety and because there will inevitably be live music performed at the *al fresco* bars that dot the beaches.

A refreshing excursion from Salvador can be done by ferry to the nearby island of **Itaparica**, where Club Med built its first installation in Brazil. Most of the island's 10,000 inhabitants make their living fishing, and the simple restaurants serve delicious seafood. Be sure to try the marinated fresh oysters.

Some 50 miles (80 km) north of Salvador is **Praia do Forte** a pristine stretch of 7 miles (11 km) of white sand beach bordered by 100,000 coconut palms. There's a sea turtle preservation project there and construction of hotels and restaurants has been limited to preserve the area's natural beauty.

Ilheus, a coastal city 240 miles (390 km) south of Salvador, is a mixture of modern and ancient architecture. The city is renowned for its lively carnival and the lovely beaches nearby, as well as being the center of 95 percent of Brazil's cocoa production.

Further south down the coast is **Porto Seguro**, the fishing village where Cabral and his explorers first set foot in Brazil. It is a largely unspoiled, tranquil area popular with younger travelers.

Inland from Salvador begins the enormous scrubby region called the *sertão*, frequently parched by drought and a tableau of human misery. The *sertanejos* who live there are often forced to leave to avoid starvation, but many return when the rains come, the others swelling the slums of the big cities.

Lace dresses flutter in the wind at an old shop in Salvador.

Beyond Salvador: Bahia is the southern-most part of a nine-state region collectively known as the Northeast. A third of Brazil's population lives in the Northeast, and the *nordestinos* are those who have benefitted least from the material progress of Brazil in the last several decades.

Those who live along the coastal regions of Bahia are predominantly of African descent, while those living inland and to the north are a Portuguese/Indian mixture, copper-skinned and short of stature.

The Northeast has wonderful white sand beaches where you can still find fishermen using *jangadas*, the ancient precursor to the windsurfer. The city of **Maceió** has the most spectacular beaches nearby, their emerald green waters reminiscent of islands in the South Pacific.

North of Maceió is **Recife**, the principal city of the Northeast with 1.2 million inhabitants. Recife's beaches are protected by coral reefs, and the most popular is in the well-to-do **Boa Viagem** sector of the city. Just to the north is **Olinda,** a colonial gem that's been beautifully conserved and a popular destination for carnival revelers.

Further up the coastline is **João Pessao**, the Americas' easternmost city. It's a pleasant, brightly painted city with a wealth of baroque architecture in its churches. Many visitors to the Northeast find João Pessoa the most congenial of all its cities.

Huge sand dunes distinguish the beaches of **Natal**, capital of the state of Rio Grande do Norte. Outside the city are other oceanside enclaves, such as delightful **Touros** (60 miles/95 km to the north), shaded by coconut groves.

Fortaleza, the capital of Ceara, pales by comparison to other Northeastern capitals. With little of its past preserved, the city is largely utilitarian, and ocean waters that wash its shores are polluted.

For a revealing look at the vast interior of the Northeast, there is a weekly steam-powered paddleboat that goes down the enormous **São Francisco River**. It departs from Piraporã on Sundays for a five-day trip.

Below, swimmers enjoy the sun before a Portuguese colonial fort, Salvador. Right, the blood of a slaughtered chicken drips on an initiate's head during a *macumba* ritual.

MACUMBA

Dusk has fallen, and the back streets of Rio de Janeiro grow quiet. Near an intersection, a car pulls up slowly to the curb, and a well-dressed woman gets out, followed by another woman clutching a paper bag. They crouch by the gutter and light several candles on the ground, then pour beer around them, and finally light up some cigarettes and leave them by the candles.

Meanwhile, in a northern suburb of Rio, the sound of drumming pulses the night. It comes from inside a kind of meeting hall where a woman is convulsed by spasms, jerking around in the room. Men dressed in white watch her from one side of the hall; women also in white watch from the other.

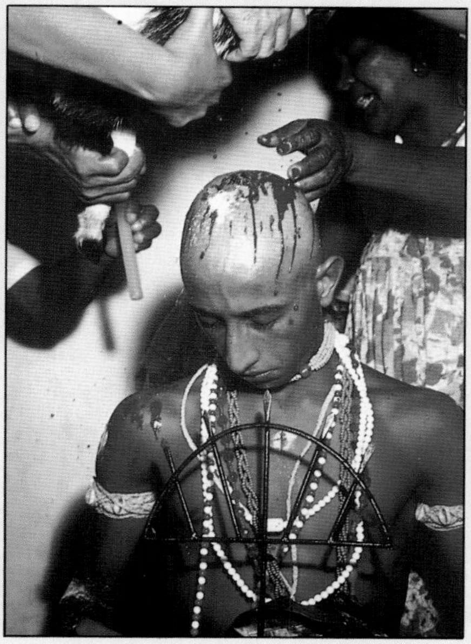

Both the street intersection and the meeting hall are typical places where you can see what in Brazil is generically known as *macumba*– the voodoo-like rituals practiced with variations throughout the country. *Macumba* came with the West Africans on slave ships, and its phalanx of deities belongs to the traditions of the Yoruba-speaking peoples. The imposition of Christianity simply resulted in each of the new, European saints taking a corresponding identity with one of the Yoruba deities. Visitors are usually welcome to watch *macumba* rites, although photography is forbidden.

Candomble is the kind of *macumba* practiced around Salvador, where slaves first disembarked. Drumming is always an element and its hypnotic rhythms frequently plunge participants into wild gyrating trances. This happens at the meeting places called *terreiros*, which are considered sacred grounds. Devotees wear white to honor Oxalá, *candomble's* equivalent to Christ and the highest of the deities. Those who wear white on Fridays (and plenty of Brazilians do) have some special favor they are asking of Oxalá.

In the south of Brazil another kind of *macumba* flourishes. Known as *umbanda*, from the Sanskrit *Aum-Bandha*, or "limit of the unlimited", it is a kind of white magic – good deeds and generosity are asked of the gods. This variation of *macumba* is a blending of Catholicism, *candomble*, and a cult called "spiritism" which started in France in the mid-19th century and soon made deep inroads in Brazil. People are visited by the spirits of deities during *umbanda* sessions, and a discerning eye can tell exactly which spirit has possessed a person.

Because street intersections form a cross, they are thought to be centers of power in *umbanda*, which is why offerings are frequently made there. It's not rare to find at curbside the charred carcass of a chicken alongside beer bottles and candle stumps the morning after a particular deity's feast day. The offerings are symbolic: smoke from the cigars or cigarettes represents the clouds; beer represents the foam of the sea.

The most important goddess of *macumba* is Iemanjá, matron of the sea. Her Christian identity is Saint Anne, and she is portrayed as light-skinned with blond hair and cloaked in flowing white and blue robes. In Salvador her feast day is August 15, but in Rio, where *umbanda* prevails, she is fêted on New Year's Eve. The beaches of Rio that night fill up with white-clad worshipers, who float candles on the water and scatter flower petals in her honor. Statues of these and other gods abound in shops dedicated to *macumba* icons. A popular figure in *umbanda* is the statue of an old black man, who is not a god but instead represents a wise African spirit.

There is also a malevolent form of *macumba* called *Quimbanda*. The chief demon of this black magic, which resembles Caribbean voodoo, is Exú, who is accompanied by a whole legion of other evil spirits. Burnt animal carcasses are a sign of offerings to Exú. ■

SLOWLY DOWN THE AMAZON

Although it is not the longest river in the world, there can be no doubt that the Amazon is the world's greatest river. At the end of the 4,000 mile (6,700km) journey that begins on the other side of the continent at the Andean Lake Lauricocha near the Pacific Ocean, the river's 200-mile (330-km) wide mouth discharges a quarter of all the world's fresh water into the Atlantic, coloring the ocean more than 60 miles (100km) from the shore.

Amazonia is a vast greenhouse of global evolution. A tenth of the world's 10 million species of living things breed here – 2,500 kinds of fish, 50,000 higher plant species and untold numbers of insects. Its thousand tributaries sprawl across eight nations, dominating Brazil, yet Brazilians are only just beginning to discover its pleasures.

It is cheaper and quicker to fly around the Amazon, nothing quite matches the romance of taking a slow boat down the world's greatest river. This vast waterway are still plied by hundreds of vessels: from ocean-going cargo ships bringing goods from overseas, to passenger ships drifting through the river's farthest reaches.

Tourist services run between the Amazon's two major ports, Manaus and Belém (*see page209*). The state-run ENASA line allows visitors to see the river in a certain style, their cruisers fitted with swimming pools, nightclubs and observation decks. The boats hug one side of the river to get a view of the jungle – the other side being almost beyond the horizon, giving the impression of sailing in a huge caramel sea.

But for the "authentic" Amazon experience as evoked by writers such as Joseph Conrad, you have to journey on one of the smaller, wooden vessels. They are known as *gaiolas* – or "birdcages" – after the crowded mid-deck levels where passengers pile over one another in hammocks.

These often antique boats still work the smaller tributaries of the Amazon from Manaus to Benjamin Constant, on the border of Colombia, then onward into Iquitos in Peru, and return. The added advantage of these journeys is that the Amazon is narrower, allowing you to see more of the river life – from fishermen paddling in canoes to dolphins diving along the water's edge.

A typical passage, from Benjamin Constant to Manaus along the Rio Negro, takes four days. Going the other way, upriver, will take up to eight, and most people choose the shorter if possible – agreeing that the romance of riverboats can wear a little thin. Finding a boat heading to or from these smaller river ports is a matter of patience and luck. The smaller companies have no fixed schedules, and captains generally choose their day of departure. The only way to arrange a booking is to wander around the port and chat to whoever is around.

Depending on which boat is currently available – and there is little choice in the matter – they can be relatively comfortable or crowded, noisy and somewhat unhygenic. Those who can afford a few extra dollars often pay for a "cabin": a small airless box with a set of bunks, but at least some space to call your own.

The boat leaves the muddy Amazon port of Benjamin Constant at night, moving into the pitch darkness with flashes of lightning in the sky but no rain. In the morning, the river turns out to be about 700 ft (200 meters) wide. Stops are made at remote jungle villages, where the whole population turns out to watch the boat unload beer, pass out a few letters and take on a cargo of bananas.

Time soon becomes incidental, marked by dawn, dusk and meals. Breakfast is Brazilian coffee and biscuits, lunch is spaghetti and fried fish, dinner rice, beans and fried chicken. Since this gets somewhat tedious in time, it's worth it to bring a few snacks and sweets to vary the diet. Water is taken from the river, so health-conscious travelers bring a large supply of mineral water.

Little in the journey changes over the four days, except that the river becomes wider and more powerful. The pleasure comes from relaxing into the rhythm of the boat, lulled by the throbbing of the engine and the cool breeze from the water. There are no mosquitoes or bugs to disturb the boat when it is moving – and when it stops there is an invasion of blue butterflies. The passengers listen to music from portable cassettes, play dominoes, or read. At dusk, Orange flashes of lightning run dramatically along the horizon.

The riverboat finally makes it to Manaus, where the dark River Negro meets the yellow River Solimoes. Disembarking at the chaotic wooden port, it is difficult to forget that flying you would have taken half an hour instead of four days. But then, the journey would hardly have had the same charm. ■

Preceding pages, the Amazon rainforest. Left: a port on the river. Above, giant water lilies.

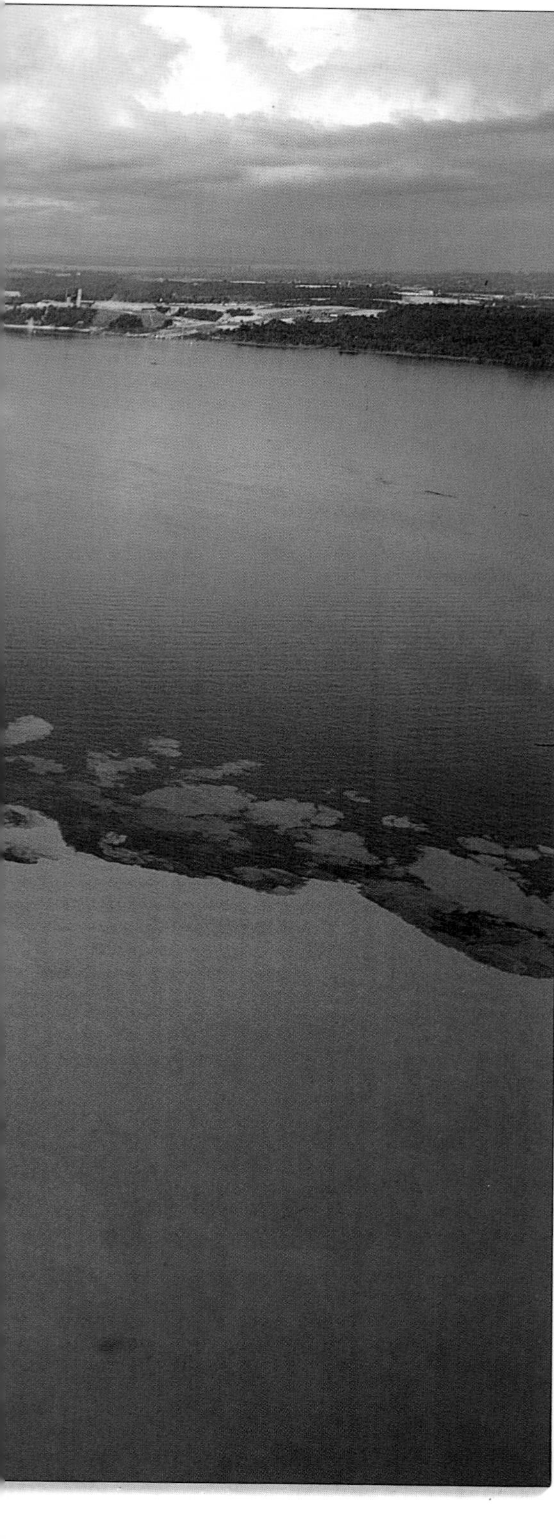

THE RIVER PORTS: MANAUS TO BELÉM

The last thing you might expect in the middle of the Amazon jungle, 1,000 miles (1,600 km) from the sea, is a thriving port city. But **Manaus** was cut from the wilderness last century: where mad conquistadors once searched in vain for gold, Brazilians found a modern El Dorado of rubber. Today, this strange outpost is enjoying a new boom as a tourist destination and one of the duty-free capitals of South America.

Arriving in Manaus by boat is dramatic, not because of the city – which is spread out on low bluffs – but because it is the meeting place of two Amazon tributaries at a 5-mile (8-km) wide junction. The dark River Negro, which looks like fizzing Coca-Cola when riverboats churn it up, hits the yellowish River Solimoes, and the two vast currents run together side by side without mingling their differently colored waters.

Not everybody has the leisure time to drift into Manaus by boat nor the energy to take the four-day bus trip from Rio de Janeiro. Most people just do as the Brazilians do and hop on an aeroplane, which within hours bring you to the heart of the city whose mystique has gripped imaginations for a century.

Champagne in the jungle: Behind the chaotic bustle of modern Manaus is the memory of its moment of glory. When the pneumatic tire was invented in 1888, Amazon rubber suddenly became a valuable material and for a brief but dazzling period at the turn of the century, Manaus became the richest city in the world. Pioneers flooded into the jungle, creating the boom town of fast fortunes and grand gestures portrayed in Werner Herzog's film *Fitzcarraldo*.

Huge rubber plantations were set up in the sinuous waterways of the Amazon, and the newly-rich rubber barons earned Manaus a name for extravagance and decadence. Quaffing champagne and lighting their cigars with $100 bills,

Left: the "meeting of the waters"; the brown river Solimoes meets the Rio Negro near Manaus, Brazil's Amazon city.

they outdid one another to prove their sophistication in this unlikely setting.

The most famous and bizarre monument to the boom days is the grand opera house, the **Teatro Amazonas**. Materials for this temple of art in the middle of the jungle were wholly imported from Europe: white marble from Italy, iron pillars from England and polished wood from France.

The sumptuous interior has four levels of Corinthian-columned balconies with red velvet chairs. The original house curtain remains, painted with Grecian nymphs lolling in the Amazon River. In its heyday, the opera house attracted such greats as the Italian tenor Caruso and today, fully restored, it can still pulll in international names.

River life: The old **port area** of Manaus is thriving. Wooden riverboats dump their exotic cargoes on to crowded wharves or straight on to the riverbank. Grunting men then lug the green bananas or crates of soft drink among ankle-deep garbage, while overhead circle black urubu birds. Out in the river is a more up-to-date floating dock for the ocean-going cargo ships which work the wide Amazon.

Houses have been thrown up around the port on precarious stilts. Among them are pool halls and dark bars, storerooms and corridors of animals kept in wooden cages. Sweeping is made easy, since scraps are brushed into the floor cracks and join the stinking debris below. A more imposing construction at the port is the stone **Customs House**, built by English engineers in 1906.

For a glimpse of the lost Indian cultures of the area, head for the **Museu do Indio** (corner Avenida Sete de Setembro and Rua Duque de Caxias), full of wooden blowpipes, feather headdresses and unexplained artifacts. Next door is one of the rubber factories still operating in Manaus, and it can be visited for free. There is even a local Amazon "beach" near the **Hotel Tropical**, where the braver swimmers can prove that the river is free of piranhas and electric eels which can so spoil a holiday.

Many tour companies head deeper

Teatro Amazonas, built so that rubber barons could enjoy opera in the jungle.

into the jungle around Manaus but need a few days to get past the disordered "development" of the region before finding virgin territory with animals. Many also offer stays in jungle lodges, with canoe trips allowing you to see crocodiles and toucans in the wild.

Boom and bust: The great rubber boom of the late-19th century collapsed as quickly as it had begun: tradition has it that a British gentleman smuggled rubber seeds out of the country saying they were for Queen Victoria's orchidorium, and soon plantations in Malaya were producing more cheaply than Brazil.

Manaus fell into a torpor that was broken in 1967, when it became a duty-free zone. Although foreigners are unlikely to be impressed by the prices, the city's airports are full of South Americans loaded down with video recorders and compact disc players. Once again fortunes are being made and lost in Manaus, but without the grand gestures of old. The background has shifted from rubber plantations to department stores, and few have time for a night at the opera.

Beyond Manaus: Further down the Amazon is the port of **Santarém**, at the confluence with the Tapajos River. Once a colonial fortress, Santarém today is a kind of Dodge City for the half million gold prospectors, or *garimpeiros*, who work in the jungle. Especially interesting is the arrival of fishermen's catches in the morning – an impressive display of the immense diversity of aquatic life and of Amazon river lore.

On the south side of the mouth of the Amazon stands proud, stately **Belém**, 90 miles (145 km) for open ocean. A city of a million inhabitants, Belém retains the graceful airs of its heyday when rubber was still king in the Amazon. The city is now primarily an export port, shipping timber, Brazil nuts (*castanhas de Para*), and a small amount of rubber.

The months of May through October are best for visiting Belém, since rains fall constantly the rest of the year. The city is only one degree south of the equator, but is cooled somewhat by tradewinds coming off the Atlantic.

ungle stays r canoe trips ring rewards uch as the ght of a ucan.

The city has an old-town with colonial-era homes and churches. There's a fort nearby commandeered by Circulo Militar – try the mouth-numbing duck soup at its restaurant.

There's a striking cathedral, **Basílica de Nossa Senhora de Nazaré**, built in 1909 with money from the rubber boom and as luxuriously baroque as those built two centuries earlier in Minas Gerais. The church is not far from the dockside municipal market called *Vero-Peso*, or "check out the weight", where fishermen bring their impressive catches.

Another Belém landmark is the **Emilio Goeldi Museum**, named after a great Brazilian naturalist. The anthropological museum has exhibits of crafts made by Indians from the nearby island of Marajó, and a small zoo is adjacent, with panthers, caymans and other jungle prowlers.

Excursions leave Belém for **Marajó Island**, in the mounth of the river. Some 200,000 people live on the island, where buffalo roam freely in the flat, swampy eastern region.

RONDÔNIA: BRAZIL'S WILD WEST

If you thought the days of the Wild West were over, consider **Rondônia**. At the beginning of the 1970s this Brazilian state was tree-tangled wilderness on the southern flank of the Amazon jungle, bordering Bolivia. It was home then to just a few thousand hardy rubber tappers who snaked through the rainforest collecting latex from wild rubber trees. Today, settlers have pushed their way pell-mell into almost every corner of Rondônia, hacking down the jungle and frequently enforcing their land claims with the squeeze of a trigger. In the 1980s, nearly one-quarter of the Rondônian rainforest was destroyed, mostly by burning, to clear land for planting and cattle pastures. During the dry season between May and October, a blanket of smoke hangs over the state as the forests are incinerated.

The last frontier: Two factors set off the land rush in Rondônia. First, changes in agriculture in Brazil's prosperous south made many peasants landless in the 1970s. Increasingly frequent freezes combined with soaring world prices for soybeans convinced many coffee farmers to cut down their bushes and plant soybeans. Peasants who had sharecropped at the edges of the coffee plantations – assuring growers a stable workforce to harvest the beans – were no longer needed for the mechanized soybean harvest, and were forced to abandon their plots.

These peasants chose Rondônia to homestead because of the extension of roadway BR 364 that started in the coffee regions of the state of São Paulo and finally reached all the way to the capital of Rondônia, the riverport of Porto Velho. Express buses carried migrant peasants directly to Rondônia, the new Brazilian frontier. This was all in line with the formula for peopling the Amazon enunciated by the Brazilian military, which then governed the country: "A land without people for people without land."

A ride up BR 364 in one of the buses that ply the paved highway provides a revealing view both of frontier life and the devastation of the rainforest. Along the highway spread vast pastures cluttered with charred stumps and tall naked trunks of once-mighty rainforest trees. On the horizon looms the high dense wall of jungle that once covered the pastures.

A boom town called **Ariquêmes** along BR 364 gives a taste of the free-for-all world of the frontier. At the bus station, or *rodoviária*, sleek buses pull in from the south, discharging loads of dazed migrants clutching their possessions in feedsacks and battered suitcases. Some are met by relatives, others simply set out on their own. A shop at the station sells T-shirts proclaiming "Rondônia–you have to see it to believe it."

In town, the dusty streets are lined by weather-beaten storefronts and filled with homesteaders shopping for provisions. Many have blond hair and blue eyes, legacies of their German forebears who settled in Brazil's south. As they wander the streets, snake-oil ven-

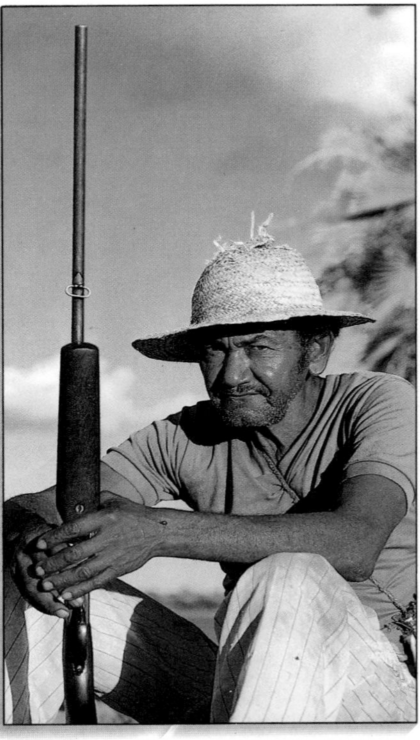

Farmers floc[k] from round Brazil to try their luck on the frontier o[f] Rondônia.

dors compete with bible-thumping evangelists for their attention. Inside noisy bars, men shoot pool and talk about the latest confrontations between squatters and well-armed land barons.

Determined settlers: Despite endemic malaria, periodic shoot-outs, and poor soils, few of these people ever have second thoughts about having left the south behind. They are proud of their tenacity and are determined to make it on this quickly expanding frontier. Talks on ecological destruction fail to move them; survival in the short term is their top priority.

Wealthy land speculators have also cashed in on the rush to settle Rondônia, buying up enormous tracts for cattle ranches. Such enterprises were subsidized by the Brazilian government until international concerns about the disastrous effect on the ecology forced them to abandon the policy. Not for nothing was the 1995 Earth Summit held in Brazil.

Those who occupied the rainforest before the land rush – the rubber tappers and Indians – have been forced further west as the frontier encroaches on their way of life. Rubber tapping has all but been abandoned in Rondônia as the trees have disappeared, despite laws enacted for their protection. Laws that require that half the jungle on any property be left standing are also honored only in the breach.

Some 300,000 Brazilians still survive collecting the fruits of the forest – wild rubber, Brazil nuts and resin. Many have migrated farther west to escape the onslaught of settlement. They now work mostly in the state of Acre, west of Rondônia on the borders of Bolivia and Peru. Key to their survival is their isolation and international pressures to protect their benign co-existence with the shrinking rainforest.

Some protected areas called "extractive reserves" have been established for these jungle harvesters. But as Brazil's population continues to grow faster than the new jobs, the pressures to clear the forest that have transformed Rondônia are likely to keep moving westward.

A canoe plies the backwaters of the Amazon basin.

THE PANTANAL, BIRD PARADISE

An enormous marsh called the **Pantanal** is perhaps the most exquisite gallery of all for observing Brazilian fauna – "a bird-lover's paradise," in the words of Brazilian geographer Osvaldo Valverde. Spreading 40,000 sq. miles (100,000 sq. km) east of the Paraguay River on Brazil's western border with Bolivia, the Pantanal is home to more than 600 species of birds, 350 kinds of fish, and an abundance of reptiles and animals. Many of these are also found in the Amazon rainforest, but seeing them there is much more difficult because of the dense free cover.

The Pantanal's menagerie of birds is mostly waterfowl and waders. There are white ibises, egrets, blue herons, ducks, green parakeets, pheasants, and the majestic white man-size Tuiuiú stork. During the rainy months of October to April, when waters are high in the north of the Pantanal, the birds feed on fish in the southern sector. From May until September, when the waters from the north flood down south, the birds move to the more shallow waters in the north. The best time of the year to visit is during the cooler and dry winter months of June, July and August; January and February are infernally hot and humid. The Pantanal can be noisy during the dry season, since that's when birds are nesting by the hundreds in swamp trees.

When the waters recede from the northern Pantanal in the winter months, wide sandy riverbanks are exposed. Brazilians like to camp on the banks during that season, but this is also when large alligators called jacarés like to sun on the sand. There are also ocelots, pimas, wild boars, jaguars, red lake deer, tapirs and a large furry rodent called capivara.

Exploring the swamps: Access to the Pantanal's edge is quite easy, but getting around inside is another matter altogether. **Cuiabá**, the capital of Mato Grosso, is one place to start. The city itself is attractive, having once enjoyed

The stunning colors of the Pantanal.

a gold boom, although the weather is intensely hot. Some 45 miles (70 km) northeast of Cuiabá there are cool waterfalls at **Chapada de Guimarães**, the source of much water that enters the northern part of the swamp. There are also striking rock formations along the escarpment.

Just south of Cuiabá is **Santo Antônio de Leverger,** on the edge of the marshland. From there it's possible to fly to hotels and cattle ranches, or *fazendas*, within the Pantanal. You can get ground transport, boats, airplane flights, and even hot-air balloon rides at these lodges for observing the surrounding wildlife. Fishing is permitted – piranhas are prized for their supposed aphrodisiacal powers – but not hunting. Poachers have already made off with many alligators and capivaras, and the many conservationists in the area keep a close lookout for human predators.

The main attraction of the area is **Baia Chacorore**, a huge shallow water basin flocked with roseate spoonbills. Its banks crawl with alligators.

It is also possible to drive into the Pantanal along the partially completed **Transpantaneira Highway**. The road is often rough and it sometimes floods, but it crosses many rivers (there are 126 bridges) and provides an intimate vantage point for watching swamplife. The road ends 90 miles (145 km) into the Pantanal at Porto Jofre, and accommodations are available along the way and at the port.

Border towns: If the Transpantaneira were completed (which appears unlikely because of opposition from environmentalists), it would connect Cuiabá to **Corumbá**, a bordertown situated along the southwest flank of the Pantanal. Although the Pantanal reaches up to the city limits, local tours reveal little – much of the wildlife has fled to more remote areas. The best way to see the swamp from Corumbá is to arrange passage on cattle boats that penetrate more deeply into the area or organize a trip through the **Caiman Fazenda**, a ranch on the highway linking Corumbá to Campo Grande.

A cayman snaps up lunch.

IGUASSÚ FALLS

Iguassú, means Great Waters in Guaraní, and it is a fitting name for the most spectacular waterfalls in the western hemisphere. Taller than Niagara Falls by 65 ft (20 meters) and twice as wide, Iguassú falls consists of 275 cascades spread across a gulf of nearly 2 miles (3 km). The torrent of brackish water pouring over the falls drops past lush subtropical vines and flitting butterflies (more than 500 species, including one of flourescent cobalt blue), a sight glimpsed by many in the 1986 film, *The Mission*.

Seeing the Devil's Throat: The falls are divided between Brazil and Argentina, and to see them properly one must visit both sides. If attempting to do so in one day (which is possible, with some effort), it's best to start out on the Brazilian side. Though more removed from the falling waters, the Brazilian vantage point gives a much more panoramic view of the immense cascade. The light there is best in the morning for photographers. This side also gives one the best look at the most spectacular section of the falls, the roaring **Devil's Throat**. Fourteen falls combine forces in their 350-ft (100-meter) fall, pounding the water below with such force that there is constantly a huge rainbow-spanned cloud of spray hovering above them. A catwalk on the Brazilian side, reached by a winding foot trail and an elevator, gives more intimate views. Helicopter rides are also available.

Crossing to the Argentine side requires no border formalities. A stop at the Argentine interpretive center can provide much useful information about the falls and its surrounding flora and fauna, a service quite lacking on the Brazilian side. A series of catwalks explores the Argentine falls, including one rebuilt in 1988 that takes visitors over the water rushing down into **Devil's Gorge**.

There are areas where it's possible to swim under the spray of the cascades,

Preceding pages: torrents pour into the "Devil's Throat" at Iguassú. Below, an aerial view of the falls.

but cuticle parasites are sometimes a problem afterwards.

Another option for exploring the falls is to climb down a series of trails and stairways to the river below, where a short boat trip takes visitors to the island of **San Martin**, making a pass close to one of the falls. Climbing back up from the canyon is quite a task, though, and should be attempted only by those in good shape.

The Argentines have created a national park adjacent to the falls, where there is a jungle trail posted with information, as well as a bird hide overlooking a swamp. A trek through the park can take most of the day. In the evening, catch a bus to **Puerto Canoas**, where the day's dying light heightens the beauty of Devil's Gorge as swallows dive into their nests in the walls behind the falling water.

The best time of the year to see Iguassú falls is autumn and spring – summers are intensely hot and are the heaviest tourist season, while the water level drops considerably in the dry winter. There are hotels on both the Brazilian and Argentine sides of the falls.

Harnessing the waters: The closest Brazilian city to the falls is **Foz do Iguassú**, near the junction of the Paraná and Iguassú rivers. This frontier town has grown phenomenally in the last two decades, largely due to the construction nearby of the world's largest hydroelectric dam. The facility, called Itaipú (Guaraní for "singing rock"), is worth visiting and offers guided tours. It was built jointly by Brazil and Paraguay, and it's powered by the waters of the Paraná River, which divides the two countries. The dam, which provides electricity mainly for far-off São Paulo, is an impressive sight, with waters roaring through its sluice gates from an immense dam above. A short film at the visitor's center tells the story of the dam's construction.

Near Iguassú falls there is a marker where Paraguay, Brazil and Argentina all converge, and a visit to the falls can easily give a glimpse of all three neighboring countries.

'he serene ;ardens ıearby.

Paraguay: Paradise Lost

When I first came to Asunción from Spain, I realized that I'd arrived in paradise. The air was warm, the light was tropical, and the shuttered colonial houses suggested sensual, tranquil lives. At night, we'd go out walking in the streets and I'd be aware of two things: the smell of jasmine and the sound of voices in the dark. But like any paradise, this one had serpents.

—Paraguayan poet Josefina Plá

Surrounded by Bolivia, Brazil and Argentina, the small subtropical nation of Paraguay lies at the heart of South America. The River Paraguay divides the country into two distinct halves: the lush, fertile east, where most of the population lives, and the barren Chaco tablelands to the west, home to a few scattered settlements, Mennonite farmers, and nomadic Indians. The River Paraguay eventually feeds into the great Rio de la Plata, linking the country historically and geographically to the other River Plate nations of Uruguay and Argentina.

But for many travelers in South America, Paraguay feels like a world apart. "An island surrounded by land" is how exiled Paraguayan novelist Augusto Roa Bastos has described his landlocked native country. The phrase refers not only to Paraguay's physical remoteness but to a kind of psychic solitude brought about by wars, dictatorships and a profound sense of ethnic unity. A visitor to the capital, Asunción, can't help noticing the profusion of monuments commemorating military rulers, crushing defeats and pyrrhic victories. Yet one is also struck by the tropical prettiness of the colonial city, and by the soft-spoken, gentle manners of Paraguayans, reminders that the Spaniards who first settled this region dreamed not of plunder but of founding an earthly paradise.

Indian traditions: In a country where almost everyone is of part Guaraní descent, schoolbooks devote considerable space to pre-Columbian Paraguay. The Guaraní were the original inhabitants of what is now Asunción.

Preceding pages: the Itaipú Dam powered by the waters of the Paraná River. Left, guards at the Pantheón Le Los Heroes in Asunción.

They were principally farmers, but they were also accomplished warriors, who bore suffering stoically. Early Spanish chroniclers reported with horror that the Guaraní were cannibals, although this custom was apparently limited to the ritual eating of prisoners of war. Their language, in the words of one Spanish priest, was "one of the most copious and elegant on the globe," and it was used as a *lingua franca* throughout the region.

The first Spanish explorer in Paraguay was Alejo García, who passed through the region in 1525 on his search for the fabled Mountain of Silver. He found his way to Peru but on his return, laden with pillaged wealth, he was killed by the Guaraní.

Asunción was founded on August 15, 1537, by Domingo de Irala, a man of letters who came seeking refuge from the miseries of the settlement at Buenos Aires. He declared this verdant spot a sort of rest-and-recreation refuge from the rigors of the conquest. The Guaraní, who were also anxious for Inca gold, were eager to form an alliance with the Spaniards and gave them their daughters as tokens of good faith.

Irala and his men soon discovered that the Incas had already been conquered and plundered by Pizarro, but the lush life in Asunción, far from the sea and the watchful eye of the Spanish crown, induced them to stay. The colonial farms were organized in a feudal manner, although there was a great degree of social mobility, as intermarriage brought the colony to a nearly classless society. But the River Plate tied the fortunes of the colony to those of Buenos Aires. When the Spanish colonial seat in Lima closed the port of Buenos Aires, Paraguay suffered as well. Spain's indifference to its fate helped sow the seed of Paraguayans' tenacious nationalism, and gave rise, perhaps, to their chronic sense of being alone in the world.

In 1588, the Spanish Jesuits opened their first missions in Paraguay, gathering hundreds of Guaraní families into towns known as *reducciones*. The Indians lived in a communal style, in long adobe buildings holding 100 families or more. Although Jesuit chroniclers and films such as *The Mission* paint an idyllic picture of mission life – a sort of

Arcadia of hymn-singing and candlelit processions – life in the *reducciones* was based on a rigid theocracy. The Guaraní learned tasks such as carpentry, leather tanning, boatmaking, tailoring, weaponry, manuscript preparation and printing. A few of the most promising boys were even given classical education. The skills of the Indians tempted Portuguese slave traders in Brazil, and the Spanish colonists, jealous of the Jesuits' wealth and power, did little to stop the raids. In 1767 King Carlos III of Spain banished the Jesuits from all Spanish territory; within a few years the missions were in ruins.

The first dictator: As the power of Buenos Aires grew, the leaders of Paraguay began to

resent their own growing insignificance. They refused to go along with the Argentine declaration of independence in 1810. A military junta led by Fulgencio Yegros declared Paraguay's independence on May 14, 1811. Yegros ruled along with a civilian lawyer named Doctor José Gaspar Rodríguez de Francia, but soon after independence Francia seized power. Congress named him supreme dictator for life in 1816. Paraguay was in danger of being annexed by either Argentina or Brazil, and against this threat Dr Francia closed the Paraguayan borders: no one was allowed in or out during his 24-year reign.

"El Supremo", as Francia was called, ruled by absolute decree. While he was a frugal and honest ruler, and a learned man who began his reign with a sincere wish to better the lot of his countrymen, his whims and punishments became more and more grotesque as he grew deranged by power and isolation. At one point Francia ordered all the dogs in the country killed; he also decreed that none of his subjects could look at him as he passed in the street. At his death in 1840, no Paraguayan priest was willing to say a funeral Mass, and a priest was finally imported from Argentina.

Paraguay immediately plunged into political chaos until the next dictator, Carlos Antonio López, was proclaimed in 1844. The constitution which accompanied his ascent to power conspicuously lacked the word "liberty", but López was an enlightened despot who re-opened the country to progress and sent students to Europe to study. Continuing border crises with Brazil and Argentina convinced López that his country's modernization should take place along military lines. Hundreds of foreign engineers, doctors, scientists, and advisers were put to work building railroads, shipyards, iron foundries and telegraphs.

On his deathbed, López advised his son and designated successor, Francisco Solano López, to consider the possibility of instituting a monarchy in Paraguay, and not to let the nation's growing military might tempt him into unnecessary war.

Disastrous conflicts: Solano López, a weak and spoiled young man, proceeded to seek the hand of the daughter of the Brazilian emperor, and was rejected. Feeling that Paraguay's neighbors did not take his country seriously, Solano López decided to intervene in Uruguay's civil war, and quickly found himself at war not only with Uruguay but with Brazil and Argentina as well. The ensuing War of the Triple Alliance was disastrous for Paraguay. The country was further ravaged by a cholera plague, and López, at this point seriously unhinged, ordered the executions of hundreds of people, including his own two brothers and scores of officers. Abetted by his famous Irish mistress, Elisa Lynch, he also executed his childhood sweetheart and other society ladies who had snubbed Madame Lynch. On March 1, 1870, he was shot by one of his own generals after refusing to surrender. "I die with Paraguay," he exclaimed, which was almost literally true. At the end of the war more than half the population of 525,000 were dead; of the survivors, only 29,000 were adult males. Paraguay was rebuilt mostly by women, who resigned themselves to a polygamous society as the church looked the other way.

Between the fall of Solano López and Paraguay's bloody Chaco War with Bolivia, the country changed presidents 32 times and endured two assassinations of presidents, six *coups d'état*, two revolutions and eight attempted revolutions. The Chaco War raged between 1932 and 1935 over a piece of barren land that was believed to contain oil and other mineral deposits. Paraguay won this war, after mediation by Argentina, Brazil, Chile, Peru, Uruguay and the United States, but once again the male population was devastated. A succession of dictators followed, until in 1954 the son of a German brewmeister, Alfredo Stroessner, seized power and ruled with an iron fist for nearly 35 years. In 1973, the exiled novelist Augusto Roa Bastos published *I the Supreme*, a fictional biography of 19th-century dictator Francia. But the parallels with Stroessner were obvious enough to ensure the writer's continued banishment.

GENERAL URQUIZA'S PALACE AT SAN JOSE.—[From a Sketch by our own Correspondent.]
PARAGUAY

Left, 17th-century Jesuit ruins at Trinidad. Above, a 19th-century etching of General Urquiza's Palace at San José.

Winds of change: *Stroessner brought running water, paved streets, and electric lights to major cities, built an airport and founded Paraguay's airline, though over these 35 years these events may well have happened without him. In the 1970s, the construction of a Brazilian-Paraguayan hydroelectric dam at Itaipú in eastern Paraguay stimulated land investment, expanded banking and financial services, and provided thousands of jobs. The giant Paraguayan-Argentine hydroelectric project at Yacryeta, proposed in 1973, began operating in 1997.

On February 3, 1989, Stroessner was overthrown by General Andrés Rodríguez, his right-hand man and father of his daughter-in-law. Rodríguez promised a free press and a gradual return to democracy after the coup and his Colorado Party was elected into office in 1991. Gleeful Paraguayans took down the photographs of Stroessner, exiled to Brazil, that graced every shop window, changed the names of streets and towns, and decapitated statues of the former president.

The winds of democracy have been blowing through South America, and many people believe that, in spite of economic and social problems, a more open society in Paraguay is now here to stay.

FROM ASUNCIÓN TO THE CHACO

For travelers unprepared for the size and dynamism of most South American capitals, Asunción fits a kind of Garcia Marquez ideal: slow-moving, flower-filled, languorous. There are few cars, no traffic lights, and the main square, the **Plaza de los Heroes**, is bright with butterflies and birds of paradise. Many of the passers-by seem to have come directly from central casting: the fruit vendors with baskets on their heads, the furtive black-market money-changers, the cluster of helmeted military police investigating a broken water pipe.

Gone is the neon sign which flashed STROESSNER: PEACE, WORK AND WELL-BEING over the square, but its focal point is still the ornate **Pantheon of the Heroes**, which was built as a copy of Les Invalides in Paris. Inside are the tombs of the two López presidents, of two unknown soldiers, and a small urn containing what remains of the dictator Francia. It's said that his bones were dug up and flung into the river by an angry mob. But no matter how Paraguayans feel about their military governments, this is a country that reveres soldiers; it's not at all unusual for passers-by to stop at this shrine and make the sign of the cross before the heroes' crypts. Diagonally across from the pantheon are shop windows that permanently display Chaco War memorabilia and accounts of battles. Across the street, on the corner of Chile and Palma, is a pleasant café called the **Lido**; a good spot to stop for fresh orange juice and a dish of rich cornbread called *sopa paraguaya*.

The oldest part of the city can be reached by following Chile down towards the Paraguay River. On a small bluff is the pastel **Presidential Palace**, the Palacio de los López. It was built in the style of the Louvre by Francisco Solano López, who imported much of the building's beautiful interiors and furniture from Paris. However, he did not have much time to enjoy the palace

View of Asunción.

since the War of the Triple Alliance broke out soon after it was constructed. Further along El Paraguayo Independiente are the tree-lined **Plaza Constitucion**, the **Congressional Palace**, and the newly renovated **Cathedral**.

One of the attractions of Asunción are the bright yellow Belgian-made electric streetcars, which Stroessner revived after the oil crisis of the 1970s. The Itaipú hydroelectric dam has given Paraguay the cheapest electricity in South America. World Bank loans for the project also enriched some Paraguayans beyond their wildest dreams. Some of their splendid new houses, which dwarf the small lots like Beverly Hills-style mansions, can be seen if you ride the streetcar out on Avenida España.

Along this route are some of Asunción's beautiful old colonial houses with wide verandahs and gardens of bottlebrush and banana trees. Also on Avenida España are the American Embassy and Library and Stroessner's former home, now a museum.

Two pretty parks in Asunción are the **Parque Carlos Antonio López**, which provides a good view of the city from the Antonio López and Rio Gallegos intersection, and **Parque Caballero**, which stretches along a riverside at the foot of Estados Unidos. It features the country home of the war hero for whom the park is named, small lakes, waterfalls and gardens. The **Botanical Gardens**, which are 4 miles (7 km) outside Asunción, are worth visiting, as is the museum of natural history on the grounds, housed in another former Lopez residence. Across the river is a **reservation** of the Macá Indians, who were brought here from their home in the Chaco as a tourist attraction. They live in rather dismal conditions, and make their living by posing for photographs (the women taking off their shirts to look more "native") and by hawking feather headbands and toy drums on the streets of the capital. Ironically, the best Indian handicrafts are to be found in the middle-class suburb of **San Lorenzo**, along the eastern highway, where a cooperative offers authentic and very beau-

iesta time n a tropical fternoon.

tiful artifacts made by Indians of the Chaco, including baskets, woven rugs, woodcarvings and pottery.

Traveling east: The Mariscal Estigarribia Highway crosses Paraguay to the Brazilian border town of Ciudad del Este, formerly Cuidad Presidente Stroessner. By express bus the trip takes about four hours, but there are interesting stops along the first half of the journey. About 14 miles (20 km) east of Asunción is **Capiatá**, which was first settled by the Jesuits in 1640. The cathedral contains a 17th-century sculpture made by the Guaraní under Jesuit instruction.

Six miles (10 km) east is **Itagua**, famous for its production of *ñandutí*, or spiderweb lace, which is woven by hand into handkerchiefs, tablecloths and hammocks. There is a three-day festival celebrating this art in mid-July, which culminates with the crowning of Miss Ñandutí.

The resort town of **San Bernardino**, 35 miles (55 km) from Asunción on **Lake Ypacaraí**, is a favorite retreat of prosperous Paraguayans. The lake, measuring 3 by 15 miles (5 by 24 km) is an idyllic spot, surrounded by tropical vegetation. Fifteen miles (24 km) down the road is **Caacupe**, another popular resort and religious shrine. On December 8, pilgrims come from all over Paraguay carrying heavy stones on their heads as penance. Unfortunately, the lovely old Basilica of Our Lady of the Miracles is being demolished and replaced by a new church.

Ciudad del Este, on the Brazilian border, has been called South America's biggest late-night shopping center. It's a bustling, rather unattractive city with a makeshift boomtown air. Brazilians arrive by the busload to buy electronics, watches and other imported goods in the huge air-conditioned malls. There are bargains to be had, particularly for residents of South America, but the city is also a magnet for con artists, who hawk everything from imitation perfume to "musical" condoms.

More impressive is the nearby **Itaipú Dam**, which can be reached by bus from Ciudad del Este. The Visitor's Center is well organized, and it offers a free film show, bus tour and a guided walking tour inside the world's largest hydroelectric project.

On the trail of the Jesuits: Most of the Jesuit *reducciones* were set up in the fertile High Paraná, southeast of Asunción along Route One. In **Yaguarón**, 30 miles (48 km) south of the capital, there is a Franciscan mission built in 1640, and a museum dedicated to Doctor Francia, the "El Supremo". The first Jesuit ruins are at **San Ignacio**, where the crumbling walls of a church, school and workshops may be seen. To the northeast is **Santa Maria**, established in 1669. It has a new church and a museum housing dozens of Indian-made carvings of saints and apostles. Ten miles (16 km) south is **Santa Roza**, founded in 1698. The church was destroyed by fire in 1883, but wooden carvings, a tower and frescoes remain. To reach the Jesuit ruins of **San Cosmé y Damian**, turn off Route One at KM 301. The 1760 mission lies 20 miles (30 km) from the main highway. Of particular interest is the sundial, all that re-

Buying up bi at Ciudad de Este, Paraguay's consumer capital.

mains of what was once a world-renowned astronomy center.

The city of **Encarnación** is the terminus for the old wood-burning train from Asunción as well as the river ferry. It's the proposed site for the Argentine-Paraguayan hydroelectric project of Yacyretá, and the port town has a prosperous look. Nearby are Japanese colonies which produce soybeans, vegetables, timber, mate and cotton. About 20 miles (30 km) northeast of Encarnación is Paraguay's most splendid ruin, **Trinidad**. The sheer size of the mission gives some idea of the scope of the Jesuit project in the New World. In addition to churches, Indian houses and crypts, there is a baptismal font and an impressive carving of the Holy Trinity, which was hollowed at the back so that a priest could hide inside and give an echoing rendition of the voice of God.

The Chaco: Some 36,000 Paraguayan lives were lost in the Chaco War, but today only twice that number actually inhabit this desolate region. The **Low Chaco**, the region nearest Asunción, is a primeval terrain of marsh and palm forest, and is used for cattle ranching. The **Middle Chaco**, around the capital of **Filadelfia**, is inhabited by Mennonite farmers and nomadic Indians. The Mennonites, a strict Protestant sect, run their own banks, schools and hospitals. They subsist on a co-operative farming system, and can often be seen in Asunción bringing eggs and butter to market. Both men and women still dress in 19th-century style, and most speak only German.

To the north of this region is the **High Chaco**, a desert of thorn forests where the only human habitation are military outposts. The roads are unpaved, and the land is rich with wildlife: jaguars, pumas, tapirs and poisonous snakes, as well as a kind of wild hog, discovered in 1975, that was thought to have become extinct during the Pleistocene Era. There is a bus service as far as Filadelfia, but travelers wishing to go to the Bolivian border must hitch rides with military or oil trucks, and be prepared for long delays when it rains.

Musicians perform with the typical Guarañi harp.

A BILINGUAL LAND

Spanish explorers in Paraguay, unlike other colonies, did not clash with the local Indians but blended to form a homogeneous, bilingual society. This idyllic situation was possible mainly because the local Guaraní had nothing the Spanish conquistadors wanted to steal. What the Guaraní did have to offer was a peaceful life in a fertile country.

It is difficult to say how much the notorious Guaraní "harems" kept by the Spaniards was a fact and how much exaggeration for the benefit of their miserable compatriots in Buenos Aires,

but it was true that a great deal of social mobility was achieved by marriage, and that *mestizo* offsprings, as in Portuguese Brazil, were not considered marginal citizens.

Sociologists also cite the relatively high position of women in Guaraní society as a factor in the continuing status of the mother tongue. But perhaps the most decisive element in Paraguayan bilingualism was the missionary work of the Jesuits. Although the Jesuits imposed Spanish on the Indians, they were impressed by the complexity and musicality of Guaraní, and produced catechisms and hymns in the native language. Ironically, as a result, the Guaraní neglected much of their original music in favour of Western music, producing a number of outstanding musicians at the expense of fostering their own culture. Nevertheless Guaraní music still has a distinctive sound.

In 1624, the Jesuit priest Antonio Ruiz de Montoya created the first Guaraní dictionary and grammar, giving the language a written form and thus a better chance for survival.

During the dictatorship of Doctor Francia (1814–40), Paraguayans of pure Spanish descent were forbidden to intermarry; this attempt to dilute the country's ruling class of course greatly increased contact between the two cultures and their respective languages. Guaraní was considered a sort of homely argot, rather than the speech of educated people, but its use became even more widespread during the Wars of the Triple Alliance and the Chaco, as a symbol of national pride and unity. On the battlefields of the Chaco wars (1932–35) Spanish was banned and Guaraní was spoken instead, as a secret language. As a result of all this, many older Paraguayans with little or no Indian heritage speak Guaraní more fluently than Spanish – ex-President Stroessner is a notable example.

In urban areas today, more than 70 percent of the population is completely bilingual; less than 12 percent speak only Spanish. In rural areas, the use of Guaraní still supersedes that of Spanish; 60 percent of the population speak only Guaraní. Before the 1970s, it was rare for teachers to use Guaraní in the classroom, but changing ideas about bilingual education have made the new generation not only fluent but literate in Guaraní.

Novels and poetry are published in Guaraní translations; there are also theater productions, television and radio shows in the language. The snatches of Guaraní a visitor is likely to hear in everyday conversation in Asunción will of course be unintelligible, but what is apparent is the influence Guaraní has had on the language of the conquistadors: the musical tones, the penchant for modesty and understatement – none of which are characteristics of Spanish.

Despite the ever-presence of the Guaraní melodies, and the 1981 Law of Native Communities which gives Indians guaranteed rights over their lands and cultures, the social position of full-blooded Indians remains inferior. ■

Left, a Guaraní woman sells cheap handicrafts outside the Guaraní Hotel in Asunción. Right, selling chipá, small cakes made from maize, in an Asunción market.

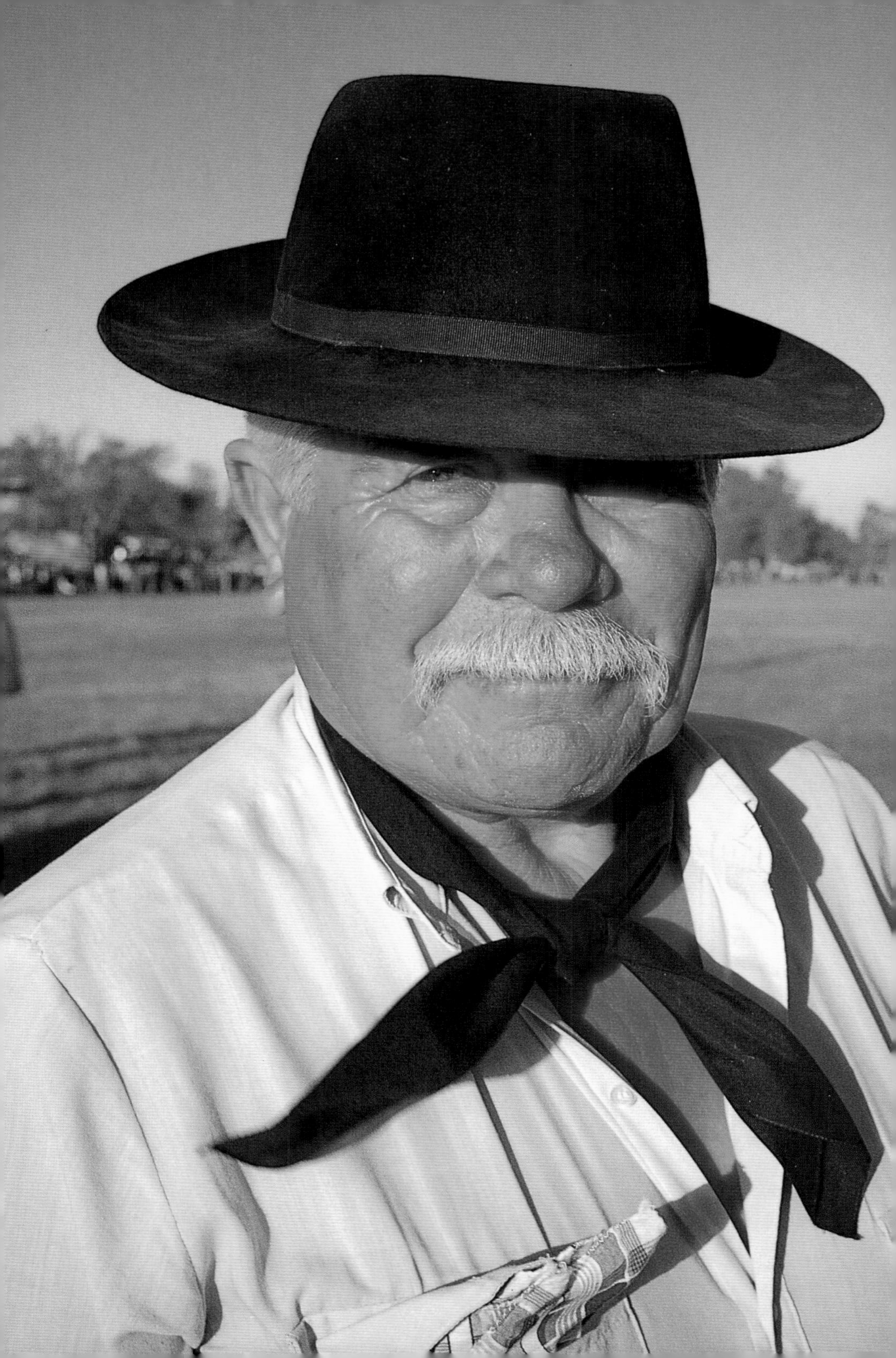

THE SOUTHERN CONE

El cono sur – the "southern cone" of Argentina, Uruguay and Chile – makes up a geological and cultural unit quite apart from the rest of South America. Sparsely populated in pre-Columbus days by roaming Indian tribes, these countries are today the most European part of the continent.

European settlement came late to the south, with many areas unexplored until the late 19th century. The newcomers were from many places besides Spain. Small colonies remain here of Germans, Boers, Britons and Swiss, all descendants of these pioneers. The attraction was the prospect of sudden wealth: several decades ago these countries were relatively affluent, riding on booms of agriculture and minerals.

Squeezed between the Pacific Ocean and the Andes mountains, the thin strip of Chile (*page 240*) is never over 110 miles (180 km) wide but has a coast that extends for 2,800 miles (4,500 km). Driving south from the northern Atacama Desert – one of the driest in the world – you pass through the moderate climate of the capital Santiago (*page 246*) with its surrounding vineyards (*page 250*) to the snow-covered forests of the Lake District (*page 257*). Beyond that are glaciers, peaks and windswept fishing villages of Chilean Patagonia (*page 261*) comparable only to the landscape of Norway.

The obscure republic of Uruguay (*page 277*) was once dubbed "the Switzerland of South America", not so much for its size as for its progressive political tradition. Once with enough money from beef to build a powerful social welfare state, the country now seems frozen in the 1920s. The capital Montevideo (*page 283*) is a quaint place where hand-cranked automobiles still groan through the streets, while the country's beautiful beaches are now mostly used by the wealthy from elsewhere in the world.

The second-largest country on the continent, Argentina (*page 293*) was at the turn of the century far and also its richest. Fired by an agricultural boom and massive Italian immigration, Argentina looked poised to dominate the region. Things haven't gone as expected since then, but the elegant capital Buenos Aires (*page 301*) is still crowded with the crumbling Parisian relics of those days. The enormously rich country has marvels from every climactic zone: the northern deserts (*page 311*), still populated by Indians; the subtropical province of Missiones (*page 312*); the lush forests around Bariloche (*page 317*); the plains of Patagonia (*page 321*), empty except for millions of sheep; and the cool, mountainous island of Tierra del Fuego (*page 324*) at the southern tip of the continent.

Preceding pages: view of Lake Nahuel Huapi near Bariloche, Argentina; and huge pieces of ice broken from the glacier melt in the "canal de los Tempanos" (channel of the icebergs) at Glacier National Park in Argentina Patagonia. Left, an Argentine gaucho.

CHILE: BETWEEN THE ANDES AND THE PACIFIC

Hernán Cortés conquered the Aztec Empire with just 550 men, and Francisco Pizarro took the Incas with a troop of 180 and a few horses. But in 1540, when Pedro de Valdivia set out towards the south from Cuzco, he discovered that conquering Chile would be a different matter.

Though the Incas exacted tribute as far south as the Bío Bío, the Araucanian Indians (or Mapuche as they are known today), the Pehuenches and other small tribes lived as hunters and gatherers, with strong bonds to the land that provided their livelihood. Valdivia subdued the docile Indians of the central valley with ease, founding Santiago in 1541. But when he marched south of the Bío Bío River, Valdivia met his match in the Araucanian warriors, for whom death in battle constituted a supreme honor. In 1554, they captured Valdivia, bound him to a tree, and beheaded him. Legend has in that the executioner ate Valdivia's heart. The south belonged to the Araucanians and the other Indians well into the 19th century. They organized a cavalry force of 10,000 men and learned to use firearms and cannons. The best the Spanish could do was to maintain garrison towns on the coast, and make marauding slave runs into Indian territory.

Eventually the Spanish conquered the Indians, initially dividing the land between officers, then later among the elite, those of direct European descent. Each land owner was given an *encomienda*, which meant the Indians of a certain area were forced to work the land. The *encomiendas* later evolved into *fundos*, with Indian tenants who worked for room and board and a small plot of their own land. To this day the *fundos* have remained an integral part of rural society and have resisted reform. The peasants who work them continue to suffer the worst conditions in Chile.

Push for independence: After Napoleon seized Spain in the late 18th century, Chile followed other Latin American nations and declared itself an independent state on September 18, 1810. In 1811 Chile opened its ports to neutral countries in open defiance of Spain's monopoly on trade. But Spain sent reinforcements to put down the rebellion, and most of the insurgents were executed or fled to Argentina.

In 1817, a man named José de San Martín

assembled an army comprised primarily of Chilean exiles and marched over the Andes to liberate Chile. San Martín left the government of independent Chile to Irish emigrant Bernardo O'Higgins and marched – on to Peru. O'Higgins ruled Chile from 1818 to 1823, and is often remembered as an "enlightened despot". He named a Scotsman, Thomas Cochrane, to head the nascent navy, built up the cities, expanded the public school system, and promoted trade. But when his power began to threaten the landed elite, he was promptly overthrown by the army.

Two political parties grew out of the conflict – Conservative and Liberal – both of which represented the elite. Women and the illiterate *mestizo* masses were excluded from the political process.

Throughout the 19th century Chile expanded into an economic force in South America, exporting copper, silver, gold and agricultural products. Great Britain invested in Chilean interests, and soon became the dominant force in its economy. Only by the end of the century did other countries make inroads into the economy. Chile emerged as the most stable nation in the region, and soon began to expand beyond its borders that reached from Concepción to Copiapó.

19th-century wars: Dictator Diego Portales won a war with a Peru-Bolivian Confederation (1836–39) taking Antofogasta, later claiming Patagonia, Tierra del Fuego and Magallanes, and founding Punta Arenas in 1847. In the Pacific War (1879–83) Peru and Bolivia declared war on Chile, but by 1881 the Chilean forces took Lima by land and sea. A treaty gave Tarapacá and Antofogasta to Chile, including the valuable nitrate and mineral mines in the desert. Eastern Patagonia could also have been won, but was signed over to Argentina since preoccupations with the war in the north prevented Chile from defending its southern claim. Chile then began to look west, and in 1888 took Easter Island.

As the mining, agricultural and shipping industries grew, the working class pushed for changes in the "have's" monopoly on power and wealth. President José Balmaceda (1886–90) proposed radical reforms: state ownership of railroads and mines, breaking the British trade monopoly and tariffs to protect Chilean industry.

The upper class didn't like Balmaceda's ideas, and congress deposed him in favor of a naval officer, Jorge Montt. Balmaceda

Preceding pages: the plains of Patagonia near Punta Arenas in the far south of Chile. Left, a 19th-century view of Valparaíso. Above, Chilean horsemen pause to light a pipe, c. 1890.

refused to step down, sparking a civil war that cost the lives of 10,000 Chileans before he committed suicide.

Reform and resistance: The 20th century brought Chile's disparities of wealth to a head, with a constant battle between reformers and the traditional power bases in the countryside, backed by industry. In the end, the downtrodden lost out.

The working class began to organize against poor work conditions and strikes broke out in the nitrate fields and the ports. The violent response of the government culminated in 1907 when thousands of nitrate workers marched in Iquique. Soldiers fired, killing an estimated 2,000 people.

In the 1920s, mining, transportation and farm workers unions consolidated, becoming a powerful force in the emerging political left. Arturo Alessandri Palma took the helm, promising reforms for the poor, but once again, opposition from the landed rich forced him out in 1924. The military strong man General Carlos Ibánez del Campo took power, but resigned during the depression that wracked Chile in 1931.

Aside from the turmoils of the 1930s Chile lived up to its claims as the most secure democracy in South America until the 1973 coup. Elections were held on schedule, vote counting was fair, and the press had a relative amount of freedom. Legislation was enacted to better the fate of the poor and the repressed, but opposition from the elite held back real changes. The Army remained a powerful factor in the power structure, participating in four civil wars, 10 fruitful coups, and several mutinies during the post-independence period.

Industrialization after World War II brought wealth to speculators and a rise in investment by international firms. But it also brought social problems. Unemployable rural workers went to the cities, and worker radicalization intensified in the 1950s.

In 1958 Jorge Alessandri Rodríguez (Arturo's son) became president with support from the traditional parties, and promises of helping the poor, but Eduardo Frei, of the new Christian Democrat Party (PDC) received 21 percent of the vote and the socialist Salvador Allende 29 percent. Change was occurring in the political landscape.

Alessandri's proposed programs to better life for the poor were cut short by a 1960 earthquake. In 1962 the opposition-controlled congress forced Alessandri to enact a land reform to break the *fundo's* control in the countryside. The 1964 elections were a turning point, and Eduardo Frei won with 56 percent of the vote over Allende's 36 percent. Frei hastened land reform and improved health, education and social services. But he met with protest from the traditional right, and pressure for accelerated reform from the left. Unemployment and inflation grew.

Socialism to Fascism: Salvador Allende won the 1970 election in spite of efforts by the right and the United States to subvert the process. It was the first ever elected socialist government, but Allende only garnered 36.5 percent of the vote, compared to Jorge Alessandri's 35.2 percent and the PDC's Radomiro Tomic's 28 percent. The PDC-controlled congress endorsed Allende's narrow victory in exchange for constitutional amendments that limited his power.

Allende and his Unidad Popular coalition socialist reforms intended to improve the standard of living for the poor – the legal road to socialism, as it was called. Initially it worked. Wages increased, land was redistributed, and the state created jobs. But opposition mounted from the middle and upper classes terrified of revolution, including the radical left who considered Allende too soft on the middle class. Fearing nationalization, local and foreign capital fled. Production declined while demand increased, spurring rampant inflation and shortages. Long lines at markets are one of the most vivid memories of the Allende years.

The right and the US government plotted to overthrow Allende, financing a 1972 truckers' strike. The truckers were soon joined by shopkeepers and professionals.Even so, Allende's Unidad Popular won 44 percent of the seats in the March 1973 congressional elections: the beleaguered leader still had strong support.

But in the early hours of September 11, 1973, tanks and troops surrounded the presidential palace, congress, newspapers and party headquarters. Some working class *barrios* were strafed from the air. Allende died when the air force bombed the Presidential Palace. Thousands of "subversives" were herded into stadiums which were quickly turned into concentration camps.

Within hours, the Allende government had

fallen in a bloody storm, and a four-man military junta took over, banning political activities and declaring a state of siege. Marxism, they declared, would be eradicated from Chile. At least 2,500 people (some estimates run as high as 10,000) were killed, and over the years many more would die as Chile's much-heralded democracy was crushed.

The leader of the coup, General Augusto Pinochet Ugarte, consolidated his power over the country through widespread repression of his foes and unmatched political cunning.

In the years following the coup, political opposition was relentlessly crushed by a security apparatus that used repression, torture and murder to its advantage. Dissidents – as well as and many innocent people – were imprisoned, tortured, sent into exile or murdered. The government nearly fell when widespread protests rocked the country in the early 1980s. But the wily general agreed to negotiate with the opposition if protests were halted, encouraging the PDC and other moderate elements to call off their forces. The moment was lost as Pinochet clamped down, arresting and exiling leaders and reaffirming his power. But the protests did create an opening, and parties gained the right to organize, register voters, start publications and hold rallies. Even so, the government retained tight control over television and broke up "unauthorized" protests.

In 1988 the tide began to turn against Pinochet. A referendum on his presidency was announced for October 5, and a series of reforms was conceded. Voters were registered, exile was abolished, and a state of emergency in effect since 1973 was lifted.

When 7 million Chileans went to the polls that day, the majority voted "No", bringing a resounding defeat to the General. Pinochet accepted his defeat, announcing that elections would be held at the end of 1989.

The new government took office on 11 March, 1990. But Pinochet did not relinquish all power. He kept cronies in eight seats in the Senate and stayed on as head of the army, ensuring no revenge was taken on either himself or those who might have perpetrated injustices during his dictatorship when some 2,000 people "disappeared." Bit by bit, however, confidence and democracy returned, helped by what some saw as an "economic miracle", which made debt and hyper-inflation seem like two more bad dreams from the past. Events came full circle at the end of 1993 when the centre-left Democratic Coalition's Eduardo Frei, son of the 1960s president, was elected president.

Above, General Augusto Pinochet, who took control of Chile in 1973 coup.

SANTIAGO: CAPITAL AMONG THE PEAKS

The conquistador Pedro de Valdivia is said to have forgotten his tortuous journey to Chile from Peru when he gazed upon the valley at the point where the Mapocho and Maipú rivers descend from the Andes on their journey to the Pacific Ocean. Surrounded in all four directions by peaks rivaling the Alps, Valdivia knew he had found the right place for a settlement.

Today, the conquistadors might not recognize **Santiago**, the smoggy home to a third of the country's 12 million people, but it has a charm unmatched in South America.

The city center: Like his home town in Spain, Valdivia marked the center of colonial Santiago with a square, the **Plaza de Armas** (1541). It served as a market and it was the place where criminals were hanged. Today, this clean, tree-lined square is a haven from the city for old men, shoe shiners, vagrants and lovers. The pink **Correo Central** (1882), which houses the most efficient postal service in South America, has an impressive iron skylight that illuminates the central corridor. Next door, the **Museo Histórico Nacional** in the Palacio de la Real Audiencia traces Chile's history from its pre-Columbian roots to the present. Like most of the city's museums, it is well worth a visit.

On the west side is the country's largest church, the **Cathedral** (1748–89) with an impressive baroque interior.

Two blocks away on Calle Catedral is the **Congreso Nacional** (1876) a neoclassical structure, home to Chile's legislative branch until it was closed in 1973. The federal courts and Sernatur are across the street.

The **Palacio de la Moneda** (1805) is four blocks south on Calle Morandé. It is an imposing structure that originally served as the mint, but later became the presidential palace. President Salvador Allende died there when the junta bombarded "La Moneda" during the 1973 military coup, and bullet holes still mar buildings facing the palace.

Paseo Ahumada, a pedestrian mall linking Plaza de Armas to the **Alameda Bernardo O'Higgins** is the heart of Santiago, offering a human collage of businessmen, street vendors and money changers.

Across the Alameda, the city's major east-west artery, is the imposing, chalky-red **Iglesia San Francisco** (1586). The church has interesting touches of Arab influences, remnants of the Spanish. Alongside is **Barrio París-Londres**, where mansions from the 1920s border sinuous streets.

Uptown from Ahumada, three blocks along Calle Augustinas, and past the 17th-century Church of San Augustín is the **Municipal Theatre**, built in 1857 and one of the finest on the continent. Theater, concerts and other cultural events are often held around the small, dimly-lit cobbled **Plaza Mulato Gil** (Metro Universidad Católica).

Green spaces beneath the Andes: Santiago's founders were careful to include trees and green spaces to bridge the gap between urban sprawl and the omni-

Preceding pages: view of the Paine National. Below, new meets old in downtown Santiago.

present Andean mountains, which lie just beyond the city's reach. In fact, Valdivia founded the city while standing atop one of its present-day parks, **Santa Lucía**, a small hill topped with terraces and a replica of a castle, which offers a view of the downtown area.

Parque Forestal (1891) follows the course of the Mapocho River (corresponding to metro stations from Mapocho to Salvador). Tropical banana trees line winding footpaths which betray the confines of this narrow park. The **Museo de Bellas Artes** is here, an approximate copy of the Petit Palais in Paris, with a fine collection of work by Chilean artists.

Parque Metropolitano covers four hills towering 2,600ft (800 meters) over Santiago. A tram goes to a terrace on the peak, commanding a view of the whole city when the smog is not too thick. There is a statue of the Virgin Mary, two pools, a zoo, a botanical garden and a wine tasting center that offers the best of Chile's vineyards. A cable car descends half the length of the mountain, to Calle Pedro de Valdivia in *the barrio alto*. **Parque O'Higgins** (metro Line 2) is an expansive open space where strolls on foot or horseback became stylish for city dwellers when it opened in the late 1800s. In **El Pueblito** there is a replica of a typical southern village.

Bellavista is the cultural heart of Santiago, the nighttime haunt of artists, writers and people who go to see and be seen. Dimly lit streets are sprinkled with raucous cafes, art galleries, and restaurants, while roving theater troupes, musicians, and hippies peddle their work. People are always very friendly and eager to chat with visitors from abroad – just pull up a seat and enjoy the atmosphere.

At night tables spill from bars along **Calle Pío Nono**, Bellavista's main drag. On the side streets, quaint homes with flowering gardens, eccentric details, and sculpted balconies weave an intriguing architectural quilt. The house where poet Pablo Neruda created many of his greatest works is on Calle A. Márquez de la Plata.

Fruit and antiques: Santiago has markets filled with vendors and customers haggling over the price of anything from exquisite antiques to a kilo of oranges.

The **Mercado Franklin** (four blocks east of the metro Franklin) is a weekend flea market that winds several blocks through an abandoned slaughter house. It offers everything from tarnished silver platters, to old books, records and plumbing supplies.

Six blocks north of the Plaza de Armas along the Mapocho River is the fresh food center, **Mercado Central**. The seafood pavilion is known for cafes that offer generous helpings of seafood at a low price.

Santiago is also a city where one finds high fashion at a reasonable price. Uptown is the **Los Leones** area on Calle Providencia (Metro Los Leones), a clean neighborhood of the affluent, where several chic boutiques and stores are located. **Parque Arauco** (Avenida Kennedy 5413) and **Apumanque** (Avenida Apoquindo/Manquehue) are fashion malls on the upper-east side of the city.

The recent relaxation of censorship laws has brought a spate of lurid new publications.

AROUND SANTIAGO

Santiago is an urban outpost surrounded by the majesty of the Andean mountains, the tranquility of rural valley communities, and the cool breezes of the coast. Travelers can easily hire a car or hop on a bus for a day to explore the variety of landscapes that lie within a few hours of the capital.

On the eastern end of the city at the foot of the Andean mountains is **El Pueblito de los Domínicos**. A creek meanders through the small village, around a cluster of adobe huts with thatched roofs. The sounds of craftsmen at work drift from the workshops where they produce leather, ceramics, metals and other materials. In **Las Condes**, people still ride their horses around nearby **Lo Barnechea**. Each weekend vendors set up an antique fair in the shadow of the town's adobe church.

Above Lo Barnechea, **El Arrayán** has become a refuge for city dwellers who have built comfortable and breezy homes on the Arrayán River valley. The **Santuario de la Naturaleza** is a park that follows the narrow Arrayán canyon. Trails wind along the river, occasionally dipping into the turgid waters, then moving up the steep canyon walls.

The Maipo Canyon: Santiaguinos venture to the **Cajón del Maipo** on weekends to take afternoon tea, nibble on *empanadas* and *kuchen* (strudel) and relax in little towns and trails along the 40-mile canyon. The valley has distinct characteristics. A sinuous road leads from **Puente Alto** southeast, against the current of Maipo and its tributaries, to finally reach its source near the 16,600-ft (5,000-meter) extinct volcano, **El Morado**. Arid peaks with names like **Punta Negra**, **Peladero**, **Lomo del Diablo** and **Yerba Buena**, meld with the changing day's sun, turning from green and brown in the day, to blue, pink, orange and red before disappearing at dusk. The narrow valley floor is lush and intensively cultivated with vineyards and pasture land. But the canyon walls open up contrasting activities: hiking, swimming, camping, or scaling the rocky peaks. There are picnic areas close to the road including **El Raco**, a wooded area with a lagoon; **Peumos del Canelo**, a grassy meadow; **las Vertientes**, an inn with a pool alongside the river; and **Fundo Estero del Manzano**, a swimming area surrounded by mountains.

Fifteen miles (25 km) from Puente Alto is **San José de Maipo**. The town was founded in 1791 when miners discovered silver in the surrounding hills, and its adobe homes and central square are testimonials to the past. At **San Alfonso** (km 40) there is hiking and camping at the **Las Animas Waterfall** facing the canyon wall. The road forks at **San Gabriel** (km 47) where the mountains darken, and the air grows thinner.

Lo Valdés (km 70) is on the southern fork of the road, a veritable oasis on the semi-arid slopes of the Morado volcano and other peaks. The **Refugio Alemán** is a pleasant inn with extensive trails to explore the snowcapped peaks surrounding the area. Nearby, **Baños de Colina** are natural hot springs in a small valley with magnificent views of the Andes and the valley below.

South of Puente Alto across the boulder-strewn Maipo River ravine is **Pirque**, an extensively irrigated area that is the birthplace of Chile's best wines. The **Reserva Nacional Río Clarillo** is in the midst of a semi-arid area where the best of indigenous cacti and flora flourish in an expansive preserve along the Río Clarillo.

Lakes to the south: Spanish aristocrats used to vacation on the sandy shores of **Laguna de Aculeo** during colonial times. The lake fills a valley 37 miles (60 km) from the capital in a wooded mountain setting. There are camping facilities, hotels and several restaurants along the shore. Twenty years ago the government built a dam where the **Tinguiririca** and **Cachapoal rivers** meet, forming the nation's largest man-made lake. **Rapel Lake** provides waterskiing, swimming and fishing.

Skiing in the Andes: The omnipresence of dizzying Andean peaks in Chile makes it one of the finest ski centers in the world. There is an abundance of natural snow on some of the most challenging runs in the world which can be enjoyed from June to September. Three resorts are within sight of Santiago.

Farellones-Colorado and **La Parva** are two ski villages above El Arrayán, just 30 miles (50 km) from Santiago, along a sinuous road that is little more than a succession of 50 hairpin curves.

Valle Nevado is a posh resort built in 1988 by the owners of Les Alps in France. It is set in a remote valley above Farellones. There is a four-star hotel and eight lifts go to slopes as high as 37,700 ft (11,500 meters) above sea level.

Portillo is one of the most famous resorts in South America, located 29,500 ft (9,000 meters) above sea level in an Andean pass 4 miles (7km) from the Argentine border at Mendoza.

A world of pottery: Pomaire (35 miles/ 60 km southwest of Santiago) has become a part of nearly every Chilean household. Pottery made from the dark clay scraped from Mallarauco Mountains is what makes this picturesque town thrive. The clay is hand-shaped into pottery and sculpture, and fired in large rustic stone ovens to be sold in the dozens of adobe homes along the dusty main street. Pomaire is also famous for restaurants that serve homemade *empanadas* and *pastel de choclo*, a delicious corn pastry.

The Pacific coast: Algarrobo (70 miles/ 110 km west of Santiago) became a resort in the late 1800s and is known for its calm seas, long sandy beaches and elegant vacation homes. Nearby **El Quisco** is a tranquil town with wide beaches complementing a small fishing port and yacht club.

Isla Negra (2½ miles/4 km south) is hidden within a cool pine forest. Its rocky coast is battered by great swells that send a delicate mist over the magnificent homes on the hills above. Nobel Poet Laureate Pablo Neruda's enchanted home is there, on a bluff above the sea. The home was sealed when Neruda died in 1973, but it is easy to spot the window where the poet pondered the sea that inspired many of his works.

athering the rapes in a ineyard near antiago.

WINE COUNTRY

The conquistadors introduced vineyards in Chile in the 16th century in order to supply the symbol of Christ's blood for the Catholic communion. Small wineries were nurtured on *haciendas* in the **Maipo Valley** throughout the colonial period by patrons doing their part for the church. Today wine is one of Chile's finest products, usually served for a purpose that is rarely spiritual.

The first commercial vineyard was established in 1851 when Silvestre Ochagavía brought French vine stock to the Maipo valley. Mining magnates began to build extensive irrigation projects as they invested in agriculture, and the vineyards spread further from the river banks.

Other land-owners started vineyards, and soon discovered that the lime-heavy soil, elevation and dry climate in the valley were the formulae for producing world-class wines.Chileans boast that when the French vines were decimated by a fungus in the late 19th century, their vines were rushed across the Atlantic to replenish the stricken vineyards. The larger labels outgrew the confines of the valley in the early 1900s and new wineries sprung up near **Los Andes** and **Rancagua**. Today, the finest reserves carry the mark of *Cajón del Maipo,* near Santiago.

Harvest time: The Maipo Vally is alive in March during the *vendímia*, or harvest, when grapes are transported to the presses in huge casks, and the air fills with the sweet smell of grapes. Many wineries have experts who provide advise on how to stock your cellar with the best of the season's run.

Several wineries are open to the public, with informative tours and generous tastings. To be lost in the cellars and vineyards of some of the best labels in the world is a connoisseur's idea of heaven, and for the novice, they are the place to go for an interesting lesson on the varieties of the much-acclaimed nectar whose different characteristics

A winemaker samples his produce in a Chilean Bodega.

are always heard about, but never quite understood.

Around the capital: The grounds of the Viña Cousiño Macul on the outrskirts of **Santiago** are themselves a work of art. It has been in the ssame family hands since 1856. A central lagoon is stocked with water fowl from around the world, surrounded by splendid hardwoods and flowering magnolias, meticulously cared for over the years. The cellars are grand stone structure where choice bottles are available for the buying.

Viña Santa Carolina, founded in the **Ñuñoa** neighborhood in Santiago (near the Estadio Nacional) in 1875, is named after the owner's wife. Though the vines have been transplanted to Molina and San Fernando, the stately colonial Casa Patronal remains, with the cellars nearby.

An hour's drive from Santiago in the direction of **Cajón del Maipu**, is Viña Concha y Toro. Melchor Concha y Toro founded the winery in 1883, and it is now the largest in Chile with more than 10 vineyards in Maipo, San Fernando and Rancagua. The original vineyard and cellars are open to the public and a visit could include a weekend trip to the mountains.

About 20 miles (32km) from Santiago, on the road to **Melipilla**, is Viña Undurraga, founded in 1885 by Francisco Ramón Undurraga. Undurraga imported select vines from France and, a first for Chile, German stock from the Rhine Valley. Like many of the other wine-makers, he also has French experts to instil the knowledge that has long since been mastered by the Chileans. Undurraga built his cellars and a magnificent colonial mansion to entertain guests, among whom is included the Duke of Windsor and the kings of Belgium and Norway. You, too, can go there today.

In 1927, José Canepa acquired choice parcels of wine country, and planted Cabernet Sauvignon, Sauvignon Blanc, and Rieseling vines in the Maipo Valley, Curicó and Lontué. This is the most modern winery in South America, and its plant on **Camino Lo Sierra** is open to the public.

'he vats.

THE MYSTICAL NORTHERN DESERTS

Northern Chile has a mysticism that sets it apart from the south. Much of the 1,100 miles (1,900 km) from Santiago to Arica seem silent, a landscape sprinkled with whitewashed adobe villages trapped by the **Atacama Desert**. Faces lose the European features of the south, and Quechua and Aymará meld with the Spanish. Society bends the rules of Catholicism, and visits by extra-terrestrials find their way into the folklore.

City amongst the sand dunes: Arica (pop. 139,000) is surrounded by the immense Atacama dunes and the sea. The downtown streets are filled with markets and stores catering to Peruvian and Bolivian smugglers who procure goods to sell across the border. Arica is also known for its beautiful beaches and late-night discos.

Plaza Aduana is a cool respite from the desert sun. **Iglesia de San Marco** (1876) nearby, is a wrought iron sanctuary designed by Gustave Eiffel. The **Morro de Arica** is a huge mountain with magnificient views of the city, the Pacific, and the desert. A museum in an old fortress recalls the battle for Arica during the War of the Pacific (1879), when Chilean troops took the city from the Peruvians.

Several travel firms offer day trips to **Lago Chungará** to the east near Bolivia, a magnificent journey up a harrowing ascent to the lake on the *altiplano* (high arid plain) at 14,500 ft (4,400 meters). The emerald lake is surrounded by snow colored peaks that rise high above the shoreline and there is a species of black ducks found only there.

Chungará is in **Parque Nacional Lauca**, where alpacas, vicuñas (deer-like llamas), vizcachas (large hares) and white geese with black-tipped wings mill along the road.

Copper mines and volcanoes: Calama (pop. 83,000) is a grimy mining center servicing the Chuquicamata copper mine, 10 miles (16 km) away. Wisps of sulfur vapor from the mine linger among

The Atacama desert is one of the driest on earth.

iew of Arica.

its bars, cheap hotels and restaurants.

There are free tours of Chuquicamata, the world's largest open-pit copper mine. It produces 750,000 tons of copper a year, and its dimensions are mind-boggling: a pit 15,800 ft (4,800 meters) long, 8,200 ft (2,500 meters) wide, and 2,000 ft (610 meters) deep, where 150 giant trucks remove 600,000 tons of ore per day. Three hours on the sinuous road to Bolivia is **Géiser del Tatío**, an impressive field of scalding geysers surrounded by high Andean peaks.

The village oasis of **San Pedro River** is 58 miles southeast of Calama. It was the most populated Atacamanian town in pre-Columbian times, only to be conquered by the Incas in 1450, and by Pedro de Valdivia in 1540. Nearby is the **Salar de Atacama** and enormous snow-capped volcanoes, including the **Licancabar**, which, at 19,300 ft (5,600 meters) is the highest in South America.

The beautiful white **Iglesia de San Pedro** (1641) is constructed of the same white *adobe* as that of the town. Next door is the impressive **Museo Arqueológico**, founded in 1955 by the Belgian missionary, Gustavo Le Paige. It traces the history of the region, and has a fine collection of pottery, mummies, and ancient Indian vestments.

The **Pukara de Quitor** is nearby, a mountainside stone fortress built by the Atacamanians against the Incan siege.

The **Valle de la Luna** (20 miles/32 km on a very bumpy road) is a mysterious valley in the midst of the desert endowed with supernatural qualities. The valley is ringed by mountains whose jagged, white ridges contrast with the dark valley floor. At twilight its formations turn brilliant colors while salt crystals in the valley shimmer in the moonlight.

On the coast west of **Copiapó** in the Third Region are **Caldera** and **Bahía Inglesa**, which comprise three successive bays with long, unspoiled beaches and warm water year-round.

Link with the past: La Serena (pop. 83,000) a quaint colonial city founded in 1543 to link Santiago with Peru, is known for its 26 churches that served many weary travelers. Remodeled in the 1950s, it is considered one of the pleasantest towns in Chile for its many gardens and buildings.

The **Iglesia San Francisco** (1627) on Calle Balmaceda has a baroque facade, with Muslim details in the interior. The **Mercado La Recova** has a good selection of regional crafts.

Tongoy (38 miles/61 km south) is a summer resort on a high peninsula overlooking the Pacific, with expansive, white beaches, restaurants and hotels.

Along the Elqui River is the narrow, serpentine **Valle del Elqui**. This lush refuge is famous for its clear blue skies, dry mountain air, steep arid mountains, and intensely cultivated pastures and vineyards that are the source of the national liquor, Pisco.

Monte Grande is a small village along the river where the Nobel prize-winning poet Gabriela Mistral spent her infancy. Her tomb is on the road to Cochiguaz. There are a number of communes in the area whose inhabitants practice meditation in what is considered to be a focal point of mystical energy.

VALPARAÍSO, AN ENCHANTED TOWN

The port of **Valparaíso**, 75 miles (120km) north of Santiago, is an enchanted town where a map is unnecessary and wandering is bliss. It is a city with a dual personality, split between the geographically flat port area and the 17 hills that tower above the bay. The port is a picaresque place with a strange brew of sailors, prostitutes, vagabonds and tourists. The hills (*cerros*) are an impressive maze of colorful homes, winding streets, narrow alleys, rickety elevator trams, hidden plazas and treacherous stairways that cling delicately to the precipitous slopes.

Muelle Pratt is the oldest part of Valparaíso's port, dating to its foundation in the 16th century. To the west is **Caleta El Membrillo**, where fishermen unload their catch. Nearby are weathered *picadas* with the freshest seafare in the city.

The nearby **Cerro Santo Domingo** is a spontaneous maze of streets and stately homes built by the emigrant merchants who founded Valparaíso.

Heading ups and downs: Valparaíso's *ascensores* are the best guide to the upper-city. For a few pesos, these romantic wooden trams make harrowing ascents to the neighborhoods high on the *cerros*. Ascensor Artillería (1893) first ran on coal, and goes to Avenida 21 de Mayo, providing a fantastic view of the bay. **Paseo Yugoslavo** is a promenade that winds along Cerro Alegre. The mountain is sprinkled with homes and gardens dating back to the early 1900s. Alegre is reached by the Ascensor El Peral.

Ascensor Concepción (1833) is the oldest elevator,reaching a neighborhood dating to the 19th century. Homes along **Paseo Atkinson** are simple, wooden structures that creep up the mountainside. **Iglesia Anglicana San Pablo** (1858) was built by British emigrants. Ascensor Barón serves the panoramic **Mirador Diego Portales** on the wes side of the bay. **Convento and Iglesia San Francisco** (1845) was also used as a lighthouse to guide ships into the port.

Southern Beaches: A road along seaside cliffs leads 11 miles (18 km) south to **Laguna Verde**, a small fishing village set in a cove and surrounded by pine-studded mountains. Its long, white beach remains unspoiled.

Quintay, 28 miles (45 km) from Valparaíso, is a fishing port surrounded by rocky cliffs. The beach is expansive, with fine white sand and provisions for camping. The fisherman's port was once a whaling station, and the abandoned facility is an eerie reminder of the past.

Viña del Mar, the garden city, is the Pacific resort – a cosmopolitan city with a spicy mix of beaches, lush gardens and nightlife. Viña is taken over in the summer by thousands of Chileans and Argentines who crowd the expensive nightspots and show-off their bodies on its golden, albeit polluted beaches.

A century ago Viña was the retreat for affluent *porteños* from Valparaíso. They built mansions with large gardens that later became the city's parks.

The **Quinta Vergara** is Viña's most

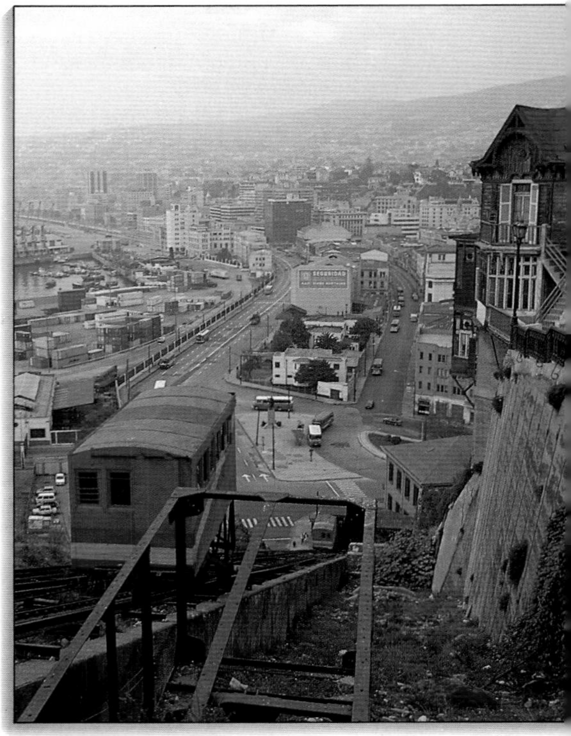

Elevators scale the different levels of Valparaíso.

elegant park, filled with exotic plants from around the world. The **Palacio Vergara** (1908) was built by Viña's founders and today houses the **Museo de Bellas Artes**. The **Anfiteatro** hosts the International Festival of Song held in February.

La Plaza is the palm-filled central square in the center of old Viña with the neo-classic **Club de Viña** (1910), **Teatro Municipal** (1930), **Hotel O'Higgins** (1935), and the **Casa Subercaseaux** on its borders.

Calle Valparaíso is a magnet to Viña's summer hustle. The pedestrian street leading west of the Plaza teems with the after-dinner resort crowd on the prowl for cafes and shopping malls. There is also an artisan fair with a good selection of crafts from across Chile.

Cerro Castillo, at the end of Calle Valparaíso, is an opulent hill sprinkled with turn-of-the-century mansions and terraces overlooking the bay. Calle Alamos winds up the hill, past Castillo Brunet and the presidential palace. The Hotel Miramar is one of the most exclusive in Viña, with terraces and a pool overlooking sea.

Avenida Peru is a misty promenade following the shore north of Cerro Castillo. The **Casino Municipal** is the premier gambling house on the Pacific side of the continent, where South America's rich play for high stakes as tourists watch in awe.

The promenade continues along Avenida San Martín, bordering long beaches mobbed by tourists in the summer. **Reñaca**, 5 miles (8 km) north, is the chic place to be at in the season. Its one-mile-long beach lies below rocky mountains covered with fashionable apartments and hotels accessible by little trams and stairways.

Horcón is a sleepy fishing village that is the legendary center of Chile's counter culture. It is set on a rocky peninsula 55 miles (90 km) north of Viña del Mar, in the midst of a eucalyptus forest with a small wharf crowded with colorful skiffs. Tourists, hippies and gnarly fishermen provide a peculiar melange in the village today.

. horse and uggy ride in 'iña del Mar.

THE LAKE DISTRICT

The Lake District is a land of extreme beauty, a seemingly endless succession of lush alpine valleys surrounded by low Andean hills and glowing, snow-covered volcanoes. The lakes, formed by the abrasive retreat of glaciers that once covered the region, are jewels of nature, whose bitter-cold waters reflect the marvels of the region. Just half of the region's population lives in the cities, and a visit to the area is a soothing journey into a tranquil wilderness, a euphoric escape from the bustle of urban life.

This natural paradise was once a forbidden fruit to outsiders. The Auraucanian Indians wiped out every settlement south of the Bío Bío River at the end of the 16th century, and the region was a dangerous place for the white man until the 1880s when the Indians were finally defeated.

A base for exploration: Concepción, Chile's second largest city (pop. 250,000) on the banks of the mighty Bío Bío, was little more than a garrison town until 1818 when Bernardo O'Higgins declared Chile's independence from Spain there. Take a stroll on the pedestrian streets near the plaza to get a feel for the downtown area. Four blocks south is **Parque Ecuador**, which winds up **Cerro Caracol** for a good view of the city. North is the **Universidad de Concepción**, a grassy campus founded in 1919.

About 18 miles east of Los Angeles, deep within a wooded Andes valley is **Salto del Laja**, the gateway to the Lake District. The frigid waters of the **Laja River** slice through some of the most beautiful scenery in Chile, and plunge 115 ft (35 meters) into a deep, rocky canyon, eternally bathed in a foggy mist. Within sight of the valley are four volcanoes that rise above the forest.

The road east snakes through huge pine forests, nearing the mountains as the valley narrows and the terrain becomes semi-arid. Huge lava fields lie nearby, flanked by mountain cypress.

The **Parque Nacional Laguna del Laja** is located in a narrow valley. In the center is a 650-ft (200 meters) high volcanic cone that holds the Laja Lagoon, and to the right is the desolate cone of the Laja Volcano. Three of the four lakes in the **Parque Nacional Conguillío** (70 miles/110 km east of Temuco) were formed by the depressions in lava fields left by the Llaima Volcano within the last 50 years. The narrow valley is covered with arucaurias as old as 1,200 years, oaks, and cypresses within sight of the Llaima (3,400 yards/3,100 meters).

Under the volcano: Villarica is one of the main resort centers of the district on the banks of the 440-sq.-mile (1,140-sq.-km) Villarica Lake. Its blue waters change hue as the sun falls, reflecting the perfect cone of the Villarica volcano. There is a Mapuche indian museum near the tourist office, and at Koerner and Pedro de Valdivia there is a replica of a *ruca*, a Mapuche Indian home. The lake is surrounded by pasture and dense forests and is scarred by

eft, bringing n the crops. **ight**, a ountry etreat.

eruptions from the still-active volcano. At night the volcano glows like the end of a giant cigar.

Pucón, a resort village on the other side of the lake, is a summer haven for affluent Chileans, and its dirt roads are filled with bungalows and hostels run by the German emigrants who have settled in the area. **Parque Nacional Villarica**, on the steep slopes of the volcano, is a bizarre mix of untouched forest and barren lava fields that seared through the woods during a recent eruption. It is possible to hike to the 6,500-ft (1,900 km) peak and peer into the steamy crater, but the weather can turn stormy at a moment's notice, so take care.

The slender **Lago Caburgua** (15 miles/24 km east) was formed when lava flows were blocked by the precipitous, densely-wooded valley. Foot trails lead to the "eagle's nest falls" which are surrounded by lush ferns that thrive on the mist. Three pristine lagoons are hidden in the small valley, and several hot springs, fed by volcanoes, gush from the ground in the area.

"Seven Lakes": The Seven Lakes that give this region its name are **Calafquén**, **Panguipulli**, **Pellaifa**, **Neltume**, **Riñihue**, **Pirehueico**, and **Lacar**, in Argentina. A little-known area, it wasn't really settled until the late 1800s, due to its remote setting and harsh winters. The lakes were formed 10,000 years ago by glaciers that covered the region, leaving behind these deep-blue pools, framed by wooded mountains and volcanoes. They are interconnected by rivers which lead to the Pacific.

Lican Ray was built for tourists on a wooded peninsula overlooking Calafquén Lake. It is said to have the nicest beach in the area and comes alive in the summer when restaurants, hotels and cafes swell with vacationing Chileans.

Panguipulli is a small, picturesque town on the banks of the lake, with an interesting Capuchin mission and church. A road leads to the tip of a wooded peninsula, with sandy beaches on the lake.

The nearby **Huilo Huilo falls** are the highest in Chile. Water shoots into the

Leading the cows home.

Neltume Lake through a lush canyon covered with ferns, and produces an eternal rainbow.

German immigrants: Valdivia sits at the confluence of several waterways that meet at the Valdivia Estuary, and the city was one of the first Spanish settlements in Chile. Its modern face is due largely to the heavy Germanic immigration in the 19th century. The streets follow the sinuous rivers, and **Calle General Lagos** near the waterfront still has remnants of European architecture that the immigrants brought with them.

The port is alive with fishermen and a thriving market. The **Austral Museum** which chronicles the German migration, is on **Teja Island**. Nearby is the **Austral University**, with a large campus along the river.

Valdivia was heavily fortified by the Spanish after 1600 to guard against Indian invasions after it was razed by the Mapuches. The best way to see them is to take a bus or boat tour of the forts along the river: Corral, Castillo de Amargos, Niebla and Mancera.

The nearby city of **Osorno**, 550 miles (880 km) south of Santiago, is the center of a cattle region with 95,000 inhabitants. It lies east to west across the **Rahue River**, surrounded by azure-green pasture lands forever nourished by the area's abundant rainfall. The city was settled by German farmers, and its shingled wooden homes and streets with names like Buschman, Amthauer and Matthei are reminiscent of a distant past. Calle Bulnes is a good street to walk along for a view of the river, but an interesting experience is the morning Feria Ganadera, Chile's largest cattle market, where burly *campesinos* haggle over animals on the block.

Puyehue Lake (37 miles/60 km east) is a popular fishing and camping spot within sight of the low Andes. The Casablanca, Puyehue, Puntiagudo and immense Osorno volcanoes are within sight of the lake's waters. Near the eastern shore are the Puyehue hot springs, which are known by locals for their therapeutic qualities. On the road to the Casablanca volcano is **Aguas Calientes**,

Colorful fishing boats at Puerto Montt.

through a virgin forest with huge ferns, holleys and manios trees.

Picturesque towns creep up to the edge of Llanquihue lake and the perfect cone of the snowcapped Osorno volcano is eternally reflected in its frigid waters. **Puerto Varas** is an immaculately kept town created in 1854 to handle lake commerce to Puerto Montt, 12 miles (19 km) to the south. Today it is a thriving stop-off point for tourists who like to gamble in the casino at Gran Hotel Puerto Varas on the shore.

Frutillar, on the northern lakeshore, is filled with interesting German homes with meticulously kept gardens and its own claim to fame: the southernmost palm tree in the world. During February it hosts the Semanas Musicales de Frutillar, a jazz festival renowned throughout South America.

On the eastern shore is **Ensenada**, a tiny village set in the shadow of the Osorno valcano and surrounded by lush forest cut by lava flows. Just to east (10 miles/16 km) the rapids of the Petrohué River are broken by strange lava formations comprised of thousands of black volcanic stones dating to an ancient eruption. The Petrohué feeds into Lago Todos Los Santos. There are daily boat excursions (at 10.45am) along the length of the lake to **Peulla**, a magnificent journey along shoreline mountains covered in dense virgin forest.

The unkempt gravel road 94 south from **Puerto Varas** to **Cochamó** is a journey through an area of great wilderness beauty. It snakes through the glacial valley, past rocky cliffs, rivers and rugged forest. **Ralún** is a stone structure built centuries ago to shelter the weary traveler along the Reloncaví estuary.

Cochamó is a tiny village on the estuary, a branch off on the Pacific through spectacular fiords that rise up to 4,900 ft (1,500 meters) straight out of the water. At Cochamó you can hire fishermen to give you a tour of the estuary in a skiff, where it's easy to spot seals, 70 lbs (30 kg) groupers, and even whales.

The center of the far south: In 1853 the adventurer Vincente Pérez Rosales founded **Puerto Montt** with a handful of German immigrants intent on settling the Llanquihue province, and the area mushroomed when the railroad arrived 60 years later. Today the city of 84,000 is a grimy port that is the gateway to Chiloé and the Patagonia frontier.

Despite its size, Puerto Montt has a small-town feeling. Many of the homes are of northern Germanic design: wooden, with pitched roofs, ornate balconies, and shingles well-weathered by the region's eternal drizzle. The cathedral in the central square is the city's oldest building, made of redwood.

Puerto Montt faces the Reloncaví sound, and a walk along the waterfront is a good introduction to the city. **Angelmó**, a contiguous fishing port, is a jewel of indigenous maritime activity. Shacks on the pier offer fresh *erizos*, *locos*, and other cold water seafare, and burly fishermen mend their nets by the skiffs on the shore. The pier is lined with artisan shops that sell a wide selection of woolen goods and wood carvings. Young boys will row you across to **Tenglo Island**, where you can walk around its fishing communities.

The fish markets of Puerto Montt.

CHILEAN PATAGONIA: THE RUGGED SOUTH

South of Puerto Montt, the land and sea become one as the country breaks into a maze of islands, fiords, rivers with myriad tributaries, lakes and wooded mountains with trees a thousand years old, Chilean Patagonia is a place of intense beauty that has somehow escaped the ravages of man.

Myth and mystery: The island of **Chiloé** emerges just out of sight of Puerto Montt – a romantic place filled with picturesque villages, a hundred tiny enchanted islands, misty waterways, and little wooden homes. It is a land cloaked in a mystical fog that awakens with the sun in lush-green forests, cool Pacific waters, and panoramic views of the Andes.

Chiloé is steeped in fishing tradition, and the magic of its culture attracts trekkers searching for the charm, customs, legends and folklore of the friendly people who live there. It is home to lively dances like the *cueca* and *vals*, local dishes like *curanto*, drinks like *chicha de manzana*, and a slew of legends, festivals and rituals all its own. Somehow it has held onto its oldest traditions.

The island is known for its 150 wooden *capillas* with distinctive shingled steeples, porticos, and glass-paned windows and three doors. Several times a year the island erupts in the largest religious festivals in Chile.

But Chiloé's people cling to paradoxical legends that explain the unthinkable: *el trauco*, a mysterious old man who leaves young women unexpectably pregnant during late night visits, or *caleuche*, a magical ship of endless party cheer that seduces fisherman who are lost forever on the high seas.

Ancud is the largest town in Chiloé with narrow streets packed with wooden commercial buildings reminiscent of its heyday as a bustling port. The **Museo Regional**, in an old fortress near the water, chronicles the history and culture of Chiloé and has numerous interesting artifacts.

Chopping wood on Chiloé.

The road south to **Quemchi** snakes past an eastern coastal area settled by European families: along gulfs that cut into the island, small inlets with oyster beds, and a few glimpses of the wooded interior mountains.

Castro (pop. 3,570) is one of the oldest cities in Chile (founded in 1567) on the shores of a protected fiord. The **Iglesia San Francisco de Castro** is an unusual wooden cathedral on the plaza. The **Museo Municipal Etnológico** explains the island traditions. In February the Festival Costumbrista Chilote is a marvelous display of island culture. There are a few *palafitos*, or rows of small houses on stilts by the water, where fishermen park their skiffs.

Nearby **Dalcahue** is famous for its Sunday artisan fair, where you can swap a pair of blue jeans for one of the fine woollen sweaters the island is well-known for.

Chonchi (16 miles/26 km south of Castro), known as the "three-floor city", is built on the side of a cliff overlooking the water. There is a nice church among several colorful *casonas* made of cypress with well-kept gardens.

Queilen is a picturesque town situated in a narrow peninsula with long beaches at each end, and elegant old homes dating back to its founding as an emigrant colony in 1900.

Ferries leave from Quellón, the southernmost port on the island.

Southern frontier: The Region Aisén del General Ibáñez del Campo, south of Chiloé, is a remote area and a visit to it gives the sensation of penetrating a new frontier. The Carretera Austral road was finished in 1988 to open up new territory for expansion, but that has yet to happen.

The region from Puerto Montt to Cochrane is still a place untouched by man, save a few fishermen and farmers. It is an amazing landscape where rocky cliffs drop into lush river valleys, dense jungles are bordered by glaciers, and turgid rivers lead to pristine lakes and the southern Andes.

With patience you can hitch during the summer, but unpredictable weather and scanty traffic pretty much rules it out in the winter. Car is the best way to go, and don't waste too much time in the towns. Bring a tent.

Chaitén (pop. 2,400) is a coastal town accessible by a six-hour ferry from Chonchi or by the carretera (km 56) offering food and lodging and nice views of the ocean and mountains. **Santa Bárbara**, 7 miles (11 km) to the north is a picturesque fishing village along a wide beach.

Emerald waters: The south is a contrasting mix of lush forest, waterfalls emerging from icy cliffs, glaciers, and valleys flanked by the icy slopes of the Andes. The road goes past the emerald green waters of Velcho Lake, Michimahuida Volcano, Villa Santa Lucía, Futaleufú and Palena.

From Santa Lucía the road follows the Río Frío along a wooded valley, reaching **La Junta** at the confluence of three rivers where there are excursions to **Lago Rossellot**, in the midst of virgin forests and **Lago Verde**.

The road continues to **Lago Risopatrón** and **Termas de Puyuhuapi**.

Produce for sale in Punta Arenas.

Nearby **Parque Nacional Queulat** is a glacial park with amazing views of the *ventisqueros*, or glaciers.

Puerto Cisne is a small village on the beach with hotels, restaurants and transport facilities. The town was colonized by Germans and Italians at the turn of the century.

Coyhaique is a large town (37,000) that is a good jumping-off point for exploring the region. Founded in 1929, it is largely a government and military center. The **Museo Regional de la Patagonia** is a good introduction to the region's history.

South of the city the land turns rugged, with trees giving way to weathered scrub, and boulders breaking through the soil. The steppe grasses begin to appear, buffetted by a wind that never ceases. The area was settled by ranchers who made their fortunes with enormous sheep and cattle *fundos*.

Puerto Aisén (pop. 13,050) is a beautifully kept town, founded to service the growing ranches in 1914.

In the region is **Laguna San Rafael**, a pristine lake which is only accessible after a journey through the fiords and archipelagos where the land meets the sea. The lake is enclosed by the **San Valentine Glacier**, which sends huge blocks of 20,000-year-old ice crashing into the water as it makes its way to the sea. A few firms offer cruises there from Puerto Montt, including luxury cruises lasting up to a week.

About 60 miles (95km) south of Puerto Aisén is **Lago General Ibañez**, the second largest lake in South America. It is a deep-blue body of water that juts into Argentina, with views of the vast pampa to the east, toward the Atlantic Ocean.

On the Chilean side it is bordered by barren, rocky mountains eroded by glaciers. Several towns with lodgings are on the shore, including **Puerto Ibañez**, **Chile Chico** and **Cochrane**.

The remote Magallanes: The southernmost province of Magallanes is a solitary place with towns called **Porvenir** (Future) and **Ultimo Esperanza** (Last Hope) that try to shake the feeling you have reached the end of the world.

A 19th-century emetery on a heep *stancia*, hilean Tierra el Fuego.

Punta Arenas (pop. 80,000) is a port city on the rolling hills above the barren, wind-swept steppe on the Straits of Magellan. It is a peculiar part of the world: the sky looks bigger here, people seem distant and less open to outsiders, while the sun glares due to years of man's abuse of the ozone layer.

Punta Arenas is known for its monuments to Yugoslav settlers and ranchers who pioneered the region. The **Magallanes Regional Museum** is a fascinating trip back in time, to the days before the Panama Canal opened, when the city boomed as the port of call at the tip of South America. **Cerro La Cruz** has good views of the city and across the straits to Tierra del Fuego.

An interesting stop is the **Zona Franca**, where you can find anything from lipstick to the finest French furs, all tax-free.

The **Tierra del Fuego**, a foreboding place across the straits from Punta Arenas, was discovered as Magellan struggled to make the passage to the Pacific in 1520. In the late 19th century the land was settled by a few ranchers who came from Yugoslavia and England to start huge sheep ranches, and cash in on the gold rush of 1881.

The wooded mountains and swamps on the western side of the island are cold and snowy in the long winter, and the rainforests on the eastern side are warmer, though wetter. And the wind never stops on the treeless pampas facing Punta Arenas where hundreds of ranches prosper.

Porvenir is the largest town (pop. 4,500) on the island, settled primarily by Yugoslavs. See the Tierra del Fuego museum. You can take a ferry across the straits from Punta Arenas to the Porrenir docks, where a sign gives the distance to every port of Chile, as well as to Belgrade. The town itself is quiet and sleepy, apparently unchanged since the turn of the century. From these, a road continues onto the Argentine side of the island and to the icy waters of Cape Horn – passing the southernmost piece of inhabited land on earth.

Right, a ranger in his wet-weather uniform at the Paine National Park.

TORRES DEL PAINE, WONDERFULLY WILD

Hidden at the far south of the Andes mountain chain, the **Torres del Paine National Park** is one of the newest nature reserves in South America. Unlike most of the range in Peru and Bolivia, this 630 sq mile (1,630 sq km) wilderness is uninhabited. But *aficionados* agree that the unique physical formations of the Paine (pronounced *pie-nee*), crowded with glaciers, lakes and animals, offer the most magnificent walking in the world. The best time to be there is December to March.

The jumping-off point for the National Park is **Puerto Natales**, a small and sleepy town set beside the Ultimo Esperanza Gulf. It boasts a few family hotels and restaurants serving the local speciality, king crab. Tour boats head out from Natales to nearby glaciers, and not far away is a huge cave where a prehistoric Myladon sloth was found frozen several years ago – today a picnic spot with a plastic replica of the animal installed.

But most people visit Puerto Natales to arrange a trip to the Paine, whether for a single day or over a week. Every morning in summer, and several times weekly at other times of the year, vans and buses make the three-hour drive along a rough dirt road to the park. The trail winds through mountain passes before descending to the foot of the Andean range, providing the first view of the **Cuernos del Paine** (horns of the Paine): twisted pillars of gray granite dusted with snow, invariably surrounded by billowing clouds.

As everywhere else this far south in the continent, weather in the Paine can be unpredictable, to say the least. The best times to visit are January to April, but even then clear skies are rare and can disappear within minutes. The famous **Torres del Paine** (towers) are even more spectacular than the Cuernos, but often difficult to see because of the changeable weather. The one thing that never seems to change is the gusting

The guanacos of the Paine National Park.

Patagonian wind, driving cold from the plains to the west.

All visitors to the park must sign on at the administration building, where *guardaparques* will give advice on condition of the trails. Hotel accommodation can be found at the **Hostería Pehoe** on a lake and the **Posada Rio Serrano**, an eccentricly converted *estancia* house. Its restaurant has mysterious sculptures made from bulbous wooden roots.

Day trips: There are several day trips that can be made from these bases, or more ambitious walks can be planned. The park has over 150 miles (250 km) of walking treks, including a seven-day circuit. Along the way are *refugios* or shelters, often primitive wood and corrugated iron edifices that barely keep out the wind and rain – sleeping bags or rugs, as well as cooking gear, are essential. Since the walking can be strenuous, people choose to make two or three day walks rather than the full circuit.

Those who make the effort are rewarded with some extraordinary views of snow-covered peaks, turquoise lakes and lush valleys. The trails are lined with orange, red and purple flowers, sometimes crossing wide pastures, other times hugging mountain sides. Much of the park is lushly forested, although a recent worm plague has left whole areas covered by dead, gray trees. The walks pass the Grey and Dickman glaciers, which can be climbed over and into.

Most routes allow walkers to see plenty of animals, most commonly the guanacos: unlike in other parts of South America, they appear unafraid of people and can be easily photographed from up close. Condors cruise between mountain peaks, hares and foxes dash about in the scrub and swans can be seen on many of the lakes.

Although the weather can turn from fair to foul and back again within minutes, the memories of the park will last well after your clothes have dried. Many people who go for a day end up staying a week: the liberating sensation of being in one of the most remote and untouched wilderness areas on earth is worth savoring for as long as possible.

/ild scenery t the end of ıe world.

EASTER ISLAND

Hidden in the endless wastes of the blue Pacific, nearly 2,500 miles (4,000 km) from the coast of Chile, the small remnant of volcanic rock named Easter Island was once the most isolated place to live on earth. But since the 1970s the Polynesian culture that left behind huge and inexplicable statues has drawn increasing attention from around the world.

Where once only one ship a year made the visit to the island, todayflights arrive regularly from Santiago. Using the village of **Hanga Roa** as a base, you can spend hours, or days, visiting this tiny south seas triangular outpost which has a population of 2,500 and measures just 15 miles (24km) across).

A puzzling past: Archaeologists now believe that Easter Island may have been first populated as long ago as AD 400. The Norwegian Thor Heyerdahl argued in his famous book *Aku-Aku* that the inhabitants came from South America, noting resemblances between the island culture and that of Tiahuanaco in Bolivia's Lake Titicaca. But in recent years this theory has been discredited and it is widely agreed that the first settlers came from Polynesia, bringing sweet potato, sugar cane and bananas to the fertile ground of the island.

Left in total isolation for centuries, the settlement prospered and spread. It created not only the remarkable stone carving culture whose remains – the famous *maoi* – can still be seen,but also the only writing system, called *rongo rongo*, known in all Polynesia and the Americas.

The first Europeans arrived on Easter Sunday 1722, when the Dutch Admiral Roggeween landed and spent a day ashore, thus giving the island its name. He recorded that the statues were still standing, the lands were neatly cultivated and "whole tracts of woodland" were visible in the distance. The population might have been as large as 12,000 people.

The picture changes in the descriptions of later arrivals. Spanish, English and French explorers in the late 18th century noted that many of the statues had tumbled, little land was under cultivation and the population was merely one thousand.

What had happened in the meantime? Simple: the population of Easter Island had outgrown its resources; the food supply failed, the forests were felled and soil began to erode. Without wood for canoes to escape from the island, tribes turned on one another in wars. The *maoi* were toppled and cannibalism became common.

The resulting ruin is seen by many today as a taste in miniature of what will most probably happen to the Earth in years to come, as the human race consumes the planet's limited resources with increasing voracity.

Grim contact: The tragedy of Easter Island becomes even more dramatic in the 19th century, when whalers and slave traders came to call. Of one thousand natives taken as slaves to the Guano islands off Peru in 1862, only one hun-

eceding ges, left d right, the *aoi* of ster Island, ysterious mnants of a st culture.

dred were released alive – of which only 15 survived the return journey, bringing smallpox to decimate the community.

By 1871, only 175 islanders remained. Today there are over 2,000 people living there, but about a quarter were born on the mainland. The building of an airfield in the 1960s has made the island a tourist attraction, and in recent years, it has become an emergency landing strip for the space shuttle, thus making the leap from the Stone Age to the present complete.

The statues: The most famous attractions of the island are the 600 or so statues (*maoi*), all basically showing the same figure. Just why this particular model was selected is, and probably always will be, a mystery.

The *maoi* is an archetype: a symbol of god and ancestor. Each was placed on a family burial platform – called an *ahu* – and transmitted *mana*, or power, to the living family chief. Sent through the statue's eyes, *mana* meant prosperity and success.

Almost all the statues are carved from the soft volcanic tufa of **Rano Raraku**, many as high as 18 ft (5,5 meters) and weighing many tons. The family dead were usually placed in a vault beneath the statue. It is not difficult to imagine what effect a fully-constructed *ahu* must have had on its family: a great inclined plane, with as many as fifteen *maoi* staring down with gleaming eyes, sending power to the future family.

Starting from **Ahu Vinapu** on the southeast coast of the island, you can visit enough statues in one day to last a lifetime. All were carved at Rano Raraku after around AD 900, where some 400 incomplete pieces remain. Each probably took a year to complete. Once finished, the *maoi* was cut out of the quarry and transported to its *ahu*, some being given heavy "hats", red stone cylinders.

All of the standing *ahu maoi* that can be seen now are modern reconstructions. In the period of the tribal wars, all the *maoi* were toppled to break the *mana* of the family chief they protected.

The most famous of the *maoi* are the

Easter Islan[d] statues.

standing sentinels embedded in the ground on the southern slope of Rano Raraku. It is these haughty-looking, long-nosed, long-eared statues that have typified the mystery of Easter Island in the imagination of the world. These statues remain eyeless: *maoi* were only given eyes once they were raised on *ahus*, at which time the *mana* began to work.

The "Bird Man cult": The most spectacular place on Easter Island is the volcano **Rano Kao**, with its steep crater and multicolored lake. The ruined village of **Orongo**, sitting on steep cliffs above the crashing sea and three foam-washed islands, is surrounded by rocks with "Bird Man" carvings: a man's body is drawn with a bird's head, often holding an egg in one hand.

Fortunately we know quite a lot about the Bird Man cult as it continued up until 1862, and survivors were able to describe it to later investigators. It involves a strange rite that probably began in the period of the wars, symbolizing a wish to escape from the tragedy of confinement on the island. The basis of the cult was finding the first egg laid by the *Manu Tara*, or sacred bird, each spring.

The chief of each tribe on the island sent one chosen servant to Moto Nui, the largest of the islets below Orongo. Swimming across the dangerous waters, the servants or *hopus* spent a month looking for the first egg. When it had been found, the successful *hopu* plunged into the swirling waters, the egg strapped to his forehead, swam to the mainland, and climbed the cliffs to Orongo.

The servant's master, named Bird Man for the year, would be given powers and privileges, although exactly what these were, nobody can say. Today there are more than 150 Bird Man carvings in the area, overlaid with fertility symbols. Nearby are markings and stones that have been interpreted as forming part of a solar observatory, where on the summer solstice the sun can be seen rising over Poike peninsula – one more mysterious attraction on this beautiful and fascinating island in the Pacific.

landers articipate in mu Pakute, e ceremony r Corpus hristi.

URUGUAY: THE ENLIGHTENED REPUBLIC

Writing more than a hundred years ago in *The Purple Land*, W. L. Hudson lavishly praised the democratic spirit of Uruguay: "Here the lord of many leagues of land and of herds unnumbered sits down to talk with the hired shepherd, and no class or caste difference divides them, no consciousness of their widely different positions chills the warm current of sympathy between two human hearts." While Hudson might be guilty of poetic exaggeration, the tiny pastoral country of Uruguay has long been perceived as a model nation, a great exception to the chaotic South American rule.

With only 72,000 sq. miles (186,000 sq. km), Uruguay has been described as a city with a large ranch attached to it. More than half of the country's 3 million inhabitants live in the pretty harbor capital of Montevideo; like some ancient Greek city-state, the capital and the country are often viewed as synonyms, by Uruguayans and visitors.

Travelers to Montevideo tend to agree that the city reminds them of somewhere else. Comparisons are made with Switzerland, for its highly literate, decorous citizenry; with Sweden, for its comprehensive welfare state and secular traditions; with New Zealand for its lush pastureland and huge sheep population. Perhaps the closest analogy to the relationship between Uruguay and neighboring Argentina is that between Canada and the United States. Like Canadians, Uruguayans share a great many cultural traditions with their next-door colossus, and point out their few differences with pride. Uruguayans are generally friendlier, more informal, and less prone to take themselves too seriously than their haughty neighbors across the River Plate. For Argentines, who flock to Uruguay's placid beaches every summer, this little country, *el paisito,* is a reminder not of another place but of another time. The great Argentine poet Jorge Luis Borges described sycamore-lined Montevideo like this: "You are the Buenos Aires we once had, that slipped away quietly over the years...false door in time, your streets contemplate a lighter past."

In the shadow of powerful neighbors: As a small country wedged between two giants – Argentina and Brazil – Uruguay's fate has necessarily been tied to its neighbors. Its first inhabitants were nomadic and warlike Indians known as the Charrua, whose rebellious spirit defeated even the tireless Jesuit missionaries of the 17th century. But in the subsequent wars fought among Europeans over the possession of Uruguay, the Indians got caught in the crossfire and were virtually exterminated; the Indian and *mestizo* population of Uruguay today is miniscule. The majority of today's Uruguayans are of Spanish or Italian descent.

The Portuguese were the first Europeans to settle the region, founding the city of Colonia in 1680. In 1726, Spain established a colony in Montevideo; the two countries battled over the area until Spain won possession in 1726. After the Napoleonic invasion of Spain in 1808, Buenos Aires declared its independence, but the Montevideo *cabildo*, or city government, decided it would be better to be ruled from across the ocean than across the river, and remained loyal to Spain. José Gervasio Artigas, the son of an old landowning family and a noted smuggler, was stirred by Buenos Aires' bid for freedom and assembled a gaucho army to join the Argentines in their fight for independence. But suddenly, in a complete about-face, the government in Buenos Aires agreed to recognize the sovereignty of Spain.

This treachery shocked the Uruguayans into creating their own nation. Artigas organized a massive exodus of 13,000 civilians and 3,000 troops across the Uruguay River, from which point they fought the Buenos Aires troops until they were driven out of Uruguay in 1815. Artigas was thus the anointed leader and father of the Uruguayan nation, but like so many South American liberators, he did not live out a life of honor and tranquility. Attempting to annex some Brazilian territory, he plunged Uruguay into four more years of war and was finally forced into exile in Paraguay.

Preceding pages: Casa Pueblo in Punta del Este, made for painter Paez Vilaró. Left, a Uruguayan gaucho takes *mate* from a gourd – keeping his water hot in a thermos flask.

But the potential for battle monuments on Uruguayan soil was not exhausted. For the next 50 years, civil wars raged between two political forces: the Blancos (whites) and Colorados (reds). Although these factions were to evolve into Uruguay's major political parties, at the time their ideological difference was perhaps comparable to the feuding houses of England's red-and-white War of the Roses. In 1872, in the interest of beef exports, peace was finally established by ceding the Blancos' influence to the countryside and the Colorados' to the city, a division that remains to this day.

A country transformed: How Uruguay emerged from this chaos to the model of civic order that it became during the first half of the 20th century is something of a puzzle. Most historians heap the credit on one man, José Batlle y Ordóñez. The son of a general who occupied the presidency between 1868 and 1872, Batlle (pronounced Ba-zhay) studied law at the University of Montevideo and then went to Paris, where he studied philosophy at the Sorbonne. He returned to Uruguay full of enlightened ideas and became a political journalist, attacking the country's dictators fearlessly. Of one general, Máximo Santos, he wrote: "The national sovereignty, honor, and dignity were crucified by his henchmen." He founded his own newspaper, *El Dia* in 1886, and gradually made his way into politics. In 1898 he became a Senator, and was elected President for the first time in 1903.

Batlle's first term in office was spent quelling another bloody war with the Blancos. On a four-year sojourn in Europe between terms, he was impressed with the Swiss social legislation and state-operated industries, and saw them as the solution to Uruguay's problems. At the beginning of his second term, he began a gradual drive towards sweeping reforms, which produced bills legalizing divorce, abolishing the death penalty, and establishing an eight-hour workday. His two principal aims were to narrow the gap between the rich and poor, and to secularize the state. He insisted that "God" be written in lower-case letters in his newspaper and forbade naming public buildings after saints. His 1918 Constitution provided for such basic rights as complete freedom of the press, the prohibition of arbitrary arrest, and decreed that prisons were for reform, rather than punishment.

After his death in 1929, Batlle's reforms had succeeded in liberalizing both parties. The widespread peace and prosperity of the past decades prevented even the conservative moneyed classes from objecting to the advance of social security and workers' rights.

A *coup d'état* in 1933 temporarily halted progress, but a 1942 constitution provided explicitly for universal health, accident and unemployment insurance, and gave illegitimate children the right to inherit.

End of the welfare state: Through the 1950s, handsome returns on wool and beef exports kept this utopia functioning smoothly, but in the early 1960s, with dropping prices and rising inflation, things began to fall apart. The growing crisis impoverished the overburdened welfare state, and speculation was rampant. In 1966, voters elected Oscar Gestido to the presidency. A Colorado who was considered a capable administrator, Gestido died before completing his year in office. He was replaced by his much more authoritarian Vice-President, Jorge Pacheco, who outlawed the Socialist Party and shut down left-wing newspapers a week after taking office. During this time, a radical group known as the Tupamaros launched a guerilla offensive in aid of the rural poor. They began by hijacking food trucks and raiding gambling casinos, but the violence escalated, and so did Pacheco's repression. In 1970 the Tupumaros kidnapped and then killed an American AID officer named Daniel Mitrione, who was believed to be training local policemen in interrogation techniques. A massive crackdown and military buildup followed, and in 1973 President Bordaberry, intimidated by the restive military, more urban violence and a looming general strike, handed over the government to the armed forces, who shut down congress and instituted a Supreme Military Council as the sole executive and legislative authority.

During the next 12 years of dictatorship, one in every 50 Uruguayans was arrested at some point for presumed subversive activity. One in every 500 was sentenced to six years or more in prison, and some 400,000 fled into exile. In contrast to the thousands executed in Argentina's simultaneous "dirty war", fewer than 300 Uruguayans were killed by the military. But most detainees were tortured, physically and psychologically. Growing civil disobedience, international outcry and a breakdown of the military's neo-liberal economic program pressured the armed forces to step down in 1985, after declaring a blanket amnesty for themselves. Uruguay's transition back to the civilian rule of the Blanco and Colorado parties has been fairly smooth, and there is every reason to believe that the country's entrenched democratic traditions will continue to prevail.

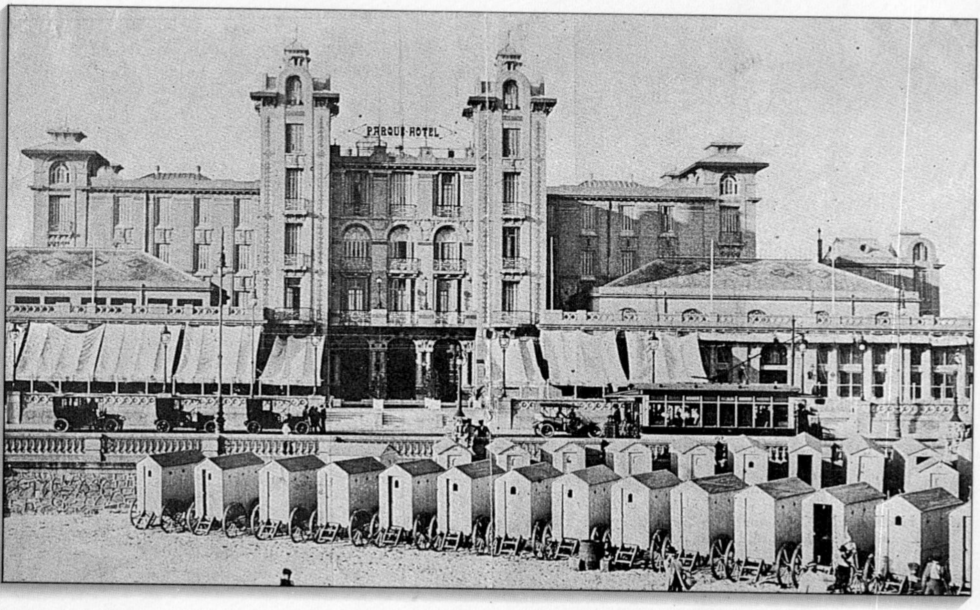

Left, an early 19th-century view of Montevideo harbour. Above, the fashionable Parque Hotel on the Montevideo beach front, c. 1920.

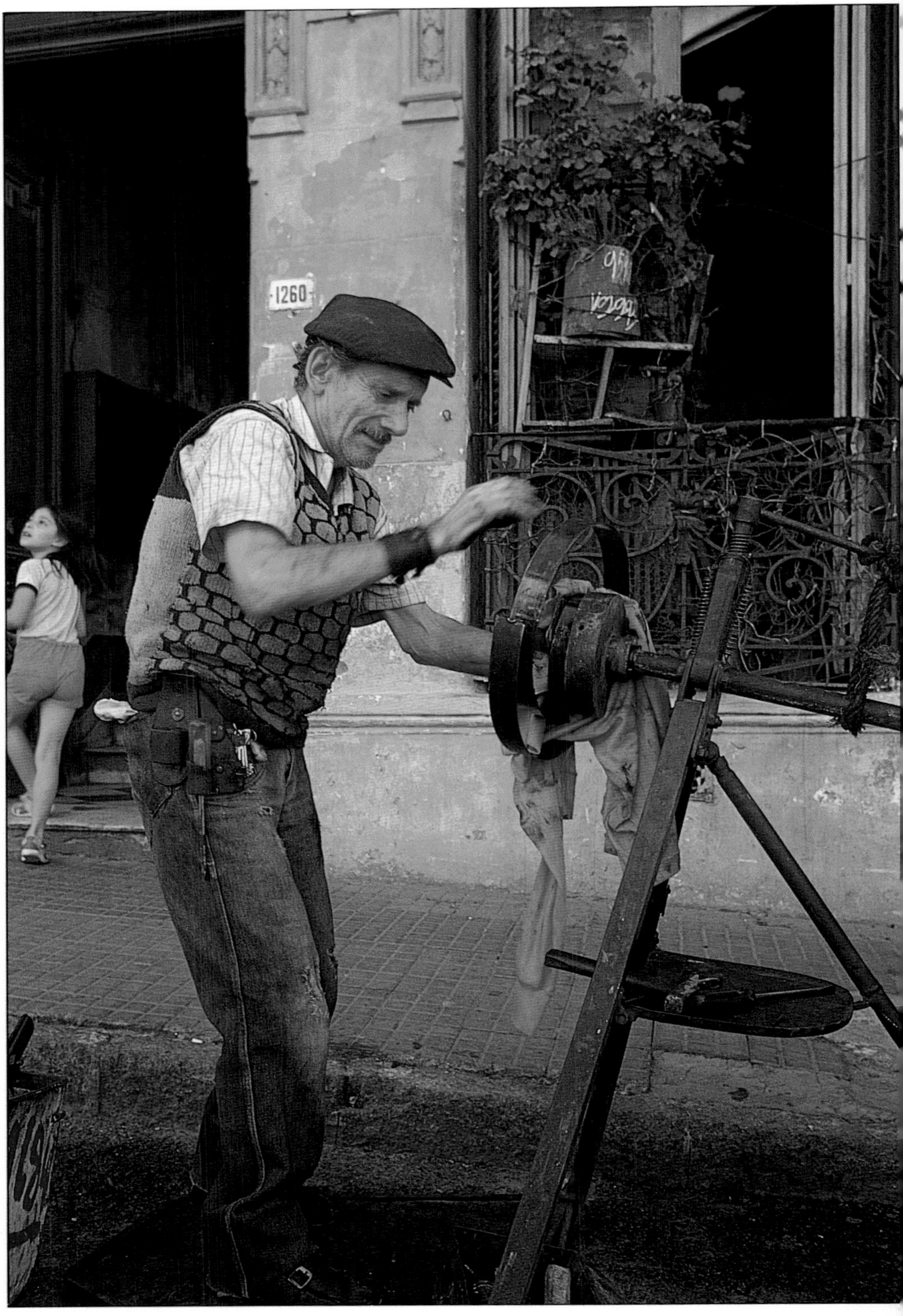
1260

MONTEVIDEO AND THE COAST

One of the most pleasant ways to travel to Uruguay is to cross the River Plate from Buenos Aires. There is a choice of hydrofoil, catamaran and ferry buses, taking between three and four hours to make the trip. From the decks, the low hill that gave Montevideo its name comes slowly into view. The word is supposedly a corruption of a Galician sailor's cry *Monte vi eu*! (I saw a hill!)

Stepping into the past: Landing in Montevideo harbor and walking through the musty customs office may give you the sensation of having traveled back in time. Old British Leyland buses and electric trolleys make their way down cobbled streets jammed with scooters, bicyclists and pedestrians. Because of Uruguay's high import duty on automobiles, many of the cars on Montevideo's streets would be considered antiques elsewhere. (Uruguayan auto mechanics are said to be among the best in the world.) The rural air of the town is reinforced every August with a farm show in the Parque Prado.

With a population of 1.8 million, Montevideo is the only town of any size in Uruguay. The country has an aging population with a median age of 47 (in the United States, it's 32). This is partly because of traditionally small families, but also due to the massive exodus of young people during the military government. Young people continue to leave Uruguay, mostly to seek wider job opportunities in Argentina or the United States. Economic hard times have given Montevideo a genteelly shabby look, although ceremonial occasions such as afternoon tea are as important as they are in Buenos Aires. Uruguayans also cling to such colonial customs as a long lunch followed by a siesta and the perpetual ritual of *mate*; you'll see people with their *mate* gourd and thermos of hot water on buses and in bank lines.

Although Uruguayans tend to use Argentina as a reference point (they call themselves *Orientales*, or Easterners, as opposed to the Argentines to the west), there are some marked differences between Montevideo and Buenos Aires. One is Montevideo's racial mixture. In the 19th century, rumors of fair treatment attracted emancipated slaves from Brazil and Argentina, but they arrived with little notion of how to live as free men. The army offered a familiar regimented life, and many joined the infantry, which reduced their numbers considerably. Uruguayans claim to have no racial prejudice, although blacks tend to occupy the bottom rungs of the economic ladder. A more subtle difference with Buenos Aires is Uruguay's strong secular tradition. The Catholic church plays no role in government, and holidays all have secular names: Christmas is Family Day, Holy Week is Tourism Week.

The best place to begin a tour of Montevideo is at the **Plaza Cagancha** (also called Plaza Libertad), on the main thoroughfare, Avenida 18 de Julio, named after the day in 1829 when Uruguay was finally freed of Argentine and Brazilian control. At the Plaza Cagancha

Preceding pages: Uruguayan girl enjoying the sun at Pocitas, Montevideo. **Left**, quick repair job in the streets of Montevideo. **Right**, looking for bargains at the Tristan Narraja fair held every Sunday.

you'll find the main tourism office, offering brochures and free city maps. If you have traveled by ferry, pause for *café con leche* and homemade croissants at the **Lusitano Café** across the street. From Plaza Cagancha, Av 18 de Julio, a busy thoroughfare, runs downhill, past the **Gaucho Museum** at No 998 (closed Sunday), which has an eclectic collection of items to show cowboy life. The street arrives at the city's main square, **Plaza Independencia**. To the left is an unattractive skyscraper known as the **Palacio Salvo**, which is, mysteriously, a beloved landmark for Montevideans. To the right is the art-deco **Hotel Victoria**, now owned by Moon's Unification Church. In the middle of the square is the subterranean tomb and equestrian statue of Uruguay's great patriot, General José Artigas. Also worth visiting in the square are the cream-colored **Government House**, now used only for ceremonial purposes, and the jewel-like **Teatro Solís**, an exact copy of the Maria Guerrero Theatre in Madrid. Even if you don't have time to attend one of its plays or concerts, you might want to have lunch in the adjacent old-world **Aguila Restaurant**. It's a bit expensive, but the dark mahogany paneling, silver and elegant service give some idea of what Montevideo must have been like in its prosperous heyday.

The Old Town: The archway at the west end of Plaza Independencia is part of the city wall that once protected Montevideo against its many invaders. It marks the entrance to the **Ciudad Vieja**, or Old Town, a neighborhood of narrow, winding streets and turn-of-the-century buildings. The heart of the Old City is **Plaza Constitución**. Here is the old *cabildo*, or town hall. Like the **Cathedral**, also in the square, it's been renovated but retains its colonial appearance. The cathedral dates from the beginning of the 19th century and is the oldest building in the city. The *cabildo* has a good **Museum of National History** dedicated to the history of the city, containing clocks, furniture and portraits. The **Stock Exchange** (La Bolsa), the **Banco da la Republica** and the

The relaxed Plaza del la Independencia

imposing **Customs House** (Aduana) are all north of the plaza and worth a look. Also intriguing is the **Palacio Taranco**, on the **Plaza Zabala**, the former home of a wealthy merchant who imported every stick of furniture and even the marble floors from France.

Following Calle Piedras down to the waterfront leads to the **Mercado del Puerto**, a lively fish market with a series of open-air restaurants at one end. Patrons sit at the counter and watch the chef cook their choice of fish or cut of meat on an enormous charcoal grill. Beef and seafood are both delicious in Montevideo; also try the hero sandwich called a *chivito*, served hot with melted cheese and bacon. Uruguayan beer is very good; it's made with spring water, not River Plate water, as in Buenos Aires.

From the old town there is a view view across the port to the **Cerro**, the 456-ft (139-meter) hill, topped by a lighthouse and fort, which gave the city its name. In 1939 the great German battleship *Graf Spee* was sunk just over a mile (2km) offshore and its anchor can be seen in the port. The city stadium was built using metal plates from the leviathan's salvaged bulkheads.

Resort town: Don't forget that Montevideo is a resort town; if it's warm you should try to visit one of the city's clean white-sand beaches. The city also has two lovely parks of historical interest. The **Prado** is located northwest of downtown (follow Agraciada north from 18 de Julio) in a neighborhood where some of Uruguay's grand old houses are still standing. It was once the property of a 19th-century financier named José Buschental, who built a 175-acre (40-hectare) estate here and married the niece of Emperor Dom Pedro II of Brazil. He brought fish from Asia to stock the streams he created on the property, as well as exotic plants and animals from around the world. This area now has a statue of Buschental, as well as 800 varieties of roses. **Parque Rodó** is located just behind the city's **Ramirez Beach**. Resplendent with palms, eucalyptus, and native ombú trees, the park

n *asado* at
e port
arkets.

was named after José Enrique Rodó, one of the most prominent 19th-century South American writers whose most famous work, *Ariel*, influenced a generation of intellectuals.

Points east: The metropolitan beaches stretch east as far as **Carrasco**, a fashionable suburb of Montevideo whose streets are shaded by big trees and whose houses belong to the few well-to-do people left in Uruguay. Along this lovely beach is the old casino, which still opens every season, though its glory days are long past. Montevideo's international airport lies just beyond Carrasco, 9 miles (14 km) from the city center.

Beyond Carrasco, the highway turns inland, but smaller roads branch off to the beaches. **Atlántida**, 35 miles (56 km) from Montevideo, is surrounded by a windbreak of cypress and eucalyptus. This beach also has a casino, golf course, tearoom and other resort amenities. Just beyond Atlántida is **Piriápolis**, a pretty town on a curving bay with an old-fashioned promenade along the beach. In the center of the curve stands the imposing Argentino Hotel, a 1920s spa with mineral baths, stained-glass windows and an elegant solarium where you may sip the curative sulfur-flavored water.

The most famous beach on the Uruguayan coast is **Punta del Este**, a jetset-studded peninsula that attracts well-heeled Argentines as well as a fair share of international celebrities and European royalty. (When general Stroessner was overthrown in Paraguay, his family happened to be vacationing here.) But "Punta", as Argentina's upper crust lovingly calls it, is primarily a *porteño* resort. At the height of summer in Buenos Aires, you will notice that a number of economic and political news articles are datelined Punta del Este – Argentina's movers and shakers are all at the beach. Punta del Este's prices make this resort an exclusive one, though not exclusive enough for some of the glamorous old-timers, who complain that the splendid old villas are being torn down to make room for condominiums offering more affordable rates. Nevertheless, one of Punta del Este's taxi companies still uses only Mercedes-Benzes. The peninsula has two long and beautiful beaches: the Atlantic one, more windswept and wild than the tranquil bay side. Those who don't share the Argentine herd instinct might find Punta del Este even more attractive off-season, when hotel rates go down and cool autumn breezes clear the sand of body-to-body sunbathers.

North of Punta del Este, the Uruguayan Atlantic coast is rich with gorgeous seascapes and deserted white-sand beaches. Along the coast highway towards Brazil, it's worth stopping at the 18th-century Portuguese fortresses of **Santa Teresa** and **San Miguel**, now beautiful national parks and popular bird sanctuaries.

A colonial relic: Two and a half hours west by car from Montevideo lies the 17th-century Portuguese town of **Colonia del Sacramento**. Colonia retains more of its original flavor than most cities in the region, partly because very little has happened here since the Portuguese founded it as a rival to Buenos

The drowsy streets of Colonia by day.

Aires in 1680. With a population of only 10,000, Colonia on a warm summer's day can have the air of an Iberian ghost town. Sights to see in the old quarter include the **Spanish Museum**, in a restored 18th-century viceroy's mansion, the **parochial church** and the **Portuguese Museum**, which has an excellent collection of mahogany and cordovan furniture.

The narrow cobbled streets of the old quarter all lead towards the river, where a still-functioning lighthouse warns passing ferries of Uruguay's treacherous coastline. You can walk along the river promenade to the remains of the colonial fortifications, which are surrounded by weeping willows. A couple of miles farther out stands a grandiose bullring, which has not been used since Uruguay outlawed bullfighting at the beginning of the century.

Once back in town, your best bet is a hearty steak lunch at the Hotel Italiano. Colonia has a number of small hotels, ranging from a luxury resort hotel with a casino to pleasant, inexpensive *pensiones*, some with views of the river. The hydrofoil runs three times daily between Colonia and Buenos Aires (the trip takes an hour); there is also the slower (three hours) but less seasick-making ferry.

The river country: For Uruguayans, a trip up the Uruguay River is the patriotic equivalent of an American tourist's pilgrimage to New England. The small, tidy villages where nothing appears to be happening were at one time the crucibles of Uruguayan independence.

Eighteen miles (30 km) up the Uruguay River from Colonia is **La Agraciada**, where the famous 33 Immortals landed from Argentina and organized a battalion to expel the Portuguese from Uruguayan soil. A statue to General Lavalleja, the patriots' leader, is on the beach. **Paysandú**, further upriver, is the town where Artigas led his followers when they fled Spanish rule in Montevideo. Today it's a popular spot for stalking the delicious *pez dorado* game fish. It's also where **Artigas Bridge** crosses the Uruguay River to Argentina.

A romantic sunset by the Rio de la Plata.

MANOS DEL URUGUAY

Rolling grasslands, English pedigree sheep and a climate similar to that of New Zealand have long made Uruguay a leading exporter of fine wool. And since the late 1960s, Uruguay has also been the source of richly colored hand knits, the creation of a knitting cooperative called Manos del Uruguay.

Manos means "hands" in Spanish, and indeed every product made by this cooperative reflects the handiwork of rural artisans who spin, dye, knit and weave the wool according to traditional methods. The finished articles, which include rugs and tapestries as well as sweaters, shawls and scarves, are on display in three pleasant shops in downtown Montevideo.

Manos knits themselves bear only a passing resemblance to typical Latin American woolens. Since the population of Uruguay is largely of European descent, Old World rather than indigenous influences prevail. A knowledge of home spinning and knitting brought over by Eastern European immigrants, combined with a need for rural housewives to find work they could do in remote areas, inspired five women to organize the knitting cooperative in 1968. With financial help from the InterAmerican Foundation and the United Nations, they sought to refine manual techniques to create articles offering more than merely rustic appeal. Manos del Uruguay started out making traditional ponchos, but by the following year was exporting sweaters to Paris.

"We always believed we should aim towards export, but without losing what is ours, what is Uruguayan, in our work," says Sara Beisso, one of Manos's founders who still serves on the board of directors.

The look of the Manos sweaters, while distinctive, is not necessarily Uruguayan. Designs blend motifs from many parts of the world with the cooperative's own inspirations. Combinations of deep colors such as russet, chocolate, black, amber, forest green, cobalt blue and crimson, predominate. The sweaters are made to be roomy and buttons are the size of a quarter or larger, handmade of wood or bone.

Two qualities characterize all Manos woolens: the silky texture of the wool achieved by hand spinning, and a subtle gradation of color tones, known as *desparejo* which comes from dyeing a single strand of wool in slightly varying intensities. Initially, the cooperative used dyes derived from bark and berries, but Manos now blends its own commercial dyes to guarantee colorfastness as well as consistency.

Over the years, Manos's styles have become more sophisticated and so has the dyeing process. Manos designer Beatriz Gulla spends much of the year traveling abroad, looking at sweater collections in Europe and the United States. "We stay in line with basic fashion tendencies, but we're not in the vanguard, of course," she says. "We want the sweaters to look like our own." Ms. Gulla and her assistants produce

eight to ten new designs each season, including a line of cotton sweaters which greet each spring and summer.

Uruguay has no fashion design schools, and Manos designers often have some training in architecture, which may explain their geometric motifs. Each season, samples of the new designs are knitted at the central Manos office on Reconquista Street in Montevideo. A committee reviews the collection at an in-house fashion show, and the designs that are chosen are then sent to the artisans affiliated with 18 branches of the cooperative throughout the Uruguayan provinces.

Each branch has a member designated as a

teacher, who demonstrates knitting the new patterns to her fellow artisans and occasionally travels to Montevideo to learn particularly complicated techniques.

For many of these rural women, becoming a Manos artisan is a source of pride as well as income; most have only an elementary education and had never aspired to any work other than grueling backcountry housework. Of the thousand artisans now affiliated with Manos, only two – a weaver and a spinner – are men. "We don't prevent men from joining, but generally they don't have the skills, or they're intimidated by so many women," says Delia Lestarpe, the president of the company, who has continued to knit during her years in office. Ms Lestarpe says that, like many women artisans, she encountered resistance from her husband when she first joined the cooperative, and she feared that the fact that she had a career would, in the eyes of their small village, imply that he was unable to provide for her. But, with time, attitudes have begun to change –"Even out there," she says.

On an average, a sweater takes 20 hours to knit, depending on the intricacy of the pattern. Knitting machines as well as knitting needles are used, but because each sweater is made from start to finish by the same artisan, all Manos garments have an individual look and feel. Each one has a tag bearing the name of the artisan and the place where it was knitted.

Manos del Uruguay produces around 100,000 sweaters a year, half of which are exported. Manos woolens can be found in boutiques in Paris, Geneva, Milan, Tokyo and New York, but prices in Uruguay are about a third of what they are abroad. In Montevideo, the two main clothing shops are at 616 Reconquista, at 1111 San José and in the carasco shopping center. There is also a home furnishings shop, offering handwoven upholstery fabric, tapestries and carpets, at 587 Reconquista.

If you've a taste for Uruguayan handicrafts, you may want to visit Montevideo's other markets. Local carvings and weavings – cushions, rugs, wallhangings – can be found at the daily fair at Plaza Cagancha and on Saturday mornings in Villa Biarritz, Parque San Martin. ■

Left, rich colors are worked into the weaving by the Manos del Uruguay cooperative which employs more than 1,000 people. Above, craftsmen at work in a pottery.

ARGENTINA: DREAMS OF GLORY

In the middle of the 20th century, Argentina was one of the richest nations on earth. Its workers had a standard of living that few could match, while the Argentine rancher was a near-mythical figure of wealth to stand alongside the Texan oil baron or railroad king. The second largest country in South America and eighth largest in the world, Argentina seemed certain to become an antipodean version of the United States.

Those hopes have never been realized, to the frustration of many Argentines. But while the blame is often laid on some spectacular mismanagement in the last five decades, the roots of decline can be traced back to the country's colonial past.

First contact: The southern stretches of South America never boasted the magnificent Indian civilizations that flourished in the Andean countries. What is now Argentina was occupied by fierce tribes of nomads, hunting across the vast plains and smearing their bodies with animal fat to keep warm. They were not overawed by Spanish explorers. Juan Diaz de Solis, the first European to set eyes on the Rio de la Plata in 1516, was set upon by Querandí Indians, killed and devoured while his crew watched helplessly from nearby boats.

The first steps at settling the region were hardly more encouraging. An attempt by the nobleman Don Pedro de Mendoza to found Buenos Aires in 1536 ended in disaster: Indian raids killed two-thirds of his men and reduced the rest to starvation, hacking the flesh from dead men's thighs for food before the site was abandoned. The Spaniards had more success pressing down from Peru into the northwestern deserts of Argentina. The towns of Salta, Jujuy, Cordoba and Tucuman were founded to supply the Andean mines with mules, food and leather.

It was not until 1580 the conquistador Juan de Garay managed to secure a permanent settlement at Buenos Aires, drawing up a grid plan on a piece of cow hide and distributing land to his 66 motley followers. Even so, it was another 100 years before the shaky outpost would be secure from Indian attacks.

Preceding pages: rounding sheep in Patagonia. Left, a gaucho chats to his *china* in an early 19th-century painting.

Finally realizing that there were no precious metals nearby and unable to press-gang Indians into work, the Spanish concentrated their efforts on plundering the riches of Peru and Bolivia. The rest of Argentina stagnated on the fringes of the Spanish empire, living out the typical colonial pattern: society was dominated by those born in Spain, who were rigidly separated from those of mixed blood – called *mestizos* – working as artisans or laborers.

Smuggling centre: The situation changed as the 18th century approached. Buenos Aires found its true vocation as a smuggling center, avoiding orders by the Spanish crown that all trade should pass through Lima or Panama. What had been nothing more than a few shacks lost on a swamp began to grow into a crowded city, with a thriving slave trade giving it a large negro population.

Fortunes began to be made in cattle hides and mule-breeding, and the Indian tribes were forced back from the pampas. It was at this time that huge tracts of land were set aside for a few Spanish families, whose names would recur again and again as the power-brokers of Argentina.

The Spanish government tried to recognize the growing power of Buenos Aires by relaxing trade restrictions and creating the vice-royalty of Rio de la Plata in 1776, but it was too late. Argentines were already realizing that they could make more money faster by being outside the empire.

Independence and civil war: The Napoleonic wars in Europe gave the initial push to the South American independence movement, cutting the colonies off from Madrid. But the major impulse in Argentina came from the misguided plans of an Englishman by the name of Sir Home Popham.

Commanding a British naval squadron on the way home from South Africa, Popham decided to capture Buenos Aires and open it up to British trade. He occupied the city for several months until the *porteños*, as the inhabitants of Buenos Aires are called, rose in rebellion and captured the whole enemy force. Reinforcements from Britain were defeated by a popular militia, showering them from the rooftops with musket fire, bricks and anything else that could be found.

The victory gave *porteños* confidence in their ability to govern themselves, and when news arrived in 1810 that Spain had been occupied by Napoleon, a junta of leading citizens declared the area independent.

When the Napoleonic wars ended, royalist forces attempted to retake Buenos Aires but were defeated. One of Argentina's greatest heroes, General José de San Martín, carried the independence struggle to the rest of South America, crossing the Andes into Chile with an army and pushing north into Peru. In Ecuador he met Simon Bolívar, the continent's other great liberator, but the two quarelled over San Martín's plans for monarchical rule. San Martín gave up on South America and went to France, where he died, lonely and disillusioned.

No sooner had independence been confirmed than arguments broke out between *porteños* – and the provincial towns. Bitter civil wars followed for the next seventy years, with Buenos Aires trying to impose a central rule over local strongmen, known as *caudillos*, and their armies of gauchos, wild *mestizo* horsemen who lived in the pampa.

The most famous of the *caudillos* was Juan Manuel de Rosas. Born of a wealthy ranching family, he arose from the chaos of the civil wars in 1829 to become governor of Buenos Aires province and *de facto* ruler of Argentina. Rosas' rule is remembered for its reign of terror, enforced by secret police, and his nationalist policies, giving Argentine goods the chance to compete against foreign trade. But after 23 years of Rosas, *porteños* finally rebelled, threw out the dictator and massacred his supporters. His protective tariffs were dismantled, flooding the country again with foreign goods, while the civil wars continued with renewed vigor.

A vision of Europe: It was not until 1886 that the final step towards nationhood was made, when Buenos Aires was separated from its province and declared the capital of Argentina. It was a victory for a new breed of politician who had a grand vision for the country. Chief among them was Domingo Sarmiento, who divided the world into "civilization" – represented by all things European – and "barbarity": the *caudillos*, gauchos and Indians.

The country's leaders were no longer unshaven soldiers but politicians dressing in collar and tie, eager to appear highly cultured and urbane. Codes were introduced to control the gauchos. Meanwhile, General Julio Roca embarked on a "Conquest of the Wilderness" in the 1880s to open up the pampas and Patagonia, still controlled by Indians. Any native standing in his path was killed, the rest herded into reservations.

Most important to shaping the economic future was an agricultural revolution. In the mid-19th century, only a fraction of the meat on slaughtered cattle had been used, most of it rotting in the open air to be picked at by wandering gauchos. But in 1876 a new method of freezing meat was developed, allowing it to be shipped across the Atlantic to the dinner tables of Europe, where beef was a rare item that fetched outrageous prices.

Cultivation of the pampas exploded to keep up with the new demands. Railways were laid across the country and Argentina was soon outstripping its rivals, Australia and Canada, in agricultural advances.

The immigrants arrive: Thousands of laborers were needed to keep the boom going. Before 1880, only a trickle of foreign workers stayed in Argentina. Overnight they became a flood, the greatest influx of immigrants in relation to population patterns in world history.

Most were peasants from northern Italy, with the next largest group coming from Spain. After a third-class passage across the Atlantic, crammed below decks in a constant battle against sea-sickness, the newcomers arrived penniless. Put up in a hotel in Buenos Aires for a couple of days, they were mostly rushed off to work in the pampas.

But Argentina's boom wealth was not shared among these new arrivals. The great landowning families of the past had refused to break up their massive holdings and after Roca's Conquest of the Desert, they snapped up even more land – getting around a 100,000-acre (40,000-hectare) limit by using false names. The immigrants were given small plots, but only to work for three to five years before moving on. Unlike North America, which was settled by millions of small landowners, Argentina remained the property of around 200 close-knit families referred to simply as "the oligarchy".

The result was a distortion in ownership that has stunted the country's growth and political life. Along with leading bankers, politicians and businessmen, the ranchers were European-educated, cosmopolitan and aloof. Soon the city of Buenos Aires was being shaped to their ideals.

The "Golden Age": As the economy expanded, the port of Buenos Aires tightened its stranglehold on the country. Its new-found importance allowed it to shed the Hispanic colonial atmosphere and become an expression of all things French. The 16th-century street plan was cast aside and streets widened into grand avenues to be lined with marble footpaths, cafes and jacarandas. *Porteño* optimism was reaching new heights.

But the political and economic inequalities of Argentina began rising to the surface. Protest movements against the oligarchs' grip produced the middle-class Unión Cívica Radical, forerunner of today's party of the same name. When it became obvious that the only thing "radical" about the movement was its name, the oligarchy allowed a democratic poll in 1916, won by Hipolito Yrigoyen. The Radical candidate was drawn through the streets of Buenos Aires by crowds of young supporters, hoping that a new age of reform was dawning.

Nothing of the kind happened, of course, and most reforms failed. But while tensions were building in the 1920s, Buenos Aires became the cultural mecca of Latin America. The rich indulged in tango parties and balls for famous writers rather than worry about

Left, the Patagonian Indians were driven from their lands in the 1880s. Above, the Plaza de Mayo in Buenos Aires, c. 1890.

social ills. A nearly senile Yrigoyen was still President of the Nation when the Great Depression hit. Nobody was surprised when, on September 6, 1930, the Argentine military marched into the Presidential Palace to take power under General José Uriburu. It was the first of many interventions.

The Age of Perón: The military handed over to a series of conservative governments in the 1930s, allowing the oligarchy to run the country as if nothing had changed in 40 years. Then, in 1943, a group of young army officers staged a successful coup. One of the figures in the new government was a man who even today, many years after his death, has a personality cult that dominates Argentine politics: Juan Domingo Perón. Born in the small town of Lobos about 60 miles (100 km) southwest of Buenos Aires, the dashing Perón had joined the Army at 16. He became an ardent admirer of Mussolini while serving as military attaché in Italy. Recognizing the changes that had been going on in Argentina, he chose to champion the disenfranchised and unprotected workers, many of whom were the children of immigrants. Perón took for himself the post of Secretary of Labor – until then an unimportant position that nobody wanted – and started a hectic program of organizing trade unions. Perón was joined in his efforts by the beautiful radio actress Eva Duarte. The two had met at a fund-raising event and soon became lovers, campaigning together for the workers. The daughter of a provincial peasant, Evita shocked high society but was worshiped by the working class for her passionate, if occasionally incoherent, speeches on their behalf.

Alarmed by Perón's growing power, a group of generals had him arrested. But Eva rallied supporters to turn out in his defence. More than 300,000 of the *descamisados* – literally, "shirtless ones" – flocked to the Presidential Palace, waving banners and chanting slogans in demand of Perón's release. The generals gave in, and the two heroes married shortly afterwards, to the general delight of their supporters. Elections were hurriedly called, and Perón romped in to become President. While he nationalized industries and started social welfare programs, Eva toured Europe in jewels and couture dresses as if she were a member of a Latin royalty.

Eva died tragically in 1952 of leukemia, at the age of 33, but the Vatican resisted calls for her canonization. The magic quickly began to wear away from Perón's rule. The cost of living was rising, government spending out of control and corruption rife. When it was rumored that Perón would distribute arms to the trade unions, the military struck, bombing the Presidential Palace and forcing Perón to flee on a Paraguayan gunboat. His supporters were purged from every level of government, and even mentioning Perón's name in public was banned.

The downward spiral: Despite the repression, Peronism lived on through 18 years of incompetent military rule. When full democratic elections were allowed in 1973, Peronist candidates won easily – and invited the aging founder back from exile in Spain to become President once again. Returning in triumph to Buenos Aires, Perón promptly died, leaving the presidency to his second wife, a cabaret dancer known by her stage name, Isabelita.

The arrangement was a disaster. Isabel lacked her husband's charisma and authority. Argentina's economy nosedived again, and rival Peronist factions began turning on one another with increasing violence. Guerilla fighting began in the mountains near Córdoba, while terrorists began letting off bombs and kidnapping prominent figures.

The military let the situation drag on until they had popular support for a coup in 1976. From then, they moved with methodical ruthlessness. The junta began a "dirty war" to purge Argentine society of everyone it suspected of left-wing sympathies. As many as 30,000 people were kidnapped, tortured and secretly executed in the campaign.

But the officers seemed incapable of running the economy, with inflation reaching record levels and poverty growing. To distract attention from his disastrous record, President Galtieri decided to take the Falklands Islands – known as the Malvinas in Argentina. The possession of these windswept South Atlantic rocks had been contentious since the British took them in 1833. It is unlikely that the junta expected British Prime Minister Margaret Thatcher to dispatch a task force to retake the islands and after a brief, bloody war, the Argentines were soundly defeated and the humiliated military were forced to call democratic elections in 1983.

Campaigning on a human rights platform, Radical candidate Raúl Alfonsin unexpectedly won the presidency. Although unable to raise Argentina from its economic slump – including a massive foreign debt inherited from the military years – Alfonsin guided the country into a new democratic era. For the first time in South American history, members of the military juntas were put on trial for their crimes in office and five were convicted. In 1989 the Judicialist (Peronist) party's flamboyant candidate, Carlos Menem, a former truck driver, won the presidential elections by a landslide, after making wage increases his main campaign proposal.

Getting down to work: Today's adolescents know no other form of government than Argentine-style democracy. For them, and their elders, work – or the lack of it for a growing number of people – is the main issue of the day.The unsmiling Argentines who populate the streets in the late 1990s know that the "fiesta" of a state-run economy with education, health care, job security and pensions for practically everyone is over – as Menem warned when he took office in 1989 and set about undoing Perón's work.

Meanwhile, Eduardo Duhalde, governor of Buenos Aires Province and Menem's would-be successor in the 1999 elections, waves the banners of social justice as he speaks of "re-Perónizing" the economy.

Left, Eva and Juan Perón, the two figures whose memory still dominates Argentina politics. Right, jubilant Argentines took to the streets on the return of democracy in 1983 after seven years of military rule.

LA CHACRA
BUENOS AIRES
ARGENTINA

Buenos Aires, a Passionate Place

Few countries are so gripped by their capital cities as Argentina is by Buenos Aires. Everyone and everything that passes through Argentina must at some stage come to "the Paris of South America".

Sprawling over the flat, empty pampas, by the shores of the muddy Rio de la Plata, Buenos Aires flaunts its European heritage and wistfully dreams of foreign shores. It is a city of immigrants who had always intended to return home, but still find themselves, somewhat uncertainly, in a strange and remote land.

But it is also a city with a creative energy that can often put New York to shame. Walk the streets at midnight, and you will see people of all ages just starting a meal in a restaurant, queuing for a cinema session or discussing theater in a cafe.

The people of Buenos Aires – known as *porteños*, or "people of the port" – are a special breed, renowned throughout South America for their contradictions. The classic image is drawn from the *porteño* middle class: urbane, charming, educated and snobbish; self-important, cynical and insecure; they can manage at different times to be wildly emotional and coldly intellectual.

Preceding pages: waiters and stuffed cows at a Buenos Aires steak house. **Left**, presidential guards on parade. **Below**, the Obelisk on Avenida 19 del Julio, the widest avenue in the world.

Obsessed with style and appearance, *porteños* turn their city into an open-air fashion parade. They are in love with the theater, public debates and the spectacle of politics in the street.Privately, the dramas of the mind exert an endless fascination: Buenos Aires has more psychiatrists per head of population than Manhattan.

But the *porteño* is famous above all for a brooding melancholy – sitting in a Parisian-style cafe and dreaming of different worlds.

A slice of Europe: Buenos Aires was founded more than 400 years ago, but it was virtually re-created at the turn of the last century. Riding the beef boom of the 1880s, the city's Hispanic colonial buildings were leveled and replaced in the image of Paris.

It was a time of tremendous wealth, when beef barons were sending their sons to Europe where they cut notorious figures in the local salons. Buenos Aires was a world center of fashion and high art, the cultural mecca of the Americas. But the cracks were already appearing in the Argentine dream, and no sooner was the city built than the long decline began.

This sense of faded grandeur makes it a fascinating place to wander through. Buenos Aires is not so much a city of "sights" as of atmospheres. Rather than visiting public buildings or sifting through museums, the main pleasure is to stroll through the city's neighborhoods, perhaps stop for a cup of coffee, stroll on again and absorb some of the everyday flavor of a city that seems to exist in a world of its own.

El Centro: The city center is carved up by wide avenues, lined by jacaranda trees and magnificent buildings that nobody has ever had the money to either knock down or restore. Bulbous cupolas protrude from their roofs, windows

BEEF AND RED WINE

Long before arriving, you will have heard that Argentina is a carnivore's paradise. Although it is exported to many parts of the world, the best beef is consumed at home with an almost religious reverence. A better-kept secret is Argentina's fine wine, especially the reds. Although the world's fifth largest producer, very little arrives overseas: nine-tenths of the wine produced is drunk within Argentina's own borders.

Taken together, a cut of beef with a bottle of red are both a simple meal and the ultimate dining experience in Argentina and part of a gastronomic ritual that goes to the heart of the country's traditions.

Steak preparation is regarded as an art, and the *parrillas* (steak houses) on every corner in Buenos Aires can seem more like temples to beef than restaurants. The most extravagant have meat in their windows being cooked in traditional gaucho fashion, with whole carcasses crucified on metal crosses around a mound of coals. Others have stuffed cows flanking the doorways, and over the tables are posters illustrating the cuts. The most expensive and leanest cut is the *bife de lomo*, roughly equivalent to a sirloin steak in other countries. The popular *bife de chorizo* is cut from the rib near the rump, while a *bife de costilla* is a T-bone.

In a class of its own is the *tira de asado*, which is a strip of rib roast usually large enough to feed two. The *parrillada* is a portable grill of mixed cuts, including plenty of offal and sausages, and is for the most committed carnivores. Two other cuts that figure on menus are *vacio* and *matambre*. *Vacio* is a cut which comprises of the bottom part of what in the US is designated as sirloin, porterhouse and the flank, and is the juiciest of all cuts. *Matambre* is like a Swiss roll with a vegetable and hard boiled egg filling. Often served cold, It can be an appetizer, or eaten inside French bread.

If you like your beef rare, order it *jugoso*; medium, a *punto*; and well done, *bien hecho*.

Steaks at an Argentine restaurant are unlikely to be sullied by vegetables, gravy or sauces. The most common accompaniment is a salad, which can vary from lettuce and tomato to a giant mixed extravaganza with artichokes and eggs. For those whose taste buds require a little more than salt and flesh, order the *salsa chimichuri*. This oregano and spice mix is traditionally a gaucho's favorite. The flavor is considered so strong that asking for it often gets a grunt of respect from the most sombre waiter – although the spices are unlikely to surprise most foreign palates.

Argentina is the world's fifth largest producer of wine and Argentines drink around 12 gallons (48 liters) per head each year. Grown near Mendoza and the drier stretches of the north near Salta, wines both absurdly cheap and amazingly good.

The *vino común*, served in jugs , is at the rougher end, but you will appreciate any of the inexpensive bottled *vino fino* on the wine list. There are around 50 varieties, and though many European grapes are used, Malbec and Torrentes are a local speciality. Continually reliable wineries include Navarro, Correas, La Rural. Escorihuela, Bianchi and Sant Elmo.

Argentines often drink their jug wine with soda water and, despite the regular consumption, it is rare for an Argentine to be seen drunk. Few people go beyond a couple of glasses.

Choosing a good restaurant for beef in Buenos Aires is easy: you're unlikely to be disappointed wherever you try. Las Nazarenas (Reconquista 1132) is the most famous. La Veda (Florida 1), open for lunchtime only, is also recommended. Cheaper and more relaxed are Chiquilín (corner Montevideo and Perón) and La Payanca (Suipacha 1015). Both serve classic steaks in warm, comfortable surroundings. ■

are framed by statues of Greek gods and hidden inside are marble stairways and chandeliers – all slightly tarnished and looking vaguely out of place.

The natural spot to start is at the pedestrian walkway of **Florida**, crammed at every hour of the day with *porteños* trying to catch glimpses of themselves in window reflections as they pass. It is lined with boutiques selling Argentina's famous leather goods, although shoppers should control themselves until reaching the cheaper **Avenida Santa Fe**. It meets Florida at the **Plaza San Martín**, where a dramatic statue commemorates one of the only heroes in Argentine history that commands universal respect.

eft, lamb arbecued in Buenos ires steak ouse. elow, njoying an pera at the agnificent olón heatre.

Intersecting Florida is another pedestrian mall, **Lavalle**, with nothing but cinemas, bingo and video game halls, cheap restaurants and bargain stores. The street can clog with people every night, especially when film sessions end at around the same time, making movement next to impossible.

Several monumental edifices in the center can hardly be avoided. The presidential palace is named **la Casa Rosada**, or "Pink House" for the tint of its masonry. It stands before the **Plaza de Mayo**, where guards in blue uniforms regularly strut and parade, surrounded by schoolchildren in white coats. Since 1980 an alternative procession has been mounted every Thursday by the white-scarfed Mothers of the Plaza de Mayo. They still demonstrate, as they did under the last dictatorship, for the return of their "disappeared" children.

On the port side of the Casa Rosada are the recycled 19th-century brick warehouses of the old Port of Buenos Aires, which are the new smart area for working and eating out. An oasis of sun and silence at the edge of the bustle of the banking district, the new **Puerto Madero** dockland development is an ideal place for a late afternoon drink on the promenade overlooking the water.

At the other end of the plaza is one of Buenos Aires' only colonial buildings, the **cabildo** or municipal palace. Inside this whitewashed edifice, which now

houses a museum, *porteños* argued for days before declaring the city's independence from Spain in 1810. Next door is the **Metropolitan Cathedral**, where General San Martín is buried.

The grand **Avenida de Mayo** stretches from here to the **Congress**, which looks like the White House in Washington. On the way, it crosses the **Avenida Nueve de Julio**, which despite being the widest avenue in the world, manages to be clogged with traffic at most hours of the day. Sticking into the air nearby is the **Obelisco**, a rather tasteless phallic object around which the city revolves.

The nearby **Avenida Corrientes** is the show business heart of Buenos Aires, lined with bright lights, art-deco theaters and cinema palaces from the 1920s. Argentines prefer to eat dinner very late and the restaurants along this street can be seen packed until 2am while on Saturday nights, the last film session does not even begin until 1.30am! Corrientes is also noted for its dozens of bookstores, crowded with browsers until the early hours of the morning. Worth visiting is the **San Martín Cultural Center** at around number 1500 Corrientes, which holds art exhibitions, film festivals and photographic displays.

Just around the corner on the Plaza Lavalle is the sumptuous **Colón Theatre**, one of the world's great opera houses that put Buenos Aires on par with Milan and Berlin. A performance here should not be missed: sitting back in wooden armchairs with plush velvet padding, looking out over six gilded tiers and gallery boxes, it is the perfect place to appreciate a little classical music or a lavish opera. Guided tours are given daily to the theater's three floors of underground workshops and the small museum commemorating appearances by such greats as Melba, Nijinsky, Pavlova and Caruso.

Cafe society: To understand Buenos Aires, the best strategy is to do as the *porteños* do: spend as much time as humanly possible in the *confiterias* or cafes of the city, doing nothing more than watch the world go by. Dominating

La Recoleta, the huge cemetery in Buenos Aires richest suburb.

every street corner, each cafe has its own distinct personality – indeed, to the *porteño*, Buenos Aires is mapped out not by streets, landmarks or *barrios*, but by key places to sit, write, think and observe.

Three of the city's oldest and most venerable *confiterias* are located within walking distance of this area. The **Ideal**, on the corner of Suipacha and Corrientes, was where the once-sizable British community in Buenos Aires met for high tea every afternoon. These days you can still have tea and cakes surrounded by polished wood, brass and marble pillars while being serenaded with waltzes which are played on an ancient electric organ.

Possibly the most famous of the *confiterias* is the **Tortoni**, on Avenida de Mayo and Piedras. In the 1920s it was the hangout of bohemians such as the writer Jorge Luis Borges, listening to tangos, experimenting with cocaine and debating poetics. Its red leather chairs, mirrors and chandeliers have changed little since that time and every Friday night, older patrons gather in a back room to hear the tango again.

Perched on the corner opposite the Congress building, the **Molino** has been a hangout for politicians and journalists for nearly a century. More sumptuous than a Viennese cafe, the Molino still tries to maintain its standards in difficult times. The aged waiters are particularly punctilious with their service, although their white outfits are often somewhat frayed from wear.

For a complete change of pace in *confiterias*, the **Cafe La Paz** on the corner of Montevideo and Corrientes is frequented by young students and artists. Something of a cross between a library reading room and a pick-up joint, the Cafe La Paz is full virtually 24 hours a day.

Remnants of the colonial city: For a taste of Buenos Aires as it was before this century, the place to head for is the artistic barrio of **San Telmo**. During the 1700s it was the riverside hub of the city, with one third of its population black. It has retained a colonial charm,

Young *porteñas* outside a discotheque.

with cobbled streets lined by low buildings, tango bars and antique shops.

San Telmo's major event is the Sunday antique market in the barrio's main square. While live jazz is played in neighboring cafes and buskers tango in the streets, hundreds of the city's artists and antique dealers set up stalls for their wares. This is the place to pick up a unique memento of Buenos Aires, like a 1952 calender with Evita's beaming face or an antique photograph album from a forgotten British settler.

The most surprising thing about the working-class suburb of **La Boca** is the sudden splash of color in the otherwise reserved city. Coming to life in the mid-19th century as the home for Genovese dock workers, this barrio by the river is famous for its houses of corrugated iron, all painted in different, dazzling tones. The Argentine painter Benito Quinquela Martin was a leading influence in the suburb's use of color earlier this century, and his home has been turned into a gallery for his paintings of dock workers. By night, La Boca has a series of gaudy restaurants where bands play renditions of kitsch classics.

The bizarre fixations of aristocratic Argentines on sex and death seem to meet in the **Barrio Norte**. The city's upper crust fled there in the 1870s when yellow fever hit Buenos Aires. Today it is the most elegant and refined of *barrios*, where old ladies in minks sit under oak trees in outdoor cafes and businessmen in European suits arrogantly order waiters about.

The neighborhood is built around a giant walled cemetery, the **Recoleta**. Hundreds of ornate marble crypts contain the remains of the city's wealthiest families, with giant angels and grim reapers adding to the unsettling effect. To the disgust of the Argentine old wealth, the Recoleta's most famous occupant is the daughter of a provincial nobody, Evita Perón. Thousands visit her tomb every year, in a crypt of black marble which has a single rose before it.

Meanwhile, the Barrio Norte boasts the city's range of *telos* – hotels rented out by the hour – where, overlooking the Recoleta necropolis, the local denizens can steal a few tense hours of passion.

A breath of fresh air: When the urban rush becomes too much and you feel the need for a view and fresh air, an easy option is to head for the **Costanera Norte**. A promenade runs along the brown Rio de la Plata, where on a clear day you may be able to pick out the coast of Uruguay on the distance. Fashionable *parrilladas* line the road on the other side of the walkway, for when the exercise loses its charm.

In October or November, a classic day can be spent at the *polo* by heading out to **Palermo** playing fields. Otherwise, a day trip can be made out to the streams and canals of the **Tigre delta**, for over one hundred years a weekend refuge for *porteños* of all ages. Trains leave regularly from the cast-iron Retiro station in central Buenos Aires, taking passengers to the quiet, tree-lined waterways within an hour. Wooden ferries leave for destinations farther into the delta, where there are modern French restaurants and guest houses that retain the atmosphere of the 1930s.

Left, tango hero Carlos Gardel looks down over Buenos Aires at night. Right, the crowded pedestrian mall of Lavalle, full of cinemas and restaurants.

LA
ESTANCIA
EL PALACIO DE LA
PAPA FRITA
SELECT
LAVALLE
ATLAS
Paramount
ROMA
Coca-Cola
John Player Special
RESTAURANT

Songs of Loneliness and Passion

You might be sitting in a dark cafe when wafting from the radio comes a mournful tune. "*Get yourself a drink*," the lyrics might say, "*For today I must forget/That I'm without a friend/And far from home...*" Or riding in a taxi, you might notice the driver's eyes glaze over as he listens to a lover's lament: "*Every day I miss you more*," croons the soloist, "*Even after all you've done...*"

The tango, Argentina's classic popular music, is anything but cheery. Its themes are loneliness and despair, jealousy and homesickness. The famous accompanying dance is a demonstration of strutting Latin machismo: passionate, erotic and flamboyant. But, so closely associated with the history of Argentina, tango is said to be a distillation of the national character. Where Brazil has the exuberant samba, *porteños* listen to the melancholy tango. True or not, the tango lingers throughout Buenos Aires like a perfume from another age.

A disreputable birth: The origins of tango can be traced to the growing slums of Buenos Aires at the end of the 19th century. Cultures from around the world were meeting in the crowded and run-down tenements of the city. Discharged soldiers were flocking from the Argentine countryside after protracted civil wars, descendants of African slaves had been drifting there for decades, while Italian and Spanish immigrants were arriving by the boatload.

Overwhelmingly male, the new arrivals gathered in the bars and brothels of the port. They shared the loneliness of exiles, mixing their national music to create the haunting tango sound. The dance was invented before lyrics were introduced, usually performed by two males while waiting in line at the local *bordello.*

Before long, the tango was gaining popularity amongst the *porteño* working class. By the turn of the century, the unique wheezing sound of the *bandoneon* (concertina) had been added to the guitar, flute, violin and piano of tango groups. Increasingly respectable, writers even began putting their names to tangos. Only the snobbish upper classes kept aloof of the new rhythm, seeing it as a sign of provincial decadence while they kept to their waltzes and polkas.

But before long, the tango reached Europe. Mothers in Edwardian England tried in vain to stem the popularity of the sensual dance, with its thrusting hip movements and intertwined limbs. Kaiser Wilhelm of Germany banned his staff from performing it. But for the rest of Europe, tango was the rage. And once the dance had succeeded in the salons of Europe, the Argentine upper crust accepted it wholeheartedly – agreeing with the French that it must be the very essence of Latin style.

"The Kid from Abasto": The invention of sound recordings allowed tango to reach a mass audience as never before. In 1917, a little-known singer named Carlos Gardel recorded the tango *Mi Noche Triste.* Almost overnight, the handsome figure became the first great tango star whose voice was heard not just in Argentina, but around the world.

Although arguments continue as to whether Gardel was born in France or Uruguay, he is remembered in Argentina as *El Pibe del Abasto* – the kid from the Buenos Aires working-class district of Abasto. From 1929 to 1935, he made a series of films that are still shown on Argentine television. His place in the local pantheon was assured in 1935 when he was killed at the peak of his career in an airplane accident in Colombia – as though Gardel were living out a tango himself. Today, record companies use new techniques to improve his old recordings and ensure his memory lives on. Of Gardel they say in Buenos Aires: "Every day he sings better."

Decline and revival: Tango enjoyed enormous popularity during the age of Perón but fell into a lull in the 1950s. Faced with new forms of popular music, it rigidified into a set of "classics" to be respected rather than enjoyed. Young people turned to more commercial music – although most schoolchildren can still recite tango lyrics by heart.

One tanguista who pushed the form in new directions was Astor Piazzola. Trained in classical and jazz music, he led a revival with his new, energetic arrangements. He can be heard on records or in the hit 1987 film *El Exilio de Gardel* (The Exile of Gardel) which won a number of awards.The tango comeback is highlighted in university courses now on offer, in the dedicated FM Tango radio station and the *Todo Tango* television show, as well as the successful Tango Argentino touring company, which has filled theaters across Europe and in the US.

Today most of the places to see tango danced in Buenos Aires are for tourists. San Telmo has a range of bars. Casa Blanca in San Telmo, Tango Mío in Barracas and La Boca and Café Homero in Palermo, both with dance shows, are well worth checking out. On Saturdays popular dance organizers rent foreign community clubs, so young and old can practice their steps. A frequent choice is the Club Croata on the corner of San Juan and Boedo, where it is easy to evoke what the tango scene might have been like decades ago.

Another remarkable gathering is held every Friday night in a back room at the Cafe Tortoni. The "cultural reunion" is a gathering of lovers of tango and romantic poetry and there will be readings and performances late into the night. As at other performances, the patrons will listen to the passionate music and tales as if transfixed, not batting an eyelid or saying a word, and when the piece is finished they will break into wild applause.

Purists mourn the waning of the tango's influence, regretting that few Argentines under 30 have been brought up learning its steps. But the rhythms are there, a melancholy undercurrent tugging at the heart strings of this remote country at the farthest tip of South America. ■

Left, singing a tango at the San Telmo markets. Above, the passionate dance.

NORTHERN DESERTS

Argentines take pride in being the most cosmopolitan country in South America. An exception would have to be their northernmost provinces. It was here that the first Franciscan monks came south from Peru to settle Argentina, building whitewashed chapels in the desert and leaving a macabre Catholic imprint.

The north is also the only part of the country where Indians still survive in numbers. Easily accessible, the region gives visitors a fascinating glimpse into Argentina's colonial past and the Andean countries just across the border.

A different world: A two-hour aeroplane flight can take travelers far away from the European order of Buenos Aires. Below, the capital gives way to the flat grazing land of the pampas, which in turn dissolves into the dry, dusty stretches of the north.

Salta is an open and relaxed town that can be used as a base to explore the surrounding provinces. Neo-colonial buildings line the straight streets that head towards the mountains, often little more than outlines obscured by dust. Despite the parched surroundings, the center of town is a green plaza with well-preserved Spanish and Italian-style buildings. Most of the city's best old colonial buildings are on Caseros Street – the **Cabildo** (city hall), the home of the Uriburu family, the San Francisco Church, the San Bernardo Convent – and along the La Florida pedestrian mall.

The city is hot and glary by day, and few people are to be seen during siesta time. The action begins at dusk, when the pedestrian malls turn into markets that are virtually monopolized by the Bolivians who have been pouring into Salta in recent years. In Buenos Aires the street vendors sell cassettes, watches and ice cream; in Salta you can also find aloe cream, spiced meat *empanadas* (called *salteñas*), cheap contraband clothing, herbs and holy pictures.

The north of Argentina is saturated by religion and any visitor to Salta will be surprised by the number of churches and statues of St Francis. Kept in the **Cathedral** are the town's pride and joy: the Virgin and Cristo del Milagro, statues carved in the 16th century and credited with miraculous powers. The ship carrying them from Spain was wrecked but the figures washed up on the Peruvian shore. Then in 1692, a sudden earthquake in Salta was dramatically halted when the statues were paraded in the streets.

The two simple, almost childlike figures are almost lost in the huge baroque altar of the church. Across the aisle, the faithful pray before a life-sized effigy of Christ fresh from the cross, complete with vast holes in his chest and a virtual fountain of fake blood. As several historians have pointed out, depictions of suffering in colonial religious art had to be horrific indeed if they were to impress local Indians as worse than much of their own lives.

The museum in the **Cabildo** gives an insight into the last few centuries. Strolling under the shadows left by white arches, the rooms are full of European-Argentine heroes from the wars of independence, with paintings of their deeds alongside medals, vests and gloves. The Indian section, covering the Incas and customs still alive today, is a collection of pots and pans, dry and unexplained.

For a change of pace, one of the most exciting trips from Salta is to take *El Tren a las Nubes* – the Train to the Clouds. Fully equipped with a dining car, this poetically-named service leaves Salta for a spectacular journey through nearby mountains. In a major feat of engineering, it climbs through the barren **Quebrada del Toro** across steel span bridges to the small town of **San Antonio de los Cobres** at 13,000 ft (4,000 meters) in the Andes.

Towards Bolivia: A highway heads north from Salta to the provincial town of **Jujuy**. The population becomes more Indian the closer you get to the Bolivian border, while the road gets rougher, the houses poorer and the religious imagery stranger. Tiny chapels can be seen in the remotest villages. One of the most curious is in **Uquaia**, which contains the *angeles caballeros*: a painting of angels dressed up as 17th-century musketeers.

The road climbs to over 9,800 ft (3,000 meters) and the countryside dries out completely along the *quebrada* (gorge) of the **Rio Grande**. Odd land formations appear: some mountains are sharp triangles, others seem to spill like molten lava, others look like decayed ants' nests. The rocks are white, red or even green and the only plants are tall, fat cactuses.

The small town of **Humahuaca** is almost in Bolivia. Arriving in early afternoon, it is an empty dust bowl, with winds sweeping from the valleys to cover everything with orange powder. The only sound comes from the 16th-century church. The bells toll the hour and in the morning the town is woken by the organ belting out dirges.

The streets of the town are narrow and winding, with Bolivian women gathering in doorways to sell herbs and potatoes. It has several guest houses and restaurants, allowing visitors to stay for several days and take walks in the lunar landscape or visit the extensive archaeological site of **Coctaca** nearby – whose mysteries are still slowly being unraveled.

Surprisingly, this small and poor town is dominated by a huge iron monument to Argentina's 19th-century war of independence. It seems incongruous that the fierce figures staring down over Humahuaca should have Indian faces. But the artistic sleight-of-hand is needed to include the northern Indians into Argentina: it brushes over the memory of newly-liberated European settlers spending the rest of the 19th century wiping out the indigenous people in the rest of the country.

The local sense of history is also revealed by the old schoolhouse in Humahuaca, which is emblazoned with the sign "Republic of Bolivia". Ask any of the students why and they look at the sign as if for the first time. Ask the school masters and they are no more helpful. It was a long time ago, they might tell you, perhaps even a century.

"But I only teach European history," they will smile, and walk away.

A monument and cacti in Argentina's dry north.

MISIONES AND THE JESUIT RUINS

Sticking out like a crooked finger from the northeast of Argentina, the subtropical province of **Misiones** boasts some strange associations. Graham Greene used its wet and steamy towns as the setting for his novel, *the Honorary Consul*, where expatriate Britons and South American revolutionaries accidentally meet.

More recently, the award-winning film *the Mission* has publicized the province's 18th-century Jesuit empire. The film was shot in its colonial ruins, dense jungles and at the Iguazú falls, considered more spectacular than those of Niagara.

A visit to the region usually begins in the provincial capital of **Posadas**, which can be reached from Buenos Aires by daily flights. The town has little to recommend it, except as a starting point to explore further north. It offers a small airport, a riverside drive, tree-lined plazas, two casinos, three discos and quiet hotels where guests sip beer or soft drinks, not always with the benefit of air conditioning.

A highway escapes north from the town into the rich green countryside, kept lush by regular downpours. The road follows the **Rio Paraná**, often in flood, with its brown waters swirling around tree tops and over the roofs of houses.

A religious empire: It was in this same region in the 1600s that the teams of Jesuit priests began setting up their mission stations. At their height in the 18th century, they housed 100,000 of the local Guaraní Indians, studying, growing grain and carving musical instruments which became renowned in the finest courts of Europe.

Today, the ruins for the greatest Jesuit mission at **San Ignacio Miní** are only two hours drive from Posadas. They are announced by the unfortunate marriage of a piece of Jesuit art in a concrete military bridge, as designed by a former governor of the province.

The Jesuit ruins at San Ignacio.

The grounds themselves are more tastefully kept. San Ignacio has been turned into a silent and elegant park, with the masonry of the ruined colonial buildings covered by a thin film of moist moss.

At these ruins in Graham Greene's *Honorary Consul*, bumbling Paraguayan guerillas who were trying to kidnap the American ambassador caught an old Englishman. But today, instead of lurking revolutionaries, there are only prowling gardeners, equipped with wooden scythes.

Busloads of visitors wander amongst the old Jesuit living quarters and cathedral, decorated with Indian carvings of angels and stars. Outside, the gravestones of the priests bear simple messages: "Here Lies Father Juan, a good man."

Other Jesuit ruins can be found nearby, mostly overgrown by jungle. Sitting amongst these shattered relics of their religious empire, it is difficult to remember what an unusual experiment flourished here for over 150 years. While the rest of South American Indians were being brutally exploited on plantations, here they were working and learning in a system which has earned the praise of many modern socialist writers. The Jesuit priests distributed grain according to need, and arranged standing Indian armies to keep out slave traders.

Only when the Jesuits were expelled from the Spanish colonies did the fatal flaw of the mission system reveal itself. The priests had ruled a paternalistic order, never training the Indians to run it themselves. With the Jesuits in exile, slave traders were more successful, the crops failed and the Guaraní Indians fled back into the jungle. Today, the descendants of those same Guaraní Indians have returned to the ruins – this time to sell plastic flutes and feathers to tourists.

Spectacular falls: The other great attraction of the Misiones province is only a few hours farther up the highway to the border with Brazil: the magnificent cataracts of Iguazú. They can be reached from the commercial center, **Puerto Iguazú**.

The nearby Iguazú falls is one of South America's most extraordinary sights. Millions of gallons of water thunder over the various cascades with such force that most visitors wear raincoats to protect against the violent spray.

While the Brazilian side of the falls is most spectacular, the Argentine side is more pleasant to explore. Obscure paths lead into the dripping rainforest, no less impressive but more serene surroundings. These trails follow various routes, with small animals scurrying for cover behind walls of thick jungle, while the red mud shows footprints of the local (and, say park rangers, harmless) variety of jaguar.

The only sight capable of crowning the Iguazú experience is **Moconá Falls**, where the River Uruguay falls into itself in a fault nearly a mile (2km) long, a few kilometers from the Brazilian town of Tenente Portela. For a panoramic view, take a ferry to Brazil from the Argentine town of El Soberbio. Boat trips are on offer in the same town for those craving a close-up white-water view.

he nearby
lls.

THE GAUCHO

Scattered through the *estancias* (estates) of the Argentine hinterland are horsemen wearing a uniform from the country's distant past: black Spanish hats, woven Indian shawls, baggy pants known as *bombachas* and carrying wicked knives called *facónes*. They are the last descendants of a breed of South American cowboys, the gauchos. Apart from the visual effect, however, their lives are only a pale shadow to those of their forebears; the real gaucho existence disappeared a century ago.

Like in many other highly urbanized societies, Argentines have romanticized their rural workers. Gauchos have been given a Kiplingesque mash of values, from a fierce sense of independence and disrespect for authority to a primitive skill of surviving in the wild. Boasting everything that the "civilized" man lacks, they have been raised to the heady heights of cultural icons. Naturally, this could only be done once the real gauchos had been destroyed by the culture that sings their praises.

From the earliest days of Spanish settlement, individuals had disappeared to the countryside and mixed with the Indians. Fleeing criminals, escaped slaves and deserting militia-men lived at the fringes of society and were known as *la gente perdida:* the lost people. They developed their own harsh, nomadic lifestyle on the pampas and tamed wild horses to ride. Slaughtering cattle that had escaped from the cities, they traded the hides for alcohol and *mate*, the bitter local tea, while learning how to hunt with the skilful use of lassoes and the *boleadores*: three balls connected by ropes that could wrap around the legs of any running target. Charles Darwin described his own hopeless attempt at handling the *boleadores*, which ended up wrapped round his own horse and a tree.

Soon called gauchos – the name may have derived from the Indian words for "orphan" – they had a growing reputation for gambling, horsemanship and knife-fighting. The first gauchos were mainly *mestizos*, of mixed Spanish and native stock. The women, called *chinas*, played a subsidiary role in this macho lifestyle. Often kidnapped from settlements in the first place, they raised children in small huts which were indistinguishable from those of the Indians.

This vagrant population had always exasperated Argentina's urban dwellers as a lawless and anarchistic element on the frontiers. But during the late 18th century, large tracts of land in the pampas began being distributed to prominent *porteños*. Fences began being put up in the grasslands and gauchos were seen as little better than cattle thieves. Many of them begrudgingly signed up as ranch hands, working for subsistence wages on the lands they had once roamed.

When the British took Buenos Aires in 1806, many gauchos were pressed into the army to

drive them out. After independence, they joined up with the private armies of provincial *caudillos*, who allowed them to indulge in their usual drinking, gambling and knife-fighting for several decades without undue molestation. But as the era of civil wars drew to a close, the days of the gaucho were numbered. New codes were introduced to regulate their movements, dress, drinking habits and diet. Thousands of gauchos were pressed into military service as punishment for not possessing a passport they could not even read.

Soon the gaucho was a symbol of the chaotic, backward Argentina that the statesmen of Buenos Aires wanted to destroy. Chief amongst these was Domingo Sarmiento, who divided the world into "civilization" and "barbarism". Gauchos, not surprisingly, were a part of the latter camp, described by Sarmiento as "biped animals of the most perverse stripe" whose carcasses were only good to fertilize the earth. Barbed wire fences hindered their movements still further and the gaucho was being eliminated as a distinct social grouping.

As this was happening in the 1870s, José Hernandez wrote in two parts his classic epic poem, the *Gaucho Martin Fierro*. Lamenting the passing of the wild frontier past, he wrote:

And listen to the story
Told by a gaucho
Who's hunted by the law,
Who's been a hard-working father
And a loving husband –
Yet in spite of all that,
Taken to be a criminal.

By 1926, when the second great literary work on gauchos appeared, *Don Segundo Sombra* by Ricardo Guiraldes, the gaucho was nothing more than a literary memory. This does not mean to say that there are not glimpses of the lost gaucho culture in the Argentina of today. In the furthest reaches of the country, on remote farms in Salta and Patagonia, hands still wear traditional gaucho dress – even if they are as likely to be driving a Land-Rover as riding a horse.

But horsemanship is still cultivated in the pampas and beyond. Visitors can take day-trips from Buenos Aires to nearby *estancias* for a *fiesta gaucha*, where – after an *asado* (barbecue) consumed with copious amounts of red wine – riding displays are put on. These include the *sortija*, where a horseman charges at full speed to try to run a needle through a small hanging ring.

The small town of San Antonio de Areco preserves a little of the old gaucho way, with restored *pulperias* or bars where the horsemen once gathered to become inebriated. A small museum commemorates the more picturesque traditions of the gauchos.Further out in the provinces, you might stumble upon a traditional Sunday rodeo, with bow-legged men in their finest hats, ponchos and kerchiefs and their wide leather chaps, recapturing life in the remotest corners of the pampa two centuries ago.■

Left and above, gauchos on an *estancia* near Buenos Aires.

Bariloche: Mountain Resort

More than anywhere else in Argentina, **San Carlos de Bariloche** is a slave to the seasons. Strategically placed between the towering Andes and the plains of Patagonia, for six months of the year the town is a booming holiday resort with a unique alpine flavor.

Summer brings hordes of travelers enjoying walks amongst the lush forests, spectacular glaciers and mountains of the surrounding Lake District. Later, the winter snows bring South America's select set of affluent skiers to the Andean slopes, filling Bariloche's restaurants by night with raucous fireside carousing.

But the other neglected months of the year are perhaps even more delightful: in spring, the valleys of the Lake District are filled with flowers and greenery, while autumn brings the slow shift of the forests' colors to red, orange, cinnamon and ochre.

An alpine atmosphere: Any mention of Bariloche to most Argentines brings the dreamy reply that it's "just like Switzerland". Certainly the alpine atmosphere is what first attracted Swiss, German and Austrian settlers to the region at the end of the last century.

Today the town itself is a reproduction of a Tyrolean skiing village. Many of the buildings are designed like chalets, while the streets are full of chocolate shops and restaurants offering Swiss fondue, trout and roast venison. By night there are several exclusive discotheques to choose from.

But the real attraction is the surrounding countryside. Bariloche's setting, by the shores of **Lake Nahuel Huapi** and rung by jagged brown mountains, is spectacular. In the distance you can spot the towering **Mount Tronador**, the highest peak in the region at 11,728 ft (3,554 meters).

Begin your visit by going to the **Patagonian Museum** near the **Civic Center**. It relates the region's history from the days when Indians roamed the countryside, covered from head to toe in animal grease for warmth, to the arrival of the first white pioneers and military expeditions. Outside in the square is a statue of General Roca, the man who headed the Desert Campaign which led to the virtual extermination of local tribes.

Into the countryside: Dozens of tour companies offer visits to the surrounding attractions, or you can hire a car in Bariloche and set off on your own to explore the dirt roads and byways of this magnificent region on the border of Chile.

The *circuito chico* or "short circuit" runs out along Lake Nahuel Huapi to the **Llao Llao hotel**. Recently refurbished and reopened after years of neglect, it reflects the glory of its heyday in the 1940s. Boats run from the docks of Bariloche to **Isla Victoria**, whose myrtle forests are said to have inspired some of Walt Disney's advisers when drawing backgrounds for the film *Bambi*.

Continuing around the circuit is the path to **Cerro Lopez**. In summer, the peak can be climbed to a refuge run by the Club Andino, where hikers can stay overnight. On a clear day the Cerro offers spectacular views over the lakes and mountains of the region to Chile. Other day drives or hikes can be taken from Bariloche to **Cerro Tronador**, **Cerro Catedral**, **Cerro Otto** and the waterfalls of **Los Cesares**. The region is world-famous for its trout fishing from November to March, and in summer there is sailing and surfboarding on the lakes.

Further afield: Also passing through some of the world's most magnificent scenery is the so-called route of the seven lakes, which winds along the border with Chile. It leads to the small backwoods town of **San Martin de los Andes**, which many travelers use as a base for hikes and camping trips.

The return trip over the **Córdoba Pass** runs through the lower regions of Neuquen province, much drier and closer to the Patagonian wastes. Fingers of stone protrude from thorny expanses, in what one English traveler in 1920 compared to the prehistoric *Lost World* imagined by popular novelist Sir Arthur

eft, St ernard dogs efore the entro ívico, ariloche.

Conan Doyle. Many of the *estancias* or ranches of the region are still English-run and worked by Chilean *peons* or weather-beaten gauchos, whose ponchos, knives and *bombachas* are definitely not worn just for tourists.

For those considering longer excursions, an overnight trip can be made to **El Bolsón**, a hippy refuge of the 1960s which sits in a valley with its microclimate. Further south, a road cuts through the serene **Cholila Valley** to **Esquel**. First settled by the Welsh, it is now the base for visiting **Los Alerces National Park** and the gateway to the **Chubut Valley**.

Connecting Esquel with the small town of **Ingeniero Jacobacci** is a small gauge railroad, made famous by Paul Theroux as the last leg of his 1979 travel book *The Old Patagonian Express*.

A taste of the "campo": For a mixture of history and adventure, take a trip out to **Estancia Nahuel Huapi** by the shores of the lake. Founded by a Texan cowboy named Jared Jones in 1889, the house still standing was a refuge for Butch Cassidy and the Sundance Kid, on the run from the Argentine authorities, having brought their Wild West ways to the new frontier of Patagonia early this century. Today the pioneer's granddaughter, the hardy Carol Jones, runs horse-riding trips into the remotest regions of her family property. The trips can last from just one morning to over 10 days, reaching into the snow-covered mountains for breathtaking views of the region. Most travelers would be satisfied with a shorter ride through the rich cattle country of the pre-cordillera ranch, watching the occasional group of deers, dashing hares or black vultures perched on rocks.

If even a half-day ride seems a little energetic, call in at the ranch just to enjoy the atmosphere. What used to be its general store at the turn of the century has been turned into a *parilla*, **El Viejo Boliche**, serving the most succulent *bifes* in the district. (To arrange horse rides, call the Jones family in Bariloche, on 00-541-0944-26508.)

Wild alphine scenery near Bariloche.

PATAGONIA: THE OUTBACK

Lost at the southern end of South America, Patagonia has for centuries been a byword for the remote and the strange.

The explorer Magellan, the first European to see this vast and windswept plain, reported it to be full of dog-headed monsters and natives with steaming heads. In more modern times, it has been a refuge for exiles and eccentrics from around the globe. Patagonia has attracted mad Frenchmen wanting to be king, tough Welsh colonists dreaming of paradise, Charles Darwin on his famous voyage and even Butch Cassidy and the Sundance Kid, coming here when the Wild West was tamed.

Today Patagonia can be easily visited from the bustling Argentine capital, Buenos Aires. Those with time on their side can leave by train or bus to fully appreciate the size of this flat, empty plain that takes up one-third of the country's landmass. Otherwise, daily flights cut across the pampas to the southern deserts, allowing a journey that only ends at the last stop before Antarctica: Tierra del Fuego.

The flight leaves behind the elegant cafes and cinemas of Buenos Aires to enter the completely different world of the Argentine outback. Below, the rich cattle country dries out and becomes divided into sheep stations. Just last century some of them were bigger than small European countries, with their owners ruling like a South American royalty. Today many are still run by the English and Scots descendants of the original owners, who still speak English in preference to Spanish.

A Welsh dream in the desert: The first stop is the city of **Trelew**, surrounded by dry bluffs and dusty scrub. It was here that thousands of Welsh colonists came after 1865 to set up a "Little Wales" in the middle of nowhere. They had decided to flee their homeland, where the Welsh culture and language was being repressed by the English, to start

A foreign train decays in the endles plains of Patagonia.

all over again in the most distant corner of the world they could ever think of: Patagonia.

Despite some early disasters, the colony began to succeed. The Welsh used their irrigation skills to make the desert bloom, and soon Patagonian wheat was winning prizes at international shows. Welsh was spoken in the streets and taught in the schools. For a brief moment it seemed that the dream would last forever.

But by the turn of the century, things were already going awry in Trelew. The Argentine government had imposed its authority on the town and many Spanish-speaking immigrants, attracted by the Welsh success, had arrived with their families. Floods devastated the area's crops. Many settlers left for Canada or Australia, but the core of the community stayed on, their Welsh nationalism slowly being diluted by intermarriage with Spanish speakers.

Today the town of Trelew looks much like other provincial Argentine towns, although the street signs are still in Welsh. The echoes of its origins can be found in the old **Hotel Touring Club,** with its cracked windows and antique wooden bar full of old men playing chess on quiet afternoons. Many of the town's elders still speak in their native Welsh to one another, although using Spanish in the streets.

For a taste of the Welsh colony as it once was, you will need to take a half-hour bus ride to the village of **Gaiman**. Built around the irrigation canals that converted the desert into an oasis, Gaiman has a number of Welsh tea houses serving up Welsh cream pastries to passing visitors. A small museum is run by local historian Señora Tegai Roberts, who can chat just as happily in English, Welsh or Spanish.

Whales and frontier towns: Easily reached from Trelew is the famous **Peninsula Valdé**, which boasts some of the world's most peculiar wildlife. Charles Darwin spent weeks here on his famous journey in the *Beagle*, and today tourists come to watch the sealions yawning by the rocky shore and hundreds of

-aces of the south: left, an elderly lady rom the Nelsh colony of Chubut; ight, a *peon*.

penguins wandering in lines to the sea. During September and October, enormous Right whales can be seen throwing up their tail fins as they mate dramatically off shore.

Flying south from Trelew, the Patagonian plain below looks increasingly desolate. One hundred years ago, a Frenchman named Orélie-Antoine de Tounens came here and declared himself king of the local Indians. The Argentine authorities, rightly considering him mad, promptly expelled him, along with most of the Indians.

The frontier town of **Comodoro Rivadavia** became important to the Argentine economy when oil was discovered nearby in 1907, but has nothing resembling rural charm. The notorious Patagonian wind that once drove settlers raving mad still blows through its prefabricated streets, which most travelers connive to avoid.

Scarcely more appealing is **Rio Gallegos**, 2,000 miles (3,000 km) south of Buenos Aires on the cool tip of South America. Unfortunately, because most flights pass through here, many travelers end up spending a night. Nothing much has happened since 1905, when Butch Cassidy and the Sundance Kid, fresh from North America, held up a bank on the main street. Stories conflict as to whether they were finally killed in Bolivia or Argentina – or whether Butch lived to a ripe old age back in the United States.

Glaciers in the Andes: Changing to a small propeller-driven plane in Rio Gallegos, a one-hour flight cuts west across the plains to the foothills of the Andes and some of the most magnificent scenery in South America. The village of **Calafate** is rung by snow-capped mountain peaks and sits next to **Lake Argentino**, which looks full of turquoise milk rather than water. This remote village is enjoying a boom as the stepping-off point to the huge blue glaciers wedged in the forest-covered countryside nearby.

The most famous is **Perito Moreno**, a 160-ft (50-meter) high wall of ice which cuts through a lake. As the poets prom-

The Perito Moreno glacier.

ise, it cracks and growls throughout the day, with enormous chunks of ice regularly falling from its side to send waves of water thundering to the shore. The glacier is still growing in four year cycles. Blocking off part of the lake, the water level rises until the glacial wall collapses in a spectacular scene that lasts for several hours.

From Calafate you can also visit the sheep *estancias* of Argentina's deep south, where the occasional gaucho figure still works. Once Argentina had 80 million sheep and was one of the world's largest wool producers. Today only 30 million remain. But sheep-raising is still a key industry in Patagonia. Between October and January every year, traveling teams of workers arrive for the shearing season.

The most notorious of the sheep stations of the far south is **La Anita**. The reason dates from 1921, when the whole of Patagonia was paralyzed by a strike of farmhands, known as peons. The organizer was a young Spanish anarchist named Antonio Soto who had wandered via the Buenos Aires stage to Patagonia. He organized the mostly illiterate workers and led them out of the sheds for months.

The mostly British *estancieros* reacted by calling on the government for help. The President responded by sending the Army to crush this "revolution". After some bouts of shooting, most of the peons surrendered – only to find the Army organizing mass executions. One of the biggest was at La Anita, although it has changed hands since then and hardly anybody remembers where the 200 or so workers are even buried.

Located a few hours from Calafate is the **Fitzroy National Park**, where you can pass from the windswept plains to lush and wet forest amongst the snow-capped Andes. Hikes through the park cross mountain streams and stretches that seem like Scottish moors. Clouds are constantly billowing overhead, but on a good day you can often catch a glimpse of Mount Fitzroy, a sheer knife of granite that is a favorite with suicidal mountaineers.

enguin olony at unto Tombo, ear Trelew.

TIERRA DEL FUEGO: LAND OF FIRE

It is the forbidding image of **Tierra del Fuego** that paradoxically lures travelers to the southernmost tip of South America. The name "land of fire" was given by the Spanish explorer Magellan who saw mysterious flames in the darkness when first passing the island. For centuries afterwards, Tierra del Fuego was feared by sailors for the icy Antarctic winds that blew their ships towards jagged rocks.

Few considered **Ushuaia**, the world's most southerly town, an attractive refuge from the storms. It progressed from a primitive whaling station to a prison colony where Russian anarchists eked out their last days.

Today the land at the end of the world can be reached by daily flights from Buenos Aires. Ushuaia is no longer the wild outpost it once was, but an odd blend of modern tourist center, Klondike-style boom-town and the gateway to one of the world's last great wilderness areas.

The end of the world: The northern half of the island is flat sheep farming land- much like the rest of Patagonia - but the south is rugged and thickly forested. Approaching Ushuaia by plane is suitably dramatic, since the town is rung by snowcapped claws of granite. The dominating peak, **Mount Olivia**, would suit a Walt Disney wicked witch for its mist-shrouded and vaguely evil appearance.

The weather lives up to Tierra del Fuego's reputation: even during the 20 or more hours of summer daylight, it shifts erratically from cold drizzle to perfectly cloudless skies, with the only constant being a gusty southern wind.

Ushuaia itself is far from a picturesque pioneering town. The Argentine government has subsidized its development and new suburbs are being flung up everywhere. The main street is like an open-air department store, with duty-free electronic goods being offered from the new factories outside town. One of

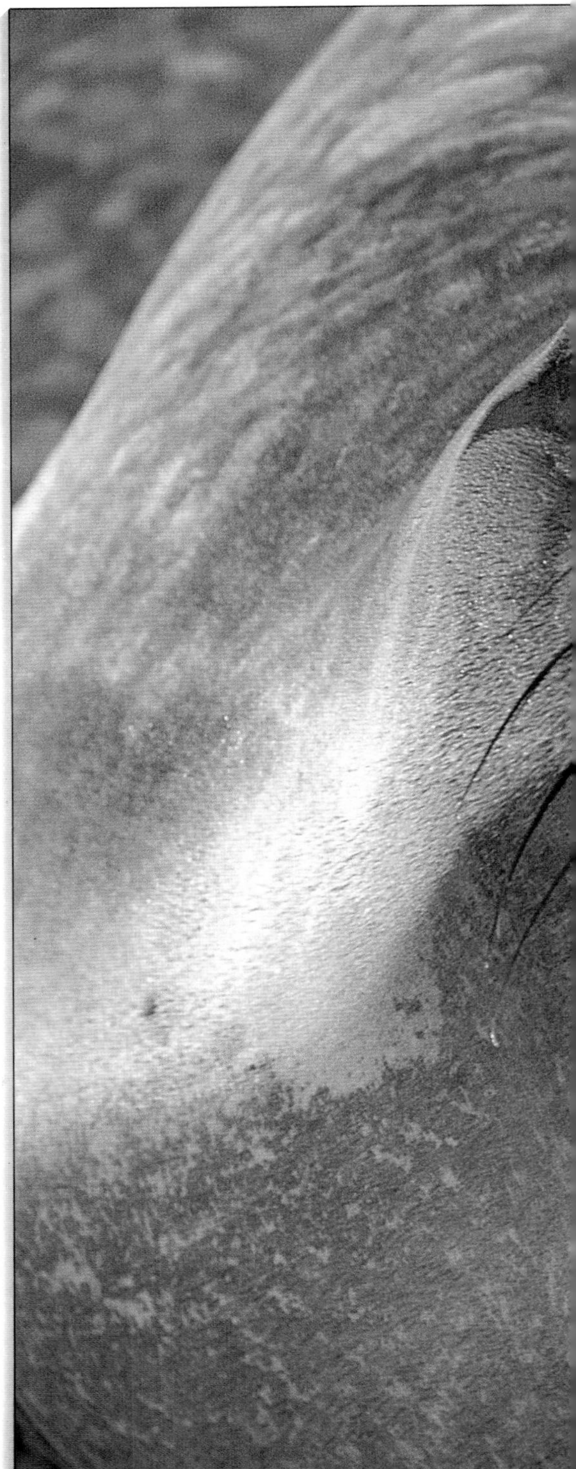

Right, an elephant seal in the far south.

the town's claims to fame is that it has the Bank of Tierra del Fuego, which is the world's first financial institution to have a branch in Antarctica.

This hubbub of development has created a new tourist infrastructure, with new hotels and restaurants to cope with the region's popularity. One place that still maintains the flavor of old Ushuaia is the **Cafe Ideal**. In a corrugated iron building, its walls are covered by photos of famous visitors and next to the television is a huge joint from a whale's spine. Seafood is standard fare, with the local specialty being *centolla* or king crab.

The **Beagle Channel**, on which the town sits, was named after the boat Charles Darwin sailed here in the 1830s for his famous wildlife studies. Boat trips can be taken on the channel past mountains dropping sheer into the water, circling islands populated by penguins or sea lions – and another covered with the remains of a wooden ship.

Just three hours' drive from Ushuaia along a winding dirt road is the first *estancia* on Tierra del Fuego, **Harberton**. Founded by the Rev. Thomas Bridges in 1888, it is open to tourists, with guides in English and Spanish. Harberton is worth visiting not just for its history, but for the beauty of its setting. Surrounded by trees and flowers, perched above the blue Beagle Channel, the *estancia* seems like the calmest place on earth.

A grisly past: The good Reverend Bridges spent much of his time here working with the local Indians and writing a dictionary of the complex Yaghan language. To his dismay, he could see before his death that the lists of words would soon be the only monument to those who spoke them.

As the British writer Bruce Chatwin has noted, Darwin's theory of "survival of the fittest" began being put into brutal practice in the 1890s. The Indians of the area, who had lit the fires that Magellan saw, occasionally killed and ate the sheep brought onto their land by European settlers. The newcomers decided to remove this "pest" en masse.

Official records show that most Indians died of disease, but the folk memory

Incessant winds make trees grow at strange angles in the far south.

persists of active resistance, battles and massacres. The most grisly tale is of white bounty hunters being paid £1 sterling for each pair of Indian ears they brought back from the wilderness. Old-timers tell of such gruesome characters as the Scotsman Alex MacLennan, nicknamed the Red Pig, famous for his drunken ravings about killing Indians. The Englishman Sam Hyslop, accredited with gunning down 80 Onas, was caught by Indians and flung from a cliff.

Windswept wilderness: The **Tierra del Fuego National Park**, where these strange events once occurred, is now the main attraction of Ushuaia because of its easily accessible wilderness area. The walking is simply magnificent, following spectacular coastline to lakes and glaciers. The park preserves the sense of being at the end of the world, with winding paths over spongy moss oozing cold water, past tough shrubs and thorny bushes as well as trees that have grown bent 45 degrees with the prevailing wind.

The path to **Bahia Ensenada** passes an encouraging altar to the Virgin of Lujan, Argentina's patron saint of travelers. There is a camping ground at the rocky beach, where you can breakfast on sweet calafate berries – the mere taste of which is said to guarantee future return to Tierra del Fuego. Boulders can be hopped down to **Bahia Lapataia**, where you can pick fresh mussels from the sea. A picturesque narrow-gauge train will take you into the Tierra del Fuego National Park along the route, on which prison inmates used to be taken to cut housing for timber.

Back in Ushuaia, the bookshops are full of books on the local Indians, but they are dull, anthropological works written as if they were still wandering around the countryside. The rumors of murders are denied or forgotten, with only a few scraps suggesting the contrary: a ledger showing that only women and children were brought back from raids; a photo in a Liverpool newspaper showing a mass grave found by police.

The final certainty is that the only fires now burning in Tierra del Fuego are from the oil rigs off its coast.

Below, Ushuaia, the world's southernmost town. **Following pages**: a desert flower.

INSIGHT GUIDES

TRAVEL TIPS

FOR THOSE WITH MORE THAN A PASSING INTEREST IN TIME...

Before you put your name down for a Patek Philippe watch *fig. 1*, there are a few basic things you might like to know, without knowing exactly whom to ask. In addressing such issues as accuracy, reliability and value for money, we would like to demonstrate why the watch we will make for you will be quite unlike any other watch currently produced.

"Punctuality", Louis XVIII was fond of saying, "is the politeness of kings."

We believe that in the matter of punctuality, we can rise to the occasion by making you a mechanical timepiece that will keep its rendezvous with the Gregorian calendar at the end of every century, omitting the leap-years in 2100, 2200 and 2300 and recording them in 2000 and 2400 *fig. 2*. Nevertheless, such a watch does need the occasional adjustment. Every 3333 years and 122 days you should remember to set it forward one day to the true time of the celestial clock. We suspect, however, that you are simply content to observe the politeness of kings. Be assured, therefore, that when you order your watch, we will be exploring for you the physical—if not the metaphysical—limits of precision.

Does everything have to depend on how much?

Consider, if you will, the motives of collectors who set record prices at auction to acquire a Patek Philippe. They may be paying for rarity, for looks or for micromechanical ingenuity. But we believe that behind each $500,000-plus bid is the conviction that a Patek Philippe, even if 50 years old or older, can be expected to work perfectly for future generations.
In case your ambitions to own a Patek Philippe are somewhat discouraged by the scale of the sacrifice involved, may we hasten to point out that the watch we will make for you today will certainly be a technical improvement on the Pateks bought at auction? In keeping with our tradition of inventing new mechanical solutions for greater reliability and better time-keeping, we will bring to your watch innovations *fig. 3* inconceivable to our watchmakers who created the supreme wristwatches of 50 years ago *fig. 4*. At the same time, we will of course do our utmost to avoid placing undue strain on your financial resources.

Can it really be mine?

May we turn your thoughts to the day you take delivery of your watch? Sealed within its case is your watchmaker's tribute to the mysterious process of time. He has decorated each wheel with a chamfer carved into its hub and polished into a shining circle. Delicate ribbing flows over the plates and bridges of gold and rare alloys. Millimetric surfaces are bevelled and burnished to exactitudes measured in microns. Rubies are transformed into jewels that triumph over friction. And after many months—or even years—of work, your watchmaker stamps a small badge into the mainbridge of your watch. The Geneva Seal—the highest possible attestation of fine watchmaking *fig. 5*.

Looks that speak of inner grace *fig. 6*.

When you order your watch, you will nc doubt like its outward appearance to reflect the harmony and elegance of the movement within. You may therefore find it helpful to know that we are uniquely able to cater for any special decorative needs you might like to express. For example, our engravers will delight in conjuring a subtle play of ligh and shadow on the gold case-back of one of our rare pocket-watches *fig. 7*. If you bring us your favourite picture, our enamellers will reproduce it in a brillian miniature of hair-breadth detail *fig. 8*. The perfect execution of a double hobnail pattern on the bezel of a wristwatch is the pride of our casemakers and the satisfaction of our designers, while our chainsmiths will weave for you a rich brocade in gold *figs. 9 & 10*. May we also recommend the artistry of our goldsmiths and the experience of our lapidaries in the selection and setting of the finest gemstones? *figs. 11 & 12*.

How to enjoy your watch before you own it.

As you will appreciate, the very nature of our watches imposes a limit on the number we can make available. (The fou Calibre 89 time-pieces we are now makir will take up to nine years to complete). We cannot therefore promise instant gratification, but while you look forwar to the day on which you take delivery c your Patek Philippe *fig. 13*, you will have the pleasure of reflecting that time is a universal and everlasting commodit freely available to be enjoyed by all.

Should you require information on any particular Patek Philippe watch, or even on watchmaking in general, we would be delighted to reply to your letter of enquiry. And if you sen

fig. 1: The classic face of Patek Philippe.

fig. 4: Complicated wristwatches circa 1930 (left) and 1990. The golden age of watchmaking will always be with us.

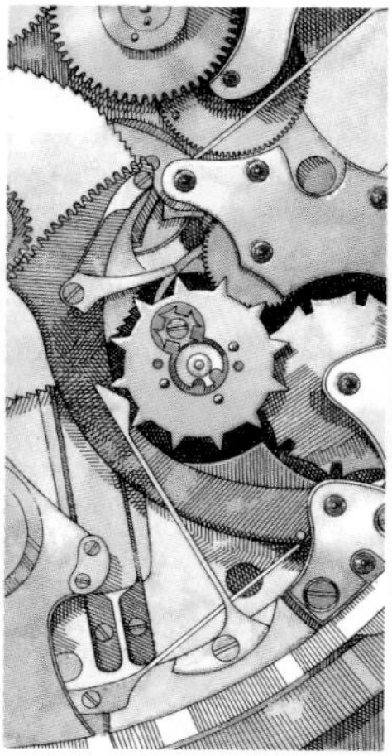

fig. 2: One of the 33 complications of the Calibre 89 astronomical clock-watch is a satellite wheel that completes one revolution every 400 years.

fig. 5: The Geneva Seal is awarded only to watches which achieve the standards of horological purity laid down in the laws of Geneva. These rules define the supreme quality of watchmaking.

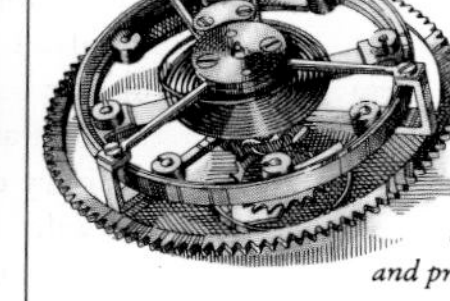

fig. 3: Recognized as the most advanced mechanical regulating device to date, Patek Philippe's Gyromax balance wheel demonstrates the equivalence of simplicity and precision.

fig. 6: Your pleasure in owning a Patek Philippe is the purpose of those who made it for you.

fig. 7: Arabesques come to life on a gold case-back.

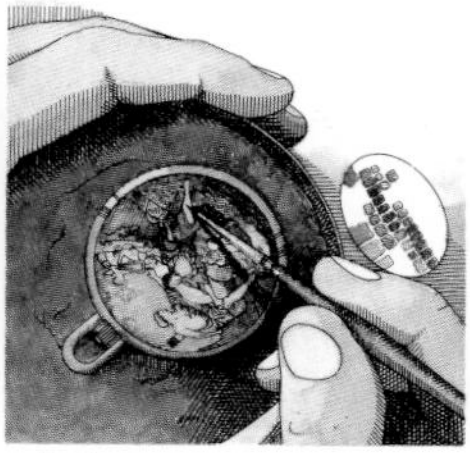

fig. 8: An artist working six hours a day takes about four months to complete a miniature in enamel on the case of a pocket-watch.

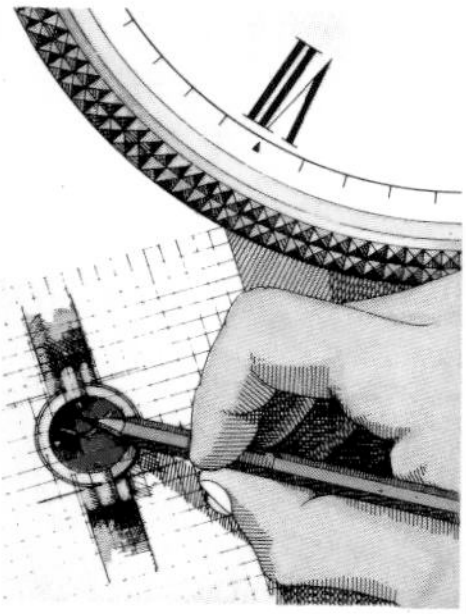

fig. 9: Harmony of design is executed in a work of simplicity and perfection in a lady's Calatrava wristwatch.

fig. 10: The chainsmith's hands impart strength and delicacy to a tracery of gold.

fig. 11: Circles in gold: symbols of perfection in the making.

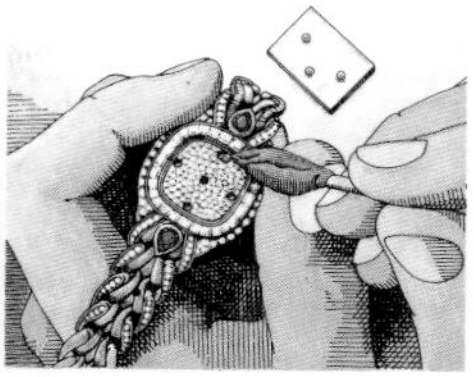

fig. 12: The test of a master lapidary is his ability to express the splendour of precious gemstones.

PATEK PHILIPPE
GENEVE

fig. 13: The discreet sign of those who value their time.

your card marked "book catalogue" we shall post you a catalogue of our publications. Patek Philippe, 41 rue du Rhône, 1204 Geneva, Switzerland, Tel. +41 22/310 03 66.

You close your laptop and adjust your footrest. A taste of Brie. A sip of Bordeaux. You lean back and hope you won't be arriving too soon.
That depends on how far you're going.
The fact that Lufthansa flies to 220 global destinations comes as a surprise to some. Perhaps we've been too busy with our award-winning service to tell everybody that we are one of the world's largest airline networks. A network that can offer you fast and convenient connections to anywhere. A network that offers rewards with Miles and More, one of the world's leading frequent flyer programmes. And above all, a network that makes you feel at home, however far you're going. So call Lufthansa on 0345 252 252 and we'll tell you the full story.
Lufthansa

Colombia
400 km
Caribbean Sea
LESSER ANTLLES
Willemstad
GOLFO
DE VENEZUELA
Pto.
Cumarebo
Santa Marta
Barranquilla
Pico Cristobal
Colón
5775
Cartagena
S. Francisco
Maracaibo
Cabimas
FALCÓN
Barquisimeto
Mara
cay
Valencia
MAGDA
LENA
CÉCAR
Lago de
Maracaibo
GOLFO
DEL DARIÉN
Sincelejo
PANAMA
El Banco
CORD. DE MERIDA
Embalse
de Guárico
Monteira
La Palma
Turbo
Ocaña
San Cristobal
VENEZUELA
Zaragoza
Magdalena
Mutatá
Cúcuta
Jurado
ANTIOQUIA
Elorza
Bucaramanga
GOLFO DE CUPICA
Arauca
Medellín
CENTRAL
Socorro
ORIENTAL
ARAUCA
Atrato
Cravo
Norte
GOLFO DE TIBUGA
Quibdó
Sogamoso
Pto. Carreño
Cabo Corrientes
Manizales
Tunja
Meta
Honda
Tomo
CHOCO
OCCIDENTAL
Pereira
Pto.
Ayacucho
Armenia
CASANARE
Cacahual
Ibagué
Bogotá
Cerro El
Nevado
4560
San Pedro de Armenia
Orinoco
CORD.
Villavicencio
Buenaventura
Vichada
San José de Ocuné
BAHIA DE
BUENAVENTURA
Cali
Pto. López
Nevado del
Huila
5750
CORD.
COLOMBIA
VICHADA
CORD.
Inirida
BA. GUAPI
Neiva
Mosquéra
NARIÑO
Guaviare
ANDES
Popayán
San José del Guaviare
GUAINÍA
Maroa
ENS. DE
TUMACO
Mariano
Patia
Pasto
Vista Alegre
Mocoa
VAUPÉS
Mitu
LOS
Tulcán
CAQUETÁ
Pto. Huitoto
Ibarra
Iauaretê
Uaupés
Quito
Pto. Leguizamo
DE
Napo
Cotopaxi
5897
AMAZONAS
ECUADOR
Pantoja
Ambato
La Pedrera
El Encanto
Julia
Volcán Sangay
5230
PLANICIE AMAZONICA
Andoas
Sta. Clotilde
Napo
Tigre
Mazán
Amazonas
CORD.
Leticia
São Paulo de Olivenca
PERU
Iquitos
BRAZIL
Pastaza
Maranon
Barranca
Benjamin Constant

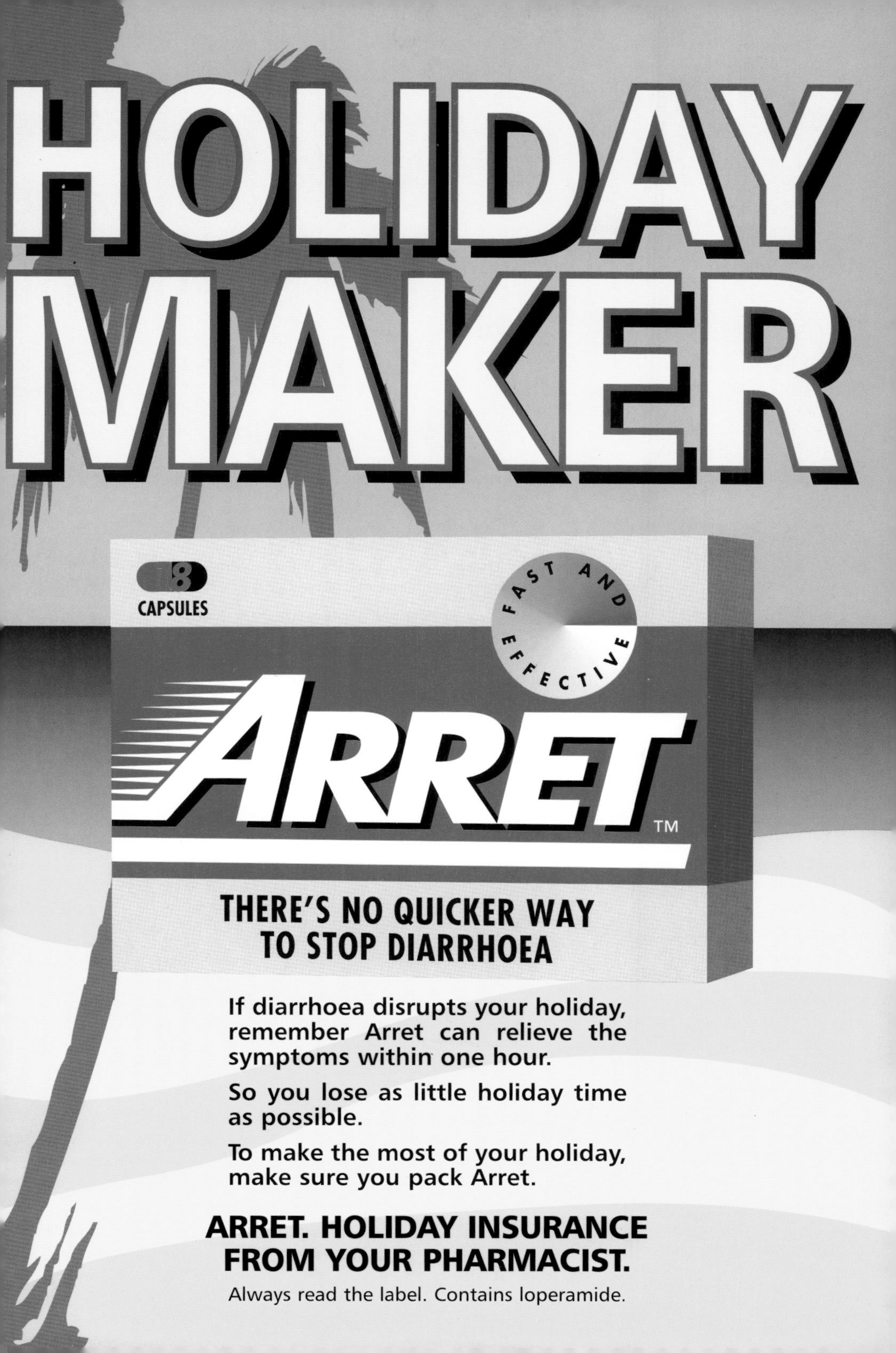
HOLIDAY
MAKER
8
CAPSULES
FAST AND EFFECTIVE
ARRET
TM
THERE'S NO QUICKER WAY
TO STOP DIARRHOEA
If diarrhoea disrupts your holiday, remember Arret can relieve the symptoms within one hour.
So you lose as little holiday time as possible.
To make the most of your holiday, make sure you pack Arret.
ARRET. HOLIDAY INSURANCE
FROM YOUR PHARMACIST.
Always read the label. Contains loperamide.

CAMEL
BAGS
YOUR TRAVEL PARTNER

Getting Acquainted

COLOMBIA

Area: 439,600 sq. miles (1,140 sq. km), bordering Panama with coasts on the Caribbean and the Pacific.
Capital: Bogotá.
Population: 33 million. Columbians are of European, African and Indian descent. Nearly half a million belong to one of 60 tribes.
Language: Spanish.
Currency: peso (US$=800 pesos, UK£=1,200 pesos. *All exchange rates are approximate*).
Weights & measures: metric.
Electricity: 120 volts.
Time zone: GMT –5hrs, same as EST.
Dialing code: 57 (Bogotá + 1).

Climate

The Colombian highlands has moderate weather all year round, while the coast is tropical.

The only seasons are wet and dry, varying per region: in Bogotá, the driest time is between December and March, and between July and August.

Government & Economy

Colombia's "limited democracy" is based on the Constitution of 1991. The president and members of the senate and house of representatives are directly elected. Indians have the right to two senate seats.

Agriculture is the most important sector of the economy, and Colombia is the world's second largest coffee producer. Manufacturing coming a close second.

Colombia has one of the strongest economies on the continent and is self-sufficient in energy. New oil and gas fields have recently been discovered in the Llanes foothills. Colombia produces about 60 percent of the world's emeralds and 70 percent of the world's cocaine.

Planning the Trip

What to Wear

The weather in Bogotá and the highlands stays moderate all year round so a light sweater will suffice in the evenings. The coast has a tropical climate: take light summer clothes. Take a thick raincoat for the uplands. Woolen clothing is necessary in the mountains.

Visas

Only citizens of China, Taiwan and Haiti need visas. Visitors are given a 90-day stay on arrival. An onward ticket may have to be shown on arrival.

Extensions of 15 days for a six month period may be applied for. Exit stamps are necessary on departure.

Health

Emergency treatment is given in hospitals. Tap water can be drunk in Bogotá without problems, elsewhere, drink bottled mineral water. Hepatitis is common, malaria tablets are advised in the Amazon jungle and there is some risk of yellow fever in coastal areas.

Money Matters

Many *casas de câmbio* change foreign currency into local money. US dollar traveler's checks can be changed at any banks at a slightly higher excgange rate. Present your passport (or a photocopy) at the desk, or you may be liable for a 10 percent tax. Do not change money on the street and avoid carrying large amounts of cash.

Credit cards are widely used, although American Express is only accepted in high-priced establishments in Bogotá is represented by the Tierra Mar Aire travel agency.

Getting There

By Air

Colombia is the northernmost country in South America and is often the visitor's first stop on the continent. There are many flights from Europe and North America to Bogotá, Cartagena and Barranquilla, with onward connections to the rest of the continent. Cheap flights are available from Costa Rica in Central America. For Australians and Asians, Aerolineas Argentinas flies from Sydney to Buenos Aires, then onward to Bogotá.

By Road

From Ecuador, buses go to and from the border at Tulcan/Ipiales. From Venezuela, you can choose between the coastal route from Maracaibo to Santa Marta, or the highland route from Caracas and Mérida to Cucuta via San Cristobal. From Brazil, the only way to enter is via Leticia in the Amazon basin and then fly to Bogotá.

Practical Tips

Emergencies

Security & Crime

The center of major cities is generally safe, but with such extreme poverty in Colombia it is worthwhile to check which outlying areas can be visited safely at night. Columbia is part of a major drug-smuggling route. Do not carry packages for other people without checking the contents. With a little common sense, Colombia is as safe as any other country.

Loss

Although most Colombians are honest and friendly, theft occurs in the larger cities and visitors should look after valuables at all times. 24-hour Tourist Police Service in Bogotá is at Carreras 7, No. 27-42, tel: 283-4930 or 334-2501. If you have lost documents, contact the police at Calles 46 y Carreras 14; for loss of valuables, go to Calle 40, No. 8-09.

Medical Services

The main medical centers in Bogotá are Cruz Roja Nacional, Avenida 68, No. 66-31, tel: 250-66/231-9027/231-9008; or Centro Medico La Salud, Carrera 10, No. 21-36, tel: 243-1381/282-4021.

Business Hours

Generally Monday to Friday, 8am–noon, then 2pm–6pm. Banks are open from 9am through to 3pm, 9am to 3.30pm on Friday.

Media

Bogotá has several daily newspapers. Both *El Tiempo* and *El Espectador* are considered the most comprehensive in terms of news coverage. The English-language *Colombian Post* is published twice a week. Drugstore Internacional, Carreras 10, No. 26-71, sells US and European papers.

Postal Services

Mail is generally very reliable in Colombia. The General Post Office in Bogotá is at the Avianca Building in the center of the city, opposite the Parque Santander. In small towns and rural areas use the Correos de Colombia.

Telephone & Fax

Telephone systems are automated and phone cards can be used. Fax services are available in large hotels, but it's cheaper to use Telecom offices. The Telecom offices in all big cities have international communication facilities to enable you to dial home.

Parks & Reserves

Permits are required to visit Colombia's parks and nature reserves. For permits and information contact: Inderena, Carrera 10 No 20-30, oficina 805, Bogotá, tel:283-0964.

Useful Addresses

Tourist Information

Bogotá: Calle 28, No. 13A-15, ground floor (Edificio Centro de Comercio Internacional). Information is also available at the bus terminal and the office in El Dorado airport.

There are branches of the Corporación Nacional de Tourismo (CNT) in all major towns and cities.

Embassies & Consulates

The following embassies and consulates are in Bogotá:
Canada: Calle 76, No 11-52, tel: 217 5555
Ecuador, Calle 100, No. 14-63, tel: 257-9947.
Great Britain, Calle 98, No. 9-03, 4th floor, tel: 218-5111 or 218-1867.
United States, Calle 37, No. 8-61, tel: 285-1300.

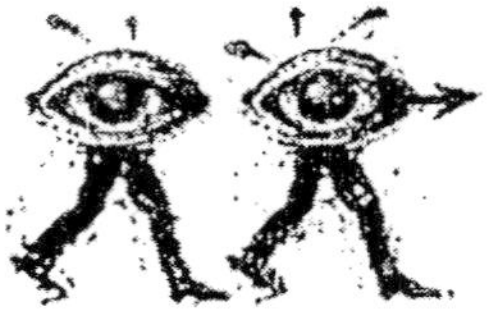

Getting Around

On Arrival

Make sure that your documentation is stamped with the date of your arrival, so that you don't have to pay double the exit tax on departure. Even with this form, foreigners pay $17 departure tax when leaving Bogotá by air.

Public Transportation

From the Airport

Registered yellow taxi services run from all the major airports to the city center, at fixed rates. Local buses also run to Bogotá airport.

By Air

The national carrier Avianca flies to all parts of the country. Less regular services are offered by SAM and Satena. Avianca also offers a non-refundable Air Pass and flies a shuttle service.

By Bus & Taxi

Bus transport along the main routes is generally good, often luxurious, but deteriorates when heading into the more remote areas. Normally, the rougher the road, the poorer the bus. The alternative on main routes is a *buseta* (minibus) or *colectivo* (a shared taxi that is more expensive but much quicker).

Within the main cities, taxis are cheap and relatively reliable. A meter clocks over the price in pesos. At night women do not travel alone in taxis.

Where to Stay

Hotels

Hotels in Colombia range from the luxurious at $130 a night to the basic at around $2 a night.

Bogotá

Some of the five-star hotels include:

Bogotá Royal, Avenidas 100, No. 8A-01, tel: 610-0066, fax: 218-3362.
Tequendama, Carrera 10, No. 26-21, tel: 286-1111, fax: 282-2860.
La Fontana, Diagonal 127A, No. 21-10, tel: 274-0200, fax: 216-0449. Recommended by many travelers.

For a hotel with some atmosphere and still perfectly comfortable though with less conveniences, try the **Hoteria de la Candelaria**, Calle 9, No. 3-11, which is in a converted colonial mansion and furnished with beautiful antiques. Tel: 342-1727.

Budget hotels, often dismal, are located between Calles 13 and 17, and Avenida Caracas and Carrera 17.

Wherever you're going we'll be there.

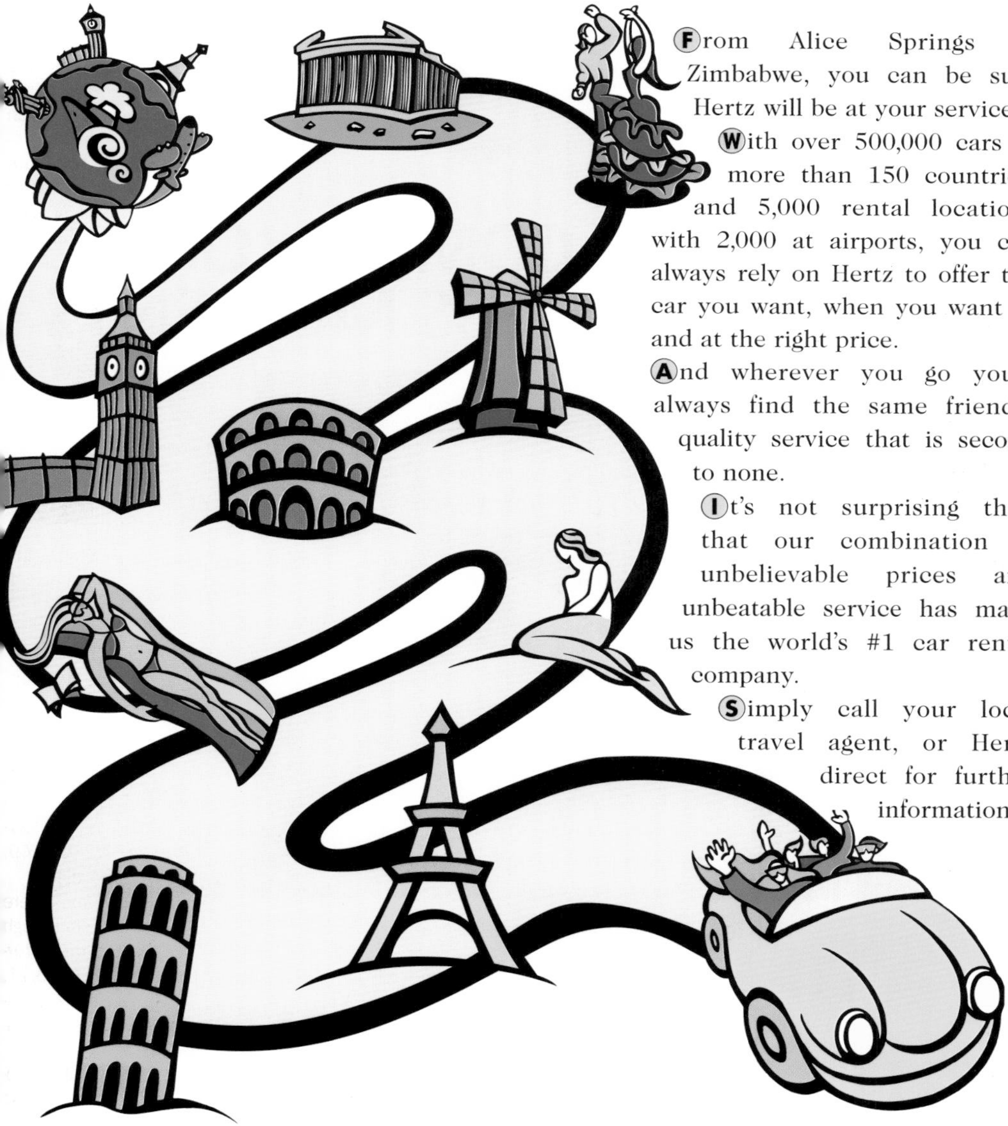

From Alice Springs to Zimbabwe, you can be sure Hertz will be at your service.

With over 500,000 cars in more than 150 countries, and 5,000 rental locations with 2,000 at airports, you can always rely on Hertz to offer the car you want, when you want it, and at the right price.

And wherever you go you'll always find the same friendly quality service that is second to none.

It's not surprising then that our combination of unbelievable prices and unbeatable service has made us the world's #1 car rental company.

Simply call your local travel agent, or Hertz direct for further information.

Highest Quality. Low, Low Prices.

Hertz

tz rents and leases Fords and other fine cars.

CARTAGENA

Cartagena-Hilton. A luxury hotel in nearby El Laguito, tel: 650-666, fax: 650-661.

Hotel de Caribe, Carrera 1 No. 2-87, tel: 650-155, fax: 653-707.

Eating Out

What to Eat

Colombian cooking varies by region, although in the big cities any kind of international cuisine can be enjoyed. A few Colombian specialties worth trying are:

Ajico: a soup of chicken, potatoes and vegetables, common in Bogotá.

Arepa: a maize pancake.

Arroz con coco: rice cooked in coconut oil, special to the coast.

Bandeja paisa: a dish of ground beef, sausages, beans, rice, plantain and avocado.

Carne asada: grilled meat.

Cazuela de mariscos: seafood stew.

Chocolate santafereño: hot chocolate accompanied by cheese and bread.

Mondongo: tripe soup.

Puchero: broth of chicken, beef, pota-to and pork, typical of Bogotá.

Tamales: chopped pork with rice and vegetables folded in a maize dough.

Where to Eat

In Bogotá, the **Casa Vieja** restaurants are considered to offer the best in regional food. They are at Avenida Jiménez No. 3-73, Carrera 10 No. 26-50, and Carrera 116, No. 20-50. **Refugio Alpino**, Calle 23 No. 7-49, serves European food. Budget meals serving *comidas corrientes*, usually a fried piece of meat with bean and rice, are found in many of the restaurants.

In Cartagena, **La Fonda Antioqueñe**, Carrera 2 No. 6-161, has traditional Colombian food, while **Paco's**, opposite the church of Santo Domingo, is also recommended.

Attractions

Culture

Museums

BOGOTÁ

Archaeological Museum, Carrera 6, No. 7-43. Open Monday–Saturday 9am–12.30pm, 1.15pm–5pm, Sunday 10am–1pm.

Museo del Oro (Gold Museum), Parque de Santander, corner of Calle 16 and Carrera 6-A. Open Tuesday to Saturday 9am–4.30pm, Sunday 10am–4.30pm.

Museo Mercedes de Perez, Carrera 7, No. 94-17, on colonial life. Open Tuesday–Sunday 9.30am–12.30pm, 2.30–5pm.

Museum of Modern Art, Calle 24, No. 6-55. Open Tuesday–Sunday 10am–7pm.

National Museum, Carrera 7, No. 28-66 in an old Panopticon prison. Open Tuesday–Saturday 9am–5pm, Sunday 10am–4pm.

For theaters and cinemas, see the *Espectaculos* section of the daily newspapers.

Nightlife

BOGOTÁ

In Bogotá, there are several good *salsa* bars around the intersection of Carrera 5 and Calle 27, although this is the seedy section of town. Others can be found in the Candelaria area – just listen out for the blaring music. Nothing gets moving until after midnight on Fridays and Saturdays. For taped tangos from Argentina, head for **El Viejo Almacén** at Carrera 5 No. 14-23.

CARTAGENA

In Cartagena, a Caribbean trio plays on weekends at **Paco's** opposite the Santo Domingo church – a good place to nurse a drink into the small hours. The bar attached to **La Quemada** has live *salsa* on Friday and Saturday nights, with dancing. For discos, head for the Bocagrande district.

Tours

Package tours as well as travel within and beyond Colombia can be arranged with **Interamerican Tours**, Calle 17, No. 6-57.

Shopping

For Colombian handicrafts, the best place is **Artesanias de Colombia**, Carrera 3 No. 18-60 next to the Iglesia de las Aguas in Bogotá. Other shops are at Carrera 10 No. 26-50 and Carrera 7 No. 23-40.

Emeralds can be bought in the *joyerias* in Bogotá's **La Casa de la Emeralda**, Calle 30 No. 16-18 or in **Joyas Verdes Ltda**, Carreras 15, No. 39-15.

The best antique shop in Bogotá is on the **Plaza Bolívar,** next to the cathedral. Pre-Columbian pottery is sold in the **Centro Internacional**. Colombian leather goods are lesser-known bargains, in shops around the city.

Further Reading

The Politics of Colombia, by Robert H. Dix (Praeger, NY, 1983).

The Search for El Dorado, by John Hemming, (Bogotá, 1984) is an account of the Spanish conquest of Colombia.

Colombia, by Francois de Tailly, (Delachaux and Niestle, 1981) has photographs and text in Spanish and English.

Whitewash: Pablo Escobar and the Cocaine Wars, by Simon Strong, (Macmillan, 1995), the incredible story of the Medellin drugs baron.

Any traveler going to Colombia should read the works of Gabriel García Márquez. His short stories and classic work *One Hundred Years of Solitude* give an invaluable insight into Colombia's past and society.

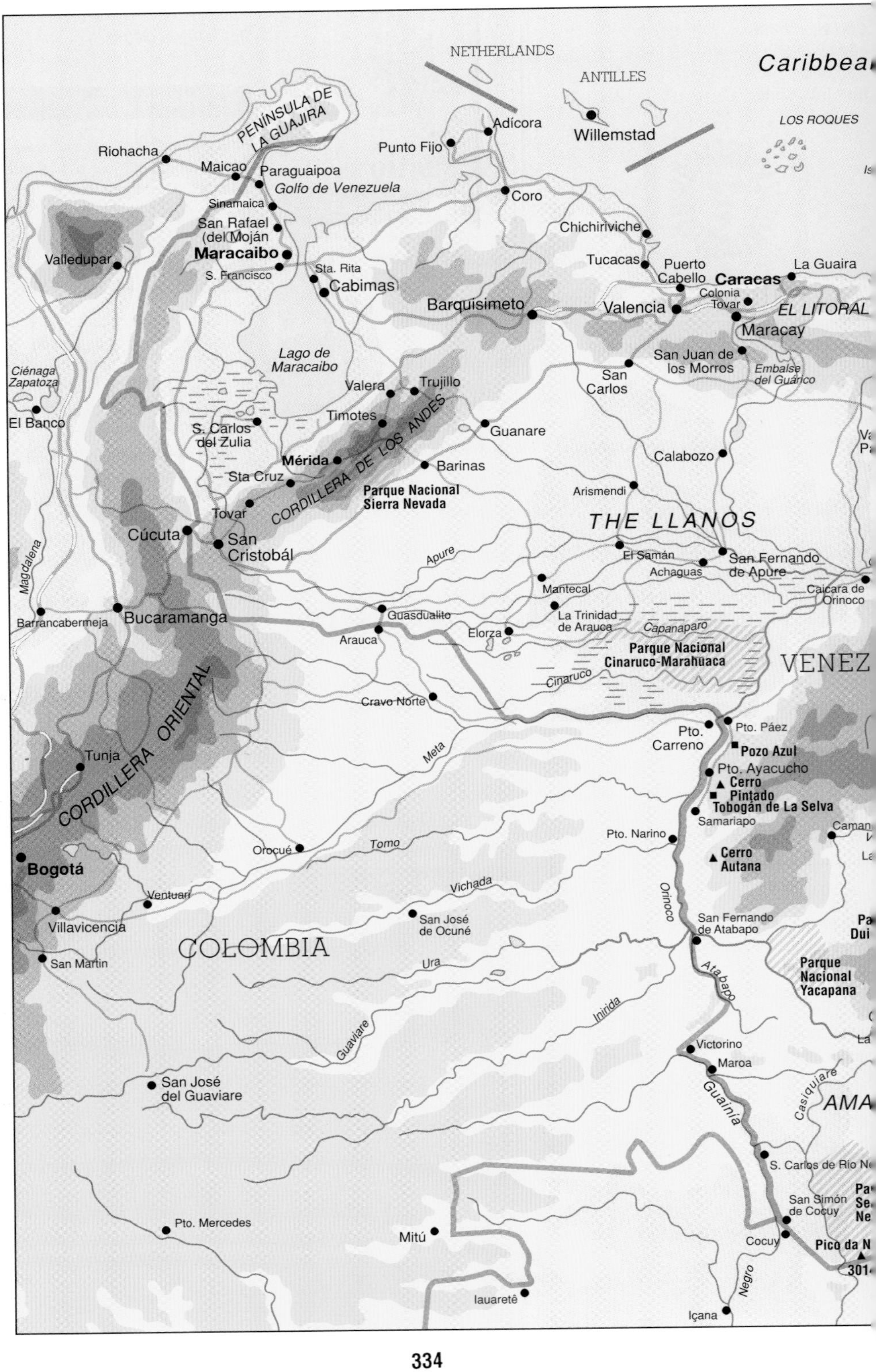
NETHERLANDS
ANTILLES
Caribbea
LOS ROQUES
PENÍNSULA DE LA GUAJIRA
Adícora
Willemstad
Punto Fijo
Riohacha
Maicao
Paraguaipoa
Golfo de Venezuela
Coro
Sinamaica
San Rafael (del Moján
Maracaibo
Chichiriviche
Tucacas
Puerto Cabello
Caracas
La Guaira
Valledupar
S. Francisco
Sta. Rita
Cabimas
Barquisimeto
Valencia
Colonia Tovar
EL LITORAL
Maracay
Lago de Maracaibo
San Juan de los Morros
Embalse del Guárico
San Carlos
Ciénaga Zapatoza
Valera
Trujillo
El Banco
Timotes
S. Carlos del Zulia
Guanare
Calabozo
Mérida
Barinas
Sta Cruz
CORDILLERA DE LOS ANDES
Parque Nacional Sierra Nevada
Arismendi
Tovar
THE LLANOS
Cúcuta
San Cristobál
Magdalena
Apure
El Samán
San Fernando de Apure
Achaguas
Mantecal
Caicara de Orinoco
Barrancabermeja
Bucaramanga
Guasdualito
La Trinidad de Arauca
Arauca
Elorza
Capanaparo
Parque Nacional Cinaruco-Marahuaca
VENEZ
Cinaruco
CORDILLERA ORIENTAL
Cravo Norte
Pto. Carreno
Pto. Páez
Pozo Azul
Pto. Ayacucho
Tunja
Meta
Cerro Pintado
Tobogán de La Selva
Samariapo
Pto. Narino
Orocué
Tomo
Cerro Autana
Bogotá
Vichada
Ventuari
Orinoco
Villavicencia
San José de Ocuné
San Fernando de Atabapo
COLOMBIA
San Martin
Ura
Parque Nacional Yacapana
Atabapo
Inirida
Guaviare
Victorino
Maroa
San José del Guaviare
Casiquiare
Guainia
S. Carlos de Río N
San Simón de Cocuy
Pto. Mercedes
Mitú
Cocuy
Pico da N
Negro
Iauaretê
Içana

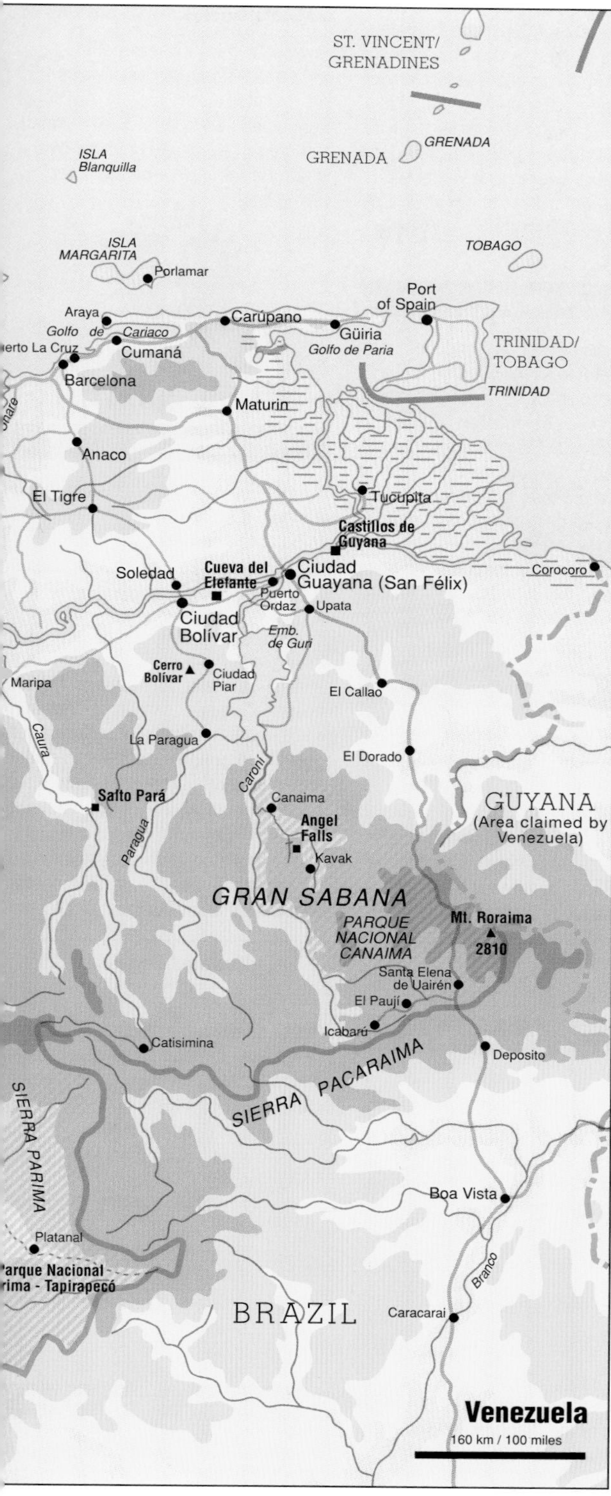

Getting Acquainted

VENEZUELA

Area: 352,00 sq. miles (912,000 sq. km), with a 1,700 mile (2,700 km) Caribbean coast, and 72 islands.
Capital: Caracas.
Population: 23 million. There is a mix of African and European descendants. The native population is fewer than 200,000. Eighty-four percent lives in the urban areas of the country's many, middle-sized cities, making an average of 50 inhabitants per square mile.
Language: Spanish.
Currency: bolívar (US$1=500Bs, £1=750Bs).
Weights & measures: metric.
Electricity: 110 volts.
Time zone: GMT –4hrs, EST +1hr.
Dialing code: 58 (Caracas +2).

Climate

Venezuela has a tropical climate with average temperatures of 27°C (80°F). Four climatic zones are represented within its boundaries: hot, mild, cool and cold.

In the Andes region the highest mountains are covered with permanent snow. Like everywhere else in the tropics, temperature depends greatly on altitude above sea-level and temperate climates can be found among mountain landscapes away from the coast. Hot temperatures prevail throughout the year in the lowlands, mainly along the coast. During December, January and February there is a slight lowering of temperature and in zones like the Caracas Valley the climate is temperate and similar to France or Spain during April and early May.

The rainy season lasts from mid-May until the end of October, but showers may fall in December or January. In Caracas, the January average temperature is 18.6°C (65°F) rising to 21°C (70°F) in July.

Government & Economy

Venezuela is a centralized federal republic formed by 22 states, a federal district, two federal territories and 62 federal departments (corresponding to Venezuela's islands in the Caribbean Sea). The government system is a representative democracy with one authority for each of the three branches of public power – legislative, executive and judicial.

Executive power rests solely with the president designated by direct, popular and secret ballot for a five-year non-renewable term. With the council of ministers, the president is answerable to the legislature – a two-chamber congress of the senate and house of representatives. While ex-presidents of the republic automatically become life members of the senate, its other members are elected, two from each state and federal district plus 55 senators proportionally representing the minority political parties.

Planning the Trip

What to Wear

Tropical worsted clothing in normal city colors is best for Caracas while in Maracaibo and the hot, humid coastal and low-lying areas, regular washable tropical clothing is best. In western Venezuela, in the higher Andes, a light overcoat and woolen sports jacket are handy. Khaki bush clothing is a must for a visit to the oil fields but men should wear long trousers except when they are at the beach. Women should wear slacks or cotton dresses with an extra wrap for cooler evenings as well as in air-conditioned restaurants and cinemas.

Visas

Entry is by passport and visa or passport and tourist card. If arriving by air, tourist cards (valid for 60 days) can be issued to citizens of the United States, Canada, Japan and Western European countries (except Spain and Portugal). If arriving by land, a visa must be obtained from a consulate before arrival – requiring a letter of reference. It is a good idea to carry your passport with you at all times as the police mount spot checks and anyone without id is detained. An exit tax of about US$25 is levied on departure.

Health

Health conditions in Venezuela are good. Water in all major urban areas is chlorinated and safe to drink. Medical care is good. Inoculation against typhoid and yellow fever is advisable and you should have protection against malaria if you plan to visit the Orinoco basin and other swampy or forest regions in the interior.

It is always good to take some form of remedy for stomach upsets and have a roll of toilet paper handy.

Money Matters

The unit of currency is the bolívar. It's best to change traveler's checks or US dollars in a *casa de cambio*. Only accept US dollars if changing money in hotels.

The majority of banks do not change traveler's checks. Many banks will accept Visa cards in their hole-in-the-wall and there are cash machines at the airport.

Public Holidays

January 1st – New Year's Day
Carnival on the Monday and Tuesday before Ash Wednesday
Holy Week Thursday–Saturday
April 19th – Anniversary of the National Declaration of Independence
May 1st – Labour Day
June 24th – The feast day of San Juan Bautista
July 5th – Anniversary of the Signing of Venezuelan National Independence Act
July 24th – Anniversary of the birth of the Liberator, Simon Bolívar
October 12th – Columbus Day (Anniversary of the Discovery of America)
December 25th – Christmas Day

Getting There

Venezuela has six international airports and 282 airdromes of which 250 are private, used mostly by small planes and helicopters. The metropolitan area of Caracas is served by the Simon Bolívar International Airport.

Practical Tips

Emergencies

The nationwide emergency telephone number, **171**, is for police, fire and ambulance services.

Security & Crime

The crime rate in Venezuela, particularly in Caracas, is high. It is recommended that you take precautions by not wearing jewelry or carrying money in a way it can be snatched. You should not walk alone in narrow streets in downtown Caracas after dark and it is strongly recommended that you not travel by car at night, particularly in the countryside where, should you have an accident or breakdown, the risk of robbery and other crimes is much greater.

Medical Services

Better hotels have physicians on call. Check with the concierge. Every town has a rotating system to ensure a pharmacy is open 24 hours. These are marked with a 'torno' sign.

In an emergency, contact the following in Caracas (02):

Hospital Universitario (UCV), tel: 606-71.11.

Clínica de Emergencia Infantil (children's emergencies) Edif. Topacio, 4th floor, Av Avila, between Avs Caracas and Gamboa. Tel: 51.61.11

Business Hours

Business hours are 8am–noon and 2pm–6pm although some stores stay open until later (8pm). As in all Latin countries, Venezuelans tend to enjoy extended lunch-hours.

Media

The *Daily Journal*, founded in 1945 by Jules Waldman, is the country's only English-language daily newspaper and is favored by newcomers to Caracas as well as international businessmen and diplomats.

The main Spanish-language papers published in Caracas with a national distribution are *El Nacional, El Universal* and *El Diario.*

Postal Services

The Venezuelan postal system is extremely slow and inefficient although efforts are being made to speed it up. As a result motorbike courier services abound in Caracas and other courier services are favored to other parts of the country.

Useful Addresses

Tourist Information

CORPOTURISMO (Corporacion de Turismo de Venezuela) is the Venezuelan State Tourist Authority with overall responsibility for matters relating to toursm. Although they claim to have a ıotel-booking or reservation service, it s strongly recommended that you nake arrangements via a local travel ıgency or tour organizer. You can conact CORPOTURISMO Torre Oeste, Piso 35-7, Parque Central, Avenida Lecuna, ;aracas, tel: (02) 507-8815 or 507-3726, telex: 27328 TURIS VC, fax: (02) 574-8489.

The special unit for information for ourists (Unitur) tel: (02) 507.86.

Embassies & Consulates

iplomatic representations in Caracas
ustralia: Quinta Yolanda, Avenida Luis oche, entre 6 & 7 Transversal, Altamia, tel: 261-46.32, fax: 261.34.48.
anada: Torre Europa, Piso 7, Avenida, Francisco de Miranda, Urg. Campo, Alegre, tel: 951-61.76.
Great Britain: Torre Las Mercedes, Piso 3, Avenida La Estancia, Urb. Chuao, tel: 993.41.11, fax: 92.32.92.
United States: Av. Francisco de Miranda, Urb. La Floresta, tel: (02) 285-22.22 or 285-31.11.

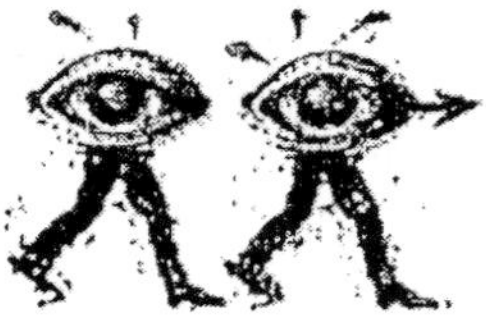

Getting Around

On Arrival

Tourist authorities warn that taxi services at the main airports are infamous for over-charging hapless tourists and anyone else who cannot speak Spanish or handle the situation well. Efforts have been made to control excesses. The airport information desk will assist you with enquiries.

Porter services are available at all the airports and hotels – a modest tip of Bs10 with the hint of more to come (perhaps totalling Bs25–30) on completion of the task will often elicit the best help available.

Public Transportation

There are 64,374 km (40,000 miles) of roads, 18,000 of which are paved and there are many freeways. Long distance bus lines operate from the Nuevo Circo bus station in the Caracas city center. Bus travel varies a lot in quality with most companies liable to run bone-shaking wrecks of buses on the same routes as luxury coaches.

The Metro

The metro runs 5.30am–11pm. It is safe and quick, probably the best way to travel around the city.

Where to Stay

Fairmont International, Torre Capriles, Planta Baja, Plaza Venezuela, Caracas, tel: 782-8433, fax: 782-4407, will book hotel rooms in Caracas and also in 102 hotels in the rest of the country. The airport tourist office is also very helpful and will make reservations. The Venezuelan Hotel Association, **Anahoven**, tel: (02) 574-3994 or 574-7172 liaises with the state tourist authority to supervise hotel standards and to deal with all customer enquiries and complaints.

Hotels

CARACAS

Avila, Av Washington, San Bernardinao, tel: 51.51.28, fax: 52.30.21. Traditional flavor in quiet residential neighborhood.
Caracas Hilton, Avenida Libertador y Sur 25, tel:503.50.00, fax: 575-0024. Well located and a favorite of the Japanese.
El Condor, 3rd Av de Las Delicias. Saban a Grance, tel: 762.99.11.15, fax: 762.86.21. Among the main shopping centers.
Tamanacolnter-Continental, Avenida Principal las Mercedes, tel: 92.45.22, fax: 208-70.04. Best hotel in Caracas.

CIUDAD GUYANA

Inter-Continental Guyana, tel (086) 22.22.35, fax: 22.22.53. Five-star hotel overlooking Caroní River and Falls.
Rasil, tel: 23.30.25. fax: 22.77.03. Central location and all facilities.

MERIDA

Posada Luz Caraballo, Av 2 No.13-80, tel: (074) 52.54.41. One of three posadas in town (Veijo Tojado, Papa Miguel). Reliable, comfortable, economical and in the center of town.,
Park, Calle 37, tel: (074) 63.70.14, fax: 63.45.82. One of the best downtown hotels.

Eating Out

What to Eat

Venezuelan cuisine is very varied because of the diverse cultural influences the country has been subjected to over four centuries. At Christmas and national celebrations the *hallaca* is paramount as Venezuela's national dish – it's a stew of chicken, pork, beef and spices used as a filling to a pie-like dough of maize, which is then wrapped in banana leaves and cooked in boiling water. One of the favorites is *Pabellon* which is considered to be the national dish combining rice, black beans, shredded beef and *tajadas* (sliced and fried ripe plantains).

In the Andes there is *pisca*, a rich and tasty soup as well as local dishes based on trout and sausage. Coro is famous for its *tarkari de chivo* (made from goat) marinated fish and goat milk preserves.

Zulia State has delicious coconut-based specialties like *conejo en coco* (rabbit cooked in coconut milk) and a selection of sweets and candies. The eastern region is widely known for its tasty seafood specialties like *consomé de chipichipi* (small clams broth); cream of *guacucos* (middle-sized clams) and *empanadas de cazón* (small shark pie). A typical and very popular Venezuelan dish is *mondongo* (a soup-like stew which uses specially processed tripe as a main ingredient). The *arepa* is traditional Venezuelan bread made from maize and served either fried or baked.

Where to Eat

Like any other great metropolis, Caracas has a huge variety of restaurants – Chinese, French, Spanish, Italian, Portuguese, Japanese, Colombian, Arabian, Argentinian, Mexican and even Trinidadian for curry lovers.

Eating out is extremely cheap by US and European standards and there are literally hundreds of restaurants catering to all tastes. From the *tascas* of Candelaria where the best Spanish cooking in the whole of Venezuela is said to be available, to the elegant and exorbitant French restaurants of Las Mercedes, there is a range of gastronomic delights to satisfy every whim.

The cheapest food is at *Fuentes de Soda* and cafes. Food in bars may cost 50 percent more and there is no need to feel reticent about asking for prices before you order as the price of a beer can often be as much as three times higher. You can save on the 10 percent service charge if you eat at the bar and not at a table. If in doubt consult the price list which by decree restaurants must put up on or near the front door. Restaurants may not charge for bread, butter or condiments.

Caracas

Las Mercedes and the Altamira–Los Palos Grandes zone offer a huge variety of cuisines and trendier, more upscale dining spots; Av. Francisco Solano, between Chacaíto and Av. Las Acacias, has a large concentration of Italian spots; Candelaria for Spanish food and tascas. An excellent source of information is Miro Popic's *Guía Gastronómica de Caracas*, updated annually, in English/Spanish, available in most bookstores and hotels.

Arábica Coffee Bar: Av Andrés Bello at Los Palos Grandes, tel: 285.34.69. Best coffee in the city; the only place in the country offering estate-grown single-variety coffees from all over Venezuela, roasted daily. Also a great choice of distinct pastries.

Tambo: Av. Francisco de Miranda, Torre Europa, ground floor, Campo Alegre, tel. 952.42.43/69.95. Two distinctive offerings under one roof: Peruvian and Japanese, reflecting the dual roots of the owner. A place to see and be seen.

Urrutia/Casa Urrutia: Av. Francisco Solano, Esq. Los Manguitos, Sabana Grande, tel. 71.04.48. Spanish cuisine with 30 years of tradition initiated by Adolfo Urrutia, with Basque–Navarrese specialties; consistent, no one ever leaves disappointed.

Bar Basque: Between the corners of Alcabala and Peligro, Candelaria, tel. 572.48.57. Tiny, friendly, inviting bar/restaurant in the same place in the heart of the Spanish zone of Caracas for some 30 years, with unwavering quality. One of the best restaurants at any price in the city. Open only for lunch.

El Buffet Vegetariano: Av. Los Jardines, La Florida, tel. 74.74.90. Half a century of consistent style and quality. Fixed vegetarian menu daily, abundant portions, no smoking, no liquor.

La Paninoteka: Av. El Empalme, La Campiña, tel. 74.83.21. Tiny place with excellent quality, honest home cooking, mostly traditional Venezuelan specialties; menu changes regularly based on requests of clients. Closed weekends.

Le Petit Bistrot de Jacques: Av. Principal of Las Mercedes, tel. 993.40.93, 91.09.75. A more authentic French bistrot you couldn't even find in Paris. Intimate setting, fixed menu written on the mirrors, classic bistrot offerings - *cassoulet, choucroute, steak frites*, homemade pastries. Closed Saturday lunch and Sunday.

Le Gourmet: Hotel Tamanaco Inter-Continental, Las Mercedes, tel. 208.-72.42. Beautiful, formal setting with a recent facelift. Premium dining with excellence guaranteed in flavor, presentation, service. Live background music. Top chef prepares primarily French cuisine but with imaginative touches.

Via Appia: Centro Coinasa, ground floor, La Castellana, tel. 263.99.23, 265.53.48. Family-run Italian eatery with great attention to details, everything prepared fresh, extremely popular place among power people in town.

El Portón: Av. Pichincha, El Rosal, tel. 952.00.27. Large place divided in various areas, with typical Venezuelan dishes and beef; live entertainment in the dining area with *música criolla*, *ranchera*, the equivalent to American country and western.

Papagallo: C.C. Chacaíto, next to the Chacaíto Metro. Long-time establishment with enormous menu and specials of the day, where one can always count on a fast, generously served economical meal. Great place for people watching; with its convenient location, a traditional meeting place; open from early morning 'til around midnight.

Verdelecho: Hotel Eurobuilding Caracas, Chuao, tel. 907.11.11, 959 11.33. Natural food, long on salads vegetarian fare with a gourmet flair.

Attractions

Culture

Museums

The following museums are recommended for a visit (most museums are closed on Monday):

Casa Natal Del Libertador, Plaza San Jacinto A Traposos, Centro, tel: 545-7693. A faithful colonial reconstruction on the original site where Simon Bolívar was born, with furnishings and memorabilia of that period.

Cuadra Bolivar, Avenida Sr 2 entre Esq. Barcenas y Las Piedras, tel: 483-3971. A reconstruction on the original site of the Bolívar family's country home "El Palmar", with gardens and patios, colonial furniture, a restored kitchen, portraits and books of the period.

Galeria de Arte Nacional, Plaza Morelos, Urb. Los Caobos, tel: 571-0170.

Galeria Felix, 3 Transversal, entre Avenida Luis Roche y San Juan Bosco, Urb. Altamira, tel: 261-4517 or 262-0204.

Jardín Botánico, Calle Salvador Allende, Ciudad Universitaria, UCV.

Museo Arturo Michelena, Esq. Urapal No. 82 (a block south of La Pastora Church), Urb. La Pastora, tel: (02) 825-853. Open 9am–noon and 3pm–5pm (closed Monday and Friday). Former residence of the famous 19th-century Venezuelan painter Arturo Michelena. It is a stony, old-style house containing the painter's personal belongings and some unfinished canvasses.

Museo De Arte Colonial, Quinta Anauco, Avenida Panteón (at the Cota Mil exit), San Bernadino, tel: (02) 518-517. Former residence of the Marqués del Toro, War of Independence hero, has been faithfully restored with a collection of colonial furniture, household implements, paintings and sculptures, surrounded by beautiful gardens.

Museo De Caracas, Palacio Municipal (Concejo Municipal), Plaza Bolívar, Esq. Las Monjas, tel: 545-6706 or 545-8688. Features wood-carved miniatures by Raul Santacan depicting scenes of life in Caracas from colonial times to the beginning of this century and the life works of Venezuela's internationally acclaimed impressionist painter Emilio Boggio (1857–1920).

Museo Historico Militar, La Planicie, Urb. 23 de Enero, tel: 415-175 or 410-808. On the site of the old Ministry of Defence buildings. It houses collections of uniforms, flags and swords.

Panteón Nacional, Plaza del Panteon, Avenida Panteon y Avenida Norte, Centro, tel: (02) 821-518. Contains the tomb of Simon Bolívar and memorials to other military heroes of the War of Independence.

Concerts

The Venezuelan Symphony Orchestra and the Caracas Municipal Symphony give regular concerts in the **Sala Rios Reyna** of the **Teresa Carreno** on Paseo Colón, one of the most important architectural works in the city.

Theaters

There are several permanent theaters and many theatrical groups. Every night there is a different presentation somewhere. The most important theaters are: **Rajatabla, Ana Julia Rojas, Alberto de Paz y Mateos, Chacaito, Luis Peraza, the National Theater** (home of the National Theater Company), **Los Cedros**, **Santa Sofia**, **La Campina**, **Sala Cadafe** and **Las Palmas.**

Nightlife

Caracas is a swinging city by night and there are many and varied discos and nightclubs. Caraqueños usually eat at home at 8pm and in restaurants between 9pm and 11pm and the partying goes on until well into the early hours of the morning. There are many small clubs, restaurants and bars on **Plaza Altamira Sur** and along the **Sabana Grande.**

Shopping

What to Buy

Venezuela's craftsmen have a prestigious position because of the variety and quality of their workmanship. For example, outstanding Quibor ceramics have pre-hispanic origins, molded using styles and techniques handed down through the generations. Baskets, hammocks, hats and other products made from vegetable fibers are to be found in the towns and villages along the Easter Coast. Beautifully woven square and round ponchos, colorful blankets and caps are sold by the Andean people while craftsmen of the *llanos* (prairies) sell four-string guitar-like musical instruments called *cuatros* as well as harps and mandolins. Craftsmen of San Franscisco de Yare make Devil's masks for their Festival of the Dancing Devils while hand-carved furniture and objects made from goat skins are among representative samples from Coro.

Where to Buy

The **Sabana Grande Boulevard** is an excellent commercial artery with hundreds of boutiques, jewelry stores, bazaars and stores. There are busy bars and coffee shops. Visit **Chacaito, CCCT, Paseo Las Mercedes, Concresa, Plaza Las Americas** – all have supermarkets, department stores, cafeterias, restaurants, beauty parlors and just about every imaginable ware on display.

Further Reading

In the Rainforest, by Catherine Caufield. A definitive report on the Amazon jungle.

The General in his Labyrinth, by Gabriel García Marquez. Traces the final days of Simón Bolívar.

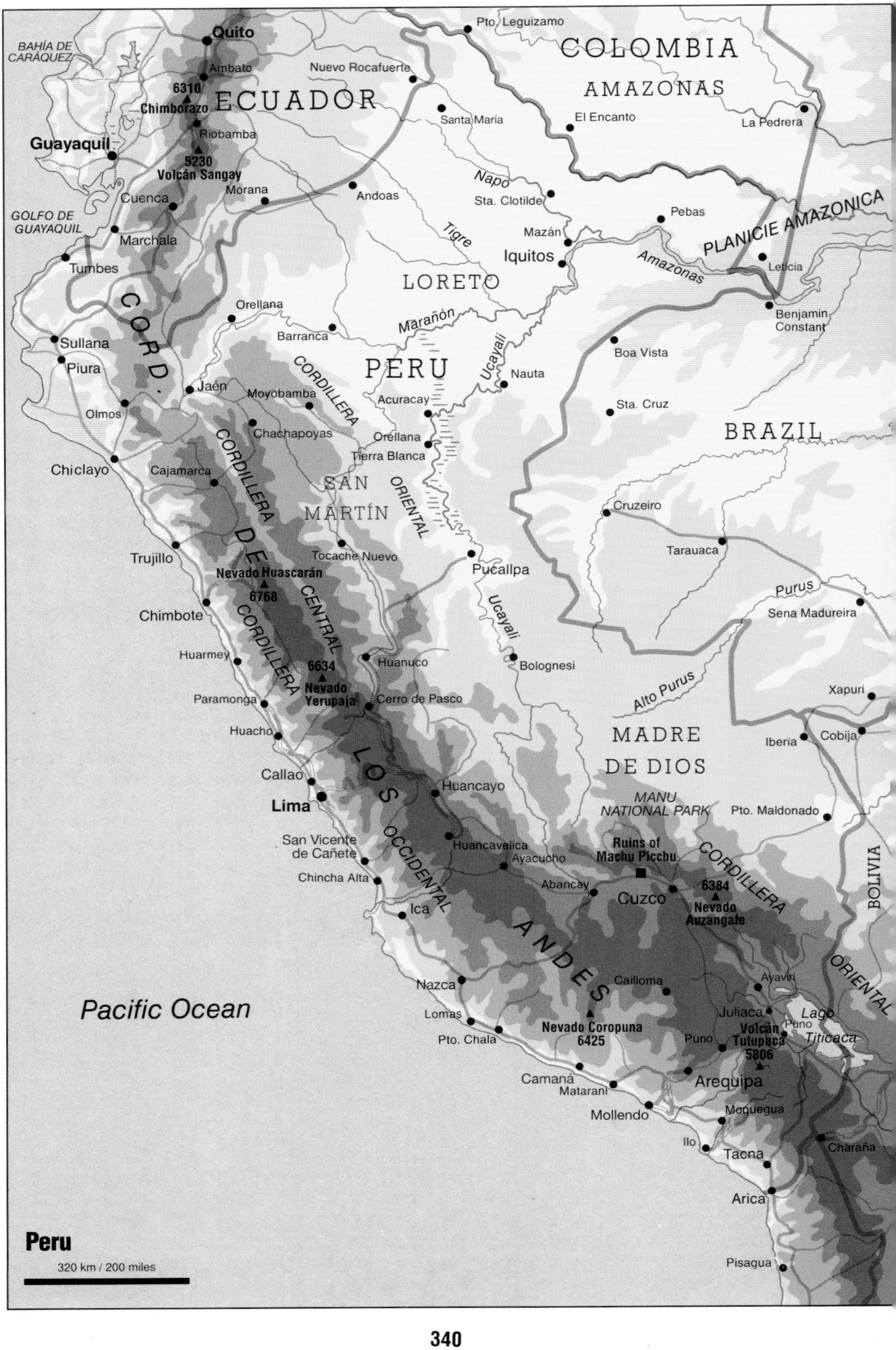
Peru
320 km / 200 miles
Pacific Ocean
COLOMBIA
AMAZONAS
ECUADOR
PERU
BRAZIL
BOLIVIA
LORETO
SAN MARTÍN
MADRE DE DIOS
MANU NATIONAL PARK
PLANICIE AMAZONICA
BAHÍA DE CARÁQUEZ
GOLFO DE GUAYAQUIL
CORD.
CORDILLERA
CORDILLERA ORIENTAL
CORDILLERA CENTRAL
CORDILLERA DE LOS ANDES
CORDILLERA OCCIDENTAL
CORDILLERA ORIENTAL
Quito
Ambato
6310
Chimborazo
Riobamba
Guayaquil
5230
Volcán Sangay
Cuenca
Morana
Marchala
Tumbes
Sullana
Piura
Olmos
Chiclayo
Jaén
Orellana
Barranca
Moyobamba
Chachapoyas
Cajamarca
Trujillo
Nevado Huascarán
6768
Chimbote
Huarmey
6634
Nevado Yerupaja
Paramonga
Huacho
Callao
Lima
San Vicente de Cañete
Chincha Alta
Ica
Nazca
Lomas
Pto. Chala
Camaná
Matarani
Mollendo
Ilo
Tacna
Arica
Pisagua
Pto. Leguizamo
Nuevo Rocafuerte
Santa María
El Encanto
La Pedrera
Napo
Andoas
Sta. Clotilde
Pebas
Tigre
Mazán
Iquitos
Amazonas
Leticia
Benjamin Constant
Marañón
Ucayali
Nauta
Boa Vista
Sta. Cruz
Acuracay
Orellana
Tierra Blanca
Cruzeiro
Tarauaca
Tocache Nuevo
Pucallpa
Ucayali
Purus
Sena Madureira
Huanuco
Bolognesi
Alto Purus
Cerro de Pasco
Xapuri
Iberia
Cobija
Huancayo
Pto. Maldonado
Huancavelica
Ayacucho
Ruins of Machu Picchu
Abancay
Cuzco
6384
Nevado Auzangate
Cailloma
Ayaviri
Juliaca
Puno
Lago Titicaca
Nevado Coropuna
6425
Puno
Volcán Tutupaca
5806
Arequipa
Moquegua
Charaña

Getting Acquainted

PERU

Area: 496,100 sq. miles (1,285,000 sq. km).
Capital: Lima.
Population: 21.5 million. Because of successive waves of immigration, Indian and *mestizo* citizens live side by side with Europeans and Chinese and Japanese. The country's coastal cities to the south include a cohesive black population.
Language: The official languages are Spanish and Quechua, although all school children must also study English. Near Puno and Lake Titicaca, Aymará is spoken.
Currency: sol nuevo (US$1=SN2, £1=SN3).
Weights & measures: metric.
Electricity: 220 volts.
Time zone: GMT–5, same as EST.
Dialing code: 51 (Lima +14).

Climate

Peru's coastline has average temperatures of between 14°–27°C (58°–80°F), while in the highlands – or *sierra* – it is normally cold, sunny and dry for much of the year, with temperatures ranging from 9°–18°C (48°–65°F). The rainy season in the *sierra* is from December to May. The jungle is hot and humid with temperatures ranging from 25°–28°C (77°–82°F).

Lima alone suffers from the climatic condition the Peruvians call *garua* – a thick wet fog that covers the city without respite for the winter.

Government & Economy

Since 1979 Peru has been governed by a democratic government under a constitution. Presidential elections are held every five years and municipal elections are held every three years. The country is divided into 24 departments and the province of Callao which is where the country's main port is located.

Fishing, mining and tourism play important roles in the economy, although the government of Alan García gradually revitalized the farming sector. Petroleum is extracted from the Amazon jungle area, providing half the domestic demand.

A slump in the manufacturing sector, caused partly by the nation's refusal to pay its huge foreign debt and the corresponding cut of new aid lending agencies, resulted in a series of problems with foreign reserves, weakening the inti in the mid-80s.

In 1992, the manufacturing sector began to return to growth when consumption was stimulated by salary increases and successful negotiations by the Fugimori government with Peru's international creditors. Agriculture and the copper and fishing industries all reached record highs and Fujimori was re-elected in 1995.

Planning the Trip

What to Bring

Tourists should bring with them any medicines or cosmetics they use. Bring any electrical equipment you might need and plenty of film for your camera as stocks are often outdated. Since Peruvians are smaller in stature than North Americans or Europeans, it may be difficult to find clothing.

Maps

Maps are available from Infotur free of charge. Larger city maps are sold at newspaper kiosks, bookstores and the **Instituto Geografico National** at Avenida Aramburu 1190 in the suburb of Surquillo, tel: 759-960. One-time use of map room and files is available from the **South American Explorer's Club** or, for the $25 membership fee, unlimited use of the club's resources and its office (with storerooms, safe deposit boxes, library, kitchen, first aid materials) on Avenida Republica de Portugal 146, tel: 0051-14-250142.

Visas

Visitors from most European countries (except Spain), the United States and Canada, do not require visas to enter Peru. With a valid passport, citizens of these countries receive a tourism card which is usually good for 90 days. Australians and New Zealanders need visas. A 60-day extension is available upon payment of $10 and presentation of a return travel ticket. Contact the Dirección General de Migraciones at Paseo de la Republica 585 in Lima.

Vaccinations are not required for entry to Peru. On departure, an $18 exit tax on international flights must be paid in US dollars.

Customs

It is illegal to take archaeological artifacts out of the country. Special permits are needed to bring professional movie or video equipment into Peru. In Cuzco, a special tax is assessed for professional photographers passing their equipment through the airport.

Money Matters

Banks, money exchange houses, hotel and travel agencies are authorized to exchange money, either from traveler's checks, cash or, in some cases, money orders. Exchange rates fluctuate daily. US dollars are the most useful currency to carry.

Most international credit cards are accepted, including Diners Club, Visa, MasterCard and American Express at hotels, restaurants and stores. Note, however, that the exchange rate may be calculated at the bank rate, which is generally not as favorable as the change house rate.

Credit card loss can be reported in Lima by calling 441-891/896. The Visa "cash advance" card is useful in major cities (the Banco de la Nacion handles these transactions).

Getting There

By Air

Peruvian Airlines, AeroPeru and Faucett have direct flights to Lima from Miami; Aerolineas Argentinas flies from Los Angeles; Faucett also has direct Miami-Iquitos service. The only US carrier with a service to Peru is Eastern Airlines. From Canada, Canadian Air has direct flights. From Europe use: Alitalia, Air France, Iberia, KLM, Lufthansa and British Airways.

AeroPeru has also been offering a 45-day excursion fare, including a stopover in Lima and one other city in Peru, from Miami to anywhere on the AeroPeru route (Guayaquil, Panama City, Santiago, Buenos Aires, Caracas, Bogotá, La Paz, São Paulo and Rio de Janeiro) for around US$759.

By Land

Peru has borders with five other countries: Chile, Bolivia, Colombia, Brazil and Ecuador. The border crossing with Chile is at Tacna on the Peruvian side, Arica on the Chilean; taxis regularly make the crossing and some long distance buses operate between Lima, Quito, Santiago de Chile and Buenos Aires. Tickets for such marathon journeys sometimes include food and overnight accommodation in resthouses.

From Bolivia, efficient minibus services will take you from La Paz to Puno; alternatively, **Crillon Tours** in Bolivia offers a hydrofoil across Lake Titicaca. The journey from Ecuador is also straight forward: take a bus to the border at Huaquillas and walk through to Tumbes. Other buses operate from there (note that the "international service" advertised in Quito still requires a change of buses at the border, so it is actually more expensive and occasionally less convenient than doing the trip with separate legs.)

All international railway links have closed due to a lack of profitability.

Useful Addresses

AeroPeru Av José Pardo 805, 3rd floor, Miraflores, tel: 47-8333
Main Tourist Office: Av Andrés Reyes 320, Lima 27, San Isidro, Lima, tel: 70-0781, fax: 42-4195

Practical Tips

Emergencies

Security & Crime

As Peru's urban centers have swelled, so has petty crime. Pickpockets and thieves – including senior citizens and children – have become more and more common in Lima and Cuzco. It is recommended that tourists do not wear costly jewelry and that their watches, if worn, be covered by a shirt or sweater sleeve. Thieves have become amazingly adept at slitting open shoulder bags, camera cases and knapsacks; keep an eye on your belongings. Officials also warn against dealing with anyone calling your hotel room or approaching you in the hotel lobby or on the street, allegedly representing a travel agency or specialty shop. Carry your passport at all times.

A special security service for tourists has been created by the Civil Guard. They are recognizable by a white braid worn across the shoulder of their uniforms and can be found all over Lima, especially in the downtown area. In Cuzco, all police have tourism police training. The tourist police office in Lima is at Avenida Salaverry 1156, tel: 714-313.

There has been much publicity about terrorism in Peru. Tourists have managed to avoid dangerous contact with political violence. It is recommended that tourists avoid areas where there are terrorism alerts or border disputes with Ecuador or Bolivia. For specific inquiries, contact your embassy.

Medical Services

Most major hotels have a doctor on call. Three clinics in Lima and its suburbs have 24-hour emergency service and usually an English-speaking member of staff on duty: Clinica Anglo-Americana, Avenida Salazar in San Isidro, tel: 40-3570; the Clinica Internacional on Washington 1475, tel: 28-8060 and the Clinica San Borja, on Avenida del Aire 333 in the suburb of San Borja, tel: 41-3141.

Business Hours

Offices normally operate from 10am–8pm with many establishments closing from 2–4pm. Banking hours are from 9am–12.30pm and from 3–6pm from Monday to Friday.

Tourist Offices

Peru's National Tourism Board offices (Infotur) – with two locations in Lima and offices in nearly every major city in the country – can offer the best information about how to get from one place to another.

In Lima the city tourism office in the passageway beside the city hall has information about the downtown area. Infotur offices are located at Av Andrés Reyes 320 (*see* Useful Adresses above) and at the national and international areas of Lima's Jorge Chavez Airport.

Embassies & Consulates

The following diplomatic representation is all in Lima:
Canada: Federico Gerdes 130 (Miraflores), tel: 444-015. It also represents Australia and New Zealand
Great Britain: 12th floor Washington Building, Plaza Washington, tel: 33-5032/28-3830.
Ireland: Carlos Povias Osores 410, San Isidro, tel: 23-0808
United States: Grimaldo del Solar 346 (Miraflores), tel: 443-621.

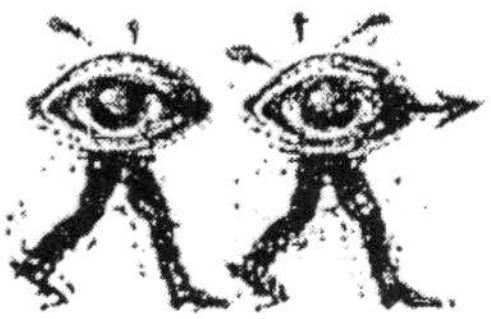

Getting Around

From the Airport

There is a bus service, the Airport Express, which runs every 20 minutes that will shuttle passengers to and from the airport and their hotels. It also will pick up passengers from other parts of town, even if they are not staying in hotels.

It costs approximately US$4–6 to take a cab from the airport downtown or to most parts of the suburbs. Since most taxis do not have meters, make sure you agree with the driver on a price beforehand. Although cabs are inexpensive anyway you look at it, walking from the airport across the parking lot to the main roadway (Avenida Faucett) to catch a cab could save half the fare. Faucett is also where you can get city buses from the airport. Ask at the Infotur office at the airport for routes and fare information.

You can also rent cars at the airport, where Avis, Budget, Hertz and National have offices open 24-hours a day. An international driver's license is needed and is valid for 30 days. For additional days, it is necessary to obtain authorization from the Touring and Automobile Club of Peru, located at Cesar Vallejo 699, Lince, tel: 403-270 or fax: 419-652.

Public Transportation

By Air

Domestic airlines Faucett, Americana and AeroPeru serve most cities in Peru. AeroPeru's main office is at Plaza San Martin, Avenida Nicolas de Pierola (La Colmena) 914, tel: 285-721/237-459; 24-hour reconfirmation and reservation line, tel: 478-333. Faucett's principal office for domestic flights is at the corner of Avenida Garcilaso de la Vega 865 (Wilson) at Quilca, tel: 338-180. Americana is located at Avenida Larco 345, tel: 478-216.

For trips over the Nazca line or special short flights, Aerocondor has an office at Jr. Juan de Arona 781, San Isidro, tel: 425-215.

By Road

Lima has a multitude of city bus lines, although most are overcrowded, slow and not recommended for tourists. Cab fares are generally so inexpensive by international standards that they are preferred.

For travel outside the city, cars may be rented, transportation can be arranged through travel agencies and buses are available to just about every part of the country.

By Train

There are train service east of Lima and south to Arequipa, Puno and Cuzco. Since trains are the most economical means of transportation, they are also sometimes the most crowded. Make sure you have a guaranteed seat and a tourist (first-class) ticket. The rail line from Lima to Huancayo is the world's highest, reaching nearly 5,000 meters (16,000 ft) above sea level. The train depot for all departures in Lima is the Desamparados Station behind the Presidential Palace, tel: 276-620/289-440.

Where to Stay

Hotels

Enturperú, the government-run hotel chain, does not have hotels in Lima but it has everything from youth hostels to exclusive luxury hotels in the rest of the country, usually going simply by the name "Hotel Turistas". Its main office and reservation center is on Avenida Javier Prado Oeste 1358, San Isidro, PO Box 4475, Lima, tel: 14-428-526/428-837. For information tel: 14-721-928. Travel agencies can also make reservations for you.

AREQUIPA

El Portal. Portal de Flores 116, tel: 21-5530. Excellent views and rooftop pool.

Hotel La Casa de Mi Abuela, Jerusalem 606, tel: 22-4582. Very popular, idyllic garden setting.

Hotel Turistas. Plaza Bolívar on Selva Alegre, tel: 21-5110.

CAJAMARCA

Hostal Laguna Seca. Avenida Manco Capac Banos del Inca. Just outside the city at the thermal baths, the waters of which enter the bathrooms of this hotel; tel: 05 (in Lima, 46-3270).

Hotel Turistas Jr. Lima 773. Tel 24-70, Reservations in Peru, tel: 42-8626. Very comfortable and central.

CUZCO

El Dorado Inn. Sol 395, tel: 23-1135, fax: 23-3112. Five star hotel with pool and sauna.

Libertador Cuzco. San Agustin 400, tel: 23-1961, (in Lima, 14-0166). The best of the five-stars.

Hotel de las Marquesas Garcilaso 256, tel: 23-2512. Colonial ambience and charming inner courtyard.

Hostal Loreto, Pasaje Loreto (the famous Inca walled lane). Popular with budget travelers.

IQUITOS

Acosta 1, Esq Huallaga & Araujo, tel 23-5974. Has swiming pool and good restaurant.

Explorama Inn/Lodge/camp. Outside the city in virgin rainforest. To make reservations in Iquitos, check at the administrative offices on Avenida de la Marina 340, tel: 23-4968.

Hotel Turistas. Malecon Tarapaca, tel: 23-1011.

LIMA

Gran Hotel Bolívar, Plaza San Martín, tel: 27-2305, fax: 33-8625. The doyen of Peruvian hotels.

Hotel Crillon, Comena 589, tel: 28-3290 to 28-3295. The hotel's Sky Room stages the best folkloric show in Lima.

Sheraton Lima Hotel & Towers, Paseo de la República 170, tel: 33-3320, fax: 33-6344. Deluxe style hotel with 500 guest rooms and swimming pool.

Hotel Residencial San Francisco, Jr. Ancash 340, tel: 28-3643. Great value budget hotel in downtown area.

Hostal Esperanza, Av. Esperanza 350, Miraflores, tel: 4424, fax: 44-0834. Beautiful hotel of middle price range.
Hostal Torreblanca, Av. José Pardo 1453, Miraflores, tel: 47-9998, fax: 47-3363. Friendly, inexpensive tourist hotel.
Renacimiento, Parque Hernan Velarde 52–54, tel: 31-8461. Secluded colonial style hotel ten minutes' walk from the center.

NAZCA

Hotel de la Borda. Kilometer 447 of the Pan American Highway, tel: in Lima: 42-40-8430. Friendly, renovated hacienda near the airport

PUNO (LAKE TITICACA)

Hotel Isla Esteves, Isla Esteves, Puno, tel 274. Reservations in Lima tel: 42-8626, fax 21-588. Government-run, connected to the mainland by causeway. Good restaurant.

TRUJILLO

Hotel Turistas. Independencia 485, Plaza de Armas, tel: 23-2741. Good value.
Hotel El Golf. Urbanization El Golf, PO Box 329, tel: 44-24-2592, fax: 44-232515 Luxury hotel with pools.

Eating Out

What to Eat

Peru's cuisine is just about as varied as its geography and ranges from scrumptious seafood to potatoes – the staple in a variety of highland dishes – to tropical fruits from the Amazon jungle.

Recommended dishes include *ceviche*, or raw fish and/or shellfish marinated in lemon juice and onions. A typical chicken entree is *aji de gallina* served in a lightly spicy creamed sauce. Also with a spicy sauce, but this one cheese based, is *Papa a la Huancaina*. For the adventurous, *cuy* or guinea pig is available stewed or fried. Hot peppers *(aji or rocoto)* are used liberally in many typical dishes.

As for desserts, the Peruvians have a variety of fruits including *chirimoya*, a large green fleshy fruit or *lucuma*, a small nut-like fruit or *tuna*, the sweet crisp fruit of the cactus. *Mazamorra Morada*, a fruity pudding dating from colonial days, is another favorite at the end of a meal.

Where to Eat

LIMA

Blue Moon. An Italian bistro hidden away in a middle class neighborhood, Pumaccahua 2526 in the suburb of Lince, tel: 70-1190.
Las Trece Monedas. Traditional Peruvian cuisine served in a colonial mansion, Jiron Ancash 536, tel: 27-6547.
El Otro Sitio. International and traditional dishes, Sucre 317 in the suburb of Barranco, tel: 772-413.
Pabellon de Caza. International cuisine in a jungle setting, complete with the squawking of exotic birds, on Alonso de Molina 1100 (beside the Gold Museum), tel: 37-9533.
La Rosa Nautica, Espigon No 4 Costa Verda, Miraflores, tel: 47-0057. Lima's best seafood restaurant on an ocean boardwalk.

CUZCO

El Ayllu, Portal de Carnes 203 (beside cathedral). Great ham-and-egg breakfasts, homemade cakes and coffee.
El Trujo, Plaz Regocijo 247. Popular, good value nightly dinner show.
Quinta Zarate, Calle Tortera Paccha. One of the many quintas or inns, specializing in *cuy* (guinea pig).

Drinking Notes

As for liquid refreshment, Peru has several beers, including Cristal, Arequipeña and Cusqueña. Its best wines are Tacama and Ocucaje. The national cocktail is *pisco sour* – made from grape brandy, lemons and egg white with a dash of cinnamon.

It is recommended that travelers drink only bottled water and that they refrain from eating food sold by street vendors.

Attractions

Culture

Museums

Peruvian officials claim that the city of Lima alone has more than 75 museums. While there are museums of all types, it is in the category of archaeology that Peruvians excel.

Gold Museum. Alonso de Molina, tel: 35-2917. A fine gold and weapons collection. Open daily noon–7pm.
Rafael Larco Herrera Archaeological Museum. Bolívar 1515, Pueblo Libre, tel: 61-1312. A private collection of pre-Columbian ceramics and artifacts; one room is reserved for erotic ceramics.
National Anthropology and Archaeology Museum. Plaza Bolívar in Pueblo Libre, tel: 63-5070. Its collection contains exquisite cloths and fabrics from Paracas, as well as ceramics from a variety of pre-Incan cultures. Open daily 9am–5pm.
Museum of Art. Paseo de Colon 125, tel: 23-4732. Although its collection is limited, it has a fine selection of colonial religious art. Open Tuesday–Sunday 9am–5pm.
Inquisition Museum. Junin 548 (No Phone). Dungeon and torture chamber of the building that once was the Inquisition headquarters for all of South America.
Amano Museum. Calle Retiro 160, Miraflores, tel: 41-2909. Guided tours by appointment only (Monday–Friday afternoons only) at this private museum with one of Peru's best collection of textiles, mostly from the Chancay culture.
National Museum. Javier Prado 2466, San Borja, tel: 37-7822. Located in the huge Banco de la Nación building, the museum concentrates on the unique art and history of the aboriginal races of Peru. Open Tuesday–Sunday 9am-5pm.

Architecture

Of the dozens of colonial buildings still standing in Lima, some have been restored and are well worth a visit.

Casa de Riva-Aguero. Camana 459, tel: 27-7678. Owned by the Catholic University, the second floor of this mansion is a folk-art museum.

Casa de Aliaga. Union 224; tel: 27-6624. One of the first homes in the city, the same family has continuously occupied this mansion since 1535 until the present. Can be visited only through Lima Tours.

Casa Osambela. Conde de Superunda 298, tel: 27-7987. Used by a collection of educational institutes, there are frequent lectures, documentaries and art exhibitions at this home.

Trekking

Preparation: The Peruvian dry season, May through September, offers the best views and finest weather. For safety reasons and for greater enjoyment, parties of three to four or more should hike together. Groups are easily formed in Cuzco, and the Tourist Office on the Plaza de Armas provides a notice board for this purpose. In Huaráz, the Casa de Guias just off the main street offers the same service.

Equipment: Supplies should include a backpack, sturdy hiking boots, sleeping bags, insulated pad, tent and a stove are the major necessities for trekking. This equipment can be hired at a number of highly visible adventure travel agencies. The cost is minimal, but quality often suffers. Inspect hired equipment carefully before departure. It can get very cold at night, and by day, the Andean sun burns quickly. Bring a good sunblock, not available in Peru, and have a hat handy. For the less adventurous, porters can be hired for the Inca Trail. In the Cordillera Blanca, *arrieros*, or mule-drivers, are quite inexpensive and readily available.

Food: All food should be brought from a major town. Very little is available in the smaller villages. Freeze-dried food is not available, but a variety of dried fruits, cheeses, fruits, packaged soups, and tinned fish can be easily acquired in a number of *supermercados, bodegas*, and open-air markets. Drinking water should be treated with iodine, and instant drink mixes like Tang can be added to offset the unpleasant taste.

High Altitude: The effects of high altitude can be significantly diminished by following a few simple precautions. Alcohol, overeating and physical exertion should be avoided for the first day or two. Drinking ample liquids helps the system adjust quickly. The sugar in hard candy stimulates the metabolism, and aspirin eases the headache. *Mate de coca*, tea brewed from coca leaves, is said to be the best overall remedy for any sickness.

Nightlife

Lima is full of colorful *peñas* where folk music and dance performances go non-stop into the early hours. Go about 9pm to get a good seat.

La Casa de Edith Barr. Ignacio Merino 250, in the suburb of Miraflores, tel: 41-0612. In bohemian Barranco suburb. Creole music.

Karamanduka. ASanchesz Carrion 135, Barranco, tel: 47-3237. Music every night.

Peña Hatuchay. Trujillo 228, tel: 247-779. Good night out, with variety show, for budget travelers.

Shopping

What to Buy

Gold, copper and silver items in Peru are a bargain and handicrafts are among the best on the continent. **Jirón de la Unión** in downtown Lima is the best place to find good quality gifts made from precious metals. The best artisan work, aside from the stores listed below, is found at the Indian markets which begin on Avenida de la Marina at Avenida Sucre and consist of a fair-like collection of stalls selling everything from furniture to sweaters. Haggling over prices is expected at the market.

Where to Buy

Antisuyo. Jiron Tacna 460 in Miraflores, tel: 47-2557. Specializes in artisan work from the jungle region and northern highlands.

Silvania Prints. Colmena 714, tel: 24-3926. Cotton handprinted with Peruvian designs and made into dresses, pillows, scarves, blouses and other colorful items.

Artesanias del Peru. Avenida Jorge Basadre 610 in San Isidro, tel: 22-8847. A co-operative with the city's best selection of artisan work from around Peru.

Further Reading

Cut Stones and Crossroads, by Ronald Wright.

Insight Guide: Peru. A detailed, beautifully illustrated companion to Insight Guide South America.

Lost City of the Incas: The Story of Machu Picchu and Its Builders, by Bingham, Hiram.

The Conquest of the Incas, by John Hemming.

The Bridge of San Luis Rey, by Thornton Wilder.

Getting Acquainted

ECUADOR

Area: 104,500 sq. miles (270,700 sq. km), bordering Colombia in the north, Peru to the south and east and the Pacific Ocean in the west.
Capital: Quito.
Population: 11 million. 50 percent of which is Quichua.
Language: Spanish and Quichua.
Currency: sucre (US$1=S/2,600, £1=S/4,000).
Weights & measures: metric.
Electricity: 110 volts.
Time zone: GMT –5hrs, same as EST (Galápagos 1hr behind).
Dialing code: 593 (Quito +2).

Climate

Ecuador's regions each have a distinct climate. The coast is hottest and wettest from January to April. The mountains are driest, and clearest between June and September, and in December. The Oriente is usually inundated between June and August, followed by a drier season until Dec- ember. As on the coast, however, a torrential downpour is never out of the question. The best months to visit the Galápagos Islands are March, April and November.

As the mountains soar the temperature drops: Quito, at 2,850 meters (9,350 ft), is cold when the sun disappears. The other regions are invariably warm and often steaming hot.

Seasonal temperature variation is minimal.

Government & Economy

There are 21 Ecuadorian provinces, including the Galápagos Islands. There has been democratic rule since 1979. The economy is based on oil, fishing, bananas, coffee and cocoa.

Planning the Trip

Visas

Visas are not required for a stay of up to 90 days. Permits (known as "T3s") for a 30-day stay are issued at the border or point of arrival and can be easily extended. For visa extensions, go to Avenida Amazonas 2639, open from 8am–noon and from 3–6pm. The immigration office in Quito is at Independencia y Amazonas 877. The main police office dealing with tourist matters is on Calle Mantúfar.

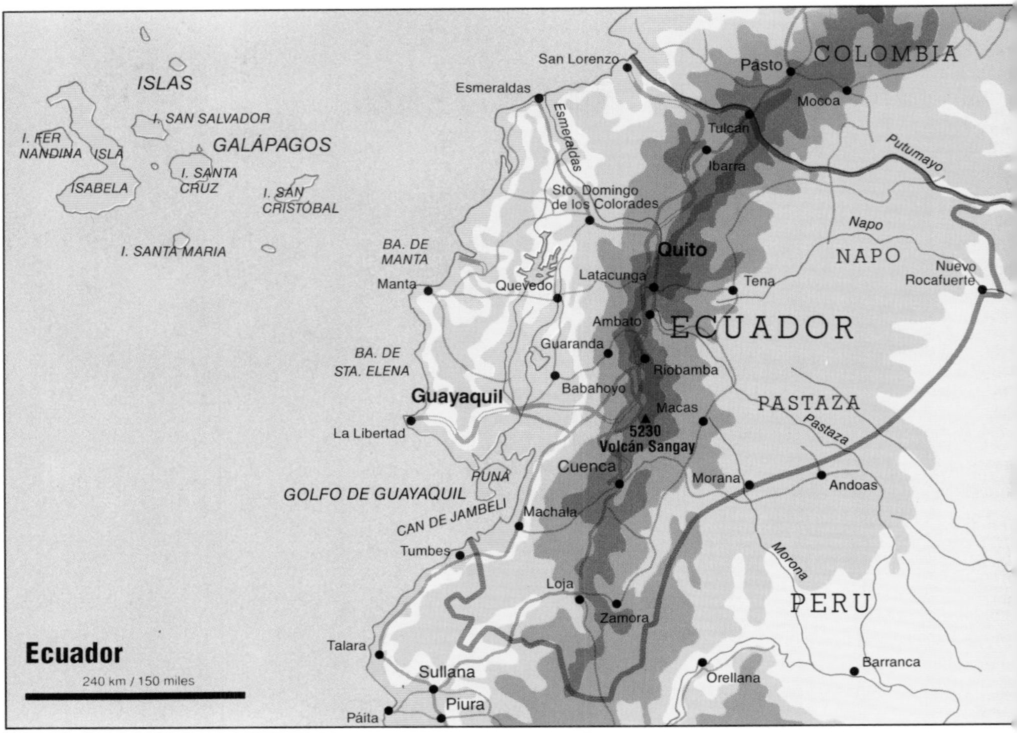

Money Matters

Travelers should bring US dollars for conversion as the dollar is highly valued and tends to fetch a higher rate of exchange at the exchange houses. Traveler's checks are also acceptable. Diners and Visa credit cards are widely accepted for meals and purchases.

Getting There

By Air

Direct flights from the United States into Ecuador are available with SAETA International (the national carrier) and American Airlines. From Europe, flights are by Air France, Iberia, KLM, and Lufthansa.

Several Latin American airlines (Aerolinaeas Argentinas, Ladeco, Varig, Visa, Avianca) offer connecting flights to Ecuador from Europe and the US.

Ecuador has two airports, Quito and Guayaquil. Ensure your carrier has made arrangements to get you to Quito if landing at Guayaquil.

By Land

Many travelers enter from Peru at the Tumbes-Huaquillas border post, changing buses at the frontier. Buses are frequent both ways. To Colombia, almost everyone takes the Quito-Ibarra, Tulcán-Pasto road.

Practical Tips

Media

The main daily newspapers sold in Ecuador are *El Comercio, Hoy, Tiempo* and *Ultimas Noticias*. Foreign papers and magazine are on sale in Quito.

Postal Services

Postal services are unreliable, but better in Quito than the provinces. The central post office is at Espejo 935 y Guayaquil in the old town. This is where the *poste restante* is located.

Telephone & Telex

The main telephone and telex office (EMETEL) is on Av 10 Augusto. The discount period is from 7pm to 7am and at weekends. There is a shortage of phone lines but there are public telephones in the best hotels in city centers. Telex and fax services are offered by all major hotels.

Embassies & Consulates

Canada: Av 6 de Diciembre 2816 y J. Orton, tel: 543-214.
Great Britain: GonzálesSuárez 111 y 12 de Octubre, tel: 560 670.
United States: Av 12 de Octubre y Patria, tel: 562-890.

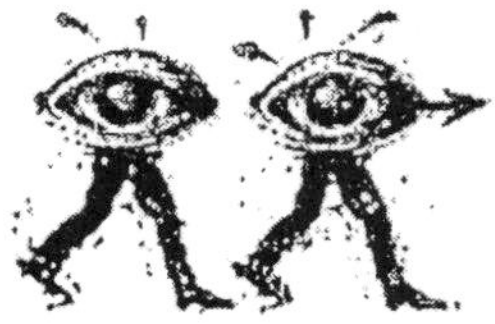

Getting Around

Public Transportation

If a road exists, some form of public transport will run along it. In the Oriente, motorized dugout canoes ply the main rivers.

Flights within mainland Ecuador are cheap. The local airlines SAETA, SAN and TAME operate flights between main cities and the Galápagos.

Where to Stay

Hotels

Quito

For budget accommodation in Old Quito, the **New Gran Casino Hotel**, tel: 516-368, and the **Viena International** are conveniently located and comfortable. In the new town, the cozy **Hostal Los Alpes**, tel: 561-128, has charming and tasteful accommodation. **Residencia Lutecia** is a cheaper option, while **Hotel Carrión**, tel: 234-620, provides every service and five-star comfort.

Guayaquil

The best area to stay is by the river, where the air is cleaner and cooler. The **Metropolitan Ramada**, tel: 565-794 and **Humboldt** hotels have good river views, while **Oro Verde**, tel: 327-999, satisfies the luxury-conscious.

Eating Out

Restaurants

Quito

Apart from the hilltop Panecillo, Old Quito has little to recommend by way of restaurants. Many places serve cheap set meals, and Chinese restaurants, *chifas*, offer adequate fare.

The streets surrounding Avenida Amazonas in the new town have many good "international" restaurants. These include the **Columbus Steak House**, the **Excalibur**, the **El Cebiche** for the national dish. The **Hotel Colón** offers a sumptuous buffet daily at lunchtime, and the pavement cafes on Amazonas are good for snacks, sunshine and street life. For local dishes try **Lo Choza**, 12 de Ocrubre 1821 y Cordero or **Taberna Quiteña**, Amazonas 1259 y Cordero.

GUAYAQUIL

In Guayaquil, the most pleasant place to eat is aboard one of the boats moored along the Malecón.

For cheaper and often more fiery seafood meals, the area just north of Parque del Centenario is good. Calle Escobedo has two popular street cafes serving breakfast.

Galeria El Taller Quisquis 1313, and **Tertulia de Hilda**, Huertado y Tunqurahua, are recommended.

Attractions

Tours

OTAVALO

Zulaytours offers cheap, comprehensive all-day tours of the villages surrounding Otavalo. The history and culture of the Indian people is outlined, and a visit to a pre-Inca cemetery is included. As each village specializes in a particular craft, the tour visits various homes to observe the different methods of production.

THE ORIENTE

Metropolitan Touring offers luxury all-inclusive, four-day tours down the Rio Napo aboard the Flotel Orellano. Cheaper and longer ex- cursions can be organized in Misahuallí. There are many guides and agencies to choose from, but Dayuma Lodge and Fluvial River Tours are two of the most established and reliable.

THE GALÁPAGOS

There are daily flights by the local internal airlines. Flights are heavily booked so you should confirm and reconfirm your seat and check in early at the airport.

All non-Ecuadorian travelers to the islands must pay an US$80 entrance fee to the national park on arrival at the airport. This can be paid in *sucres* or dollars. Keep the receipt, since you may have to show it again.

The Galápagos archipelago is almost entirely a national park, and no visitor is allowed to enter it without a qualified guide on an organized tour. The great bulk of visitors go on a cruise around the islands, taking at least three nights – the more, the better. If you are going to spend the cash to come all this way, it is a pity to miss out on what must be classed as one of the world's great travel experiences.

For many, a trip on one of the largest cruisers is the most comfortable and convenient way to visit the islands. The best two are the **Galápagos Explorer** run by SAN/Saeta from San Cristóbal island, and the **Santa Cruz** run by Metropolitan Touring. Both take around 80 passengers on three or four day cruises – one covering the northern islands, another the southern. You can also combine both trips to make a seven-day cruise. Passengers visit the islands in groups of 10 on motorboats (*pangas)* accompanied by English-speaking naturalist guides.

The cost works out to between US$135 and US$225 per person per night on a twin-share basis (all inclusive, except for bar and airfare). In the United States and Europe, bookings can be made through: **Galápagos Inc**, 7800 Red Rd, S Miami, Fl. Tel: 1 (305) 665-0841. Fax: 1 (305) 661-1457. Toll-free in the US: 1 (800) 327-9854.

There are literally dozens of yachts operating cruises around the islands, most of which work out of Puerto Ayora, although a growing number are basing themselves in Puerto Baquerizo Morena to deal with the influx of tourists from SAN/Saeta flights. They can take anything from 6–20 people.

Galápago Sub-Aqua, Av. Charles Darwin, Puerto Ayora, Isla Santa Cruz. Tel/fax: 593-4-314510, offers scuba and diving tours and instruction.

Excursions

Among Ecuador's snow-capped peaks, Chimborazo, Cotopaxi, El Altar and Tungurahua are certainly the most challenging.

Twenty kilometers (12 miles) north of Quito is Mitad del Mundo, where a monument and museum mark the equator. The road passes two dozen or so colorful billboards painted by prominent Latin American artists. On a clear day, a train or bus ride along the Avenue of the Volcanoes from Quito to Riobamba is breathtaking.

Shortly before Santo Domingo on the Quito road is Tinalandia, with excellent accommodation and meals. This tranquil hotel is set amidst lush subtropical vegetation inhabited by over 150 species of birds.

Nightlife

Nightlife in Ecuador often involves frequenting bars with astonishingly loud music. In Quito, the new town has its share of discos, as well as two reasonably authentic English pubs, the Reina Victoria on the street of the same name, and nearby, El Pub. They nicely complement the cruising double-deckers. The best *peña* is the Taberna Quiteña which has two venues, one on Avenida Amazonas, the other on Calle Manabí in the old city.

In Guayaquil, countless all-night discos play the latest American and *latino* tunes, and some good Colombian *salsa*. They are not places for the faint-hearted.

Otavalo has a couple of *peñas* which get rather lively on Friday and Saturday nights. In addition to excellent local music, they regularly feature groups from Colombia, Peru and Chile.

Shopping

Otavalan goods are the best buys in Ecuador. If you cannot make it to Otavalo, there are stores in Quito, Guayaquil, Cuenca and Baños where prices are only slightly higher than in the market.

Cuenca is perhaps the best place to buy quality gold and silver jewelry, and is – along with Montecristi – a center of Panama hat production. Shops and stalls on Avenida Amazonas in Quito sell everything Ecuador has to offer.

Further Reading

Ecuador – A Travel Journal, by Henri Michaux. 1928.
Ecuador and the Galápagos Islands: A History, by Victor. W. Von Hagen, 1949
Four Years Among The Ecuadorians, by Friedrich Hassaurek. 1861–1865.
Galápagos: A Natural History Market, by Michael Jackson, 1987.

In The Eyes Of My People, by Pablo Cuvi, 1985.
Insight Guide: Ecuador. A companion guide in the same series, with stunning photography and detailed travel information by local experts.
Otavalo – Weaving, Costume and the Market, by Lynn Meisch, 1987.
The Voyage of the "Beagle", by Charles Darwin, 1835–1836.
Travel Among The Great Andes of the Ecuador, by Edward Whymper, 1891.

Getting Acquainted

BOLIVIA

Area: 424,200 sq. miles (1,100,000 sq. km).
Capital: Sucre is the legal capital but La Paz is the effective capital.
Population: 7.3 million. Seventy percent live in and around La Paz, Oruru and Lake Titicaca. About two-thirds are of pure Indian stock most of the rest are mestizos, or mixed Spanish and local descent, locally referred to as *cholos*. About 1 percent are of African heritage, and a fraction of pure European and Japanese descent.
Language: Quechua, Aymará and Spanish.
Currency: boliviano (US$1=B$5, £1=B$8).
Weights and measures: metric
Electricity: 110 volts in La Paz, 220 volts elsewhere. Check first.
Time Zone: GMT –4hrs, EST+1.
Dialing code: 591 (La Paz +2).

Climate

The Bolivian highlands, where the average temperature is 10°C (50°F), is the most popular region to visit. Rain falls heavily from November to March here, but May to November is very dry.

The average temperatures in La Paz are between 6°–21°C (42°–70°F) during summer and 0°–17°C (32°–63°F) in winter. Naturally, the higher mounains are colder while the Amazon basin is hot and wet all year around.

Government & Economy

Bolivia may have suffered an average of one coup per year since independence from Spain in 1825, but it has had civilian rule since 1982. The President is elected by popular vote every four years under the 1967 constitution. The country is divided into nine departments, each controlled by a delegate appointed by the president.

Bolivia has La Paz for an effective capital, as the seat of the Government and Congress, with the legal capital being the small city of Sucre, where the Supreme Court sits.

Bolivia is the poorest country in South American. More than half the population subsist on agriculture. Until the collapse of prices in 1985, tin was the major export earner for the country. Today, Bolivia still mines quantities of gold, silver and zinc. Natural gas is exported. The biggest moneyspinner is coca growing, which the government hopes to curb – it employs thousands of peasants and contributes an undetermined but significant sum to the official economy.

The economy showed signs of growth in the 1990s, but the country's profound poverty, combined with widespread corruption, continues to fuel discontent among the people.

Planning the Trip

What to Wear

The Bolivian highlands can be bitterly cold at night all year round. Bring warm clothes and take a jumper out with you even when the day is warm – the temperature is likely to drop dramatically when the sun sets.

Note that winter is the dry season and it rarely snows in La Paz or Potosí. Winter nights do not go much below freezing in the capital, but can be bitter cold higher up in the Andes.

Visas

Citizens of the United States and most European countries do not need visas; Australians, New Zealanders and most Asians do. At the border, the guards will grant entry for between 30 and 90 days. The immigration office for visa extensions: Avenida Gonzalvez 240. On departure, a US$20 tax is levied.

Health

Travelers of all ages arriving by air in La Paz are likely to need a half day's rest to become accustomed to the altitude. Don't walk too far for the first few days, drink plenty of *mate de coca* and you will adjust. A yellow fever vaccination certificate, at least 10 days old, is officially required before leaving the country. If going to the Amazon basin, take malaria tablets, Chagas disease is endemic in the Yungas and warmer parts of Bolivia. Avoid huts with thatched or leaf roofs.

Money Matters

Banks, hotels and street money changers all offer similar rates of exchange for foreign currency – the black market is more or less dead. Take money in US dollars and change it in larger cities. Credit cards are not always accepted outside of major hotels and restaurants. Visa cash advances are possible from the Banco de La Paz in the capital.

Getting There

By Air

Bolivia has good air connections. The national Bolivian airline, Lloyd Aero Boliviano (LAB), and American, fly direct from the United States to La Paz. From Europe, Lufthansa has a service via Lima. AeroPeru flies regularly from Lima to La Paz. Lan Chile flies connections from Santiago and Arica, LAB from Caracas, Lima.
AeroPeru, Calle Colón 157, tel: 370-002-4.
Lloyd Aero Boliviano (LAB), Avenida Camacho 1460, tel: 367-701/367-718.

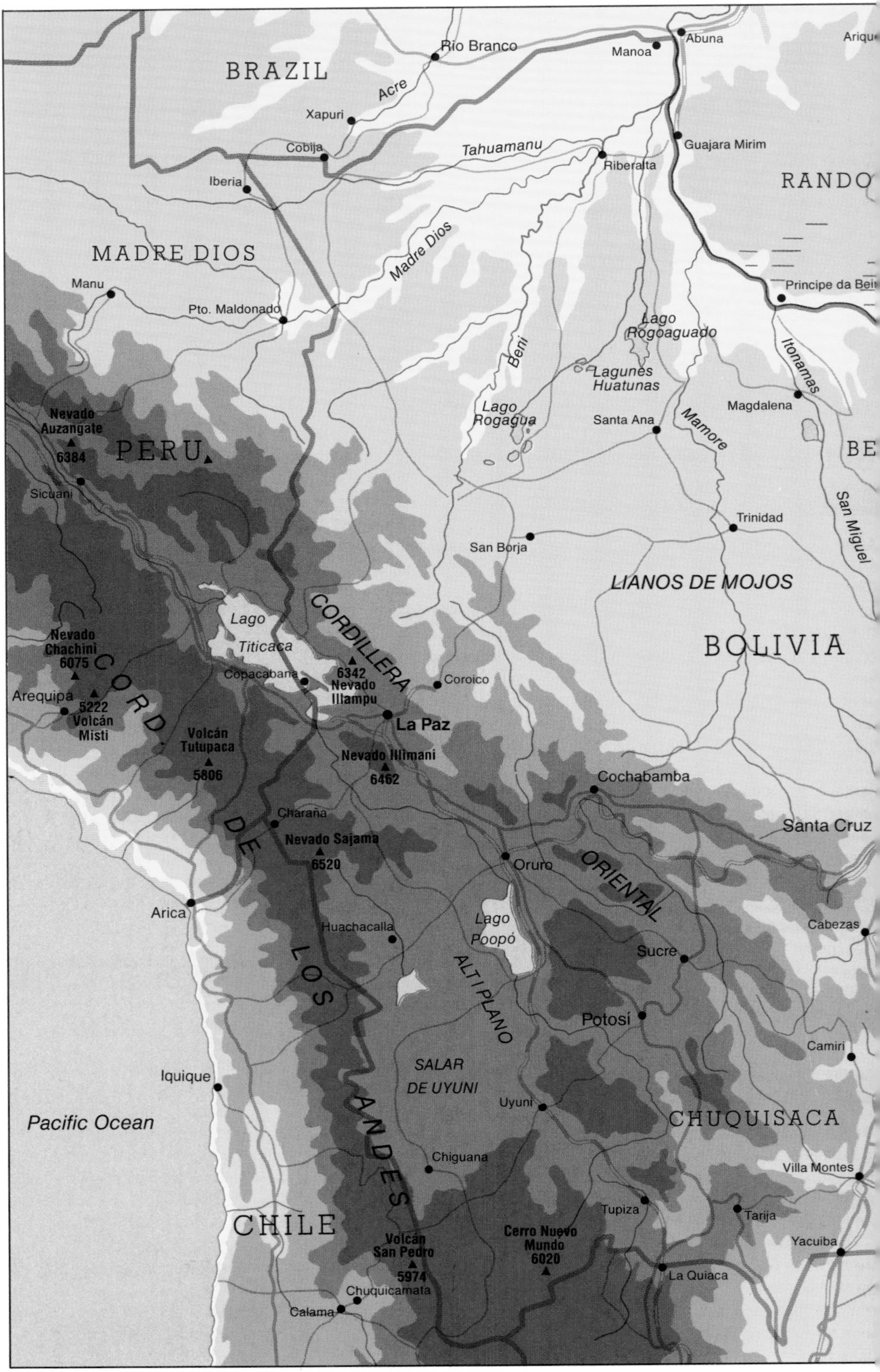

BRAZIL
Rio Branco
Manoa
Abuna
Ariqu
Acre
Xapuri
Cobija
Tahuamanu
Riberalta
Guajara Mirim
RANDO
Iberia
MADRE DIOS
Madre Dios
Manu
Pto. Maldonado
Principe da Bei
Lago Rogoaguado
Beni
Lagunes Huatunas
Itonamas
Lago Rogagua
Santa Ana
Magdalena
Mamore
Nevado Auzangate 6384
PERU
BE
Sicuani
San Miguel
Trinidad
San Borja
LIANOS DE MOJOS
Lago Titicaca
CORDILLERA
BOLIVIA
Nevado Chachini 6075
Copacabana
6342 Nevado Illampu
Coroico
Arequipa
5222 Volcán Misti
CORD.
La Paz
Volcán Tutupaca 5806
Nevado Illimani 6462
Cochabamba
Santa Cruz
Charaña
DE
Nevado Sajama 6520
Oruro
ORIENTAL
Arica
Lago Poopó
Huachacalla
Cabezas
Sucre
ALTI PLANO
LOS
Potosí
Camiri
SALAR DE UYUNI
Iquique
Uyuni
Pacific Ocean
ANDES
CHUQUISACA
Chiguana
Villa Montes
Tupiza
Tarija
CHILE
Volcán San Pedro 5974
Cerro Nuevo Mundo 6020
Yacuiba
La Quiaca
Chuquicamata
Calama

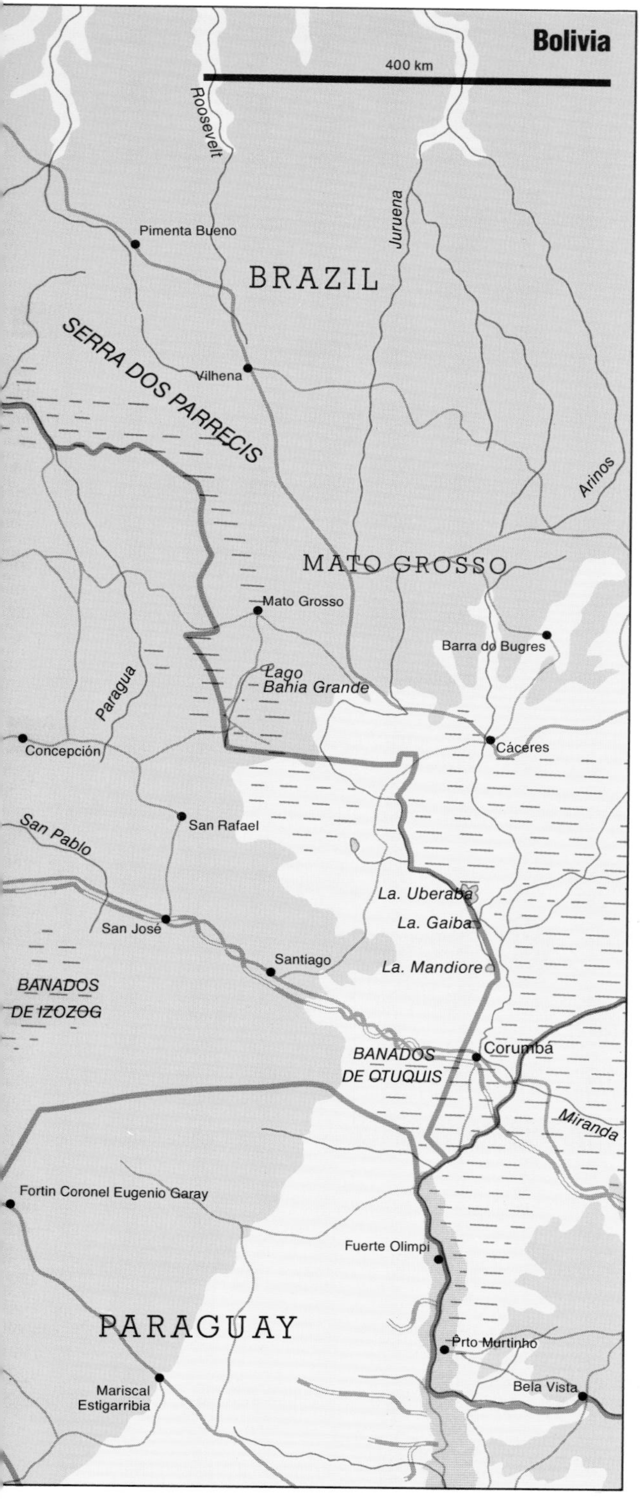

By Land

The great majority of travelers enter Bolivia via Lake Titicaca in Peru. Many companies offer minibus connections between Puno and La Paz. Crillon Tours offers a luxury hydrofoil service both ways across the lake, allowing a stopover on the Island of the Sun, a meal in Copacabana and drinks on the water – as well as a visit to the Museum of the Altiplano with audio-visual displays, which gives an excellent introduction to Bolivia. Crillon Tours is at Avenida Camacho 1223 in La Paz (tel: 350-363, 374-566, fax: 391-039), with an agent in Puno.

It is also possible to travel from Argentina by land, crossing the frontier at La Quiaca and continuing by bus or train – a slow but fascinating journey. From Brazil, the so-called "Train of Death" comes up from Corumba in the jungle to Santa Cruz. It's not particularly comfortable but favored by more adventurous travelers. To and from Chile, there are train and bus links.

Practical Tips

Medical Services

Major hotels have doctors on call. The Clinica Americana in La Paz (6 de Agosto 2821, tel: 323-023), or the Clinica Santa Isabel (opposite the Hotel Crillon,) are competent and well-run. They can usually handle any problems that you may encounter.

Business Hours

Normally 9am to noon and 2pm until 6pm. Banks are only open until 4.30pm. Government offices close on Saturday.

Newspapers

In La Paz, you can choose from *El Diario, Hoy* and *Ultima Hora*. or the weekly, English-language publication the

Bolivian Times. Other cities have their own local papers.

Postal Services

The main post office in La Paz is at Avenida Mariscal Santa Cruz y Oruro, open Monday–Saturday 8am–10pm, Sunday 9am–noon. The outbound mail is quite efficiently posted to the rest of the world. The poste restante keeps letters for three months.

Telephone & Telex

Telephone calls can now be made by satellite to the United States and Europe, although an operator is required. Call from your hotel or the Entel offices in La Paz, Edificio Libertad, Calle Potosí and Ayacucho 267.

Consulates & Embassies

Canada: Av 20 de Octubre 2475, tel: 375-224
Great Britain: Also representing Australian and New Zealand, Avenida Arce casi Campos 2732, tel: 357-424, fax: 391-063.
United States: Avenida Arce 2780, Consulate on Avenida Potosí, tel: 350-251, fax: 359-875.

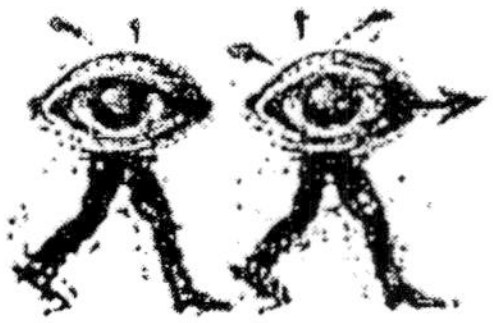

Getting Around

From the Airport

To get from El Alto, above La Paz, you can choose a taxi for US$10, or less, or a minibus for about $2 which runs along the main street of the city to your hotel.

Public Transportation

The bus network in Bolivia is well-developed, although the quality of service depends on the conditions of roads (of which only some 2 percent are paved). Luxury services run between La Paz, Cochabamba and Santa Cruz; quite rough services to Potosí. A wide choice of services are available to Coroico and Copacabana. Trains run from La Paz to Oruro and Potosí, but these are only for the hardy and those with plenty of time: worth paying for a pullman seat if it's available. To get off the beaten track, trucks are the standard transport in the Andes. Most tour companies also offer services to major cities and attractions.

Within La Paz, taxis are probably the best way to get around. They can be hired privately to go anywhere in the city for about US$1.40 or caught as *colectivos*, sharing with passengers along a fixed route for about 30 centavos.

By Air

The domestic airline LAB covers routes between all major cities. Fares are comparatively cheap. It can be worthwhile to avoid a back-breaking bus journey, especially from La Paz to Potosí (on this route, it is necessary to fly to Sucre then take the four-hour bus journey to Potosí. Crillon Tours offers a comfortable minibus connection that can be arranged in La Paz – their office is at Avenida Camacho 1223, tel: 374-566, fax: 391-039).

Where to Stay

Hotels

La Paz

Sheraton, Avenida Arce, tel: 356-950/391-593.
Plaza, Avenida 16 de Julio, tel: 378-311, fax: 343-391.
Presidente, Potosí 920 y Sanjines, tel: 367-193, fax: 354-013.

For a budget hotel, the best is the **Residencial Rosario** at Illampu 704, tel: 326-531, fax: 375-532. Recommended by budget travelers as the cheapest in La Paz is the **Andes**, Avenida Manco Capac 364, tel: 323-461.

Potosí

Hostal Colonial, Hoyos 8, tel: 24809.
Claudia, Avenida Maestro 322, tel: 22242.

Eating Out

What to Eat

Bolivian food varies by region. Lunch is the main meal of the day and many restaurants offer an *almuerzo completo* or three-course fixed menu. Traditional foods of the highlands are starchy, with potatoes, bread and rice. Their meats are highly spiced. Trout from Lake Titicaca is excellent.

Many restaurants in La Paz serve international cuisine – from Japanese to Swiss. These are mostly along Avenida 16 de Julio (the Prado) and Avenida 6 de Agosto.

Where to Eat

Los Escudos, Edif. Club de la Paz, tel: 322-028.
Casa del Corregidor, Calle Murillo 1040, tel: 353-633. (International and local dishes)
Club de la Prensa, Calle Campero.
Vienna, Federico Zuazo, tel: 391-660.

Drinking Notes

The usual tea, coffee and soft drinks are readily available in restaurants and cafes, as is the *mate de coca* in tea bags. For a coffee, head for the Cafe La Paz, corner Camancho and the Prado.

Bolivian beer, brewed under German supervision, is surprisingly good. The favorite drink of everyday Bolivians is *chicha*, the potent maize liquor produced near Cochabamba. Keep in mind that altitude intensifies the effects of alcoholic beverages – both the intoxication and the hangover. Also remember that most Bolivians drink to get drunk.

Attractions

Culture

Museums

La Paz

Museum of Ethnography and Folklore, Calle Ingari 916. Open Monday–Friday 8.30am–1pm, 2.30–6pm. Exhibits relating to Indian culture.

Museo Tiahuanaco. Relics from the site, on Calle Tiwanaku just below the Prado. Open Tuesday–Friday 9am–noon, 2–6pm, Saturday–Sunday 10–11.30am.

National Art Museum. In restored colonial building, cnr. of Comercio and Socabaya near the Plaza Murillo. Open Tuesday–Friday 9.30am–12.30pm, 3–7pm, Saturday 9.30am–1.30pm.

Tours

Most tour companies offer services to major cities. For information on trekking and adventure tours, call Expediciones Guarachi, Plaza Alonso de Mendoza, tel: 320-901, fax: 392-344.

Nightlife

La Paz has several *peñas*. Try the most popular, **Peña Naira** on Sagarnaga, tel: 325-736, just above Plaza San Francisco, open every night with a US$5 cover charge. Others are at the **Casa del Corregidor** and **Los Escudos** restaurants (listed under Where to Eat section above).

Bars are not the most pleasant places to be in La Paz, frequented for inebriation rather than relaxation.

Shopping

The **artisan's market** in La Paz is along Calle Sagarnaga, between Mariscal Santa Cruz and Isaac Tamayo. You can pick up ponchos, vests, jackets and mufflers of llama and alpaca wool, as well as some extraordinary tapestries. Many also sell various types of Andean musical instruments, as well as various small sculptures. A little haggling is expected, but don't overdo it – after all, many of these handicrafts take months to make. Prices vary depending on the quality, but are a fraction of what they'd be if bought from the United States or Europe.

Further Reading

The Open Veins of Latin America, by Galeano, Eduardo. A study of South America's sad history of exploitation.
The Incredible Voyage, by Jones, Tristan. Including several months sailing about Lake Titicaca.
We Eat the Mines and the Mines Eat Us, by Nash, June. On life and death in the Bolivian tin mines.

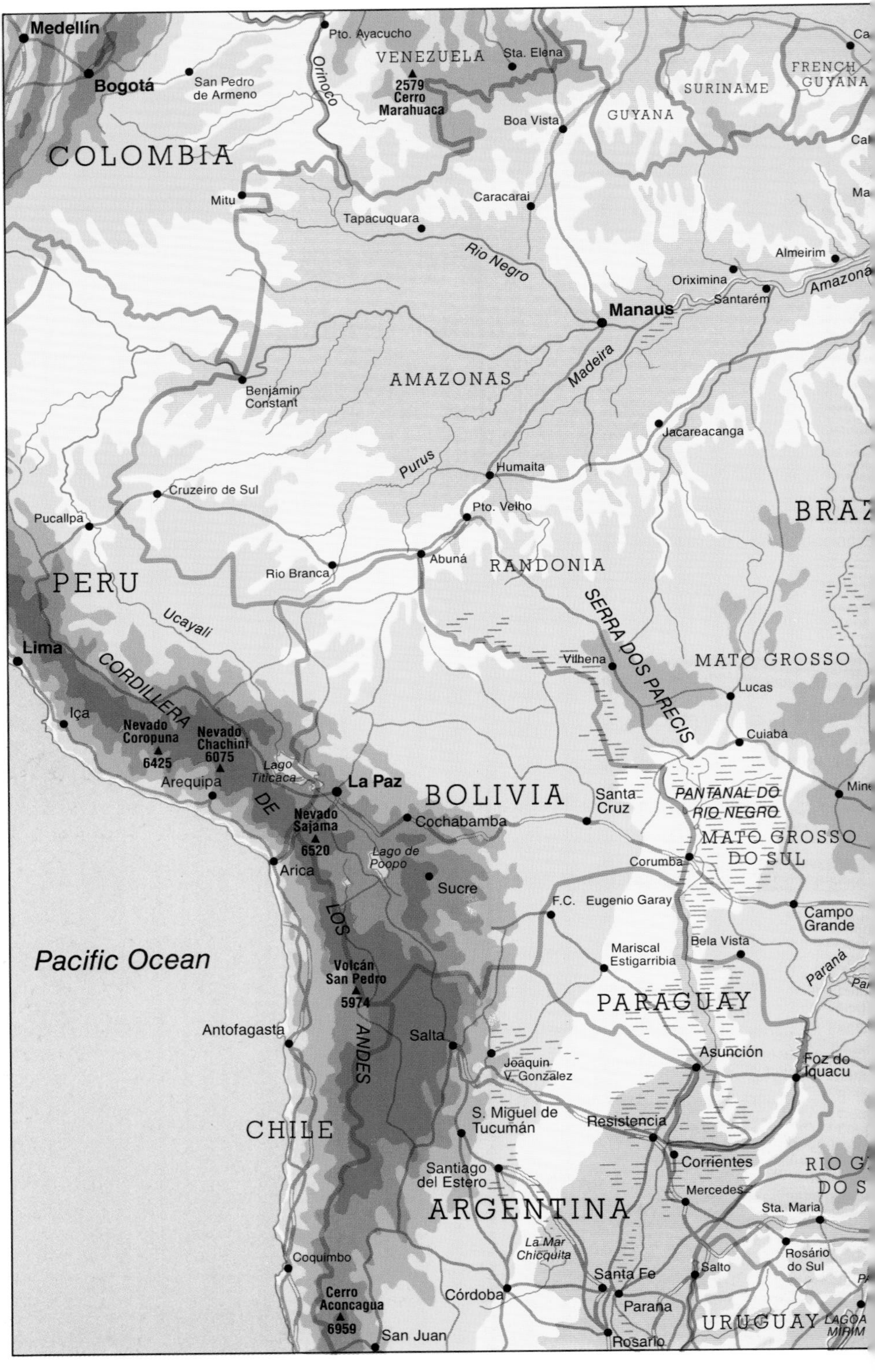
Medellín
Bogotá
San Pedro de Armeno
COLOMBIA
Pto. Ayacucho
Orinoco
VENEZUELA
2579 Cerro Marahuaca
Sta. Elena
Boa Vista
GUYANA
SURINAME
FRENCH GUYANA
Mitu
Tapacuquara
Caracarai
Rio Negro
Almeirim
Oriximina
Santarém
Amazonas
Manaus
Madeira
AMAZONAS
Benjamin Constant
Jacareacanga
Purus
Humaita
Cruzeiro de Sul
Pucallpa
Pto. Velho
BRAZ
Abuná
Rio Branca
RANDONIA
PERU
SERRA DOS PARECIS
Ucayali
Lima
CORDILLERA DE LOS ANDES
Vilhena
MATO GROSSO
Lucas
Cuiabá
Iça
Nevado Coropuna 6425
Nevado Chachini 6075
Lago Titicaca
Arequipa
La Paz
BOLIVIA
Santa Cruz
PANTANAL DO RIO NEGRO
MATO GROSSO DO SUL
Nevado Sajama 6520
Cochabamba
Lago de Poopo
Arica
Sucre
Corumba
F.C. Eugenio Garay
Campo Grande
Pacific Ocean
Mariscal Estigarribia
Bela Vista
Paraná
Volcán San Pedro 5974
PARAGUAY
Antofagasta
Salta
Joaquin V. Gonzalez
Asunción
Foz do Iquacu
CHILE
S. Miguel de Tucumán
Resistencia
Corrientes
Santiago del Estero
Mercedes
RIO G DO S
ARGENTINA
Sta. Maria
La Mar Chicquita
Rosário do Sul
Coquimbo
Santa Fe
Salto
Cerro Aconcagua 6959
Córdoba
Parana
URUGUAY
LAGOA MIRIM
San Juan
Rosario

Getting Acquainted

BRAZIL

Area: 3,285,600 sq. miles (8,512,000 sq.km).

Capital: Brasília.

Population: 154 million. Over half the population are white or near-white, 11 percent are Afro-Brazilians and the rest are of mixed race.

Language: Portuguese.

Currency: real (US$1=1R$, £1= 1.5R$.

Weights and measures: metric.

Electricity: Mostly 127 volts; 220 in Brasilia, Florianópolis, Fortaleza, Recife and São Luis; 110 in Manaus.

Time zone: Major cities and eastern half of country GMT –3hrs (EST +2hrs); Mato Grosso and the north GMT–4hrs (EST +1hr); Acre and western Amazonas GMT –5hrs (EST).

Dialing code: 55 (Brasilia +61, Rio de Janeiro +21),

Climate

In jungle region, the climate is humid equatorial, characterized by high temperatures and humidity, with heavy rainfall all year round.

The eastern Atlantic coast from Rio Grande do Norte to the state of São Paulo has a humid tropical climate, also hot, but with slightly less rainfall than in the north and with summer and winter seasons. Most of Brazil's interior has a semi-humid tropical climate, with a hot, rainy summer from December to March and a drier, cooler winter (June–August).

Mountainous areas in the southeast have a high-altitude tropical climate, similar to the semi-humid tropical climate, but rainy and dry seasons are more pronounced and temperatures are cooler, averaging from 18°–23°C (64°–73°F).

Part of the interior of the Northeast has a tropical semi-arid climate – hot with sparse rainfall. Most of the rain falls during three months, usually

March-May, but sometimes the season is shorter and in some years there is no rainfall at all. The average temperaature in the northeast is 24°–27°C (75°–80°F).

Brazil's South, below the Tropic of Capricorn, has a humid subtropical climate. Rainfall is distributed regularly throughout the year and temperatures vary from 0°–10°C (30°–40°F) in winter, with occasional frosts and snowfall (but the latter is rare) to 21°–32°C (70°–80°F) in summer.

Government & Economy

Brazil is a federal republic with 27 states, each with its own state legislature. Since the federal government exercises enormous control over the economy, the political autonomy of the states is restricted. The overwhelming majority of government tax receipts are collected by the federal government and then distributed to the states and cities. The head of government is the president with executive powers and, in fact, exercises more control over the nation than the American president does over the United States. The legislative branch of the federal government is composed of a congress divided into a lower house, the chamber of deputies, and an upper house, the senate.

In February 1987, however, the federal congress was sworn in as a national constitutional assembly to draft a new federal constitution for Brazil. The constituent assembly completely revised Brazil's constitution in 1987–88. The constitution approved in 1988, opened the way for direct presidential elections every five years.

Brazil is almost self-sufficient in food production and is the world's largest producer of coffee. It has huge reserves of metals and minerals and has seen expansion itechnology-based industries in recent decades.

Planning the Trip

What to Wear

Brazilians are very fashion-conscious but actually quite casual dressers. What you bring along, of course, will depend on where you will be visiting and your holiday schedule. São Paulo tends to be more dressy; small inland towns are more conservative. If you are going to a jungle lodge, you will want sturdy clothing and perhaps boots. However if you come on business, a suit and tie for men, and suits, skirts or dresses for women are the office standard.

If you come during Carnival, remember that it will be very hot to begin with and you will probably be in a crowd and dancing nonstop. Anything colorful will be appropriate.

Visas

Most Asian, Australian, US, Canadian and French citizens are required to arrive with a visa; Britons and Germans are not. Your passport will normally be stamped for a 90-day stay.

Customs

You will be given a declaration form to fill out in the airplane before arrival. Customs officials spot check half "nothing to declare" arrivals.

Health

Brazil does not normally require any health or inoculation certificates for entry, nor will you be required to have one to enter another country from Brazil. If you plan to travel in areas outside of cities in the Amazon region or in the Pantanal in Mato Grosso, however, it is recommended for your own comfort and safety, that you have a yellow fever shot (protects you for 10 years, but is effective only after 10 days, so plan ahead). It is also a good idea to protect yourself against malaria and Dengue fever in jungle areas. Consult your local public health service and be sure to get a certificate for any vaccination.

Don't drink tap water in Brazil. Although water in the cities is treated and is sometimes heavily chlorinated, people filter water in their homes. Any hotel or restaurant will have inexpensive bottled mineral water, both carbonated (*com gas* or "with gas") and uncarbonated (*sem gas* or "without gas"). If you are out in the hot sun, make an effort to drink extra fluids.

Money Matters

Banks and hotels will exchange your foreign currency into *real*, introduced on July 1, 1994. Banks in major cities will change cash and traveler's checks. Unless you don't have the time, it's best to exchange money at the parallel rate. Ask at your hotel where the nearest money exchange (*casa de câmbio*) or tourist agency is located. If you keep exchange slips, you can convert back into foreign currency US$100 worth of *reales*. Credit cards are widely used and dollars cash are becoming more frequently used for tourist transactions.

Holidays

January 1. New Year's Day (national holiday); **Good Lord Jesus of the Seafarers** (four-day celebration in Salvador; starts off with a boat parade)
January 6. Epiphany (regional celebrations, mostly in the Northeast)
January (3rd Sunday).Festa do Bonfim (one of the largest celebrations in Salvador)
February 2. Iemanjá Festival in Salvador (the Afro-Brazilian goddess of the sea corresponds with the Virgin Mary)
February/March (movable). Carnival (national holiday; celebrated all over Brazil on the four days leading up to Ash Wednesday. Most spectacular in Rio, Salvador and Recife/Olinda)
March/April (movable). Easter (Good Friday is a national holiday; Colonial Ouro Preto puts on a colorful procession; passion play staged at Nova Jerusalem)

April 21. Tiradentes Day (national holiday in honor of the martyred hero of Brazil's independence – celebrations in his native Minas Gerais, especially Ouro Preto)
May 1. Labor Day (national holiday)
May/June (movable).Corpus Christi (national holiday)
June/July. Festas Juninas (a series of street festivals held in June and early July in honor of Saints John, Peter and Anthony, featuring bonfires, dancing and mock marriages)
June 15–30. Amazon Folk Festival (held in Manaus)
June/July. Bumba-Meu-Boi (processions and street dancing in Maranhao are held in the second half of June and beginning of July)
September 7. Independence Day (national holiday)
October. Oktoberfest in Blumenau (put on by descendants of German immigrants)
October 12. Nossa Senhora de Aparecida (national holiday honoring Brazil's patron saint)
November 2. All Souls Day (national holiday)
November 15. Day of the Republic (national holiday, also election day)
December 25. Christmas Day (national holiday)
December 31. New Year's Eve (on Rio de Janeiro beaches, gifts are offered to Iemanjá).

Getting There

By Air

Around two dozen airlines fly to and from Brazil on a variety of routes. Although most incoming flights head for Rio de Janeiro, depending on where you are coming from, there are also direct flights to São Paulo and Brasilia, Salvador and Recife on the northeastern coast, and to the northern cities of Belém and Manaus on the Amazon River. A tax of US$20, paid in local currency, is levied on international flights. Flight time from New York is around nine hours, from Europe around 12 hours. Varig Brazilian airlines is the national carrier.

By Road

There are bus services between a few of the larger Brazilian cities and major cities in neighboring South American countries, including Asunción (Paraguay), Buenos Aires (Argentina), Montevideo (Uruguay) and Santiago (Chile). While undoubtedly a good way to see a lot of the countryside, where the distances are great, you sit in a bus for several days and nights.

Practical Tips

Emergencies

Medical Services

Should you need a doctor while in Brazil, the hotel you are staying at will be able to recommend reliable professionals who often speak several languages. Many of the better hotels even have a doctor on duty. Your consulate will also be able to supply you with a list of physicians who speak your language. In Rio de Janeiro, the Rio Health Collective (English-speaking) runs a 24-hour referral service, tel: (021) 325-9300 *ramal* (extension) 44 for the Rio area only.

Check with your health insurance company before traveling – some insurance plans cover any medical service that you may require while abroad.

Business Hours

Business hours for offices in most cities are 9am–6pm Monday through Friday. Lunch "hours" may last hours.

Banks open from 10am–3pm Monday through Friday. The *casas de câmbio* currency exchanges operate usually from 9am–5.30pm.

Tipping

Most restaurants will usually add a 10 percent service charge onto your bill. If you are in doubt as to whether it has been included, it's best to ask (*O serviço está incluido?*). Give the waiter a bigger tip if you feel the service was special. Although many waiters will don a sour face if you don't tip above the 10 percent included in the bill, you have no obligation to do so.

Hotels will also add a 10 percent service charge to your bill, but this doesn't necessarily go to the individuals who were helpful to you.

Media

A daily English-language newspaper, the *Latin America Daily Post,* circulates in Rio de Janeiro and São Paulo, carrying international news from wire services, including sports and financial news, as well as domestic Brazilian news. The *Miami Herald*, the Latin America edition of the *International Herald Tribune* and the *Wall Street Journal* including a selection of international weekly magazines are available on many newsstands in the big cities.

Postal Services

Post offices generally are open from 8am–6pm Monday–Friday, 8am to noon on Saturday and are closed on Sunday and holidays. In large cities, some branch offices stay open until later. (The post office in the Rio de Janeiro International Airport is open 24 hours a day.)

Post offices are usually designated with a sign reading *correios* or sometimes "ECT" (for *Empresa de Correios e Telégrafos* – Postal and Telegraph Company).

Telephones & Telexes

Pay phones in Brazil use tokens which are sold at newsstands, bars or shops, usually located near the phones. Ask for *fichas de telefone* (the "i" is pronounced like a long "e" and the "ch" has an "sh" sound). Each *ficha* is good for three minutes, after which your call will be cut off. Insert several tokens into the slot and the unused tokens will be returned when you hang up. The sidewalk *telefone público* is also called an *orelhão* (big ear) because of the protective shell which takes the place of a booth – orange for local or collect calls, blue for direct-dial long-distance calls within Brazil. The latter requires a special, more expensive token. You can also call from a *posto telefônico*, a telephone company station (at most bus stations and airports), where you can either buy tokens, use a phone and pay the cashier afterward, or make a credit card or collect call. Phone cards, available from telephone offices, are being introduced. For international calls, buy a 100 unit card at least, calls are rated either cheap or normal, depending on the time of day.

Useful Hints

To understand Brazilian addresses, here's what the Portuguese words mean: *Alameda* (abbreviated Al.) = lane; *Andar* = floor, story; Av. or *Avenida* = avenue; *Casa* = house; *Centro* = the central downtown business district also frequently referred to as a *cidade* or "the city"; Cj. or *Conjunto* = a suite of rooms or a group of buildings; *Estrada* (abbreviated Estr.) = road or highway; *Fazenda* = ranch, also a lodge; *Largo* (Lgo.) = square of plaza; *Lote* = Lot; *Praça* (Pça.) = square or plaza; *Praia* = beach; *Rio* = river; *Rodovia* (Rod.) = highway; *Rua* (abbreviated R.) street; *Sala* = room.

Ordinal numbers are written with ° or a degree sign after the numeral, so that 3° andar means 3rd floor. BR followed by a number that refers to one of the federal interstate highways, for example BR-101.

Telex, telephone, fax numbers are given with the area code for long-distance dialing in parentheses. *Ramal* = telephone extension.

Tourist Information

Brazil's national tourism board Embratur, headquartered in Rio de Janeiro, will send information abroad. Write to: Embratur, Rua Mariz e Barros, 13, tel: 273-2212, 9° andar, Praça da Bandeira, 20000 Rio de Janeiro, RJ, Brazil. Each state has its own tourism bureau.

Government Tourism

Manaus: Emamtur, Rua Tarumã, 379, tel: (092) 234-2252. Information Center: Airport.

Rio de Janeiro: Riotur – Rua da Assembleia, 10, 8-9° andares, tel: (021) 242-1947/242-8000; Flumitur – Rua da Assembleia, 10, 8° andar, tel: (021) 398-4077. Information Centers: International Airport, Bus Station, Corcovado, Sugar Loaf, Cinelândia Subway Station, Marina da Gloria.

Salvador: Bahiatursa – Praça, Municipal, Palácio do Rio Branco, tel: (071) 241-4333. Information Centers: Airport, Bus Station, Mercado Modelo, Porto da Barra.

São Paulo: Anhembi Centro de Feiras e Congressos, Av. Olvavo Fontoura, 1209, tel: (011) 267-2122. Information Centers: Praça da República, Praça da Liberdade, Sé, Praça Ramos de Azevedo, Av. Paulista in front of Top Center and at the corner of Rua Augusta, Shopping Morumbi, Shopping Ibirapuera.

Consulates & Embassies

Canada: Brasilia: SES, Av. das Nações 16, Q 803, lote 16, s1. 130, tel: 223-7665. São Paulo: Av. Paulista, 1106, tel: 287-2122.

Great Britain: Brasilia: SES, Av. das Nações, Q 801, cj. K, lote 8, tel: 225-2710. Rio de Janeiro: Praia do Flamengo, 284, 2° andar (Flamengo), tel: 552-1422. São Paulo: Av. Paulista, 1938, 17° andar (Cerqueira Cesar), tel: 287-7722.

United States: Brasilia: SES, Av. das Nações, lote 3, tel: 223-0120. Rio de Janeiro: Av. Pres. Wilson, 147, (Centro), tel: 292-7117. São Paulo: Rua Pe. João Manoel, 933, (Jardim America), tel: 881-7917.

Getting Around

From the Airport

Until you get your bearings, it is better to take a special airport taxi for which you pay a fixed rate in advance at the airport according to your destination. If you decide to take a regular taxi, check out the fares posted for the official taxis so that you will have an idea of what is a normal rate.

Public Transportation

By Taxi

Taxis are the best way for visitors to get around. It's easy to get "taken for a ride" in a strange city. Whenever possible, take a taxi from your hotel where someone can instruct the driver.

By Bus

Comfortable, on-schedule bus services are available between all major cities, and even to several other South American countries. Remember that distances are great and bus rides can take a few days. It is possible to take stops along the way.

By City Bus

Since just a small percentage of Brazilians can afford cars, public transportation is used a great deal. The larger cities have special air-conditioned buses connecting residential areas to the central business district including routes from airports and bus stations that pass by many of the larger hotels. You will be handed a ticket as you get on. Take a seat and an attendant will come around to collect your fare which is charged depending on the route.

The regular city buses are entered through the back door (often quite a high step up) and after paying the trocador, who will give you change, move through the turnstile.

Robberies are committed on crowded buses, even in broad daylight. If you are bent on riding the regular city buses, try to avoid the rush hour when passengers on certain lines are packed tight. Don't carry valuables, keep shoulderbags in front of you and your camera inside a bag. Avoid calling attention to yourself by speaking loudly in a foreign language. In short, be discreet.

By Boat

Local boat tours and excursions are available in coastal and riverside cities. There are also options for longer trips.

Amazon River boat trips last a day or two to up to a week or more. These range from luxury floating hotels to more rustic accommodations. Boat trips can be taken on the São Francisco River in the Northeast and in the Pantanal marshlands of Mato Grosso, popular for angling. The Blue Star Line will take passengers on its freighters which call at several Atlantic coast ports. Linea C and Oremar have cruises out of Rio which stop along the Brazilian coast on the way down to Buenos Aires or up to the Caribbean. Book well in advance for the longer trips .

Cities along the coast (and along major rivers) offer short sightseeing or day-long boat tours. Many towns have local ferry service across bays and rivers and to islands. Schooners and yachts, complete with crew, may be rented for an outing.

By Train

Except for crowded urban commuter railways, trains are not a major form of transportation in Brazil and rail links are not extensive. There are a few train trips, which are tourist attractions in themselves, either because they are so scenic or because they run on antique steam-powered equipment.

In the southern state of **Paraná**, the 110-km (66-mile) Curitiba-Paranaguá railroad is famous for spectacular mountain scenery.

The train to Corumbá, in the state of Mato Grosso do Sul, near the Bolivian border, crosses the southern tip of the **Pantanal** marshlands. There are train links all the way to São Paulo, over 1,400 km (840 miles) away – a long ride. The most scenic part is the 400-km (240-mile) stretch between Campo Grande and Corumbá.

In the **Amazon** region, you can ride what is left of the historic Madeira-Mamoré Railway – the 27 km (16 miles) of track between Porto Velho and Cachoeira de Teotônio in the state of Rondônia. The Madeira-Mamoré runs on Sundays only and strictly as a tourist attraction.

By Air

For travel within Brazil, the major airlines are Transbrasil, Varig and Vasp with several other regional carriers which service the smaller cities.

Different lines have similar prices for the same routes. To get the best value call up for several quotes. There is a 30 percent discount for night flights (*vôo econômico or vôo noturno*) with departures between 10pm and 6am.

Transbrasil, Vasp and Varig also offer air passes which must be bought outside Brazil. Costing around US$440, it is valid for 21 days and is limited to five coupons. Ask your travel agent about these – they are a good deal if you plan to travel extensively within Brazil.

The large airlines also cooperate in a shuttle service between Rio and São Paulo (with flights every half hour), Rio and Brasilia (flights every hour) and Rio and Belo Horizonte (usually about 10 flights per day). Although you may be lucky, a reservation is a good idea.

Where to Stay

Hotels

Rio de Janeiro (City)

Caesar Park (luxury), Av. Vieira Souto, 460, Ipanema, tel: (021) 287-3122, fax: (021) 521-6000.

Copacabana Palace (luxury), Av. Atlântica, 1702, Copacabana, tel: (021) 255-7070, fax: (021) 235-7330.

Intercontinental Rio (luxury), Rua Perfeito Mendes de Morais, São Conrado, tel: (021) 322-2200, fax: (021) 322 5500.

Ambassador, Senador Dantas 25, tel: (021) 297-7181, fax: (021) 220-4783.

Luxor Copacabana (luxury), Av. Atlântica, 2554, Copacabana, tel: (021) 257-1940, fax: (021) 255-1858.

Meridien-Rio (luxury), Av. Atlântica, 1020, Leme, tel: (021) 275-9922, fax: (021) 541-6447.

Ouro Verde (luxury), Av. Atlantica 1456, Copacabana, tel: 542 1887, fax: 021 542 4597.

Rio Othon Palace, Av. Atlântica 3264, tel: (021) 521-5522, fax: (021) 521-6697.

Sao Paulo (City)

Caesar Park (luxury), Rua Augusta, 1508/20, Cerqueira Cesar, tel: (011) 253-6622, fax: (011) 288-6146.

Maksoud Plaza (luxury), Alameda Campinas, 150, Bela Vista, tel: (011) 251-2233, fax: (011) 253-4544.

Moferrej Sheraton (luxury), Alameda Santos, 1437, Cerqueira Cesar, tel: (011) 253-5544, fax: (011) 280-8670.

São Paulo Hilton, Av. Ipiranga, 165, Centro, tel: (011) 256-0033, fax: (011) 257-3137.

Brasilia

Brasilia Carlton, Setor Hoteleiro Sul, Quadra 5, Bloco G, tel: (061) 224-8819, fax: (061) 226-8109.

Eron Brasilia, Setor Hoteleiro Norte, Quadra 5, Lote A, tel: (061) 321-1777, fax: (061) 226-2698.

BELO HORIZONTE

Belo Horizonte Othon Palace, Av. Afonso Pena, 1050, Centro, tel: (031) 273-3844, fax: (031) 212-2318.

SALVADOR

Bahia Othon Palace (luxury), Av. Presedente Vargas, 2456, Ondina, tel: (071) 247-1044, fax: (071) 245-4877.

Club Mediterranee (luxury), Estr. Itaparica-Nazaré, km. 13, Itaparica, tel: (071) 833-1141, fax (071) 241 0100. Reservations in Salvador, tel: (071) 247-3488.

OLINDA

Quatro Rodas Olinda, (luxury) Av. José Augusto, Moreira, 2200, Casa Caida tel: (081) 431-2955, fax: (081) 431-0670.

RECIFE

Boa Viagem, Av. Boa Viagem, 5000, Boa Viagem, tel: (081) 341-4144, fax: (081) 341-1627.

Recife Palace Lucsim (luxury), Av. Boa Viagem, 4070, Boa Viagem, tel: (081) 325-4044, fax: (081) 326-8895.

MANAUS

Amazonas, Praça Adalberto Vale, Centro, tel: (092) 234-7679, fax: (092) 234-7662.

Ana Cassia, Rua dos Andradas, 14, Centro, tel: (092) 232-6201, fax: (092) 232-1153.

Tropical Manaus (luxury), Praia de Paula Negra, tel: (092) 238 5757, fax: (092) 238-5221.

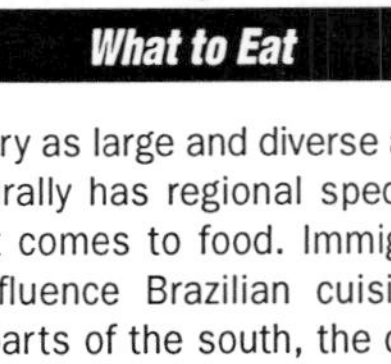

Eating Out

What to Eat

A country as large and diverse as Brazil naturally has regional specialties when it comes to food. Immigrants, too, influence Brazilian cuisine. In some parts of the south, the cuisine reflects a German influence; Italian and Japanese immigrants brought their cooking skills to São Paulo. Some of the most traditional Brazilian dishes are adaptations of Portuguese or African foods. But the staples for many Brazilians are rice, beans and manioc. Lunch is the heaviest meal of the day and you might find it very heavy indeed for the hot climate. Breakfast is most commonly *café com leite* (hot milk with coffee) with bread and sometimes fruit. Supper is often taken quite late.

Although not a great variety of herbs is used, Brazilian food is tastily seasoned, not usually peppery – with the exception of some very spicy dishes from Bahia. Many Brazilians do enjoy hot pepper (*pimenta*) and the local *malagueta* chilis can be infernally fiery or pleasantly nippy, depending on how they're prepared. But the pepper sauce (most restaurants prepare their own, sometimes jealously guarding the recipe) is almost always served separately so the option is yours.

Considered to be Brazil's national dish (although not found in all parts of the country), *feijoada* consists of black beans simmered with a variety of dried, salted and smoked meats. Originally made out of odds and ends to feed the slaves, nowadays the tail, ears, feet, etc. of a pig are thrown in. *Feijoada* for lunch on Saturday has become somewhat of an institution in Rio de Janeiro, where it is served *completa* with white rice, finely shredded kale (*couve*), *farofa* (manioc root meal toasted with butter) and sliced oranges.

The most unusual Brazilian food is found in Bahia, where a distinct African influence can be tasted in the *dendê* palm oil and coconut milk. The Bahianos are fond of pepper and many dishes call for ground raw peanuts or cashew nuts and dried shrimp. Some of the most famous Bahian dishes are *Vatapá* (fresh and dried shrimp, fish, ground raw peanuts, coconut milk, *dendê* oil and seasonings thickened with bread into a creamy mush); *moqueca* (fish, shrimp, crab or a mixture of seafood in a *dendê* oil and coconut milk sauce); *xinxim de galinha* (a chicken *fricasse* with *dendê* oil, dried shrimp and ground raw peanuts); *caruru* (a shrimp-okra gumbo with *dendê* oil); *bobó de camarão* (cooked and mashed manioc root with shrimp, *dendê* oil and coconut milk); and *acarajé* (a patty made of ground beans fried in *dendê* oil and filled with *vatapá*, dried shrimp and *pimenta*). Although it is delicious, note that the palm oil as well as the coconut milk can be too rich for some delicate digestive tracts.

Seafood is plentiful all along the coast, but the Northeast is particularly famed for its fish, shrimp, crabs and lobster. Sometimes cooked with coconut milk, other ingredients that add a nice touch to Brazilian seafood dishes are coriander, lemon juice and garlic. Try *peixe a Brasileiro*, a fish stew served with *prião* (manioc root meal cooked with broth from the stew to the consistency of porridge) and a traditional dish served along the coast. One of the tastiest varieties of fish is *badejo*, a sea bass with firm white meat.

A favorite with foreign visitors and popular all over Brazil is the *churrasco* or barbecue, which originated with the southern gaucho cowboys who roasted meat over an open fire. Some of the finest *churrasco* can be eaten in the South. Most *churrascarias* offer a *rodizio* option: for a set price diners eat all they can of a variety of meats.

The cooler climate in Minas Gerais will whet your appetite for the state's hearty pork-and-bean cuisine. Try *tutu* (mashed black beans thickened with manioc meal into a mush) or *feijão tropeiro* (literally, mule skinner beans: *fradinho* beans, bacon and manioc meal). Mineiros eat a lot of pork and produce some very tasty pork sausage called *linguiça*.

Minas is also corn country and a dairy state, lending its name to Brazil's fresh, bland, white *queijo minas* cheese.

A few exotic dishes found in the Amazon include those prepared with *tucupi* (made from manioc leaves and having a slightly numbing effect on the tongue), especially *pato no tucupi* (duck) and *tacacá* broth with manioc starch. There are also many varieties of fruit that are found nowhere else. The rivers produce a great variety of fish, including piranha. River fish is also the staple in the Pantanal.

In the arid inland areas of the Northeast, life is frugal, but there are some tasty specialties, like *carne seca* or *carne de sol* (dried salted beef, often served with squash) and roast kid. Bananas (especially certain varieties that are only eaten cooked) are often served together with other food. Tapioca (the starch leached out of the manioc root when it is ground into meal) is popular all over the Northeast in the form of *beijus* (like a snowy white tortilla, usually stuffed with shredded coconut) and *cuscuz* (a stiff pudding made of tapioca, shredded coconut and coconut milk).

Two Portuguese dishes that are popular in Brazil are *bacalhau* (imported dried salted codfish) and *cosido*, a glorified "boiled dinner" of meats and vegetables (usually several root vegetables, squash and cabbage and/or kale) served with *pirão* made out of broth. Also try delicate palmito palm heart, served as a salad, soup or pastry filling.

Salgadinhos are a Brazilian style of finger food, served as appetizers, canapés, ordered with a round of beer or as a quick snack at a lunch counter – a native alternative to US-style fast food chains. *Salgadinhos* are usually small pastries stuffed with cheese, ham, shrimp, chicken, ground beef, palmito, etc. There are also fish balls and meat croquettes, breaded shrimp and miniature quiches. Some of the bakeries have excellent *salgadinhos* which you can either take home or eat at the counter with a fruit juice or soft drink. Other tasty snack foods include *pão de queijo* (a cheesy quick bread), and *pastel* (two layers of a thinly rolled pasta-like dough with a filling sealed between, deep-fried). Instead of French-fried potatoes, try *aipim frito* (deep-fried manioc root).

Drinking Notes

Brazilians are great social drinkers and love to sit for hours talking and often singing with friends over drinks. During the hottest months, this will usually be in open air restaurants where most of the people will be ordering *chope*, cold draft beer, perfect for the hot weather. Brazilian beers are really very good. Take note that although *cerveja* means beer, it is usually used to refer to bottled beer only.

Brazil's own unique brew is *cachaça*, a strong liquor distilled from sugar cane, a type of rum, but with its own distinct flavor. Usually colorless, it can also be amber. Each region boasts of its locally produced *cachaça*, also called *pinga*, *cana* or *aguardente*, but traditional producers include the states of Minas Gerais, Rio de Janeiro, São Paulo and in the northeastern states where the sugar cane has long been a cash crop.

Out of *cachaça*, some of the most delightful mixed drinks are concocted. Tops is the popular *caipirinha*, also considered the national drink. It's really a simple concoction of crushed lime – peel included – and sugar topped with plenty of ice. Variations on this drink are made using vodka or rum, but you should try the real thing. Some bars and restaurants mix their *caipirinhas* sweeter than you may want – order yours *com pouco açucar* (with a small amount of sugar) or even *sem açucar* (without sugar). *Batidas* are beaten in the blender or shaken and come in as many varieties as there are types of fruit in the tropics. Basically fruit juice with *cachaça*, some are also prepared with sweetened condensed milk. Favorites are *batida de maracujá* (passion fruit) and *batida de coco* (coconut milk), exotic flavors for visitors from cooler climates. When sipping *batidas*, don't forget that the *cachaça* makes them a potent drink, even though they taste like fruit juice.

If you've never tasted coconut juice – the colorless liquid contained in the shell – you can stop at a street vendor. Restaurants or bars that serve *água de coco* will usually hang the *cocos* near the door (pronounced similar to cocoa; so if you want hot chocolate, ask for *chocolate quente*, otherwise you'll probably get a coconut). The top is lopped off and after drinking your fill, ask to have the *coco* split open to sample the soft, gelatin-like flesh that is beginning to form inside the shell.

Finally there is wonderful Brazilian coffee. *Café* is roasted dark, ground fine, prepared strong and taken with plenty of sugar. Coffee mixed with hot milk (*café com leite*) is the traditional breakfast beverage throughout Brazil. Other than at breakfast, it is served black in tiny demitasse cups, never with a meal. (And decaffeinated is not in the Brazilian vocabulary.) These *cafezinhos* or "little coffees", offered the visitor to any home or office, are served piping hot at any *botequim* (there are even little stand-up bars that serve only *cafezinho*). However you like it, Brazilian coffee makes the perfect ending to every meal.

Attractions

Culture

Museums

Brazil's historical museums are unlikely to be the highlight of your visit. With rare exceptions, there are just not enough resources available for proper upkeep and acquisitions. What follows is a partial listing. Temporary exhibits are announced in the newspapers under *Exposicoes*.

Rio de Janeiro

City Museum (Museu da Cidade), Estrada de Santa Marinha, Parque da Cidade, Gávea, tel: (021) 322-1328. Tuesday–Sunday noon–4.30pm.

Folk Art Museum (Museu do Folclore Edison Carneiro), Rua do Catete 179, tel: (021) 285-0891. Tuesday–Friday 11am–6pm, weekends 3–6pm.

Indian Museum (Museu do Indio), Rua das Palmeiras, 55, Botafogo, tel: (021) 286-8799. Tuesday to Friday 10am-5pm, weekends 3–6pm.

Museum of Modern Art (Museu de Arte Moderna), Av. Infante D. Henrique, 85, Parque do Flamengo, tel: (021) 210-2188. Tuesday–Sunday noon–6pm.

National History Museum (Museu Histórico Nacional), Praça Rui Barbosa, Centro, tel: (021) 240-7978/ 220-2628. Tuesday–Friday 10am–5.30pm; weekends, holidays 2.30–5.30pm.

National Museum (Museu Nacional), Quinta da Boa Vista, São Cristóvão, tel: (021) 264-8262. Tuesday–Sunday 10am–4.45pm.

National Museum of Fine Arts (Museu Nacional de Belad Artes), Av. Rio Branco, 199, Centro, tel: (021) 240-0068. Tuesday and Thursday 10am–6.30pm, Wednesday and Friday noon–6.30pm, weekends 3–6pm.

Sao Paulo

Museum of Brazilian Art (Museu de Arte Brasileira), Rua Alagoas, 903, Pacembu, tel: (011) 826-4233. Tues-

day–Friday 2–10pm; Saturday, Sunday, holidays 1–6pm.
Museum of Contemporary Art (Museu de Arte Contemporanea), Parque do Ibirapuera, Pavilhão da Bienal, 3° andar, tel: (011) 571-9610. Tuesday–Sunday 1–6pm.
Museum of Image and Sound (Cinema) (Museu da Imagem e do Som), Av. Europa, 158, Jardim Europa, tel: (011) 852-9197. Tuesday–Sunday 2–10pm.
Museum of Modern Art (Museu de Arte Moderna), Parque do Ibirapuera, Grande Marquise, tel: (011) 549-9688. Tuesday–Friday 1–7pm; Saturday–Sunday 11am–7pm.

MANAUS

Indian Museum (Museu do Indio), Rua Duque de Caxias, Av. 7 de Setembro, tel: (092) 234-1422. Monday–Saturday 8am–11am, 2–5pm, Saturday 8am–11am.
Museum of the Port of Manaus (Museu do Porto de Manaus), Rua Vivaldo Lima 61, Centro, tel: (092) 232-4250. Tuesday–Sunday 8–11am, 2–5pm.

OURO PRETO

Inconfidencia Historial Museum (Museu da Inconfidência), Pça Tiradentes. Tuesday–Sunday noon–5.30pm.

SALVADOR

Afro-Brazilian Museum (Museu Afro-Brasileiro), (old medical school/Faculdade de Medicina building), Terreiro de Jesus, tel: (071) 243-0384. Tuesday to Saturday 9–11.30am, 2–5.30pm.

Concerts

Concerts are Brazil's forte. Musical forms have developed in different parts of the country, many with accompanying forms of dance. While the Brazilian influence (especially in jazz) is heard around the world, what little is known of Brazilian music outside the country is just the tip of an iceberg.

Take in a concert by a popular singer or ask your hotel to recommend a nightclub with live Brazilian music: bossa nova, samba, choro and seresta are popular in Rio and São Paulo – each region has something different to offer. If you are visiting at Carnival, you'll see and hear plenty of music and dancing in the streets, mostly samba in Rio and frevo in the Northeast. There are also shows all year long designed to give tourists a taste of Brazilian folk music and dance. If you like what you hear, get some records or tapes to bring back with you.

The classical music and dance season runs from Carnival through mid-December. Besides presentations by local talents, major Brazilian cities (mainly Rio, São Paulo and Brasilia) are included in world concert tours by international performers. One of the most important classical music festivals in South America takes place in July each year in Campos do Jordáo in the state of São Paulo.

Amazon Boat Excursions

The government-owned ENASA service for tourists ply the Belém-Manaus-Santarem-Belém run over 12 days. The modern boats have air-conditioned cabins, swimming pool, etc. Contact offices in Avenida Pres Vargas 41, Belém, and Rua Marechal Deoforo, Manaus for details.

Hammock space on the somewhat irregular ENASA passenger boats can be booked from Belém to Manaus and vice versa. Other services make the run, often in better conditions than ENASA boats. They take five to six days from Manaus to Belém, as well as working along the more remote tributaries to Colombia and Peru.

Arranging passage on a boat is a matter of patience and luck in most cases as there are no fixed schedules for bookings.

Shopping

What to Buy

One of the major attractions of shopping for **gemstones** in Brazil, besides the price, is the tremendous variety not found anywhere else. Brazil produces amethysts, aquamarines, opals, topazes, the many-colored tourmaline – to name a few of the most popular buys – as well as diamonds, emeralds, rubies and sapphires.

Although you may find some tempting offers, unless you are an expert gemologist, it's wise to buy from a reliable jeweler. Whether you are selecting a gift for someone (or treating yourself) or whether you have an investment in mind. The three leading jewelers operating nationwide are H. Stern, Amsterdam Sauer and Roditi, but there are other reliable smaller chains. The top jewelers have shops in the airports and shopping centers and in most hotels.

Another good buy in Brazil is leather goods, especially shoes, sandals, bags, wallets and belts which can be found at handicraft street fairs. The finest leather comes from Brazil's south.

Further Reading

Brazil and The Brazilians, by Bruce, G. New York, NY: Gordon Press Pubs., 1976.
Brazil on the March, by Cooke M. New York, NY: Gordon Press Pubs., 1976.
Brazil, by Denis, Pierre. New York, NY: Gordon Press Pubs., 1977.
The Cloud Forest, by Matthiessen, Peter. New York: 1961.
Insight Guide: Brazil, Rio de Janeiro and *Amazon Wildlife* complete the picture of the country, with detailed, expert text and outstanding pictures.

Getting Acquainted

PARAGUAY

Area: 157,000 sq. miles (406,800 sq.km).
Capital: Asunción.
Population: 4.3 million. Eighty percent of Paraguayans are mestizo. There has also been heavy immigration from Korea, Japan and Taiwan.
Language: Spanish and Guaraní.
Currency: guoraní (US$1=G2,000, £1=G3,000).
Weights and measures: metric.
Electricity: 220 volts.
Time zone: GMT–3hrs in east, –4hrs in the west (EST +3hrs, EST+1hr).
Dialing code: 595 (Asunción +21).

Climate

The climate is subtropical. Summers (December to February) are very hot and humid; spring and fall are milder. In winter (June to August) temperatures can drop to 5°C (41°F) but it never snows. Dress is casual; mosquito repellant and an umbrella are advisable year-round.

Government & Economy

Paraguay is a highly centralized authoritarian republic. It has a powerful executive branch, a bicameral legislature, and a national judiciary. Departments and municipalities are centrally administered. Major General Andrés Rodríguez who in 1989 led a coup that overthrew the nearly 35-year dictatorship of General Alfredo Stroessner was replaced by Juan Carlos Wasmosy, the country's first elected president.

Agriculture is the main export with manufacturing increasing in importance during the last two decades.

Planning the Trip

Visas

The entry requirement is a passport. Tourist cards good for 90 days are issued at the border and cost $3. Citizens of France and Asia need visas.

Customs

Alcohol, tobacco and electronic items for personal use are admitted to the country duty-free.

Health

It's safer to stick to bottled water or soft drinks in the capital, tap water should not be drunk elsewhere. Dengue fever and malaria are endemic in the interior of Paraguay. Malaria tablets are advisable if you plan to travel in the countryside. Innoculation against tetanus, typhoid and paratyphoid are recommended before arrival.

Should you need any prescriptions, there is also a 24-hour drugstore in Asunción: Farmacia Franco Americana at Estrella 434.

Money Matters

It is not possible to convert guaraní into another currency outside the country – so only change what you think you will need for your trip. A *Casa de cambio* will accept traveler's checks, though they may ask to see purchase records of the checks. Street money changers offer the best rates for currency conversion. Visa and Mastercard are both widely accepted.

Public Holidays

The following are the public holidays observed in Paraguay: January 1; Feb-

ruary 3; March 1, Maundy Thursday; Good Friday; May 1, 14, 15; June 12; August 15, 25; September 29; Oct. 12; November 1; December 8 and 25.

Getting There

By Air

Paraguay can be reached by international airlines which include South American as well as international air carriers such as Aerolineas Argentinas, American Airlines, Iberia, Air France, Ladeco, LAPSA (Paraguay's state airline), Lloyd Aéreo Boliviano (the cheapest), Pluna and Varig.

By Sea

There is a passenger boat service that shuttles up the Parana River between Buenos Aires and Asunción. The journey takes five days and can be suspended during the dry season.

By Land

There is a luxury bus service that serves Asunción and Ciudad del Este , Pedro Juan Caballero and Encarnación by way of Argentina, Uruguay and Brazil.

Practical Tips

Emergencies

A satisfactory ambulance service is not available; it's best to transport the patient by private means or taxi. Have someone phone the hospital, stating the nature of the illness and asking that a doctor receive the patient in the emergency room. To contact the police, dial 445-008.

For emergencies, you should contact any of the Asunción emergency rooms:

Centro Paraguayo del Diagnóstico, Gral Díaz 975 y Colón, Asuncíon, tel: 947-722.

Hospital Bautista, Avda. Rep. Argentina and Campos Cervera, tel: 600-171 or 600-174.

Business Hours

The timetables are similar to those of Central America. Many shops and offices open at 6.30am.

The siesta which is between noon–3pm is observed during the hot season and offices then open again until 7pm. Banks are open from 7.30–11am and are closed Saturdays. Dinner is served somewhat earlier than in neighboring countries, that is, 8.30–11pm.

Religious Services

The state religion is Roman Catholicism. There is a Sunday Mass in English at Padres Oblatos de Maria Chapel, on Gómez de Castro and Quesada. Other churches include the Anglican Church at Av. Espãna 1261, the Mormon Church at Av. España and the Brasilia Synagogue at Gral. Diaz 657.

Media

Radio is the only effective means of communication that reaches the population. The most popular is Radio Ñandutí, a talk and news station which was recently re-opened after being shut down by Stroessner's government. Two privately-owned television networks operate in Asunción; all TV drama programs are imported from the United States and the neighboring countries. Channel 8 shows CNN in English.

Newspaper quality has improved considerably since press censorship was lifted in 1989. The widest-circulating dailies are: *Hoy, Diario Noticias*, *El Diario*, and *Ultima Hora* (an afternoon daily).

Telecoms

It is wise to send important letters by registered mail. Long-distance calls can be made from antelco office on N.S. de Asunción and Presidente Franco. Telex and fax services are also available. International calls are requested either as ordinario or urgente, urgent calls costing twice as much.

Tourist Information

The Direccion Nacional de Turismo is at Palma 468 in Açuncíon, information on roads, maps, etc. are available at the Touring & Automobile Club of Paraguay at 25 de Mayo y Brasil.

Consulates & Embassies

Great Britainb: Pte. Franco 706, tel: 444-472 or 449-146.
United States: Avd. Mcal. Lopez 1776, tel: 213-715.

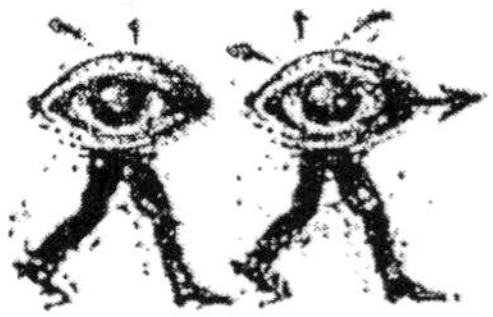

Getting Around

Public Transportation

Buses are the main means of transport within Paraguay; the main terminal is on the outskirts of Asunción at Rep. Argentina and Fernando de la Mora. "Executive" buses vary according to company; this means at least a reserved seat and possibly air conditioning and video films.

Taxis are inexpensive. The main taxi stand downtown is in front of the Hotel Guaraní on the Plaza de los Heroes. Electric streetcars are a novel way of transport if time is not pressing.

By Car

Petrol is cheap and acar hire relatively inexpensive Calle Brase. Touring y Automóvil Club Paraguayo, Calle Brasil, tel: 210 550.

Where to Stay

Hotels

ASUNCIÓN:

Cecilia Hotel, Estados Unidos 341, tel: 210-033/034, fax: 497-111. Has a good restaurant
Chaco Hotel, Caballero esq. Mcal. Estigarribia, tel: 492-066/9, fax: 444-223. Rooftop pool.
Excelsior Hotel, Chile 980, tel: 495-632/5. The best. Modern with conference facilities.
Guaraní Hotel, Ind. Nacional y Oliva, tel: 491131, fax: 443-647. Central, tried and tested.
Hotel de Yacht y Golf Club Paraguay, PO Box 1795, tel: 36117, fax: 36120. Sporting with all the trimmings.

Eating Out

What to Eat

Paraguayan specialties include *surubí*, a mild river fish; *sopa paraguaya*, a rich cornbread; *soyo*, a beef and vegetable soup; *empanadas* and fresh tropcal juices. There are several good German restaurants featuring *wurst*, potato salad, *schnitzel*, etc.

Where to Eat

ASUNCIÓN

Bar Asunción, Estrella y 14 de Agosto. Fastfood and Paraguayan specialties.
La Piccola Góndola, Av Mcal López y Juan de Motta. Good Italian food.
Amstel, Av Rep Argentina 1384. Expensive; good traditional food.
La Preferida, 25 de Mayo y Estados Unidos, tel: 491-126. Part of the Cecilia Hotel group. Excellent international cuisine.
Sukiyaki, Avenida Constitucion near Brasil. Japanese.
Tallyrand, Mcal Estigarribia 932, tel: 441-163. Best and most expensive. French cuisine and wild game.

Drinking Notes

Paraguayan beer is made according to German methods and is excellent. The national wine is not recommended. The local sugar cane liquor, *caña*, is popular but just about any imported liquor is available here at low prices.

Attractions

Culture

Theater Restaurants

A typical evening entertainment is a restaurant floor show, which emphasize Paraguayan harp and guitar music, and sometimes the typical bottle dance. Prices vary according to the quality of the show, but generally are about $10 per person. Recommended spots include:
Hermitage, 15 de Agosto 1870.
Hotel Casino, Ita Enramada Cacique Lambare y Rio Paraguay (out of town).
El Jardín de la Cerveza, Avd. Rca. Argentina y Castillo.

Museums

Museu Nacional de Bellas Artes, Iturbe y Estigarribia, 8am–3pm. Spanish and Portuguese art.
Museu Etnográphico Andrés Barbero, Av España 217, 8–11am, 3–5.30pm. Crafts and photographs.

Tours

For tours, you can check with the recommended tourist agencies such as: Inter Express, Luis A. de Herrera and Yegros, and the Time Tours, 15 de Agosto y General Díaz, tel: 493-527.

Cinemas

There are 12 movie theaters in Asunción, showing mostly porn and B-grade violence. Centro Cultural de la Ciudad, EV Haedo 347, shows some quality foreign films.

Casinos

Hotel Itá Enramada, outside the city in Lambare. Tel 33041.

Shopping

Ñadutí (*guaraní* for "cobweb") lace is one of Paraguay's most typical handicrafts, used to decorate bedcovers, tablecloths, mantillas, etc. Motifs are taken from the fauna and flora of Paraguay. Another traditional item is *ahopoi*, embroidered cotton used for making clothing, tablecloths, etc. Other good buys are guitars and harps, gold and silver filigree jewelry, tooled leather, and ponchos of cotton and wool.

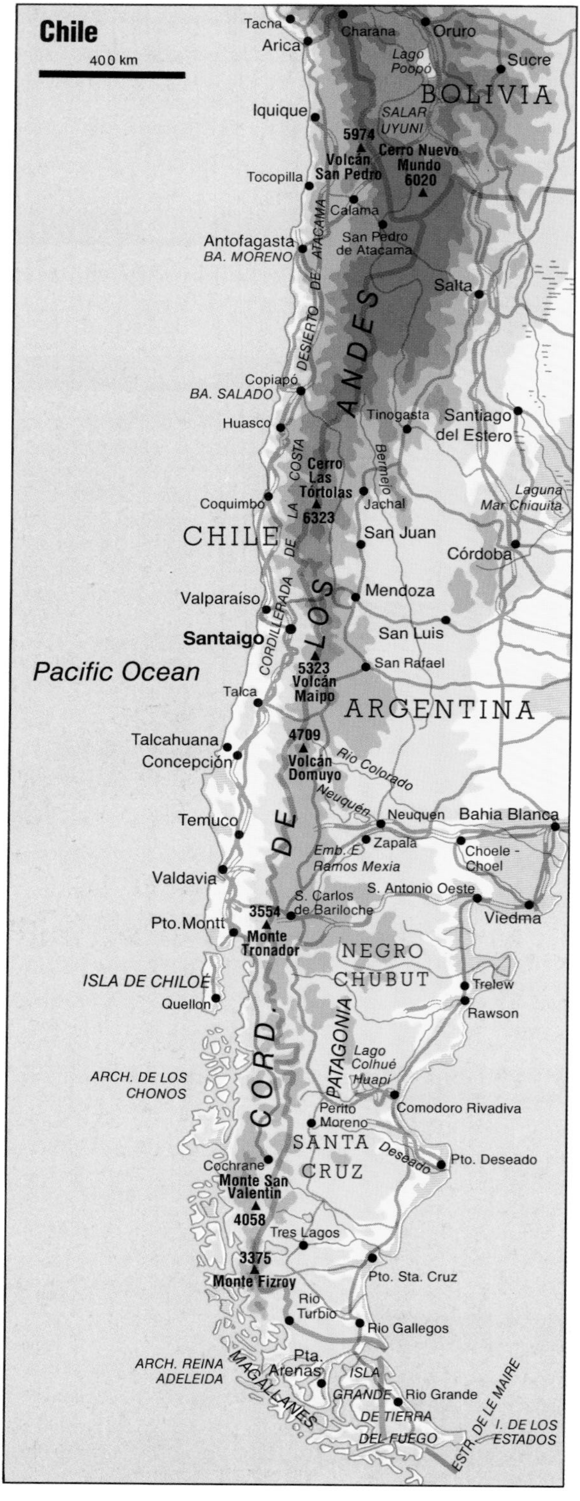

Getting Acquainted

CHILE

Area: 292,100 sq.miles (756,600 sq. km).
Capital: Santiago.
Population: 14 million, 90 percent are mestizo.
Language: Spanish.
Currency: peso (US$1=$400, £1= $600).
Weights & measures: metric.
Electricity: 220 volts.
Time zone: GMT –4hrs, EST +1.
Dialing code: 56 (Santiago +2).

Climate

The central valley (Santiago, Valparaíso, Viña del Mar) has a Mediterranean climate with summer (January and February) averaging 28°C (82°F), and in winter average 10°C (50°F). Evenings are chilly and it rains in winter but the weather is generally pleasant.

In the coast, it is humid, cloudy and windy, so it feels colder than inland. The lake district has a pleasant temperate climate, but winds can be chilly. The mountains are cold and it rains a lot, so bring dry clothing and rain gear.

Patagonia is almost always cold, with sudden, unpredictable changes of weather. Fog, rain and high winds are not uncommon even in the summer.

Government & Economy

Until 1990, Chile's government was a military dictatorship known for its horrendous human rights record, but a peaceful transference of power to a civilian government took place when President Azócar was elected.

Chile is a relatively stable country with a solid free market economy. Theft is rare, corruption low. Travelers are impressed with the clean streets and amiable people. It is one of the safest countries on the continent.

Planning the Trip

What To Wear

In winter bring a light coat, and lots of long sleeve shirts and sweaters since hardly any buildings are heated. A wool cap, gloves and scarves are a must. In the desert always pack a sweater or jacket. If you are in the *altiplano*, bring along some heavier clothes for the night.

During summer, the sun is strong. Bring along a hat and sunglasses, but do not forget a light jacket and a sweater for the cool evenings and for trips to the Andes. The common weather denominator in Chile is that the nights are chilly, so be prepared.

Visas

Passport and tourist card only are required for entry by all foreigners except citizens of France, New Zealand, China, India and all African countries who need visas. Tourist cards valid for 90 days are issued upon arrival, and this can be renewed for another 90 days for about US$8 at the immigration office on Calle Moneda in Santiago. The recommended way to stay longer (than the 180 days allowed for the tourist) is to go to a border country and return; application for a visa extention involves a great deal of paperwork.

Maps

Pick up the *Mapa Caminero de Chile*, which is one of the best of the country. Ask the Sernatur booth on Paseo Huerfanos for a map of Santiago and for other information.

Customs

All bags are searched for agricultural products that may harbor disease. If you have any food with you, eat it or dispose of it.

Clearance at border posts inland can be a bit more cumbersome. As at international entry points, bags here are thoroughly searched for agricultural products, and contraband searches are more frequent. Still, delays are not that long.

Health

Chile's hygiene standards are good. City water is safe, as is the food in most restaurants. No vaccinations are required to enter Chile and the country is free of malaria and yellow fever.

Acute mountain sickness (called *puno*) is something you may run into crossing in to Chile over the Andes or during treks above 3,000 meters (10,000 ft). It is totally unpredictable and requires more than anything, to get to a lower altitude. If you must stay at a high altitude, rest for a few days, drink lots of fluids but do not smoke or consume any alcohol.

Money Matters

Changing money is no problem in Chile. There is a thriving quasi legal black market that is about 12 percent higher than the official rate in *casas de câmbios* all over downtown Santiago. (Also see notes under On Arrival section below.)

You can change most currencies, but US dollars bring the best rates by far. Outside Santiago, however, you must have dollars in cash, or you may have a problem traveling from one place to another or making your purchases for food and lodgings. Diners' Club, Visa and MasterCard are taken, but American Express is less useful.

Public Holidays

Public holidays in Chile include: January 1, May 1, May 21 (Navy Day), August 15, September 18 and 19 (Independence Day), October 12 (Columbus Day), November 1 (All Saints Day), December 8 (Immaculate Conception), December 25.

Getting There

By Air

Chile has a number of international flight services from the major US and European cities. Chilean airlines Lan Chile and Ladeco have several flights a week from New York and Miami, and from Tahiti, a connection point to Australia and New Zealand. There are numerous discount connections from Europe by way of Brazil or Argentina, or even Peru and Venezuela.

By Land

To and from Argentina: A number of bus companies including TurBus, Chile Bus and Pluma shuttle between Santiago and Mendoza, and Buenos Aires. There are also several *colectivos* that go to Mendoza from the Terminal Norte, for about $20.

At Puerto Montt there is a bus and boat service to Argentina. From the north, long and arduous bus services ply Antofogasta and Salta, Argentina.

Practical Tips

Emergencies

Perhaps because of the country's authoritarian past, police *(carabineros)* are in great abundance, always willing to help a needy gringo for no fee.

Call **119** for any other emergency.

There are several good hospitals in Santiago, such as **Clinica Las Condes, Santa Maria** and **Clinica Aleman** (Av. Vitacura 5951, tel: 229 0515). Check with your embassy for a list of certified physicians.

Business Hours

Business hours are 8.30am–12.30pm, 2–6pm Monday to Friday. Banks open 9am–2pm, Monday to Friday. Exchange houses are open during regular business hours, though many are open on the weekends.

Media

There are several dailies. *El Mercurio*, *La Tercera* and *La Segunda* generally toe the government line. *La Epoca* is an opposition paper and is a bit more objective.

Postal Services

The post offices are open daily 9am–8pm, and until about noon on Saturday and Sunday. The system is more reliable than most in South America. The Poste Restante (Lista de Correos) in Santiago is in the main post office building in the Plaza de Armas

Telephone & Telex

Chile has the most efficient and cheapest telecommunication system on the continent. Entel dominates international telephone and telegraph communications but national international calls have been opened up for competition. Coin-operated telephone boxes can be used for local and long-distance calls. Entel, CTC and VTR Communicaciones have offices in most cities. VTR operate telex services.

Embassies & Consulates

Canada: Ahumada 11 (10th floor), tel: 696-2256.
Great Britain: El Bosque Norte 0125, Casilla 72-D, tel: 231-3737, fax: 231-9771.
United States: Merced 230, tel: 710133.

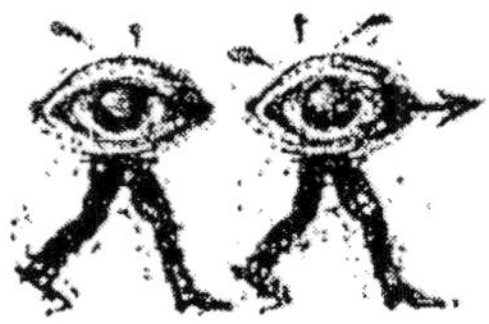

Getting Around

On Arrival

Arriving in Chile is a breeze. You should get through customs easily unless you are exceptionally unkempt. There are frequent buses from the airport, taxis cost about $15 to the center of town. The exchange house outside customs offers the official rate, so just change what you need for the first day until you get to Santiago.

An official of the tourism office (SERNATUR) at the airport gives lodging suggestion and orientation. The Sernatur office in Santiago is at Av. Providencia 1550 (Casilla 14082), tel: 236-1416.

Public Transport

Chile's private intra-city bus service is excellent. The roads are well maintained and buses are new, comfortable, and run on time. All lines leave Santiago from Terminal Sur (points south and Argentina) and Terminal de Buses Norte (north). During off times, you can bargain for a cheaper fare, always ask before you pay full fare.

Santiago's chaotic bus system is privately owned. Fares are cheap. They all go down the Alameda, but there is no logical route numbering. The only way to find your bus is to look for the street on the marquee or ask the driver.

Hitchhiking in Chile is safe, but difficult. Truckers will pick you up sometimes, but motorists are reluctant to stop, so don't depend on it.

On Departure

Leaving Chile is prompt and efficient. If you fly out you must pay a US$12.50 exit tax, so save enough pesos or dollars or you will not be going anywhere.

Where to Stay

Hotels

There are several good hotels in Chile especially in the main cities. These include:

Santiago

Hotel Carrera, Teatinos 180, tel: 698-2011, fax: 672-1083. Overlooking the presidential palace, this is Santiago's most famous grand hotel.
Hotel Foresta, Victor Subercaseaux 353, tel/fax: 639-6261. A beautiful place overlooking Santa Lucia Park.
Hotel Santa Lucia, Vicuña Mackenna, tel: 635-3879, fax: 222-6065. Rooms have televisions, telephones, clean baths.
Sheraton San Cristobal, Avenida Santa Maria 1742, tel: 233-5000, fax: 223-6656. Overlooking the river and the barrio alto.

Viña del Mar

Cap Ducal, Av. Marina 51, tel: 6326-655, fax: 655-478. Moderate.
Hotel O' Higgin, Plaza Vergara, tel: 882-016, fax: 883-537. Vina's famous grand hotel.
Hotel San Martin, San Martin 667, tel: 689-191, fax: 689-195. Moderate

Arica

Hotel El Paso, Calle Velasquez, tel: 231-965.
Hotel Lynch, Patricio Lynch 589, tel: 231-581, fax: 251-959. Inexpensive.
Residencial La Blanquita, Maipu 472, tel: 232-064. Clean rooms and good hot showers. Budget.
Savona, Yungay 380, tel: 232-319, fax: 231-606. Laundry, quiet and comfortable. Inexpensive.

Puerto Montt

Colon Apart Hotel, Pedro Montt 65, tel: 694-290, fax: 264 293. Modern seafront hotel with self-catering suites.
Hotel Montt, Antonio Varas 301 tel: 253-651, fax: 253-652.
Hotel Vientosur, Ejército 200, tel: 258-701, fax: 258-700.

Hotel Vicente Perez Rosales, Antonio Varas 447, tel: 252-571, fax: 255-473. The oldest hotel in town.

Motels

Santiago

There are several dives that cost a couple of dollars a night around the Terminal de Buses Norte, along General MacKenna, Amunategui, San Pablo and San Martin, but most of these *pensiones* and *residenciales* will cost much more in emotional toil.

Hotel Caribe, San Martin 821, tel: 696-6681. This is the best with clean rooms and communal showers.

Residencial Londres, Londres 54, tel/fax: 638-2215. Near the San Francisco Church on the Alemeda. It's a much nicer neighborhood, close to the subway and downtown.

Vegas Hotel, Londres 49, tel: 632-2514, fax: 632-5084. The haunt of prostitutes and lovers, it is a clean place with showers and romantic amenities that will do for a night. $5 per 12 hours.

Viña Del Mar

There are a few *residenciales* near the bus station with rooms from $5 to $10, but they fill early, especially in the summer. The best bet is to stay across the bay in Valparaíso.

Garden Hotel, Serrano 501, Near Plaza Sotomayor, tel: 252-777. Decent rooms.

Hotel Reina Victoria, Plaza Sotomayor 190, tel: 212-203.

Residencial Lily, Blanco Encalada 866, tel: 255-995.

Eating Out

What to Eat

Lunch is the main meal in Chile, and restaurants will have a cheap lunch menu for under two dollars. It starts with a simple salad with oil and lemon juice, followed by a hot bowl of *cazuela* or soup with meat, chicken or seafood, or *empanadas* (pastries stuffed with meat, onions, a boiled egg and a couple of olives) may substitute the soup. In summer don't miss *humitas*, seasoned pureed corn wrapped in corn husks, or *pastel de choclo*, a corn casserole.

Seafood is a hot favorite in Chile. Try *picarocos, jaiva* (crab) and *locos* (abalone) if you can find it. The main course usually consists of specially prepared rice and chicken, meat or fried fish. Dessert is a must followed by a cup of instant coffee.

At night, sandwiches are the fare, and Chile is famous for its *churrasco* steak sandwich with avocado, *chacarero* (steak with green beans), or *completos* (hot dogs with tomatoes, avocado and mayonnaise).

Drinking Notes

Wine is by far the best drink in Chile. *Undurraga, Concha y Toro, Carmen, Santa Rita, Pirque* – they're all worth sampling.

Where to Eat

Restaurants

Santiago: **Bellavista** is the place to eat at night, where the hippest crowd gathers. **El Tallarin Gordo** has some of the best Italian food in Santiago, on Purisima near Antonio Lope de Bello. Dinner about $5 per person. Other eating places include **Pio Nono** and **Antonio Lope de Bello.** Dinner there is about $4 per person.

Venezia is the haunt of the bohemian crowd, **Galindo** is a great place for a real Chilean lunch. At **Dardignac** and **Constitution**, lunch is only about $1.

Apoquindo

Uptown, at Bosque Norte, Isidora Goyenechea streets in Apoquindo are filled with high class restaurants.

Coco, La Concepcion 236, tel: 231-5626. Expensive seafood.

Fra Diarolo, París 836. Local and Italian food.

El Huerto, tel: 233-2690. On Orrego Luco a block from Providencia, has excellent vegetarian dishes in a beautiful garden setting.

Giratorio, 11 de Septembre 2250, tel: 232-1827. An elegant rotating restaurant on the top floor of a skyscraper with an excellent full course dinner for $10 per person.

Viña del Mar

For cheap dinners, it is best to eat sandwiches and platos del dia at the innumerable cafes throughout the city. The recommended restaurants are:

Cap Ducal. Most famous in Viña, with great seafood on the water. About $18 per person.

Mare Nostro. On 4 Norte between 1 and 2 Orients.

The best seafood costs about $15 per person.

Parillada Argentina, Valparaíso 121; **Casino Chico**, Valparaíso 99; and **Club de Vina** on the plaza, all offer affordable menu del dias for lunch.

Easter Island

Hotel Hanga Roa, Av Pont tel: 223-299. Expensive, as are nearly all on the island, but the most luxurious.

Rapa Nui Inn, Av Policarpo Toro, tel: 223-228. Comfortable with local hospitality.

Attractions

Culture

Museums

There are several museums worth a visit in Santiago and these include:

Museo de Arte Precolombiano, Bandera 361. Catalogs 4,500 years of civilization prior to the conquest. Open Tuesday to Sunday, 10am–12.30pm, 2–5pm.

Museo Nacional de Bellas Artes. On Santa Lucia in Parque Forestal. The oldest and one of the largest art museum in South America. Has 3,000 works of art. Open Tuesday to Saturday, 10am–6pm, Sunday and holidays 10am–1.30pm.

National Museum of History, 951 Plaza de Armas. Chile's history from prehistoric to modern times. Open Tuesday to Saturday, 10am–6pm, Sunday and holidays, 10am–1pm.

Galleries

In Bellavista and Providencia, check out the art galleries. Must sees include: **Galeria del Arte Nocturon**, **El Cerro**, **La Fachada**, **Carmen Waugh** and **Eidophon** and **Plaza Mulato Gil Praxis**, **Epoca**, **Fundacion Nacional de la Cultura** and **Plastica 3**.
See listings in the local papers.

Theaters

Most theaters are downtown, and offer a good selection. There are **Abril**, **El Angel y La Comedia**, **Moneda**, **El Trolley** and **Sala America**. In Bellavista, there are **El Conventillo**, **Arte Camera Negra** and **la Feria**. In Providencia, **Galpon de Los Leones** and **Apoquindo**. Check papers for listings, call for reservations. For opera and concerts, try **Teatro Municipal** and **Teatro Oriente**. For movies, there are theaters downtown and in Providencia. Check the papers for listings, call for times.

Bars & Nightclubs

It seems Chile still has not recovered from more than a decade of curfews and states of siege, when it was dangerous or illegal to venture out at night.

Santiago

Check out the sidewalk cafes and bars along Pio Nono and side streets in Bellavista for the more bohemian crowd, or the discos in barrio alto. Near Avenida Providencia, along Suecia is **Red Pub**, **Olivers Bar**, and **El Otro Pub**. On Tobalaba, try **Punta R**. Near Manuel Montt on Providencia is the **Phone Box Pub**, with English cuisine and drink.

Viña del Mar

They say Viña is where it's at in the summer. There are dozens of bars and cafes, and people-watching opportunities along the pedestrian streets around the plaza are abundant. Go to Renaca for the best dancing, at **Topsy**, and **Renaca Club**. In Viña,why not try **Scala** on Caleta Albarca.

Shopping

Chile's open, import oriented free market economy offers a selection of just about anything you want to buy. Fashion is top notch and affordable. Argentine leather is about the same price here as in Buenos Aires. For the latest fashion, check out the department stores and chic boutiques on Providencia near Los Leones and Manuel Montt. Uptown ones are **Parque Arauco** and **Apumanque**, both large fashion malls.

Stores are open Monday through Friday, 10.30am–7.30pm and Saturday, 9.30am to 1.30pm. Most, except for the malls, are closed Sunday.

Further Reading

For a history of pre-Columbian Chile, check out *Chile – The Legacy of Hispanic Capitalism* (Brian Loveman, OUP, New York, 1979).

An insightful primer on Chile since the 1973 coup is Jacobo Timmerman's *Al Galope Muerto*, published in English.

For a look at the inner workings of Pinochet's security apparatus and its role in the assassination of Orlando Letelier in Washington D.C., try *Labyrinth* (Taylor Branch and Eugene M. Propper, Penguin Books, New York, 1982).

For stories about travels in the south, try *The Old Patagonia Express*, (Paul Theroux, Penguin Books, New York, 1980).

Insight Guide: Chile is a companion volume with depth and detail for the discerning traveler matched by wonderful photographs

Getting Acquainted

URUGUAY

Area: 68,000 sq. miles (176,200 sq. km).
Capital: Montevideo.
Population: 3.9 million.
Language: Spanish.
Currency: peso (US$1=Ur$7, £1=Ur$10).
Weights and measures: metric.
Electricity: 220 volts.
Time zone: GMT –3hrs, EST +2hrs.
Dialing code: 598 (Montevideo 2).

Climate

Fertile grasslands alternate with wooded hill country and lush river valleys. The climate is temperate. Montevideo lies at about the same latitude as Buenos Aires, but it's windier and the air is drier. June, July and August can be quite cold and damp. Heavy sweaters and jackets are a must. Spring (September, October, November) and fall (March, April, May) are pleasant; summers (December, January, February) are hot but tempered by the cool Atlantic breezes which make Uruguayan life more tolerable during these months.

December through March are heavy tourist months and hotels should be reserved in advance.

Government & Economy

With the exception of the 1973–85 military dictatorship, Uruguay has enjoyed a liberal democratic system for the past century. Presidents are elected for five years, and cannot run for consecutive terms. The constitution, modeled on Switzerland's, has traditionally provided for a wide array of social services, but the current economic crisis has made many of these benefits seem quite theoretical.

Chief exports of the country are beef and wool, followed by rice, citrus and fish products, and some consumer goods. The country was hit hard by the oil crisis of the 1970s. In the early 1980s, it had the highest per capita foreign debt in Latin America. Current aims are to improve the country's infrastructure of roads, railways, etc. and to take advantage of a well-educated population to produce skilled labor and high-valued exports. With a population of nearly 4 million, it is the smallest Spanish-speaking country in South America.

Planning the Trip

What to Wear

Dress follows European standards as in most South American cities: ties are necessary for business and some cultural evening occasions, as are skirts and stockings for women; jeans and running shoes are the universal casual dress.

Visas

A valid passport is required for most visitors. Exceptions are nationals of other American countries, who need to show identity documents, and citizens of Western Europe, Israel and Japan.

Travelers must fill out a card at the customs counter that has to be surrendered on departure. The stamp on passports is usually good for three months and can be extended for a small fee at the Migraciones Office on Calle Misiones 1513, Montevideo, tel: 960-471.

Customs

There are no special restrictions on liquor, tobacco, or electronic products brought in for personal use.

Public Holidays

Uruguay has a strong secular tradition whereby Christmas is known as Family Day; Holy Week is Tourism Week, celebrated with horse shows, etc. Carnival is celebrated with lively parades of minstrels known as *murgas*, and businesses close on Monday and Tuesday of that week. Other holidays are: January 1 and 6, April 19, May 1 and 18, June 19, July 18, August 25, October 12, November 2, December 8.

Getting There

By Air

Uruguay is serviced by a number of international airlines which fly to Montevideo: Aerolineas Argentinas, United Airlines, KLM, SAS, Air France, Varig, Lufthansa and Iberia. Uruguay's state airline, Pluna, flies to Montevideo from Spain, Portugal and most of the South American capital cities. From Buenos Aires, flight time to Montevideo is about 40 minutes. It's also possible to take a ten-minute flight from Buenos Aires to Colonia which is a 2-hour bus ride from Montevideo.

By Sea

The most enjoyable way to travel to Montevideo is by night ferry, which leaves Buenos Aires at 9pm, arriving at 8am the following morning. The cost is around a third of the air fare, and includes a sleeping berth or, for a bit more, a private cabin. There are also three daily ferries from Colonia. The hydrofoil (*aliscafo*) shuttles the river from Buenos Aires to Colonia three times daily. The trip takes 50 minutes, but can be rough on windy days. The ticket includes a connecting bus service to Montevideo.

By Land

There is a daily bus service from Buenos Aires. The trip takes 10 hours. Buses also run on the Pan-American Highway from Rio de Janeiro to Montevideo and on to Colonia.

Practical Tips

Business Hours

Most shops are open 9am–noon and 2–7pm Monday to Friday. On Saturday they stay open from 9.30am–12.30pm. In Montevideo, banks are open between 1 and 5pm and are closed on Saturday.

Money Matters

Most banks and exchange houses make a small charge for changing US dollar traveler's checks into US dollars, which are widely accepted. Credit cards are frequently not taken outside Montevideo.

Religious Services

Most Uruguayans are nominally Catholic. There is a Methodist church (in Carrasco) and an Anglican church in Reconquista 522 with services in English. Montevideo has a synagogue.

Media

There are four television stations in Montevideo; one is state-run. A large percentage of programs come from Argentina. Uruguayans are avid newspaper readers; dailies include the prosaic *El Dia* and *El País* as well as the left-leaning *Republica* (good for film, theater and other social happenings) and the Communist *La Hora*. There are also a number of interesting weeklies – *Busqueda* is considered foremost.

Postal Services

Postal services have improved since postal workers were forbidden to strike, but letters should be sent airmail. There is a convenient downtown office in the Intendencia.

Telephones & Telexes

The new telephone center (Antel) on San Jose between Paraguay and Ibicuy is the most efficient place to make international calls. Telex and telefax services are also available. Pay telephones require tokens (fichas) which may be purchased at Antel or at newsstands.

Tourist Information

The main tourist office is on Plaza Fabini (Entrevero). It offers free maps, information on hotels, etc. The main bus company (Onda) and money exchange houses are also located here. The tourist office at the Terminal Tres Cruces bus terminal is open 7am–11pm.

The Tourist Commission is located at Lavalleja 1409. For information on current hotel prices, go to the Centro Hoteleria at 1213. They also give away maps. There is also an American Express office at Mercedes 942, which opens from 1–5pm, Monday to Friday.

Embassies & Consulates

Canada: Tagle 2823, tel: 62-3630
Great Britain: Marco Bruto 1073, tel: 623-597.
United States: Lauro Muller 1776, tel 23-6061.

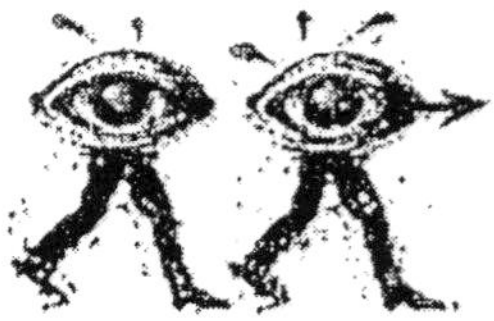

Getting Around

Public Transportation

By Air

Internal flights within Uruguay are quite inexpensive. Tamu, the military airline, offers further reduced prices to most Uruguayan destinations.

By Road

The nation's bus system is quite good. There are a number of competing companies whose rates can vary.

In Montevideo, taxis are cheap though not always plentiful. The city bus system is a mixture of old British Leyland buses and ancient electric trolleys, but the service is fairly efficient. Bus no. 104 (catch it on 18 de Julio) makes a slow but scenic tour of the beaches as far as Carrasco.

By Train

The railway system was built by the British in the 19th century and hasn't been over-modernized. In January 1988, all passenger services were withdrawn. Only lines between Tacuarembó-Rivera and Montevideo-25 de Agosto run, but check service details once you are in the country.

Where to Stay

Hotels

MONTEVIDEO

Columbia Palace, Rambla Rep de Francia 473, tel: 960-001, fax: 960-192.
Hotel International, Colonia 823, tel: 90-5794. First class modern hotel on a quiet street. Recommended for business travelers.
Hotel Lafayette, Soriano 1170, tel: 92-2351. Top businessmen's best bet.
Hotel Victoria Plaza, Plaza Independencia 759, tel: 98-9565. Hotel owned by Rev. Moon's Unification Church. Secretarial services, fax, roof-garden restaurant, nightclub.

PARQUE

Hotel Mediterraneo, Paraguay 1486, tel: 905-090. Small, charming hotel converted from a mansion.
Playa Ramirez, Old-fashioned resort hotel with 1930s decor. Pool, beach views, tearoom, ballroom, casino.

PUNTA DEL ESTE

Hotels are invariably expensive, especially in season. Recommended include: **Americana** (tel: 80794), London (tel: 41911), **La Posada del Gobernador** (tel: 3108), Peninsula tel: 41533).

COLONIA

Recommended hotels include: **Rincon del Rio** (tel 3002), Esperanza (tel 2922) , **El Mirador** (tel: 2004), Italiano (tel: 2103).

Eating Out

What to Eat

Most Uruguayans are of Spanish or Italian descent, and customs generally follow those of Southern Europe. Breakfast consists of coffee and croissants; lunch is the main meal and is served between 1 and 3pm. Dinner tends to be quite late. On weekends restaurants are jammed at midnight. Restaurant portions, particularly meat, are often enormous; it's all right to order one dish for two.

Uruguayan cooking, like Argentine cooking, consists of two staples, beef and pasta. Uruguayans also like seafood. Try *calamares a la plancha* (grilled squid), *cazuela de mariscos* (seafood stew), and *lenguado* (sole) *a la provenzal.* Ice cream and pizza are excellent snacks as is *chivito*, a Dagwood-type sandwich. For dessert, try a custard, *isla flotante*.

Where to Eat

Montevideo

Mercadodel Puerto, Calle Piedras. Closed Sunday. Expensive grills, good atmosphere.
El Fogón, San Jose 1080. Grilled beef a specialty; seafood excellent.
El Águila, Buenos Aires 694, next to Teatro Solis. Elegant service with a continental menu.
El Palanque, In the Puerto market complex. Grilled beef and seafood. Open Sundays.
Doña Flor, Artigas y Avenida Espana. Classy French cuisine.

Drinking Notes

For coffee or snacks, try the **Cafe La Pasiva** in the Plaza Independencia or the **El Lusitano** at 18 de Julio across from the Plaza Cagancha. Uruguayan wine is drinkable but nothing special. Beer is made with spring water and is very good, especially Norteña.

Attractions

Concerts

The Teatro Solis offers concerts from national and visiting companies. Season starts March through November. The Teatro Circular, on Rondeau behind the Plaza Cagancha, offers a series of theater productions.

Bars & Nightclubs

Jazz is available at Alianza Frances and Brazilian music at Clave de Fu, Pocitos. For tango dance and music, try Tangueria del 40, Hotel Columbia, in the Ciudad Vieja. The most popular discos are Caras y Caretas, Punta Gorda and San Tehno on Maldonado 1194. Gambling is available at the Parque Hotel and the Hotel Carrasco in Carrasco.

Getting Acquainted

ARGENTINA

Area: 1,074,000 sq. miles (2,780,400 sq. km).
Capital: Buenos Aires.
Population: 33.5million.
Language: Spanish.
Currency: peso (US$1=1 peso, £1=1.5 peso).
Weights & measures: metric.
Electricity: 220 volts.
Time zone: GMT –3hrs, EST +2hrs.
Dialing code: 54 (Buenos Aires +1).

Climate

Most of Argentina lies within the temperate zone of the southern hemisphere. The northeastern part is very humid and subtropical but has a mild winter. The pampas are temperate while the southern part of the country has colder temperatures and rain most of the year.

Rainfall varies in the humid pampa (which comprises the province of Buenos Aires, and some of the Córdoba and La Pampa provinces) from 99 cm (39 inches) in the eastern parts to about 51 cm (20 inches) near the Andes.

Summer months in Buenos Aires are indeed very hot and the majority of the people leave soon after Christmas for the beaches and mountain resorts. The city is almost empty during the months of January and February. Wintertime is very pleasant as the thermometer doesn't drop drastically.

Government & Economy

The The Republic of Argentina is made up of 24 provinces. The government is a Federal Republic with a senate and chamber of deputies and a president as head of state. Argentinia is one of the world's richest farming economies: agriculture and livestock production provides over 50 percent of export earnings. The manufacturing sector is well-developed and the country is virtually self-sufficient in oil.

Planning the Trip

What to Wear

In general, the local atmosphere is somewhat formal, especially in the winter months. As Buenos Aires is a very cosmopolitan city, fashion is very important, and the people are always up-to-date with the latest styles. Dressing in Buenos Aires for dinner is customary. The Argentine man will always wear a suit or at least a sports coat with a tie. Women are always very well dressed.

Visas

Tourists coming to Argentina must have their valid country passports and a visa is not necessary for citizens of the US and Western Hemisphere countries (excluding Cuba) and Japan, who can stay for three months. In some cases a tourist card is all that is required which must be verified with a travel agent. Citizens of bordering countries of Brazil, Chile, Paraguay and Uruguay only need their ID cards.

Money Matters

It is not a good idea to change money on the street – use *casas de cambio* where possible. There is no market rate only an official exchange rate which is listed in major, daily newspapers. It is difficult to change traveler's checks in small towns, and the *casas de cambio* charge large commissions. Credit cards are accepted in most establishments, but a supplement is often added. .

Getting There

By Air

Ezeiza International Airport (EZE) is the arrival point for all foreign travelers. It is located about 30 minutes from downtown Buenos Aires. However, there is another airport, Jorge Newberry, located within the city and used mostly for domestic flights as well as for shuttling to and from bordering countries. The following are airlines most commonly used: Aerolíneas Argentinas, British Airways, Canadian Pacific, Air France, Aeroflot, Avianca, KLM, Swissair, Lufthansa, Lan Chile, Varig, Viasa. Local travel can be on Austral, Aerolíneas Argentinas and LADE.

By Sea

Few cruise ships call at Buenos Aires. There are boat connections between Uruguay and Argentina: Tigre to Carmelo and Montevideo to Carmelo. Ferry services run to Colonia from Daraena Sur and a hydrofoil service runs between Montevideo and Colonia four times a day during the summer. The English-language daily, *Buenos Aires Herald*, has listings of all sailings to Argentina.

By Land

Most tourists do not arrive by land. However, for the more adventurous, this can be accomplished by bus, train or car. Bus services are available from Chile, Bolivia, Paraguay, Uruguay and Brazil. Large air-conditioned buses are usually used for long distance overland travel. But travelers must remember to exercise to ensure personal safety.

In 1994, the government withdrew its funding for Ferrocarriles Argentinos and some train services were suspended.

Traveling by automobile is possible. Most of the roads are paved but cautious driving is absolutely essential. Speed limits are posted and should be followed closely. The **Automobile Club of Argentina**, located in Buenos Aires on Avenida Libertador 1850 (tel: 802 6061/7061), is very helpful and can provide the traveler with maps and useful information.

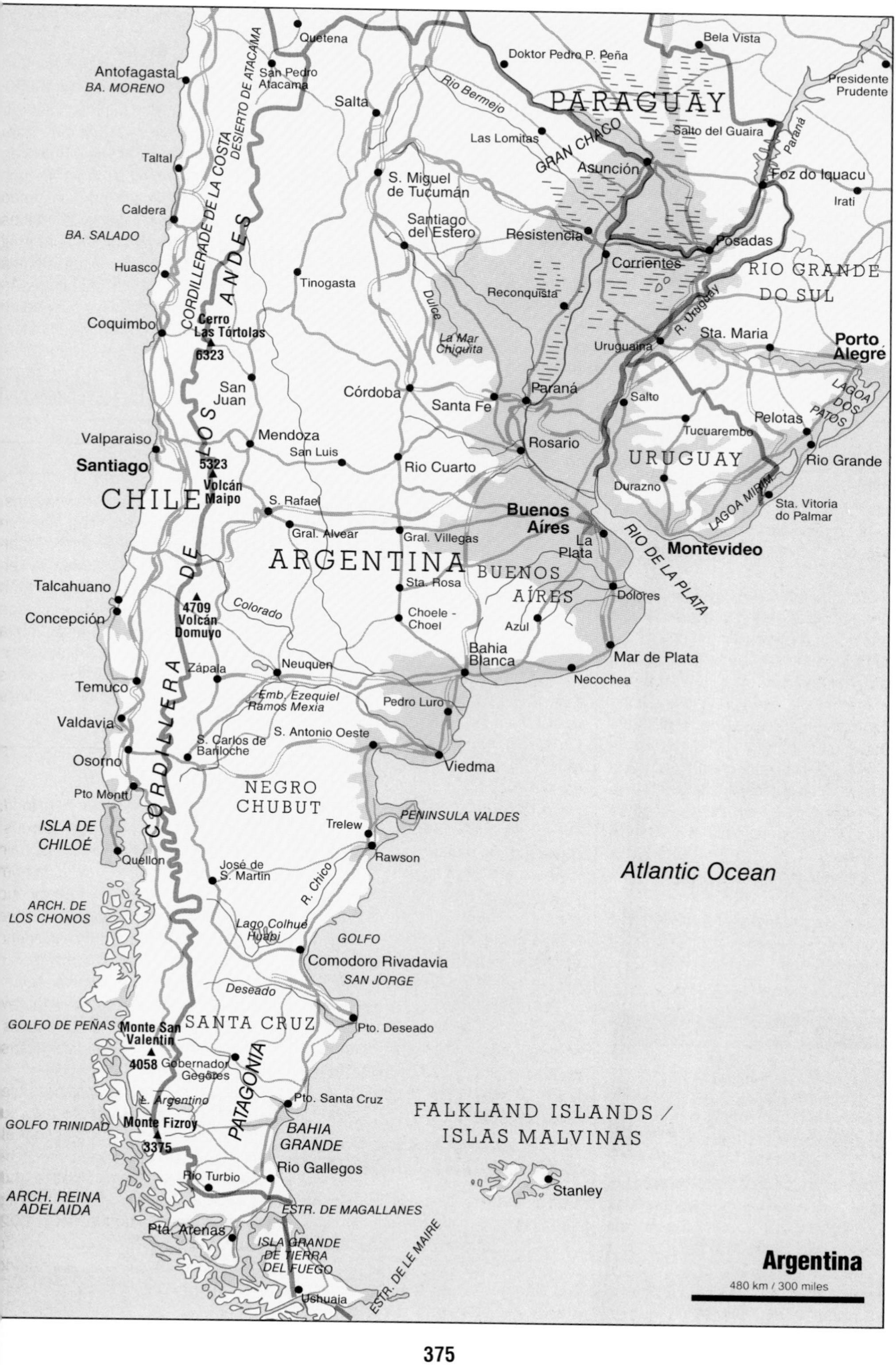
Quetena
Antofagasta
BA. MORENO
San Pedro Atacama
DESIERTO DE ATACAMA
Salta
Doktor Pedro P. Peña
Bela Vista
Rio Bermejo
PARAGUAY
Presidente Prudente
Las Lomitas
GRAN CHACO
Salto del Guaira
Paraná
Taltal
CORDILLERA DE LA COSTA
Asunción
S. Miguel de Tucumán
Foz do Iquacu
Irati
Caldera
BA. SALADO
Santiago del Estero
Resistencia
Posadas
Huasco
Tinogasta
Corrientes
RIO GRANDE DO SUL
Dulce
Reconquista
R. Uruguay
Coquimbo
Cerro Las Tórtolas
6323
La Mar Chiquita
Uruguaina
Sta. Maria
Porto Alegre
San Juan
Córdoba
Santa Fe
Paraná
Salto
LAGOA DOS PATOS
Valparaiso
Mendoza
Tucuarembo
Pelotas
San Luis
Rosario
Santiago
5323
Rio Cuarto
URUGUAY
Rio Grande
Volcán Maipo
Durazno
CHILE
S. Rafael
Buenos Aires
LAGOA MIRIM
Sta. Vitoria do Palmar
Gral. Alvear
Gral. Villegas
La Plata
Montevideo
CORDILLERA DE LOS ANDES
ARGENTINA
BUENOS AIRES
RIO DE LA PLATA
Talcahuano
Sta. Rosa
Dolores
Concepción
4709
Volcán Domuyo
Colorado
Choele - Choel
Azul
Bahia Blanca
Mar de Plata
Zápala
Neuquen
Necochea
Temuco
Emb. Ezequiel Ramos Mexia
Pedro Luro
Valdavia
S. Antonio Oeste
S. Carlos de Bariloche
Osorno
Viedma
Pto Montt
NEGRO
CHUBUT
PENINSULA VALDES
ISLA DE CHILOÉ
Trelew
Quellon
Rawson
José de S. Martin
Atlantic Ocean
R. Chico
ARCH. DE LOS CHONOS
Lago Colhue Huapi
GOLFO
SAN JORGE
Comodoro Rivadavia
Deseado
GOLFO DE PEÑAS
Monte San Valentin
SANTA CRUZ
Pto. Deseado
4058
Gobernador Gegores
PATAGONIA
L. Argentino
Pto. Santa Cruz
GOLFO TRINIDAD
Monte Fizroy
3375
BAHIA GRANDE
FALKLAND ISLANDS / ISLAS MALVINAS
Rio Turbio
Rio Gallegos
Stanley
ARCH. REINA ADELAIDA
ESTR. DE MAGALLANES
Pta. Arenas
ISLA GRANDE DE TIERRA DEL FUEGO
ESTR. DE LE MAIRE
Ushuaia
Argentina
480 km / 300 miles

Practical Tips

Emergencies

Security & Crime

As in any other part of the world, be cautious and use a little common sense. When registering at the hotel, don't leave luggage unattended. If carrying valuables, ask to have them locked in a safe. Carry money in different parts of your clothing rather than all in a wallet or purse. Don't display large amounts of cash when making purchases. Although dealing with foreign currency can sometimes be confusing, the bills here are clearly marked.

Buenos Aires and most of the bigger cities are very much alive till the late hours of the night. You can go out to dine, dance to the wee hours and still go at 4 or 5 in the morning to get a *bife* (steak). But a little caution can prevent a bad experience: don't walk on desolate streets and try not to walk alone. If driving, lock the car and don't leave any valuables in it. It is common for thieves to break the windows of cars to steal radios or cassette players.

Crime is on the rise, mainly in the large cities. Fortunately, the crime rate doesn't compare with other cities of the same population. Just exercise a little caution.

Medical Services

The health care in this country is good. Hospitals have trained personnel, who have studied at home and abroad. There are excellent specialists in most of the medical fields, who make it a point to attend international medical congresses, to inform themselves on the recent advances in medical science and to bring these to Argentina.

Medical equipment is very costly, but all efforts are coordinated in order to maximize benefits. In some sections of the country, the hospitals may not have up-to-date equipment, but what is available is adequate for an emergency situation.

For emergencies in the Buenos Aires area, you can contact the following:

British Hospital, Perdriel 74, tel: 23-1081.
Children's Hospital Pedro Elizalde, Bustamante 1399, tel: 28-5898.
City Medical Attention, tel: 34-4001.
Coronary Mobile Unit, tel: 107.
Poison Unit, tel: 87-6666.
Fire Department, tel: 23-2222.
Police, tel: 101.

Business Hours

Monday through Friday, the business hours are from 9am–6pm, and the banking hours are from 10am–3pm. The stores open 9am–7pm. In some parts of the country, stores stay open from 9am–1pm and from 4–7pm. All government agencies as well as the banks close on public holidays.

Media

Several newspapers are available. The local papers are *La Nación, Clarín* and *La Prensa*. The English paper is the *Herald*. There are newspaper and magazine stands throughout the city, where these and some foreign papers, as well as many international magazines, may be found.

There are five stations, and cable TV is also available. Most of the programs are brought in from the US and some Europe. Many drama series are locally made. Soap operas are also popular with the afternoon viewers.

The radio stations carry a variety of programs. The BBC is on from 5pm to about 12.30am. A number of stations carry international top hits, local tango music as well as talk programs.

Postal Services

The main Post Office is located on Sarmiento 189, and operates Monday to Friday, 8am–10pm. Other small post offices are found throughout the city. The hotels are the best source stamps.

Telephone & Telex

Telephone services are run by Telcom in the north and Telefónica Argentina in the south. Phone cards are available. Domestic calls can be made from public telephone boxes using tokens, bought from news stands. In main cities the Centros de Llamadas offer good telephone and fax services. International public phones have a ddi sign. Many telephone offices send international faxes. In Buenos Aires you can make international calls and send faxes from the communications office on Av. Corrientes 705. Open 24-hours.

Useful addresses

Tourist Information

There are tourist offices in most big towns in Argentina. The following are in Buenos Aires:

National Direction of Tourism, Santa Fe 883, tel: 312-2232, fax: 313-6834.
Casa de Turismo, Av. Callo 237, tel: 40-7045.

There are also tourist information centers along Florida Avenue, a pedestrian boulevard. Here in these booths, the traveler can obtain maps of the city and a bilingual (Spanish and English) tourist information newspaper called *The Buenos Aires Times*. It offers complete listings of what is happening in the city, as well as other pertinent and useful information. *Where*, a booklet giving a complete list of shopping, dining and entertainment, can be obtained in most hotels.

The provinces of Argentina have offices in Buenos Aires where the tourist can obtain valuable information. Pamphlets about special events, attractions, lists of hotels, restaurants, etc are readily available. All are located in the center of town and can be easily located. Look in the phone book.

Airlines

Airlines in Buenos Aires:

Aerolineas Argentinas , Calle Peru 2 tel: 393-5122.
Austral Lineas Aereas, Corrientes 485, tel: 235-0505.
LADE, Calle Peru 710, tel: 361-0853.
LAPA, Santa Fe 1970, Floor 2, tel: 311 2492.

Embassies & Consulates

The following are in Buenos Aires:
Australia: Santa Fé 846, 8th floor, tel: 312-6841
Canada: Suipacha 1111, 25th floor, tel: 803-7070
Ireland: Santa Fé 846, 12thg floor, tel: 774-7611
Great Britain: Dr Luis Agote 2412/52, tel: 803-7070
United States: Cerviño 4320, tel: 774-7611.

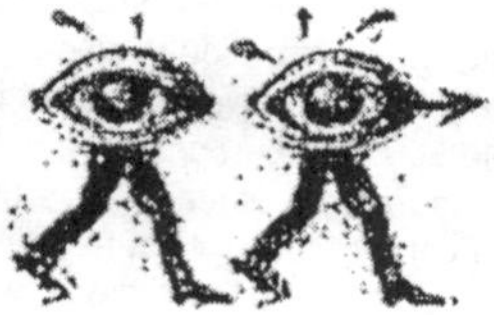

Getting Around

Public Transportation

By Air

Traveling by air in Argentina is done on the local airlines, which are Austral, Aerolíneas Argentinas and Lade. Jorge Newberry Airport, also known as "Aereoparque", is used for national traffic. For those tourists who wish to visit several cities, the Aerolineas Argentinas 30-day Visit Argentina ticket can be used to stop off in towns.

The ticket is made up of four flight coupons which can be added to make up eight in total. Austral sells similar tickets called Jetpaq. They cost around US$450, US$120 for extra coupons, must be purchased outside Argentina and in conjunction with an international flight ticket. Reconfirmation 24-hours before the time of your flight is strongly recommended.

By Bus

The buses are a very good way to get around Buenos Aires, which is a very large city. They are one of the means of mass transportation that is usually prompt and very inexpensive. However, try not to get one during the rush hour as the queues are very long. Any part of the city can be reached. Bus stops are located throughout the city. The number and destination are clearly marked. Long distance travel on buses is also available.

A very large and modern bus terminal is located in Retiro. Information regarding bus destinations can be obtained at the terminal from the different companies.

By Train

Most train services were suspended in 1994, when the government withdrew funding from Ferrocarriles Argentinos and few provinces were able to maintain services. For up-to-date information contact: Ferrocarril Nacional Roca (southern) tel: 230-021; Ferrocarril Nacional Urquiza (north-eastern) tel: 555-214; Ferrocarril Nacional Sarmiento (western), tel: 870-041; Ferrocarriles Argentinos, tel: 331-3280.

By Subway

The subway system, better known as the **Subte**, is the fastest and definitely the cheapest way to get around Buenos Aires. The rides are quick, taking no more than 25 minutes, and the waiting is between three to five minutes. The art work that can be observed at some of the stations is quite unique and has an interesting background. Many of these painted tiles were baked by artisans in Spain and France at the beginning of the century and around the 1930s.

By Taxi

These can be easily recognized – black with a yellow roof, and are readily available 24 hours a day. The meter registers a number that will correspond to the amount of the fare appearing on a list. These must be shown to the passenger by law. A bit of advice: be careful when paying and make sure the correct bill is given; quick exchanges of bills have been known to take place, especially with the tourist who doesn't know the language or the currency.

By Sea

Traveling to Uruguay on the ferry is a pleasant trip, inexpensive and entertaining. A well known company is Ferrytur, located on Florida 780, tel: 394-2103.

Private Transportation

Car Rentals

Remises are private automobiles, with a driver, that can be rented by the hour, excursion, day or any other time period. They are more expensive than taxis, and a list of these can be found in the telephone directory or at the information desks of the hotels.

Where to Stay

Hotels

Buenos Aires

FIVE STAR

Buenos Aires Sheraton, San Martín 1225, tel: 311-9000, fax: 318-9353. Magnificent view of river and port.
Claridge Hotel, Tucumán 535, tel: 314-7700, fax: 314 8022. Old-fashioned British style.
Libertador Hotel, corner of Córboda & Maipu, tel: 322-2095, fax: 322 9703. Modern, central.
Marriot Plaza Hotel, Florida 1005, tel: 318-3000, fax: 315-3008. For the rich and famous with renowned Plaza Grill.

FOUR STAR

Carrson. Viamonte 650, tel: 393-0029. Faded, charming elegance.
Gran Hotel Colón, Carlos Pelegrini 507, tel: 325-0717, fax: 325 4567. Rooftop pool.

THREE STAR

Gran Hotel Hispano, Av de Mayo 861, tel: 345-2020. Antique building popular with budget travelers.
Hotel Phoenix, San Martín 780, tel: 312-4323, fax: 311-2845.Old world charm in beautiful turn of the century building.
Hotel San Antonio, Paraguay 372, tel: 312-5381. Old-fashioned European-style *pension*.
Waldorff Hotel, Paraguay 450, tel: 312-2071, fax: 312-2079. Modern, near shopping streets.

IGUASSÚ

Hotel International de Iguassú. Reservations in Buenos Aires, tel: 311-4259, fax 312-0488. Located in the National Park where the falls are, offering a magnificent view of its spectacular casades. Very modern and with all the facilities.

Hotel Salta. Buenos Aires 1, tel: (087) 211-011. Best hotel in Puerto Iguazú, in the main square.

JUJUY

Hotel Termas de Reyes, tel: 0382, telex: 66130 NASAT. Located about 12 miles (19 km) from the city, offers thermal baths in all rooms, good facilities and heated pool.

MENDOZA

Hosteria Puente del Inca, Ruta 7, Las Heras, tel (061) 380 480, fax 380-477. Secluded, with Aconcagua in sight.

Hotel Aconcagua, San Lorenzo 545, tel: (061) 243-321. A few blocks from the main shopping area, very modern architecture, pool and air-conditioned rooms. Good restaurant.

Plaza Hotel, Chile 1124, tel: (061) 233-000. A traditional hotel, located in front of a beautiful plaza, with lovely antique furnishings.

BARILOCHE

Edelweiss Hotel, Av San Martín 232, tel: (0944) 261 65, telex: 80711 EDEL AR. A large hotel, with up to 90 rooms plus several suites. A five-star hotel located in town and close to everything.

Hotel Tronador. Reservations in Buenos Aires 311-6684. A unique small lodge-type hotel with excellent food, offering fishing, horseback riding, hiking and beautiful surroundings for relaxation. Located in front of the Mascardi Lake, southwest of Bariloche. Open from November to April.

CARLOS PAZ

El Ciervo del Oro, Hipólito Yrigoyen 995, Carlos Paz, tel: 22498. A lovely small lodge-type hotel right on the lake, with pool, excellent food and very cozy.

VILLA GENERAL BELGRANO

Hotel Edelweiss, tel: 6317/6284. Villa Gral. Belgrano, in the sierras, Córdoba. A very well-run hotel, with swimming pool, tennis courts and recreational activities for children. Set in the scenic sierras of Córdoba, the temperature is very good. Excellent place to stay if attending the Oktoberfest or just relaxing a few days in the summer. Nearby tours available to La Cumbrecita and the many lakes surrounding the area for fishing.

USHUAIA

Del Glacier, Camino Clacier Martial, tel: (0901) 306036, fax: 39638. A new 4-star hotel above the city.

Malvinas Hotel, Deloqui 615, tel: 22626.

Cabo Hornos Hotel, Ave. San Martin y Rosas, tel: 22187. Clean, comfortable.

CALAFATE (LAGO ARGENTINA)

Hotel La Loma, B Roca y 15 Febrero, tel: 91016. Located in the National Glacier Parks, has 27 rooms, centrally located with lovely views. Open from October to April. Several languages spoken.

Eating Out

What to Eat

It is possible to eat out every day of year and still not savor the cuisine of all the restaurants of Buenos Aires. Dining out here is a delightful experience. Food, wine and service are excellent, for the most part. Argentina is well known for its beef, and most visitors prefer this to other types of foods. The typical meal will be *empanadas* (meat pastries, although the filling will vary according to the region), *chorizos* or *morcillas* (pork blood sausages), an assortment of *achuras* (sweetbreads) of course, this is only the appetizer. For the main course, a good *bife de chrozo*, or *tira de asado*, or *lomo* are the most popular choices, accompanied by various types of salads. To finish off, one might choose a nice flan (custard), topped with *dulce de leche* and some whipped cream. Don't think of calories, just enjoy.

Where to Eat

A complete listing of all restaurants in Buenos Aires would be impossible. The most popular are the listed here:

Dining out is a favorite pastime of porteños, but the menu is not the only attraction. Restaurants are a place to socialize, to see and be seen, and share a bottle of wine until the wee hours of the morning. Nevertheless, porteños take eating seriously. A list of recommended eateries follows, but don't be afraid to try any clean, well-lit place that catches your fancy. There are hundreds of good restaurants in the city, where the food is almost universally fresh and well-prepared in a simple Southern European style.

Restaurants in Buenos Aires open for lunch at noon, and for dinner around 8pm. But no one dines out in the evening before 9pm, with restaurants really coming alive between 10pm and 11pm. Weekends, restaurants stay busy much after midnight.

REGIONAL ARGENTINE

El Ceíbal, Güemes 3402, tel: 823-5807; Cabildo 1421, tel: 3402. Great place to try specialties from Northern Argentina, including *locro* (corn chowder), *humitas* (*tamales*) and *empanadas*. Inexpensive.

PARILLAS (STEAKHOUSES)

Chiquilín, Montevideo 321, tel: 373 5163. Italian Pasta and Argentinean Asado.

El Mirasol, Davila 202, tel: 315-6277. Upscale parrilla in posh Puerto Madero, elegant atmosphere, reservations. Expensive.

El Palacio de la Papa Frita, Lavalle 735. Inexpensive and popular.

La Cátedra, Cerviño 4699, tel: 777-4601. In the heart of the pleasant Palermo district, nice atmosphere, grilled beef but also interesting international cuisine and fresh salads. Moderate.

La Chacra, Avenida Córdoba, tel: 322 1409. Huge portions.

La Estancia, Lavalle 941, tel: 326 0330. Classic Asado-Restaurant in the heart of the city.

La Veda, Florida 1, tel: 331-6442 Basement floor, dark wood panelling excellent steak poivre, tango dinne show most evenings. Reservations Expensive.

Los Años Locos, Av. Costanera R. Obligado, tel: 783-5126. The most popular of the riverfront parrillas. Moderate.
Río Alba, Cerviño 4499, tel: 773-5748. Also in Palermo, popular restaurant famous for brochettes and enormous filet mignon steaks. Moderate.
There are lots of trendy steak restaurants along Avenida Costanera (at the Rio de la Plata), for example **Los Años** or **El Rancho Inn**.

POPULAR EATERIES

Barbaro, Tres Sargentos 415, tel: 311-6856. A BA landmark, a charming, old world version of the hole-in-the-wall bar, a great place for a simple midday meal or for music, beer and bar food in the evening. Inexpensive.
Chiquilín, Sarmiento 1599, tel: 373-5163. One block from Corrientes, with the quintessential BA-restaurant atmosphere, serving very reasonable pasta and beef specialties. Fills up quickly on weekends. Inexpensive.
El Trapiche, Paraguay 5099, tel: 772-7343. Typical neighborhood restaurant in Palermo, with cured hams, tins of olive oil and bottles of wine decking the walls and ceiling. Great grilled beef, homemade pastas and seafood. Inexpensive.
La Casa de Esteban de Luca, Defensa and Carlos Calvo. In the heart of San Telmo, restored colonial-era home of the Argentine "poet of the revolution", popular Sunday lunch after the San Telmo fair. Inexpensive.
Pippo, Montevideo 345. No frills but great atmosphere and unbeatable prices. Try a *bife de chorizo* (T-bone steak), or a bowl of *vermicelli mixto* (pasta noodles with pesto and bolognaise sauce), washed down with the house red and seltzer.
Restaurant Dora, L.N. Alem 1016, tel: 311-2891. An upscale version of a popular eatery with rave reviews on the enormous steaks and simple seafood dishes, a downtown "don't miss".
Rodi Bar, Vicente Lopez 1900, tel: 801-5230. Cozy, neighborhood restaurant nestled amongst the famous gourmets of the Recoleta, featuring simple homemade food.

Attractions

The Argentine people are extremely cultured and a wide range of activities are available. Museums, galleries, theaters, bookstores and several libraries are among the places to be visited. Be sure not to miss any of the ones listed below while in Buenos Aires.

Culture

Art Museums

Ornamental Art Museum. Displays art of the period between the 15th and 19th centuries, housed in a beautiful baroque style home. Located on Ave. Libertador 1902. Open all week 3–7pm. Closed Tuesday. Tel: 802-6606. Houses the Museum of Oriental Art. Open Wednesday–Monday 3–7pm (closed January). Tel: 801-5988.
National Gallery. Thirty four halls displaying more than 300 pieces on permanent exhibition. Many Argentine painters as well as famous works by Van Gogh, Picasso, Manet, Rodin, Renoir, etc. Located on Ave. Libertador 1437. Open Tuesday to Friday 1.30–7.30pm, Saturday 9.30am–7.30pm, Sunday 1.30–7.30pm. Closes January–February. Tel: 803-8817.
The Jose Hernandez Museum of Argentine Motifs. This houses the most complete collection of folklorist art in the country. Many gaucho artifacts, earthenware, silverware, musical instruments, etc. Located on Ave. Libertador 2373. Open noon -8pm, closed Monday. Tel: 802-9967.
Museum of Modern Art. Wonderful collection of works by Matisse, Utrillo, Dali, Picasso, etc. On Corrientes 1530, 9th floor. Open Monday to Friday 10am–10pm, Saturday to Sunday noon–10pm. Tel: 469-426.
Historical Museum of the City of Buenos Aires. On Republiquetes 6309, Saavedra open daily for tours. Closed in February. Tel: 572-0746.

Theaters & Concerts

The theater season in Buenos Aires usually opens in March, with a large number of varied plays to please everyone. The Argentines like to go to see a good play and are highly critical. There is always something worth seeing. Check the local paper or with the hotel for the current and best ones available. Recitals and concerts are promoted by the Secretary of Culture in an effort to bring culture to the people. The public responds enthusiastically by attending all events. Open-air concerts are very popular on hot summer evenings and are held in any one of the numerous parks in the city.

Teatro Colón: Most of the renowned performers of the world are well acquainted with this magnificent theater. The building is in the Italian Renaissance style with some French and Greek influence. It has a capacity for 3,500 people, with about 1,000 standing. The acoustics is considered to be nearly perfect. Opera is one of the favorite programs for the season. In 1987, Luciano Pavarotti performed *La Boheme* here and tickets were sold out well in advance. Ballets are another favorite, performed by greats such as Nureyev, Godunov and the Bolshoi Ballet. The local company is very good and many of its members go on to become international figures. The Colón also has a magnificent museum, where all of the theater's history and its mementos are stored. It is an enlightening experience to have a guided tour of the theater and the museum. This can be arranged by calling 382-0554 for an appointment. Tours: Monday–Friday 11am–3pm, Saturday 9am, 11am and noon, closed Sunday. Tickets can be purchased at the box office located on Calle Tucumáno. Closed January to February.

San Martín Theatre: Sarmiento 1551. Offers a variety of plays and musicals. Check the local paper for performances.

Tours

Estancia Getaway: Visitors to Buenos Aires have the chance to get away from the buzz of the city, in the small town of San Antonio de Areco, about 70 miles (110 km) away. In this peaceful location, with beautiful scenery, the Aldao family has converted the Estancia La Bamba into a country inn, with all the facilities to make a stay comfortable and memorable. For more information tel: 392-0394 or 392-9707.

Shopping

A few words of advice before mentioning some fine places to go shopping; there are two main streets for good shopping.

The most known and the most "touristy" is **Florida**. Anything the average tourist might want to buy can be found here. The next main street is **Avenida Santa Fe**. Many shopping galleries are located on either side of the avenue, and once again nice things are available. The exclusive part of town, with the most expensive boutiques, is located in the Recoleta area, along Avenue Alvear, Quintana, Ayacucho and some little side streets. The antique stores in this area are exquisite – and so are the prices!

The fine jewelry stores are located at the beginning of Florida and on **Avenue Alvear**. Also, Sterns is located in the lobby of the Sheraton Hotel. The garment district is known as **Once**, and is accessible by taxi.

Buenos Aires also has a number of factory outlets, where good quality merchandise is available from a larger selection and best of all – the price is right. People who live here are well acquainted with these and will shop here rather than in stores. The only inconvenience is that they are usually located far from downtown.

Nightlife

The nightlife in Buenos Aires is quite a bit more active than in most major cities of the world. Argentinians enjoy staying up late. People walk carefree in the late hours of the night. Crime, although on the rise, is still not a major concern. The center part of town, on Calle Florida and Lavalle, at midnight might appear to most as midday.

Discos, nightclubs, cabarets and bars can be found in most of the city. Hear the latest hits from around the world and dance into the morning at, for example, **Cemento**, located on Estados Unidos 1238, or for a more formal crowd, dance at **Le Club**, on Quintana 111, or at **Hippopotamus**, Junin 1787. Other possibilities are:

Roxy, Rivadavia 1900. Raggae and rock.

New York City, Av. Alvarez Thomas 1391, tel: 552-4141. Popular with older clubbers.

El Cielo, Costanera. For the trendy and influential.

El Dorado, Hipolito, Yrigogen y 9 de Julio. Young and interesting crowd.

Tango Shows

A good tango show will be found almost everywhere, but the best shows are in Buenos Aires. Reservations are suggested for the following where such shows are staged:

Taconeando, Balcarce 725, tel: 362-9596 or 362-9599.

Casablanca, Balcarce 688, tel: 331-4621. Excellent show, prices include drinks.

El Caminito de Jan Telmo, Balcarce. Good show, price includes some drinks.

Cano 14, Talcahuano 975, tel: 393-4626.

Mesón Español, Rodriguez Peña 369, tel: 350-516. Good food, good music.

Michelango, Balcarce 4332, tel: 331-5392. In a converted monastery.

Sports

Trekking

There are many tour operators in Las Heras, Mendoza, which specialize in climbing and trekking tours. One of the best is **Servicios Especiales Mendoza**, Amigovena 65, 5500 Mendoza, fax: (061) 244-721.

Skiing

The main ski resorts in Argentina are **The Cerro Catedral Complex**, located near Bariloche; **Valle de las Leñas**, in the south of Mendoza Province; **Los Penitentes**, a small resort near the town of Mendoza.

There are also a number of small facilities located throughout the southern provinces, including one in **Tierra del Fuego** and another near **Esquel**. Contact a travel agent for details and reservations. Package tours are available and they tend to keep down the costs of a ski vacation.

Horseback Riding

Spend from half a day to a week riding under the open skies of the Andean foothills, near the town of Bariloche. Similar to dude ranching operations in the United States, but more rugged, with camping beneath the stars. Contact Carol Jones, Estancia Nahuel Huapi, Casilla 1436, Neuquen, Argentina, or Hans Schulz, Casilla 1017, Bariloche, Argentina, tel: (0944) 23835/26508, telex: 80772 polva ar.

Further Reading

Argentina: A City and a Nation, by Jamesd R. Scobie, New York: Oxford Univ. Press, 1964.

The Uttermost Part of the Earth, by E. Lucas Bridges, New York: Dutton, 1949.

In Patagonia, by Bruce Chatwin, New York: Summit Books, 1977.

Tierra del Fuego, by R. Natalie Goodall, Buenos Aires: Ediciones Shanamaiim, 1979.

Tales of the Pampas, by W.H. Hudson, Berkeley: Creative Arts Book Co., 1979.

Idle Days in Patagonia, by W.H. Hudson, London: Everyman's Library, 1984.

Two Thousand Miles' Ride Through the Argentine Provinces, by William Mac Cann, William. Reprint of 1853 edition.

The Cloud Forest, by Peter Matthiessen. New York: Viking, 1961.

Life Among the Patagonian Indians, by George Musters.

Perón: A Biography, by Jposeph Page, New York: Random House, 1983.

Santa Evita by Tomás Eloy Martinez, Transworld, 1997

Insight Guide: Argentina and *Insight Guide: Buenos Aires* are companion guides in the series, Their detailed, practical information, backs up the entertaining essays and stunning photography – the hallmark of the whole Insight Guides series.

Art/Photo Credits

Fiora Bemporad 296, 297
Nair Benedicto 168/169
Biografia de la Pampa 292
Camera Três Fotografic 193, 203, 206, 208/209, 210, 214, 215
Country of New York Library 34, 35, 36, 59, 76, 225, 240, 278, 279
Vautier de Nanxe 212
Tui de Roy 1
Eduardo Gil 14/15, 16/17, 18/19, 22/23, 26/27, 28/29, 30, 38/39, 40, 41, 42, 43, 44, 45, 46, 47, 48/49, 50, 51, 52L&R, 53, 54, 55, 56/57, 58, 62/63, 64, 67, 72, 74/75, 79, 82/83, 84, 86, 87, 88, 90, 92, 93, 94, 95L&R, 99L&R, 100, 101, 106/107, 108, 109, 110, 111, 112, 113, 114, 115, 117, 118, 119, 120/121, 126/127, 128, 129, 130, 131, 133, 134, 135,136, 137, 138, 139, 140, 141, 142L&R, 143, 144/145, 150/151, 152, 153L&R, 154, 155, 156, 157, 160, 161, 162, 163, 164, 166, 167, 196, 197, 200R, 211, 213, 218, 219, 222, 224, 226, 227, 228, 229, 230, 231, 232/233, 236, 238/239, 244/245, 246, 247, 249, 250, 251, 252, 253, 254, 255, 256, 257, 258, 259, 260, 261, 262, 264/265, 266, 267, 268/269, 270, 271, 272, 273, 274/275, 276, 280/281, 282, 283, 284, 285, 286, 287, 288, 289, 290/291, 298/299, 300, 301, 302, 304, 306, 307, 308, 309, 311, 312, 313, 314, 315, 316, 318/319, 321L&R, 322, 323, 324/325, 326, 327, 328
Manfred Gottschalk 234/235
Marcos Joly/Focus 2
John Maier 9, 20/21, 170/171, 172, 174/175, 176, 182/183, 184, 185, 187, 188L&R, 191, 192, 194, 195, 198/199, 200L, 202, 204, 205, 207, 216/217
Kal Muller 32/33, 220/221
Tony Perrottet 3, 68/69, 85, 91, 96, 97, 98, 103, 132, 158, 159, 165, 201, 263, 320
Royal Library of Copenhagen 78
Steven Rubin 243
Selio Villon 102, 104, 105
Bill Wassman 70/71
David Welna 186, 189, 303, 305

Maps Berndston & Berndston

Visual Consultant V. Barl

Index

Argentina

Bolivia

Brazil

Chile

Colombia

Ecuador

Paraguay

Peru

Uruguay

Venezuela

The Insight Approach

The book you are holding is part of the world's largest range of guidebooks. Its purpose is to help you have the most valuable travel experience possible, and we try to achieve this by providing not only information about countries, regions and cities but also genuine insight into their history, culture, institutions and people.

Since the first Insight Guide – to Bali – was published in 1970, the series has been dedicated to the proposition that, with insight into a country's people and culture, visitors can both enhance their own experience and be accepted more easily by their hosts. Now, in a world where ethnic hostilities and nationalist conflicts are all too common, such attempts to increase understanding between peoples are more important than ever.

Insight Guides:
Essentials for understanding

Because a nation's past holds the key to its present, each Insight Guide kicks off with lively history chapters. These are followed by magazine-style essays on culture and daily life. This essential background information gives readers the necessary context for using the main Places section, with its comprehensive run-down on things worth seeing and doing. Finally, a listings section contains all the information you'll need on travel, hotels, restaurants and opening times.

As far as possible, we rely on local writers and specialists to ensure that the information is authoritative. The pictures, for which Insight Guides have become so celebrated, are just as important. Our photojournalistic approach aims not only to illustrate a destination but also to communicate visually and directly to readers life as it is lived by the locals.

Compact Guides
The "great little guides"

As invaluable as such background information is, it isn't always fun to carry an Insight Guide through a crowded souk or up a church tower. Could we, readers asked, distil the key reference material into a slim volume for on-the-spot use?

Our response was to design Compact Guides as an entirely new series, with original text carefully cross-referenced to detailed maps and more than 200 photographs. In essence, they're miniature encyclopedias, concise and comprehensive, displaying reliable and up-to-date information in an accessible way.

Pocket Guides:
A local host in book form

However wide-ranging the information in a book, human beings still value the personal touch. Our editors are often asked the same questions. Where do *you* go to eat? What do *you* think is the best beach? What would you recommend if I have only three days? We invited our local correspondents to act as "substitute hosts" by revealing their preferred walks and trips, listing the restaurants they go to and structuring a visit into a series of timed itineraries.

The result is our Pocket Guides, complete with full-size fold-out maps. These 100-plus titles help readers plan a trip precisely, particularly if their time is short.

Exploring with Insight:
A valuable travel experience

In conjunction with co-publishers all over the world, we print in up to 10 languages, from German to Chinese, from Danish to Russian. But our aim remains simple: to enhance your travel experience by combining our expertise in guidebook publishing with the on-the-spot knowledge of our correspondents.